VILLA JULIE COLLEGE LIBRARY
STEVENSON, MD 21153

UNEMPLOY INSURAN IN THE UNITED STATES

The First Half Century

Saul J. Blaustein

with

Wilbur J. Cohen
and
William Haber

1993

WITHDRAWN

W.E. UPJOHN INSTITUTE for Employment Research
Kalamazoo, Michigan

HD
7096
.U5
B5397
1993

Library of Congress No. 93-13480

Copyright © 1993
W.E. Upjohn Institute for Employment Research
300 S. Westnedge Avenue
Kalamazoo, Michigan 49007-4686

The facts presented in this study and the observations and viewpoints expressed are the sole responsibility of the author. They do not necessarily represent positions of the W.E. Upjohn Institute for Employment Research.

Cover design by J.R. Underhill.
Index prepared by Shirley Kessel.
Printed in the United States of America.

Preface

In 1980, as the work of the National Commission on Unemployment Compensation was drawing to a close, its Chairman, Wilbur J. Cohen, and I discussed and agreed to pursue the idea of producing a new updated edition of "Unemployment Insurance in the American Economy" by William Haber and Merrill G. Murray, published in 1966 by Richard D. Irwin, Inc. Clearly, much had happened in unemployment insurance since the mid-1960s, and it was time to consider a new volume. Merrill Murray had passed away several years earlier, and Professor Haber was in no position to undertake the task by himself. He did endorse the idea, however, and agreed to join us in the undertaking.

We asked the Upjohn Institute to support the project as it had the writing of the 1966 volume. The Institute agreed, making some of my time available for the research and writing involved. Richard D. Irwin, Inc. released its rights to the 1966 edition for use in preparing the new one. The Upjohn Institute assumed responsibility for its publication. Other professional activities and health problems caused lengthy interruptions in the project. Before the work could be completed, both Cohen and Haber died, in 1987 and 1988 respectively.

As was the case with Haber and Murray, Cohen's connections with unemployment insurance traced back to its creation and early years. Cohen's contributions to the account of early developments enriched that part of the book. Haber, in turn, was stimulated to recall other aspects of the story not previously covered.

While the structure of the 1966 volume's early chapters was largely followed and some of its text retained, only part of the ground covered in the Haber-Murray book is included in the present volume. New material about the program's early years and the addition of 25 more years of experience greatly expanded the size of the new book. The result was to divide it into two volumes, with the second volume dealing primarily with unemployment insurance issues. The expansion of content and its restructuring into two volumes made the work more than a second edition of the 1966 book, although it is clearly a descendant to a large degree. Because of the long delays in completing the entire work, the decision was made to publish the first volume now.

The planned second volume will cover issues in the program, its relationships with other government programs, and some conclusions.

In the rewriting and expansions that I needed to accomplish after Cohen and Haber passed away, I have tried to remain faithful to their views and ideas on the subject. Disagreements that emerged with respect to earlier drafts were few and not of major consequence. Both men would, I am confident, be content to be cited as contributing authors of this volume. My association with them over many years has been and remains a source of inspiration and pride for me. The same sentiment applies with regard to Merrill Murray, a close and valued long-time colleague.

An undertaking of this magnitude could not have come so far without the support and assistance of many people. Early drafts of the book were reviewed by two key individuals. One was William Papier, for decades the Director of Research and Statistics in the Ohio Bureau of Unemployment Compensation and secretary of that state's Advisory Council. The other was Murray Rubin, long a legislative and policy analyst in the Department of Labor's Unemployment Insurance Service and later a consultant on unemployment insurance. Mr. Rubin died in 1990. Their thoughtful comments and suggestions were of significant value in enhancing the quality and integrity of the book. Valuable help with regard to statistical and statutory information came from staff of the Unemployment Insurance Service in the Labor Department who also reviewed much of the draft manuscript. Among them, I am especially indebted to Joseph Hickey, Virginia Chupp, and James Manning.

The support of the Upjohn Institute has been critical to the successful completion of this volume, not only for its financial backing but for the human resources made available. Christopher O'Leary and the Institute's Director, Robert Spiegelman reviewed the final draft, contributing to its further improvement. Moreover, since I was no longer present at the Institute during the later years of work on the book, I came to rely increasingly on Chris O'Leary. He played an important role by supplying me with research information, occasional guidance for other staff assisting me, or simply by being available for discussion of subject matter whenever I felt the need for it. I am also grateful to several members of the Institute's support staff for research and secretarial assistance. Irene Krabill and Ellen Maloney typed the manuscript, patiently enduring many revisions and changes through successive drafts. Final editing and preparation for publication by Judy Gentry added to the quality and polish of the finished product. Typesetting of the manuscript by Natalie Lagoni was her usual deft contribution. To Bob Spiegelman I am especially grateful for his constant encouragement, support, and great patience.

While many have helped generously, only I can take the full responsibility for any shortcomings and errors in this book.

Saul J. Blaustein
Tucson, Arizona
April 1993

Contents

List of Tables

I

The Changing Unemployment Problem and Its Implications for Unemployment Insurance

Some unemployment is inevitable in a free, dynamic society. In an economic system that places a premium on private enterprise and free choice, not all economic activity runs smoothly. Ebbs and flows occur in business, including seasonal and cyclical variations. Business undertakings do not always work out. The same is true for public policies and government programs. Above all there is change, constant change, in the structure and patterns of economic activities. All of these factors can and do result in some unemployment. Decisions of individuals to enter the labor market to seek jobs, or to leave jobs they have held to find other employment, may also lead to unemployment if the demand for workers is less than the supply of labor offered, or if job seekers and employers with openings do not match or do not find each other right away. Even if "full employment" were attained, there would still be some unemployment simply because the labor market requires time to serve its function. Full employment, in the sense that everyone who wants to work is working all the time, does not appear to be likely or necessarily desirable.

A substantial share of involuntary unemployment represents temporary job loss with assured or good prospects for reasonably prompt recall to the same employer. But recall can also be less certain and long delayed, especially during a business recession. Much permanent job loss and subsequent unemployment is a consequence of significant changes that occur constantly in the economy. New products, new technology, altered markets and consumer tastes, increased foreign competition, and shifts in government procurement and regulatory policies all can and do cause dislocations of labor. The ensuing unemployment of displaced workers may be due to their inability to fit into new types of jobs. The search for a new job is often not smooth or easy.

Unemployment insurance is a "first line of defense"[1] against involuntary unemployment, whether it be structural, cyclical, long term, or short term. An understanding of trends in the extent, duration, and nature of unemployment, as well as employment and labor force trends, is therefore of prime importance to those interested in understanding and evaluating the unemployment insurance program.

Labor Force Growth

Unemployment insurance became fully established in the United States during the late 1930s in the wake of the Great Depression. Soon after came World War II, and the economy went on a war footing; unemployment virtually disappeared and civilian labor shortages became a central problem. By 1947, the postwar readjustment was substantially over. Most of the ensuing period was one of prosperity and comparatively full employment. The year 1947, therefore, is a good starting point for the purpose of considering those changes in the labor force that affect the character and operation of the unemployment insurance program. These changes and trends are here reviewed over the next forty-three years—to 1990, the threshold of the closing decade of the century.

Beginning at an average level of 59.4 million persons in 1947, the civilian labor force grew to nearly 125 million by 1990, an increase of 110 percent.[2] This growth averaged about 1.5 million a year during the

---

1. This phrase was used early to identify unemployment insurance as the primary and preferred form of income support for involuntarily unemployed workers, with public work relief used as a supplementary form of support, if needed. See, for example, Lampman 1962, p. 229.

2. Labor force data, including employment and unemployment statistics, are developed from sample household surveys (the Current Population Survey) conducted monthly by the U.S. Bureau of the Census and published by the Bureau of Labor Statistics. The data refer to persons 16 years of age and over. The numbers cited for years prior to 1950 generally come from *Handbook of Labor Statistics* (December 1980), hereafter cited as *HLS* 12/80. The numbers cited for years 1950-1953 generally come from *Handbook of Labor Statistics* (June 1985), hereafter cited as *HLS* 6/85. Data for subsequent years are from the January 1991 issue of *Employment and Earnings*, a monthly publication of the U.S. Department of Labor's Bureau of Labor Statistics, hereafter cited as *E&E* 1/91.

entire period, but about 2 million annually after 1965 compared with 840,000 a year before then (*HLS* 12/80, table 1; *E&E* 1/91, table A-1).

One of the most important elements of this growth during the period was the striking rise in the number of women in the labor force. Women accounted for 61 percent of the total increase in the forty-three years after 1947 when their labor force participation rate was only about 32 percent; that rate was 57.5 percent in 1990. By contrast, the male participation rate declined from 87 percent in 1947 to 77 percent in 1990.[3] Women made up almost 45 percent of the labor force in 1990 compared with 28 percent in 1947. In 1990, over 58 percent of all married women living with their husbands were in the labor force, compared with about 20 percent in 1947 (*HLS* 6/85, table 50; *E&E* 1/91, table 8).

Unemployed married women who file claims for benefits may present special concerns for the unemployment insurance program. Determining their continued eligibility for benefits can pose difficulty in some cases when uncertainty surrounds their current labor force attachment, i.e., their availability for work. As a group, they have tended to move in and out of the labor market more than other groups. For example, 28 percent of all married women (spouse present) between 25 and 44 years of age who worked at some time in 1987 were out of the labor force for three or more weeks during that year (14 percent were out for twenty-six or more weeks). These figures compare with 8 percent for all men in this age group (3 percent for twenty-six or more weeks), also in 1987.[4]

The higher proportion of wives in the workforce means relatively fewer workers are the sole providers for their families. Insured unemployed workers in 1990 are thus much more likely to be from multi-earner families than was the case in 1947. This change has prompted some question about how critical the unemployment insurance program's role is in alleviating hardship.

Another major component of civilian labor force growth was the increase in the number of young workers, 16 to 24 years of age, from

---

3. Participation rates from *HLS* 12/80, table 2, and *E&E* 1/91, table A-2. The participation rate for a population group (e.g., women age 16 and over) is the number of that group in the labor force divided by that group's total population.

4. Based on tabulations supplied by the Bureau of Labor Statistics from the March 1988 household survey.

11.7 million in 1947 to 21 million in 1990. Virtually all of this increase occurred after 1960, reflecting the coming of age of the baby boom generation born in the approximately fifteen-year period following World War II. The numbers in this age group leveled off in 1979 and 1980, and declined somewhat since then, as most of that generation was 25 years of age or older by that time. By 1980, the 16-24-year-old age group accounted for 23 percent of the labor force; it was down to 17 percent by 1990, the same proportion as in 1960 (*HLS* 12/80, table 3; *E&E* 1/91, table 3). Young persons also show a greater tendency to move in and out of the labor force than do older workers. Those with enough work experience qualify for unemployment benefits when jobless, but some may stir eligibility questions because of the circumstances of their job separation or the uncertainty of their availability for work, especially if they are also going to school. Most unemployed youths do not qualify for benefits.

Older labor force participants, age 55 and over, increased in number from 10 million in 1947 to 15.4 million in 1990, but their proportion of the labor force fell from 16.8 to 12.3 percent over this period. Older women accounted for most of the increase, more than tripling in number from about 2 million to 6.6 million in this time. The number of men age 65 and over in the labor force declined from 2.4 to 2.0 million, reflecting the strong trend toward retirement since the mid-1950s (*HLS* 12/80, table 3; *E&E* 1/91, table 3). The increase in both the availability and value of pensions, including Social Security, during this period accounted for much of this trend. Dual receipt of pensions and unemployment benefits by some older workers produced a significant issue for the program.

Labor force growth is expected to continue, though at a slower rate, beyond the end of this century. A mid-range projection[5] sees a workforce of almost 151 million by the year 2005, representing an increase of about 21 percent over the 15-year period, compared to 33 percent growth during the previous fifteen years. Women will continue to account for the majority of the increase—about 58 percent of it—rais-

---

5. Based on Fullerton (1991, pp. 31-44). This article reviews projections prepared by the U.S. Bureau of Labor Statistics using alternative assumptions about labor force and population changes to derive high, medium, and low growth projections from 1980 decennial census baseline levels; adjustments for a shift to a 1990 census baseline are not expected to affect significantly the medium-level projections.

ing their proportion of the labor force to over 47 percent and their participation rate to 63 percent, from 1990 levels of 45 and 58 percent, respectively. While the number of workers in all age groups will increase, the largest proportionate rise (about 44 percent) is expected in the number of older workers, age 55 and over, increasing from about 15 million in 1990 to 22 million in 2005. Moreover, the labor force participation rate for persons in this age group will rise to 35 percent, reversing a decline in the prior fifteen years. By 2005, baby boomers born in the first years of the post-World War II period will have moved into their later 50s, still in the workforce and not yet at the usual retirement age. Also by 2005, the baby boom generation will account for less than half the labor force and all of them will be over the age of 40. Overall, the labor force will be somewhat older and more experienced than in 1990.

These changes are likely to have broad effects on unemployment insurance. More experienced, prime-aged workers tend to have lower rates of unemployment than their younger counterparts. They are also more likely to qualify for benefits if unemployed. While the rising number of women may increase the concerns associated with unsteady labor force participation, as women workers gain greater experience and acceptance in all kinds of jobs, their steadiness as participants may very well improve. Child care and other family responsibilities may also create fewer interruptions in employment for women as their numbers concentrate increasingly in the older age groups.

Employment Trends

Employment growth roughly paralleled total labor force growth from 1947 to 1990, although changing economic conditions produced more variability in the employment trend. Over the entire period, when employment more than doubled from about 57 million to 118 million, the average annual increase in employment was 1.4 million. During recession years, however, the level of employment declined or, as in 1980, failed to grow to match the rise in the civilian labor force. In general, employment growth did not keep up as well with labor force increases in the 1970s and early 1980s as it did in the two prior decades.

Actually, the growth in nonagricultural employment from 1947 to 1990 of 66 million about matched the growth in the labor force, while employment in agriculture declined from 7.9 to 3.2 million. Among nonagricultural industries, the rates of increase were uneven. Wage and salary employment more than tripled, from about 25 million to 85 million in private service-producing industries over the 43-year period, but grew less than 50 percent, from 18.5 million to 25.0 million in goods-producing industries.[6] Government employment rose from 5.5 million to 18.3 million, mostly in state and local government. As a proportion of all employees, production and nonsupervisory workers declined over the years. Nonproduction workers in manufacturing accounted for about 16 percent of all manufacturing employment in 1947 and 32 percent in 1990. In a number of industries, the employment of production workers actually declined over the period, or rose very little. Production employment in primary metals hovered around 1 million in most years since 1950, but was down sharply in later years to less than 600,000 by 1990. In transportation equipment manufacturing, production worker employment fluctuated between about 1 million and 1.5 million over the years and averaged 1.2 million in 1990. Employment levels declined from 1950 to 1990 in textile mills, food and kindred products, and leather goods manufacturing. Sizable long-term employment declines also occurred in mining, particularly in coal mining, although a temporary surge came in the 1970s and early 1980s with rapid expansion of oil and gas drilling.[7]

Between 1950 and 1990, employment gains were proportionately much larger in the South and West than in the Northeast and North Central states. While nonagricultural employment more than doubled over this period nationally, it increased more than sevenfold in Florida, nearly fourfold in California, and more than threefold in Texas. It doubled in New England and the East North Central states, and it

---

6. *E&E* (1/91, table B-1). Data for 1990 are preliminary.

7. Most data cited on industry employment are based on monthly surveys of employing establishments. They are published in *HLS* 12/80, tables 72-76; *E&E* 1/81, tables B-1 and B-2; *E&E* 5/88, tables A-1 and B-1; and *E&E* 1/91, tables 65 and 66.

increased somewhat over 50 percent in the mid-Atlantic region.[8] Increasing industrialization in the more rapidly growing states provided expanding job opportunities which, along with the good climate, attracted workers from elsewhere in the nation. Heavy concentrations of federal defense and space agency procurement contracts in California, Florida, Texas, and a few other states in the South and West contributed strongly to their rapid industrial growth. The energy crises of the 1970s stimulated oil and gas industry expansion in several Rocky Mountain and Gulf Coast states. The areas benefitting from all these developments in turn became more vulnerable to the business cycle, to federal procurement policy changes and budget reductions, and to wide swings in world petroleum prices. As these events occurred during the 1970s and 1980s, many of the "boom" areas experienced their first serious encounter with substantial industrial unemployment. The states involved found it necessary to reexamine the adequacy and solvency of their unemployment insurance programs.

Another notable employment trend with increasingly important implications for unemployment insurance has been the growing popularity of a variety of work patterns as alternatives to full-time and year-round employment. There have always been part-year temporary and seasonal jobs, as well as part-time jobs (less than thirty-five hours per week). Since about the mid-1950s, the number of people who work part time has increased dramatically. This trend reflects the rising labor force participation by women, many of whom cannot or prefer not to work full time. In 1990, 11.5 percent of all men who worked during the year worked at part-time jobs, compared with 27.7 percent of all women who worked; the comparable proportion for teenagers in 1990 was nearly two-thirds (*E&E* 1/91, table 7). Another element in this trend has been the growing interest of older workers in more limited employment, including many who retire early from regular full-time work. Some employers have organized their job arrangements to make possible alternative work schedules. Flextime, job splitting, and other forms of work sharing have emerged as new options for workers (Best 1981).

---

8. Changes cited based on data in *HLS* 12/80, table 79; and *E&E* 1/90, table B-8. The divisions of states applied are from the standard "Regions and Geographic Divisions of the United States," U.S. Department of Commerce, Bureau of the Census.

The number of persons who work part time by choice grew from an average level of about 5 million in 1957 to 16.7 million in 1990, more than a threefold increase over the period when all employment doubled.[9] Women accounted for most voluntary part-time workers (about 70 percent during the mid- and late-1980s), and about three-fourths of these women were employed in clerical, sales, and service occupations.[10] The rate of growth in voluntary part-time employment slowed during the 1970 to 1990 period, rising an average of about 2.9 percent a year compared with a 6.2 percent annual rate of increase during the prior thirteen years. The smaller increases, and even decreases, in the number of teenage workers during the later 1970s and 1980s contributed to the slower growth in part-time employment.

Some workers are employed part time not by choice but for economic reasons. They include, for example, persons who worked less than 35 hours a week because of slack work, job changing, material shortages, and inability to find full-time work. They represent the underemployed. Their number fluctuates with economic conditions. During the 1970s, it ranged between annual averages of 2.4 million and 3.7 million; it rose during the 1980s, reaching a high of 5.4 million in 1987, of whom about 32 percent usually worked full time.[11] The majority of the latter were men, while most of those who usually worked part time were women.[12]

The implications of these employment trends for unemployment insurance are not entirely clear. For example, should unemployed workers who voluntarily work part time and who qualify for benefits remain eligible if they refuse full-time jobs that are otherwise suitable? When full-time employment is scarce, to what extent should unemployed full-time workers receiving unemployment benefits be urged or required to accept part-time work? Dealing with workers whose

---

9. Based on workers in nonagricultural jobs. The number in 1957 was 5.2 million but includes 14- and 15-year-olds who are not included in later data. *HLS* 1975, p. 77, table 22; *E&E* 1/91, table A-1, table 1, and table 7.

10. *HLS* 12/80, table 23; *HLS* 6/85, table 20; *E&E* 1/81, table 35, and other January issues for 1984-1990, tables 33 and 34.

11. After 1987, the number of workers employed part time for economic reasons fell slightly to 5.2 million in 1988 and then to 4.9 million in 1989 (*E&E* 1/90, Tables 31 and 33).

12. *HLS* (12/80, table 24 and 25); *E&E* (1/88, tables 31 and 33). Those who usually work part time prefer more work but have been on short-time for so long that they can no longer be regarded as full-time workers.

employers place them on short-time or who are usually employed on a part-time basis may become a more active area of concern for unemployment insurance.

Trends in Unemployment

The annual average level of unemployment in the nation varied from 1947 to 1990 between a low of 1.8 million in 1953 to more than 10.7 million in 1983 (table 1.1). The higher levels of more recent years are due, in part, to the growth of the labor force. Rates of unemployment (the number unemployed as a percent of the total labor force) overcome this effect of labor force growth. The rates are thus useful when assessing the significance of unemployment. Between 1947 and 1990, the annual average civilian unemployment rate has varied over a range from 2.9 percent in 1953 to 9.5 percent in 1982 and 1983.

The pattern of unemployment during the post-World War II era has been largely a cyclical one. Recession year rates ranged from 5.5 percent in 1954 to 9.5 percent in 1982-83. At no time, however, did these rates come close to the levels experienced during the depression of the 1930s, which dominated the economic climate that helped shape the nation's unemployment insurance system. Although the 1954 unemployment rate of 5.5 percent represented a recession peak in that period, it is notable that until 1988, the nation's unemployment rate had not averaged that low for any year after 1970, except for 1973. The annual rate was less than 5.0 percent in fourteen of the twenty-four years from 1947 to 1970; it was more than 6.0 percent in eleven of the twenty years from 1971 to 1990. Indeed, the unemployment rate was never as high as 7.0 percent for any year from 1947 to 1974; the rate averaged 7.0 percent or higher in nine of the sixteen years from 1975 through 1990. While the pattern was generally cyclical throughout, the entire forty-four-year period saw a significant rise in the rate of unemployment along with the cyclical swings. This difference between the earlier and later years of the period is a fairly crucial one for unemployment insurance, considering the various effects on the program of the more serious unemployment of the later period. These effects and

Table 1.1   Average Annual Levels and Rates of Unemployment and Percentage Distribution of the Unemployed by Duration of Unemployment: 1947-1990

Year	Number unemployed (in thousands)	Rate of unemployment	Percentage distribution of the unemployed by duration of unemployment[a]		
			Less than 15 weeks	15 to 26 weeks	27 weeks and over
1947	2,311	3.9	82.8	10.1	7.1
1948	2,276	3.8	86.4	8.5	5.1
1949	3,637	5.9	81.2	11.8	7.0
1950	3,288	5.3	76.2	12.9	10.9
1951	2,055	3.3	85.3	8.1	6.7
1952	1,883	3.0	87.7	7.9	4.5
1953	1,834	2.9	88.5	7.2	4.3
1954	3,532	5.5	77.0	14.0	9.0
1955	2,852	4.4	75.4	12.9	11.8
1956	2,750	4.1	80.6	10.9	8.4
1957	2,859	4.3	80.4	11.2	8.4
1958	4,602	6.8	68.4	17.1	14.5
1959	3,740	5.5	72.2	12.5	15.3
1960	3,852	5.5	75.2	13.0	11.8
1961	4,714	6.7	67.5	15.4	17.1
1962	3,911	5.5	71.4	13.6	15.0
1963	4,070	5.7	73.3	13.1	13.6
1964	3,786	5.2	74.3	12.9	12.7
1965	3,366	4.5	77.6	12.0	10.4
1966	2,875	3.8	81.7	10.0	8.3
1967	2,975	3.8	84.9	9.1	5.9
1968	2,817	3.6	85.4	9.1	5.5
1969	2,832	3.5	86.7	8.5	4.7
1970	4,088	4.9	83.8	10.4	5.7
1971	4,993	5.9	76.3	13.3	10.4
1972	4,840	5.6	76.1	12.3	11.6
1973	4,304	4.9	81.2	11.0	7.8
1974	5,076	5.6	81.5	11.1	7.4
1975	7,830	8.5	68.3	16.5	15.2
1976	7,288	7.7	67.9	13.8	18.3

Table 1.1   (continued) Average Annual Levels and Rates of
Unemployment and Percentage Distribution of the
Unemployed by Duration of Unemployment: 1947-1990

Year	Number unemployed (in thousands)	Rate of unemployment	Percentage distribution of the unemployed by duration of unemployment[a]		
			Less than 15 weeks	15 to 26 weeks	27 weeks and over
1977	6,855	7.0	72.1	13.1	14.8
1978	6,047	6.0	77.2	12.3	10.5
1979	5,963	5.8	79.8	11.5	8.7
1980	7,448	7.1	75.5	13.8	10.8
1981	8,273	7.5	72.4	13.6	14.0
1982	10,678	9.5	67.4	16.0	16.6
1983	10,717	9.5	60.7	15.4	23.9
1984	8,539	7.4	67.9	12.9	19.1
1985	8,312	7.1	72.3	12.3	15.4
1986	8,237	6.9	72.9	12.7	14.4
1987	7,425	6.1	73.3	12.7	14.0
1988	6,701	5.4	75.8	12.0	12.1
1989	6,528	5.2	78.9	11.2	9.9
1990	6,874	5.4	78.1	11.8	10.1

SOURCES: *Employment and Earnings,* January 1981, table A-1, and January 1991, table A-1; *Handbook of Labor Statistics*, August 1989, table 33, and December 1980, table 38; *Employment and Earnings,* January 1981, table 17; *Employment and Earnings*, January 1986, table A-16, January 1988, table A-16, January 1990, table 13, and January 1991, table 14.

a. Weeks unemployed in current spell of unemployment as of the week surveyed each month.

the response will occupy a great deal of the discussions in later chapters of this book.

Long-term Unemployment

Higher rates of unemployment are accompanied by higher levels of long-term unemployment (table 1.1). In years when the average unemployment rate was below 4.0 percent, the proportion unemployed for fifteen or more weeks (as of the time of the monthly labor force surveys) ranged between 12 and 18 percent of all unemployed persons. It ranged from about 19 to 39 percent in years when the rate exceeded 5.0 percent. Since the higher proportions unemployed for long periods occur when the total number of all unemployed is high, the rise in the number of long-term jobless is even more extreme. For example, in 1969 when unemployment averaged 2.8 million and 3.5 percent of the labor force, long-term unemployment (fifteen or more weeks) averaged less than 400,000 persons, including only about 133,000 unemployed twenty-seven or more weeks. In 1975, when unemployment averaged over 7.8 million (less than three times the 1969 level) and 8.5 percent of the labor force, the number unemployed fifteen or more weeks exceeded 2.5 million, over six times the 1969 level; the number unemployed twenty-seven or more weeks that year was about 1.2 million, almost nine times the 1969 level.[13]

The annual averages in table 1.1 do not convey the full extent of unemployment experienced by labor force members throughout the year. Table 1.1 data are based on a snapshot, a cross-section picture taken by a sample household survey (see footnote 2) of the labor force status of the adult population as of a single week in the middle of each month and averaged for all twelve months of the year. In each monthly cross-section survey, persons are counted as unemployed if that is their status in the week on which the survey focuses, and the duration of their unemployment is measured by the number of successive weeks they have been jobless and seeking work as of the surveyed week. This duration measure, thus, is truncated; it excludes any additional weeks of unemployment the unemployed may continue to have before their current spells end. Nor does the duration measure include unemploy-

---

13. Even adjusting for a 12 percent increase in the total labor force over the 1969-75 period does not alter the significance of this pattern very much.

ment in other spells they may have in the same year. (Generally, about a third of all persons with any unemployment during a year experience two or more spells of joblessness in that year.[14]) Also missed by the monthly surveys are persons with very short spells of unemployment which begin and end between the survey weeks.

By contrast, another view examines the adult population's total labor force experience as accumulated throughout the year. This longitudinal perspective, also provided by a survey,[15] develops counts of the total number of weeks each person was employed and unemployed during the year. The unemployment experience data derived from this information are presented in table 1.2 for each year beginning with 1957, the first for which work experience survey data are available. A comparison of the total number of people experiencing unemployment during the year (table 1.2) with the annual average level of unemployment in the survey weeks of the year (table 1.1) shows that the total runs about 2 to 4 times higher than the average level for the same year. In 1969, for example, a year of relatively low unemployment, 11.7 million people experienced some unemployment, over four times the average level of 2.8 million that year. In 1982, a severe recession year, 26.5 million experienced some unemployment, nearly two-and-one-half times the average unemployment level of 10.7 million that year.

As noted above, the duration of unemployment measured as of the surveyed week is limited to the number of weeks those unemployed in that week had been seeking work in their current spells. The proportion who had been unemployed fifteen or more weeks at that time, therefore, is limited, since additional unemployment beyond the surveyed week or in other spells during the year is not reflected. On the other hand, when duration or the total number of weeks of unemployment is measured on the basis of all experience in the year, the proportion with a total of fifteen or more weeks of unemployment is higher, usually much higher, than the proportion unemployed this long in their current

---

14. For example, about 5.8 million, over 32 percent of all workers with some unemployment in 1990 (almost 5.9 million, 31 percent in 1991) had more than one spell that year (*Bureau of Labor Statistics News* 1992, table 3).

15. The work experience survey is taken in March of each year as a supplement to the regular household survey for that month. This supplement obtains information about each person's employment and unemployment experience during the preceding calendar year. For further description of the work experience survey, see Mellor and Parks (1988, pp. 13-18).

Table 1.2   **Persons with Unemployment During Year and Percentage Distribution by Extent of Unemployment, 1957-1990**

		Persons with unemployment[a]			
		Percent of all persons in	Weeks unemployed during year (percentage distribution)[b]		
Year	Number (millions)	labor force during year	Less than 15 weeks	15 to 26 weeks	27 or more weeks
1957	11.6	14.7	68.5	17.8	13.7
1958	14.1	17.9	59.6	20.5	19.9
1959	12.2	15.3	65.9	19.1	15.0
1960	14.2	17.2	64.6	19.6	15.8
1961	15.1	18.4	62.3	21.2	16.5
1962	15.3	18.2	64.2	20.7	15.1
1963	14.2	16.7	64.1	21.1	14.8
1964	14.1	16.2	66.8	19.8	13.4
1965	12.3	14.1	71.8	18.3	9.9
1966	11.4	13.0	76.2	15.5	8.3
1967	11.6	12.9	77.5	14.7	7.8
1968	11.3	12.4	78.8	13.9	7.3
1969	11.7	12.5	77.9	14.6	7.5
1970	14.6	15.3	69.1	19.2	11.7
1971	15.9	16.3	63.1	21.5	15.4
1972	15.3	15.4	65.6	20.4	14.0
1973	14.5	14.2	70.5	18.5	11.0
1974	18.5	17.9	66.9	20.6	12.5
1975	21.1	20.2	57.1	24.0	18.9
1976	20.4	19.1	59.0	22.8	18.2
1977	19.5	17.8	62.3	21.9	15.8
1978	17.7	15.8	65.9	20.7	13.4
1979	18.5	15.8	66.7	20.5	12.8
1980	21.4	18.1	58.8	23.4	17.8
1981	23.4	19.5	58.6	24.1	17.4
1982	26.5	22.0	51.6	26.0	22.4
1983	23.8	19.6	52.5	25.0	22.4
1984	21.5	17.4	61.0	23.6	19.4
1985	21.0	16.7	58.3	23.8	17.9
1986	20.7	16.2	57.3	24.3	18.4

Table 1.2   (continued) Persons with Unemployment During Year and Percentage Distribution by Extent of Unemployment, 1957-

		Persons with unemployment[a]			
		Percent of all persons in	Weeks unemployed during year (percentage distribution)[b]		
Year	Number (millions)	labor force during year	Less than 15 weeks	15 to 26 weeks	27 or more weeks
1987	18.5	14.3	58.6	23.8	17.6
1988	17.1	12.9	60.9	22.7	16.4
1989	17.3	12.9	63.1	23.0	13.9
1990	19.8	14.7	60.6	24.1	15.3

SOURCES: *Handbook of Labor Statistics,* December 1980, table 49; *Monthly Labor Review,* June 1981, p. 50, table 2; *Handbook of Labor Statistics,* August 1989, table 50; *Bureau of Labor Statistics News,* 1990, p. 5, table 3; and *Bureau of Labor Statistics News,* 1991, p. 5, table 3.
a. Includes unemployed age 14 and 15 years old from 1957 to 1965 and excludes them thereafter.
b. Excludes unemployed who did not work but looked for work during the year.

spells as of the surveyed week. Again, using 1969 and 1982 as examples, the proportions accumulating fifteen or more weeks of unemployment during these years were 22 and 48 percent, respectively, (table 1.2) compared with 13 and 33 percent, respectively, unemployed this long in their current spells as of the time surveyed (table 1.1).

Dealing with longer-term unemployment, especially during recession, has been one of the most difficult of all problems faced by unemployment insurance. The program's response over the years through liberalized benefit duration provisions and extended benefits during high-unemployment periods has probably altered the structure and reach of the system more than any other factor.

Characteristics of the Unemployed

Reflecting labor force and employment trends, the unemployed became younger and increasingly female over the years through the 1970s, though somewhat less so in the 1980s. Table 1.3 indicates these changes. Since the mid-1960s, women have averaged over 40 percent of the unemployed; they were closer to a third of the unemployed in the early 1950s. Their rising rate of labor force participation has also affected the family circumstances of unemployed men. In 1990, for example, about 69 percent of unemployed husbands had wives in the labor force, compared with about 32 percent in 1958.[16]

Teenagers (age 16-19) and young adults (age 20-24) together also comprised over 40 percent of the unemployed from the mid-1960s, but less than this share after 1982. Teenagers alone were about 30 percent of the total in the late 1960s, compared with less than 20 percent in the 1950s and after 1981. The young adult group's share of unemployment peaked in the 1970s. Older workers, age 55 and over, as a proportion of the unemployed, declined from about 15 percent in the early 1950s to less than half that level by the end of the 1970s. Early retirement has contributed to this trend, especially among men. Except in recession years 1975-76, new entrants and reentrants to the labor force made up about 40 to 45 percent of the unemployed during the 1970s, reflecting the high concentration of women and teenagers. This proportion fell below 40 percent in the 1980s with the declining size of the teenage group.

New entrants and reentrants typically do not qualify for unemployment insurance. Nor do workers who leave their jobs voluntarily. The latter group accounted for another 10 to 15 percent of the unemployed.[17] For those reasons alone, about half the unemployed are not likely to be eligible to receive unemployment benefits. Other factors, such as unemployment continuing beyond the duration limits of unemployment insurance, further reduce the proportion of the unemployed who receive benefits. New entrants, reentrants, and job leavers tend to make up smaller proportions of the unemployed during recession periods when involuntary layoffs of regular established workers mount steeply.

Total year unemployment experience data also show the increasing importance of women and youths over the years. The proportion of women among all persons experiencing any unemployment during the year rose from about 33 percent in 1957 to about 43 percent in 1990

---

16. *HLS* (6/85, table 57); *E&E* (1/91, table 8). 1958 is the first year for which this information is available.

17. Data for new entrants, reentrants, and job leavers based on *HLS* 12/80, table 39; *HLS* 8/89, table 37; *E&E* 1/86, table 12, 1/88, table 12, and 1/90, table 12.

Table 1.3   Women and Selected Age Groups as Percentages of All Unemployed, Selected Years, 1950-1990

	Percentage of all unemployed (annual averages)[a]			
Year	Women (age 16 and over)	Teenagers (16-19)	Young adults (20-24)	Older workers (55 and over)
1950	31.9	15.6	17.1	15.4
1955	35.0	15.8	13.9	16.6
1960	35.5	18.5	15.1	13.4
1965	43.6	26.0	16.5	12.6
1970	45.3	27.0	21.1	10.1
1975	44.1	22.4	23.3	8.6
1976	45.6	23.3	22.9	8.9
1977	46.8	24.0	23.0	8.6
1978	49.5	25.8	23.6	7.6
1979	49.4	25.6	23.1	7.4
1980	44.2	22.0	23.7	6.5
1981	44.7	21.3	23.9	6.6
1982	42.1	18.5	22.4	7.1
1983	41.6	17.1	21.7	7.4
1984	44.4	17.6	21.5	7.8
1985	45.6	17.7	20.9	7.4
1986	45.0	17.7	20.0	7.0
1987	44.8	18.1	19.6	6.6
1988	45.5	18.3	18.8	6.9
1989	46.0	18.3	18.7	7.2
1990	44.7	16.7	17.8	7.3

a. Percent calculations based on data in: *Handbook of Labor Statistics*, December 1980, table 30, and August 1989, table 27; *Employment and Earnings,* January 1981, table 15, January issues of 1985-1991, table 17.

(*HLS* 12/80, table 49; *Bureau of Labor Statistics News* 1991, p. 5, table 3). Teenagers and young adults (age 20-24) together accounted for about 28 percent of all persons with unemployment in 1959, increased to about 43 percent of the total in 1978, and diminished to 32 percent in 1987.[18]

How individuals with unemployment during the year are distributed by their household or family status gives some sense of the significance of their unemployment in family terms. Table 1.4 summarizes this information for the 18.5 million who experienced any unemployment in 1987, the latest year for which such information was available as of 1992. Almost one-fifth lived alone or with unrelated individuals and, for the most part, were self-supporting. The rest of the unemployed lived in families. Nearly one in three of all unemployed were family heads, if we assume that husbands headed husband-wife families. Only about 10 percent of this group were under 25 years of age. Wives of husband-wife families were 18 percent of all unemployed, with about one out of seven under age 25. The remaining groups consisted of other family members, mostly the children of family heads. These groups accounted for about 30 percent of all persons with unemployment during the year; over two-thirds of them were teenagers or young adults. Combining persons who lived alone with all family heads, 52 percent of individuals experiencing unemployment in 1987 were the sole or principal providers for their households. The rest were wives and other family members, nearly half of whom were under 25 years old. As noted earlier, to the extent that these latter groups consisted of new entrants and reentrants to the labor force, or persons who tended to quit their jobs or leave the labor force, their eligibility for unemployment benefits would have been limited or nil. Those who received benefits were more likely to be concentrated among the unemployed who lived alone, were family heads, or wives of heads.

Not included in the unemployment counts based on the monthly surveys are persons who indicate that they want to work but have not looked for a job for a month or more because they think they cannot

---

18. Cooper (1960, tables 6 and 9). The 1959 figure includes 14- and 15-year-olds while the teenagers in the 1978 and 1987 figures do not. Data for 1978 are based on Young (1979, table C-1). Data for 1987 are based on tabulations supplied by the Bureau of Labor Statistics from the March 1988 household survey.

Table 1.4   Persons with Unemployment During 1987 by Family Status and Age

Family status	Total with unemployment Number (thousands)	Total with unemployment Incidence rate[a]	Percentage distribution By family status	Percentage distribution By years of age[b] 16-24 years	Percentage distribution By years of age[b] 25 or more years
All unemployed	18,535	14.3	100.0	31.6	68.4
Unrelated individuals[c]	3,581	16.1	19.3	27.3	72.7
Family heads	6,061	12.0	32.7	9.7	90.3
Husbands[d]	4,472	10.8	24.1	7.8	92.2
Other family heads[e]	1,589	17.3	8.6	15.1	84.9
Non-head family members	8,893	15.5	48.0	48.2	51.8
Wives[d]	3,412	10.4	18.4	14.8	85.2
Other non-heads	5,481	22.2	29.6	68.9	31.1

SOURCE: Based on tabulations supplied by the Bureau of Labor Statistics from the March 1988 household survey.

a. Number with unemployment as a percent of all persons who worked or looked for work during year.

b. Percentage distributions by the two age groups shown are for each family status category and add horizontally to 100.0 percent.

c. Lived alone or with unrelated persons in households.

d. In husband-wife families.

e. Persons without a spouse present but with children or other relatives in household; women comprised 78 percent of this group in 1987.

obtain one given current labor market conditions or personal factors which they feel deter employers from hiring them. These "discouraged workers" averaged almost 1.4 million in recession year 1982; they averaged about 850,000 in 1990. Women accounted for 57 percent of this group in 1990 (*Bureau of Labor Statistics News* 1991, table A-12).

Types of Unemployment

Any classification of unemployment by type is necessarily arbitrary. For convenience, however, unemployment will be discussed under the headings of short-term unemployment, cyclical unemployment, and unemployment due to structural and technological developments. Short-term unemployment includes unemployment from several sources—frictional unemployment, short-term layoff (a temporary state without loss of the employment relationship), and seasonal unemployment.

The way the unemployment insurance program responds to the unemployed depends to a fair degree on the type of unemployment generating the claims for benefits. The ensuing discussion will refer to how or why a particular type of unemployment makes a difference for unemployment insurance. It should be understood that the program does not necessarily identify the unemployed individual by type of unemployment to determine benefit rights. Moreover, it often is not possible to clearly classify the unemployed by type, especially at the outset of their unemployment. General analysis of unemployment by type can be useful, however, in helping to evaluate program policies and in guiding administration of eligibility rules regarding the current availability for work and job search of unemployment benefit recipients.

Short-term Unemployment

Most unemployment is of short duration. The proportion varies with business conditions, but usually about 70 to 85 percent of the unemployed have been out of work less than 15 weeks, and from 40 to 55 percent have been unemployed less than five weeks, as reported in the monthly surveys. The proportion with less than fifteen weeks of unemployment tends to run lower when experience is reported and totaled over a full year. It has usually ranged from about 60 to 75 percent, but fell below 60 percent during most of the 1980s and in recession years (tables 1.1 and 1.2).

Much short-duration unemployment is what is sometimes referred to as "frictional" unemployment. It simply may take a little time for qualified job seekers and employers with openings to find each other. Some frictional unemployment is a necessary ingredient of a dynamic economy and represents people who enter or reenter the labor market to look for work they soon find, or who are idle for a short period while changing from one job to another. Such mobility of labor characterizes a healthy economy if the jobless periods are short. Some of this unemployment can be reduced or shortened through improved labor market information and organization; not all of it can be eliminated. Workers terminated from jobs through no fault of their own and who have another job lined up to begin in a short time or good prospects for one, may draw unemployment benefits in the meantime to compensate for lost wages.

The bulk of short-term unemployment, however, is caused by constant changes in the need for labor during the year due to temporary changes in consumer demand, inventory adjustments, model change-overs, seasonal factors, and a host of other reasons. Work reduction usually takes the form of short layoffs after which the workers return to their former jobs. These workers typically draw unemployment benefits during such layoffs.

An important component of short-term unemployment is the result of pronounced seasonal reductions in employment. Outdoor work, food processing, and other activities affected by the weather are examples of seasonally oriented employment patterns. Consumer demand for and production of apparel is also markedly seasonal, as is the use of vacation, travel, and holiday-related services. Swings in employment levels follow these seasonal variations. It is possible for seasonal unemployment to last or accumulate to fifteen or more weeks for some workers, as in construction work. The seasonal adjustment factors used by the U.S. Bureau of Labor Statistics to eliminate seasonal variations in the monthly levels of unemployment during 1989-90 ranged from 0.875 in September 1989 to 1.186 in February 1990 for males age 20 and over. This means that adult male unemployment resulting from seasonal influences alone may cause the unemployment level of this group to fluctuate from nearly 13 percent below the annual average in September to almost 19 percent above the average in February. The range is narrower for unemployed adult women but much wider for teenage unemployment.[19]

Compensation of seasonal unemployment has always been an issue for unemployment insurance. Concerns include fears about potentially heavy drains on funds since benefits paid to the seasonally unemployed may substantially exceed the taxes paid into the funds by their employers. Concerns also include uncertainty about the unemployed worker's availability for work and the administrative agency's ability to test or monitor availability and job search adequately during the off season. There is some evidence that the availability of unemployment compensation has actually increased worker attachment to seasonal employers and some types of seasonal unemployment (Lester 1962, pp. 49-50; Hamermesh 1977, pp. 64-72).

Some states have attempted to identify specific industries or occupations as seasonal and pay benefits only to employees laid off during the normal season of operation, but without significant results (Murray 1972). Federal law prohibits the payment of benefits to professional school employees, under specified conditions, during summer or other between term breaks, and to professional athletes in their off season. Although the bulk of seasonal employment is covered by unemployment insurance, some industries that operate for only a short season are excluded under state laws that cover only employers who operate for twenty or more weeks in the year. The minimum amount of past employment or earnings required of unemployment insurance claimants to qualify for benefits works to exclude some seasonally employed workers from drawing any benefits.

Cyclical Unemployment

When it occurs, cyclical unemployment caused by business recessions generates national concern. Although it may vary in intensity

---

19. *E&E* (7/89, table 1, and 1/90, table 1). Reported monthly unemployment counts are divided by the adjustment factors to "deseasonalize" the data to permit month-to-month comparisons unobstructed by regular seasonal influences.

across regions, cyclical unemployment is usually nationwide in impact and more in the public view than other types of unemployment. Total unemployment levels run comparatively high, and long-term unemployment accumulates more than usual.

Most business recessions since World War II have been relatively mild and of short duration. Those occurring in 1957-58 and in 1974-75 were quite severe. The recession of 1981-82 was also very serious and came soon after the brief recession of 1980, which was more regional in nature. Unemployment rates in 1982 and in 1983 averaged higher than in any year since the 1930s. During recessions, unemployment tends to concentrate heavily in manufacturing, particularly in the durable goods manufacturing industries. Employment declines during these periods in manufacturing, construction, and trade, however, may be partially offset by continuing employment gains in government and in the finance and service industries. For example, between July 1974 and July 1975, when total nonagricultural employment (seasonally adjusted) declined by about 2.1 million, the employment drop of 2.9 million in the first three industry groups noted above was partially offset by a gain of nearly 1 million in the last three. Between mid-1981 and mid-1982, the corresponding offset was far less significant, largely because of a decline in government employment.[20]

As table 1.5 shows, unemployment levels and rates rise sharply when the economy slips into recession. There were eight recessions between 1947 and 1989.[21] The percentage increases in unemployment to peak year averages from the previous year range from 22 to 93 percent. The latter, occurring in 1954, reflects the very low level of unemployment of the prior year; the 1954 peak unemployment level and rate were actually lower than those of any other recession year. The low end of the range of percent increases in unemployment represents the opposite situation in 1961 when unemployment rose from a relatively high level in 1960, reflecting incomplete recovery from the 1958 recession. The short and less widespread recession of 1980 produced a com-

20. Based on data in *Monthly Labor Review* (September 1975, p. 87, table 11); *E&E* (7/82 and 7/83, table B-1).

21. During late 1990, the ninth recession since 1947 began.

paratively limited rise of 25 percent in average unemployment over the 1979 level. The weak and faltering recovery in 1981 did not prevent further unemployment increases that year, near the end of which began the next recession. While unemployment averaged only 29 percent higher in 1982 than in 1981, the rise from 1979 to 1982 came to nearly 80 percent. The unemployment rate in 1982 and in 1983 averaged 9.5 percent, the highest level of the entire post-World War II era and well above the previous high of 8.5 percent in 1975. The 1975 unemployment level was 54 percent above that of 1974, but 82 percent above the level in 1973 when unemployment began its rise. If the increases are measured from low to peak months of unemployment during recession, the swings are considerably larger. For example, unemployment (seasonally adjusted) rose from a low of 4.1 million in October 1973 to a peak of over 8.5 million in May 1975, an increase of 108 percent (*E&E* 6/74 and 6/75, table 1).

Table 1.5   Percentage Increases in Number and Rate of Unemployment in Recessions, 1947-1991

Recession year[a]	Percentage increase from prior year	
	Number unemployed	Unemployment rate
1949	59.8	55.3
1954	92.6	89.7
1958	61.0	58.1
1961	22.4	21.8
1970	44.5	40.0
1975	53.8	51.8
1980	24.4	22.4
1982	29.1	27.6
1991	22.6	21.8

SOURCES: Recession years based on periods designated by the National Bureau of Economic Research, Inc. as given in Zarnowitz (1992, table 11.7); percentages based on the *Economic Report of the President,* February 1975, table C-25 and C-26; and the *Economic Report of the President,* February 1992, table B-37 and B-33.
a. Calendar year of peak unemployment.

The large and rapid rise in unemployment as a recession develops brings on very heavy use of unemployment insurance. It is then that the reserve funds, if sufficiently accumulated during low unemployment periods, can come into play to help compensate for the extensive loss of wage income. The program serves two of its vital roles by helping to brace so many workers against the financial shocks of job loss and hard-hit communities against serious loss of purchasing power.

During recessions, unemployment increases not only in number but also in duration. The average proportion unemployed fifteen or more weeks at the time of the monthly surveys rose 61 percent from 1957 to 1958, 71 percent from 1974 to 1975, and 61 percent from 1979 to 1982 (18 percent from 1981 to 1982). The proportion unemployed 27 or more weeks increased 71, 105, and 91 percent, respectively (19 percent from 1981 to 1982). Long-term unemployment sometimes continues to rise beyond the peak recession year. The proportion out of work 27 or more weeks rose another 20 percent from 1975 to 1976 and 44 percent more from 1982 to 1983.[22] As noted earlier, the combination of much heavier concentrations of unemployment in the long-term categories and the much higher levels of unemployment produce very large increases in the number of long-term unemployed in recessions.

The impact of the rise in long-term unemployment in recessions has fallen heavily on unemployment insurance. The program's response to this problem, involving adjustments in its benefit duration limits, is a major development that has altered some of the character of the program over the years. How unemployment insurance deals with long-term unemployment, particularly in recession periods, constitutes one of its major policy issues.

Structural Unemployment

Perhaps the most serious type of unemployment is structural unemployment, the result of basic change that is taking place all the time in many aspects of the economy. The sources of such change are numerous. They include technological modifications in industrial production, the replacement of old products and services by new ones that serve

---

22. These increases based on data in table 1-1. The comparatively limited increase from 1981 to 1982 in the proportion unemployed long term reflects the higher levels of long-term unemployment lingering after the 1980 recession.

their purposes more effectively or at less cost, the geographic reloca-tion of production facilities, the closing of obsolete and inefficient plants, shifts in consumer tastes and preferences, the substitution of new materials or new forms of energy for those that are more costly or which have become less available, shifts in various policies of govern-ment that affect private economic activity, and the impact of foreign competition.[23]

The list of causes of structural unemployment can be extended; all have their effects on employment. Old jobs may disappear entirely and new job opportunities may emerge. Workers who have worked regu-larly in the same occupations or for the same employers, sometimes for many years, may suddenly face transformed situations which require substantial adjustment on their part to meet new work conditions or which simply eliminate their jobs with no comparable employment alternatives available. For many workers, permanent layoffs induced by any of these factors may be the beginning of long periods of unem-ployment or of unstable employment. Regaining steady employment may call for difficult adjustments, such as retraining or relocation, or the willingness to try something quite different, often at lower pay or under less favorable working conditions. Some affected workers may never go back to work, or to a regular job. They may choose early retirement instead, if they can, or simply leave the labor force con-vinced after prolonged and futile job search that they cannot find work. Another employment effect of structural change is the curtailment of job opportunities for new entrants to the labor force who have particu-lar skills and training for which there is less demand, or no skills at all in a labor market in which more skills are in demand.

Structural changes and their effects on employment have ranged from limited, isolated instances that attract little but local attention to major events affecting thousands of workers. The latter can take on the proportions of a national crisis and may affect entire industries. Some changes occur suddenly while others may develop over an extended period with substantial accumulation of employment effects.

Several examples are worth noting briefly to illustrate various kinds of structural unemployment. The twentieth century witnessed a major

---

23. Racial, ethnic, sex, and age discrimination by employers in their hiring practices may be considered another source of structural unemployment.

shift from reliance on coal to reliance on petroleum as the principal source of energy. Employment in the coal mines declined from an average level of 438,000 in 1945, already less than half the peak level of 1923, to 133,000 in 1969 (*Historical Statistics of the United States* 1979, p. 608). This trend reversed itself somewhat in the 1970s, a result of the Arab oil embargoes, skyrocketing petroleum prices, and the recognition of an energy crisis in which coal, especially low sulphur coal, regained some favor. By 1980, coal mining employment had increased to 246,000, approaching twice the 1969 level. Many Appalachian coal fields, long the prime examples of depressed areas awash with structural unemployment, showed signs of revival in the 1970s. However, few of the miners left stranded by the earlier mine closings benefitted from the new employment opportunities. It was a new generation of younger workers which filled the demand. Moreover, mining technology has changed greatly, raising productivity and requiring different skills. New coal fields were developed in the West. The structure of the industry and its location have altered dramatically. In the 1980s employment in coal mining subsided to less than 200,000 again as oil became plentiful and lower in price.[24]

The shift of the textile industry from New England to the South left in its wake widespread and lasting depression in the former mill towns. Only decades later did New England show strong signs of economic revival with the development of its electronics and other high technology, often defense-related industries to significant levels. But a large part of a whole generation was left stranded in the meantime.

The rise of trucking, automobile, and air transportation sent the nation's railroads into a steep, long decline, wiping out hundreds of thousands of jobs in that industry. Foreign imports have captured significant shares of American markets for many products—steel, television sets, and automobiles, to name a few. The result has been substantial losses of jobs in these import-sensitive domestic industries. Employment in the automobile industry plunged from a peak average of over 1 million in 1978 to 70 percent of that level in 1982. Besides the foreign competition, the shift of car production to more automated

---

24. Data on employment in coal mining for the years 1980 to 1990 from January issues of *Employment and Earnings*, each following the year of reference, table 30 for the first three years and table 28 for the next seven years.

processes and to concentration on smaller, more fuel-efficient vehicles led to the general expectation that with diminishing labor intensity in this industry, employment may not regain former high levels at least for many years. In the mid-1980s, average employment did move up toward 900,000, but then fell to about 800,000 in 1990. The story for the nation's steel industry has been even grimmer. From an average level of almost 600,000 in 1965, employment at blast furnaces and steel mills fell over the years to about 200,000 by 1990.[25]

Successful foreign competition has stemmed, in part, from a major shift in government policy, dating back to the early 1960s, to cooperate with other countries in lowering tariffs and other trade barriers on a wide range of goods in order to promote trade expansion for all. Firms and jobs in some industries in the United States have been adversely affected as a result, while other industries have gained. Other policies and actions by the federal government have also produced employment effects in certain industries leading to structural unemployment. Deregulation of the airlines and restrictions on the lumber industry in the cutting of California redwood trees are but two cases in point.

Ups and downs in military procurement usually have strong effects on employment. A well-known example was the cutback in government purchases of military aircraft around 1970. The effect on aircraft manufacturing, particularly in the State of Washington, was devastating. Employment there fell deeply and rapidly. Despite the exodus of many workers, unemployment remained high in the Seattle-Tacoma area for some years. Structural unemployment was not confined to the workers laid off by the aircraft plants, but also included workers laid off by supplier subcontractors, as well as many in the area's secondary services and trade industries that depended heavily on the health of the primary aircraft industry. Yet, several years later that industry recovered handsomely with the booming demand for new planes from the commercial airlines. The cold war's dramatic end at the close of the 1980s has set off a major reevaluation of the nation's huge defense budget. The likely results are significantly reduced outlays for military procurement, base closings, and cutbacks in service personnel, all producing serious employment dislocation in the coming years.

---

25. Employment trends were examined using Bureau of Labor Statistics (1991) page 148 for blast furnaces and steel mills and page 331 for the auto industry.

These examples emphasize several important points about the employment effects of structural change. One is that while the change leads to loss of jobs in a particular industry or location, there are often contrary forces that result in new jobs elsewhere. Over time, the aggregate level of employment may not decline; it may even rise. The aggregate, however, hides the painful dislocation and usually long-term unemployment of workers whose jobs have disappeared. Because of a mismatch of skills and location, those workers are not the ones likely to reap the advantage of the new jobs created by the change. Sustained or higher total employment levels also obscure the effects of the replacement of lost high-wage, full-time factory jobs by more low-wage or part-time trade and service jobs. From 1982 to 1990, a period of substantial structural change and concern about displaced workers, about 18 million jobs were added, a gain of 18 percent in employment. Despite productivity improvements, the average earnings of workers over this period could hardly keep pace with inflation; indeed, for most workers real earnings fell.[26]

Another point to be noted is that the decline that may occur in a particular industry or area because of a shift in demand, as for coal and military aircraft, can eventually reverse itself with subsequent shifts. The passage of time, however, is critical for those workers initially affected.

A third point is that structural unemployment is often the handmaiden of cyclical unemployment. It is when business in general turns down that the weakest and most marginal elements of the economy suffer most. Obsolete and cost-inefficient plants closed, many never to open again. Distinguishing between cyclical and structural unemployment at such times is difficult. If the recovery is strong and subsequent economic growth is vigorous, then unemployment will fade, including long-term unemployment. But the period of recession and subsequent recovery is usually the occasion for improvements in efficiency of operations, for applications of new technology, and for building new

---

26. See *E&E* (1/92, table A-1) for employment data, and (1/92, table C-1) for earnings data. The latter shows an increase of 29 percent in the average weekly earnings of production and nonsupervisory employees on private nonagricultural payrolls from 1982 to 1990; over this time, consumer prices rose 34 percent. See *Monthly Labor Review* (1991, p. 80, table 33) for Consumer Price Index.

modern plants in new locations. What remains are stubborn pockets of clearly structural unemployment, unrelieved by these developments.

Structural unemployment is the most difficult and most worrisome type of unemployment of all. Its total number may not account for a very large share of all unemployment nationally (and how to define the structurally unemployed for counting purposes is itself a debated question), but it can be quite significant for an affected community or industry, and it is a substantial component of long-term unemployment. The financial hardship for individual workers and their families can be severe and steadily worsening. Deterioration of morale, of mental and physical health, and even of the social fabric of a community is not an uncommon consequence of structural unemployment. The fears generated by the announcement of a permanent plant closing with mass layoffs, or the introduction of new technology that will replace labor, can arouse strong resistance and unrest among the affected workforce. Government involvement is frequently the result as efforts to forestall or ease the problem turn political. The political response has ranged from the establishment of public programs, such as those provided under the Area Redevelopment Act of 1961, the Manpower Development and Training Act of 1962, and many successor, including the Job Training Partnership Act of 1982. Other legislative efforts were designed to regulate the timing of plant closings and employer responsibility for effects on workers and communities. The 1962 legislation was a response to the widespread fears of automation's effects on jobs at that time. Other legislation has provided for special unemployment benefits and adjustment assistance for workers dislocated because of the adoption of particular government policies, most notably with regard to foreign imports or industry regulation (see Rubin 1980).

Unemployment insurance comes into play at the outset of structural layoffs, buying time to work out alternative possibilities and vocational readjustments. The time needed, however, may be more than unemployment insurance alone can provide. Advance warning of plant shutdowns and of permanent mass layoffs, therefore, appears desirable (Freedman 1980, p. 15). At least sixty days advance notice of plant closings by large employers (100 or more employees) and of mass layoffs, permanent or very long-term (six months or longer), became a mandatory federal requirement in 1988 after many years of unsuccessful legislative effort.[27] Concern persists about potential workforce dislocations portended by widening prospects for the application of computerized electronic or robotic operations to many factory and office processes in coming years.[28] Structural unemployment seems destined to be a continuing problem for our society.

The Insured Unemployed

The discussion thus far has dwelt on employment and unemployment trends based on data reported from the monthly household labor force surveys and the yearly work and unemployment experience surveys. Trends in employment covered by unemployment insurance programs and in insured unemployment have not closely followed the total employment and unemployment patterns all of the time. To obtain a firmer grasp of the unemployment insurance system and the role it plays, it is important to understand the differences in these trends and the reasons they have been different.

Covered employment has increased proportionately much more over the years than has total employment. In 1990, it is estimated that an average of about 111 million jobs were covered under all state and federal unemployment insurance programs. That number compares with average covered employment of 34 million in 1950 (*Economic Report of the President* 1981, table B-34; *Economic Report of the President* 1992, table B-40). The 226 percent increase over this period was more than double the percentage increase in all employment over the same period. The difference is due to the extension of unemployment insurance coverage, through state and federal legislation, from very limited beginnings to where about 97 percent of all wage and salary jobs are now covered. Employment that was not covered as of 1990

---

27. Public law 100-379 specifies that sixty days advance notice must be given to employees of firms with 100 or more employees when a plant closing is expected to result in at least fifty workers losing their jobs. Furthermore, the law requires that sixty days advance notice be given when 50 or more workers, amounting to at least 33 percent of a firm's workforce, will be laid off for six months or more. A similar rule applies to six-month layoffs of 500 employees regardless of the firm size.

28. See, for example, Norman (1981, pp. 30-32); and Hunt and Hunt (1983).

consisted mainly of self-employment, domestic household service, agricultural employment on small farms, and employment of elected government officials.

The insured unemployed are workers who file claims for unemployment benefits for a week of unemployment. Each week the number of claims is compiled from all local claims offices throughout the nation and aggregated to state and national totals.[29] The total of all insured unemployment ranged between annual averages of about 1.8 million and 4.9 million during the 1970s and from 2.1 million to 4.6 million between 1980 and 1990 (table 1.6). During the two decades prior to 1970, that total exceeded two million only in recession years. In nonrecession years, insured unemployment was less than half of all unemployment. Federally mandated programs which extend the duration of unemployment benefits when unemployment is high have become a significant factor in swelling the insured unemployed total in those times.

A number of reasons explain the large differences between total and insured unemployment levels. The most important is that total unemployment includes new entrants and reentrants into the labor force who have not yet found jobs. Lacking recent work experience, they do not qualify for unemployment benefits. As noted earlier, they accounted for about 40 to 45 percent of all unemployed during the 1970s and 35 to 40 percent during most of the 1980s. Others among the unemployed who are not insured include (1) workers from jobs not covered by unemployment insurance, a more significant group in earlier years; (2) those who exhaust their unemployment benefits and remain unemployed, an important group in recession periods; (3) unemployed workers who leave their jobs voluntarily and therefore, in most cases, are disqualified from receiving benefits, a group that usually accounts for from 10 to 15 percent of all unemployed; (4) jobless workers who for various reasons do not qualify or are determined to be ineligible for benefits; and (5) unemployed workers who do not file for benefits even though they are eligible. On the other hand, a small percentage of the insured unemployed receive partial unemployment benefits because they currently have some limited employment and earnings while

---

29. For a description of the compilation and uses of these data, see Blaustein (1979).

Table 1.6   Total and Insured Unemployment, 1970-1990 and Selected Years, 1950-1965 (Numbers in thousands)

Year	Total unemployment (number)	Insured unemployment				
		All programs[a]		State programs		
		Number	Percent of total unemployment	Number	Percent of all programs	Rate[b]
1950	3,288	1,605	49	1,513	94	4.5
1955	2,852	1,399	49	1,265	90	3.4
1960	3,852	2,071	54	1,908	92	4.7
1965	3,366	1,450	43	1,328	92	2.9
1970	4,088	2,070	51	1,805	87	3.4
1971	4,993	2,608	52	2,150	82	4.1
1972	4,840	2,192	45	1,848	84	3.0
1973	4,304	1,793	42	1,632	91	2.5
1974	5,076	2,558	50	2,262	88	3.4
1975	7,830	4,937	63	3,986	81	6.1
1976	7,288	3,846	53	2,991	78	4.4
1977	6,855	3,308	48	2,655	80	3.7
1978	6,047	2,645	44	2,359	89	2.8
1979	5,963	2,592	43	2,434	94	2.9
1980	7,448	3,837	52	3,350	87	3.9
1981	8,273	3,410	41	3,047	89	3.5
1982	10,678	4,594	43	4,061	88	4.7
1983	10,717	3,775	35	3,396	90	3.9
1984	8,539	2,565	30	2,474	97	2.7
1985	8,312	2,693	32	2,611	97	2.8
1986	8,237	2,746	33	2,650	97	2.8
1987	7,425	2,401	32	2,000	97	2.3
1988	6,701	2,135	32	2,081	98	2.0
1989	6,528	2,205	34	2,158	98	2.1
1990	6,874	2,575	37	2,522	98	2.4

SOURCES: Total unemployment—Table 1.1. Insured unemployment (All Programs)—*Economic Report of the President, 1981*, p. 272, *Economic Report of the President, 1988*, p. 295, and *Economic Report of the President, 1992*, p. 343, table B-40.
a. Includes federal unemployment compensation programs for veterans (UCV), ex-servicemen (UCX), federal civil service employees (UCFE), the railroad unemployment insurance program, the federal-state extended benefit programs, temporary extension programs, and state regular unemployment insurance programs. Does not include federal supplemental benefits program.
b. State insured unemployment as a percent of employment covered by state unemployment insurance programs.

awaiting return to full-time employment; they are not included in the total unemployment count.

Insured unemployment varies during the year because of seasonal factors, but in patterns that do not coincide entirely with those for total unemployment. Levels are high in the winter months for both, but relatively more so for the insured. As a result, insured unemployment tends to be a much higher proportion of all unemployment in those months than at other times. Total unemployment levels rise sharply in May and June when large numbers of students leave school and look for summer work, but these new entrants or reentrants into the labor market add few, if any, claimants to the insured unemployment count. The insured-total ratio tends to be the lowest in these months. During 1977, for example, that ratio ranged between 39 percent in June and 56 percent in the winter (Blaustein 1979, p. 221). In 1986 and 1987, the monthly ratios reached their lowest levels in late summer and fall, rather than in May or June, perhaps reflecting the accelerating economic activity at the time unrelated to seasonal factors and which especially limited layoffs and unemployment of insured workers (*Economic Report of the President* 1988, table B-42).

The insured-to-total unemployment ratio was lower in the 1980s than in prior years (table 1.6). It was only 43 percent in 1982, a severe recession year; normally, the ratio exceeds 50 percent at such times. In the recession of 1975, the ratio averaged 63 percent; including recipients of the Federal Supplemental Benefits program enacted at the time for the very long-term unemployed, the ratio was 78 percent. During the eight years following 1982, the ratio dropped off sharply to between 30 and 37 percent. The ratio had averaged less than 40 percent in only one year between the end of World War II and 1982.

The low ratios of the 1980s have stirred debate about the reasons for the decline and their implications concerning the effectiveness of the unemployment insurance system. Attempts have been made to explain the various factors accounting for the difference between insured and total unemployment and for the ratio's decline in the 1980s. Not all of the difference can be accounted for or measured. There is recognition, however, that statutory changes adopted early in the 1980s affecting extended benefits during high unemployment periods made those benefits available later and terminated them sooner than had been the pattern during previous recessions. These changes helped to keep insured unemployment, including extended benefit recipients, unusually low in 1982 and 1983. Moreover, increased qualifying requirements and stiffened disqualification rules backed by their closer administration also appear to have barred more unemployed workers during the 1980s than before from eligibility for unemployment insurance, although it has been practically impossible to measure these effects.[30]

Insured unemployment levels have generally increased over the long span of years, reflecting rising employment levels, wider coverage by unemployment insurance, and longer duration of benefits, among other factors. Insured unemployment can and does at times fluctuate considerably from year to year because of cyclical factors. The fluctuation is more readily apparent in the insured unemployment rate (IUR)—insured unemployment computed as a percent of covered employment.[31] Table 1.6 shows annual IURs, based on state unemployment insurance programs, for the 1970s, 1980s, and selected earlier years. The annual rates ranged between 2.0 and 6.1 during the 1970s and 1980s. They were below 2.5 in the late 1960s, above 4.0 in the early 1960s, and varied from 2.7 to 6.5 during the 1950s (*Unemployment Insurance Financial Data, 1938-1982*). Total unemployment rates (TURs) show similar fluctuations though at higher levels (table 1.1).[32] The relative swings in IURs tend to be larger. For example, the

---

30. Studies of declining insured unemployment relative to total unemployment have noted other factors. These include a rise in the incidence of exhaustion of regular benefits as long-term unemployment has worsened; changes in the demographic and industrial mix of the unemployed resulting in greater concentrations among those less likely to qualify for benefits; the treatment of unemployment insurance as taxable income since 1979 probably discouraging some filing for benefits; and the new restrictions on benefits payable to pensioners beginning in the 1980s. For further discussion, see Burtless (1983, pp. 225-249); Burtless and Saks (1984); and Corson and Nicholson (1988).

31. Rates are computed each week by dividing the number of insured unemployed for the week by the level of covered employment averaged over a period of four calendar quarters lagged from six to nine months before the week involved. An annual rate is also calculated for average state insured unemployment for a year taken as a percent of average employment covered by state programs during the same year.

32. Total unemployment rates are not truly comparable with insured rates, not only because of differences between the two measures of unemployment noted above, but also because the total rate is based on the total labor force (the employed plus the unemployed) while the insured rate is based on covered employment only.

percentage increase in the IUR from 1974 to 1975 was 79 percent compared with 52 percent for the TUR; from 1969 to 1970 the corresponding increases were 62 and 40 percent; and from 1957 to 1958 they were 81 and 58 percent. The increases in the 1954, 1961, and 1982 recessions were not so different between the two rates.

It is noteworthy that the IURs for the years 1987 to 1990 were less than 2.5 percent. The only other period since 1947 when they were equally low was from 1966 to 1969. It may be conjectured that the low rates of the late 1980s may reflect the more restrictive tendencies in state unemployment insurance laws in recent times, especially as the TURs of the late 1980s exceeded 5.0 percent while those of the late 1960s were 4.0 percent or less.

Since unemployment insurance is mostly operated on a state basis, it is important to know something about the geographic distribution of unemployment. IURs permit comparisons among states with regard to their insured unemployment which varies greatly in number because of state-size differences. The range of insured unemployment *rates*, however, is also quite wide among the states (see table 1.7). With a national rate of 4.7 in the recession year 1982, state IURs ranged from 2.0 in Texas and 2.3 in South Dakota to 7.4 in Oregon and 7.6 in Michigan (leaving Puerto Rico aside, which is not typical because of its relative underdevelopment). In the comparatively low unemployment year of 1989, insured unemployment dropped to a national rate of 2.1, but ranged from 0.9 in Virginia and 1.1 in South Dakota, Nebraska and Hawaii to 3.1 in Idaho and Rhode Island (again leaving aside Puerto Rico and also Alaska with its very high winter unemployment).

In short, insured unemployment rates can be several times as high in some states as in others. This diversity is due partly to differences among state unemployment insurance laws, particularly with respect to provisions that affect the duration of benefits and qualifying requirements. It is mainly due, however, to interstate differences in economic characteristics and economic conditions, differences that are also important factors for the financing of unemployment insurance benefits.

As compared with all unemployed in recession year 1982, proportionately more of the insured were male and less were under twenty-

Table 1.7   Rate of Insured Unemployment by State, 1982 and 1989 (Annual averages)

	1982	1989
United States	4.7	2.1
Alabama	5.5	2.2
Alaska	6.2	4.4
Arizona	4.1	1.7
Arkansas	5.7	2.9
California	5.3	2.5
Colorado	2.9	1.6
Connecticut	3.4	1.8
Delaware	3.5	1.2
District of Columbia	3.9	1.7
Florida	2.5	1.1
Georgia	3.4	1.4
Hawaii	3.6	1.1
Idaho	7.3	3.1
Illinois	5.7	2.1
Indiana	5.0	1.2
Iowa	4.6	1.6
Kansas	4.1	2.0
Kentucky	6.0	2.1
Louisiana	4.5	2.5
Maine	4.7	2.2
Maryland	4.3	1.5
Massachusetts	3.9	2.8
Michigan	7.6	2.9
Minnesota	4.2	1.9
Mississippi	6.0	2.5
Missouri	4.4	2.1
Montana	5.3	2.7
Nebraska	2.8	1.1
Nevada	4.8	1.6
New Hampshire	2.8	1.1
New Jersey	4.7	2.3
New Mexico	3.8	2.1
New York	3.8	2.3

Table 1.7   (continued) Rate of Insured Unemployment by State, 1982 and 1989

	1982	1989
North Carolina	4.7	1.4
North Dakota	3.6	2.0
Ohio	6.1	1.9
Oklahoma	2.9	1.6
Oregon	7.4	2.8
Pennsylvania	6.8	2.6
Puerto Rico	9.1	4.7
Rhode Island	6.1	3.1
South Carolina	5.7	1.6
South Dakota	2.3	1.1
Tennessee	5.1	2.0
Texas	2.0	1.6
Utah	4.6	1.3
Vermont	5.1	2.0
Virginia	2.6	0.9
Virgin Islands	4.7	1.7
Washington	6.8	3.0
West Virginia	7.3	2.8
Wisconsin	5.9	2.2
Wyoming	3.7	2.0

SOURCES: *Unemployment Insurance Financial Data, 1938-1982* and annual supplements.

Table 1.8   Selected Characteristics of the Insured Unemployed and of All Unemployed, 1982

Characteristic	Percentage distribution within each characteristic	
	Insured unemployed[a]	All unemployed
Sex		
Male	64	58
Female	33	42
Information not available	2	—
Age		
Under 25 years	17	41
25 to 44 years	52	43
45 years and over	26	16
Information not available	4	—
Duration of current spell of unemployment		
Less than 5 weeks	33	36
5 to 14 weeks	43	31
15 or more weeks	24	33
Industry of last employment[b]		
Construction	17	10
Manufacturing	34	26
Trade and services	20	33
Other industries	16	10
Gov't. workers, no prior work experience	0	21
Information not available	13	—

SOURCES: Data for all unemployed based on *Economic Report of the President, 1992* (tables B-31 and B-39); and *E&E* (1/83, tables 12 and 15). Percentages for the insured unemployed based on data supplied by the Unemployment Insurance Service, U.S. Department of Labor; the data represent weighted averages of percentage distributions in the mid-months of the four calendar quarters of the year.

NOTE: Totals may not add to 100 percent due to rounding.

a. Under state unemployment insurance programs.

b. For all unemployed, only wage and salary workers identified by industry.

five years old (table 1.8). Larger proportions of the insured had worked in construction and manufacturing, and smaller proportions had been unemployed for more than fifteen weeks. The considerable numbers of new entrants and reentrants included in the all-unemployed total account for most of these differences since they are predominantly women and youths, many with little or no prior work experience.[33]

Concluding Observations

The flourishing economic climate during much of the half century following the establishment of the federal-state unemployment insurance system contrasted sharply with that of the depressed 1930s when the system was formed. Strong employment growth and moderate unemployment, compared with depression levels, made the demands on the program much lighter than originally anticipated. Although cyclical recessions temporarily increased unemployment, recoveries usually proceeded well enough to avoid seriously prolonged national stagnation, at least until the 1970s. Unemployment insurance gradually extended its coverage of the workforce and the duration of benefit protection of the insured employed. Long-term unemployment, particularly the very high levels common during recession periods, posed one of the foremost challenges for unemployment insurance. The response led to a major addition to the program's structure.

As the nation prospered in the decades following World War II and avoided sliding back into depression, numerous changes accumulated which altered much of the economic context in which unemployment insurance operated. Prominent among them were changes in the composition of the workforce, in the patterns of employment, in the industrial make-up of the economy, and in its industrial geography. These and other related developments influenced the levels and character of employment and unemployment. In turn, the program was affected and under pressure to react appropriately.

---

33. Similar data for the insured unemployed in 1990 or the late 1980s are inadequate for comparison because information about these characteristics was not available for very significant proportions of the insured unemployed.

A different tone distinguished the character of the economy after the 1960s. Growth slowed, faltered, and at times, stalled. Recessions marked the early and mid-1970s and early 1980s. Recoveries between recessions were weak. The resulting heavy unemployment fallout in these years placed severe strains on unemployment insurance and produced a financial crisis for the system. The ensuing pressures on the program to adjust were substantial. It is not yet time to gauge the full consequences for unemployment insurance of these circumstances or of the adjustments that have been made thus far, but it is clear that the program has become more restrictive.

Economic recovery and expansion in the 1980s persisted longer than usual. Employment grew steadily and the unemployment rate declined to pre-1980 levels. A sense of unease, however, lingered about the future. Concerns have continued with the eventual impact of many successive years of huge federal budget deficits, of unending trade deficits, and of heavy corporate and consumer debt. The unemployment insurance system was generally solvent as of early 1990, but how long it can remain so given a substantial and widespread rise in unemployment is a troubling question. Also troubling is the large gap between total and insured unemployment and the doubt it casts on whether the approximately two-thirds of the unemployed in recent years who have not received benefits are appropriately excluded, or whether they include many barred from benefits because the program has grown overly restrictive.[34]

Economic developments, although significant, are not the only factors that influence unemployment insurance. This book considers how the program evolved in response to these various factors and to the controversies that emerged in the process. Unemployment insurance operates in a dynamic setting; change is constant, a phrase that seems to be an oxymoron. The program must adapt and adjust in order to continue relevant, viable, and faithful to its purposes.

---

34. Recession conditions reappeared in the early 1990s. Although by many measures, this recession did not seem as serious as that of the early 1980s, a persistent underlying public perception of fundamental weaknesses in the economy has served to undermine the confidence required for a good recovery and restored economic vigor.

2

The Broad Objectives
of Unemployment Insurance

Unemployment insurance serves a number of purposes. Its primary objective is to alleviate the hardships that result from the loss of wage income during unemployment. Other objectives are also significant. They have been a source of controversy, however.

More than ten years after the passage of the Social Security Act, a congressionally sponsored review of its various programs stated, with respect to unemployment insurance, that "there is still some disagreement as to its primary purpose and as to its basic principles. It is generally conceived of as a multi-purpose program, although different groups emphasize different aspects of it" (U.S. Congress, House, 1946, p. 368). Views about the program's objectives continued to differ and evolve in succeeding decades. The more broadly they were stated, the wider the agreement about them tended to be. More elaboration or specificity on particular purposes usually evoked greater disagreement.

This chapter reviews the basic objectives advanced during the early efforts to establish unemployment insurance in the United States. It also notes a few later statements of purposes for the ongoing program. Each of the broad objectives generally indicated for unemployment insurance is then considered and, to some extent, explored for its significance. It should be noted that these discussions do not cover the purposes of specific elements of the program, such as those of the qualifying requirement, the maximum benefit amount, and the taxable wage base. Those are treated in subsequent chapters concerned with different elements of the program.

Early Expression of Objectives

The strong focus of social insurance generally on relieving hardship and forestalling poverty was stated long ago by Dr. I. M. Rubinow, a physician, actuary, and one of the earliest and foremost proponents of social insurance in this country. In his study of the subject, after discussing different social insurance programs for dealing with contingencies involving interruption or termination of worker earnings, Rubinow noted that "the purpose of every one of the measures described is to give relief in the case of human destitution." He contrasted this with the purpose of public poor relief which is "to grant the necessary minimum for a physiological existence, and that only." Further, "the ideal purpose of social insurance, the purpose to which the best insurance systems tend,...is to prevent and finally eradicate poverty, and the subsequent need of relief, by meeting the problem at the origin, rather than waiting until the effects of destitution have begun to be felt" (Rubinow 1913, pp. 480-81). This purpose was the predominant objective of the British and other European unemployment insurance programs adopted before 1935, as it was for some of the early efforts to enact state unemployment insurance laws in this country.

A competing point of view emerged in the United States, however, articulated forcefully by Professor John R. Commons of the University of Wisconsin. Commons saw, as the primary purpose of a program to compensate workers for joblessness the prevention of unemployment in the first place. His idea was to hold employers responsible for the involuntary unemployment of their employees. A comparable conception had been established as the basis for workers' compensation, which Commons had administered in Wisconsin. He was a leading advocate of employer initiatives in reducing labor turnover and irregular employment, seen widely in the early 1920s and prior years as a major source of unemployment. He wrote that "neither the wage earner nor the state can prevent unemployment. All that they can do is partly to relieve it. ...But the business-like way of doing it is to place the responsibility on the businessman who alone is in a position to prevent it" (Commons 1922, p. 21). He regarded the European unemployment insurance plans as paternalistic. If full responsibility and all the costs of compensation were placed on individual employers, they would be motivated to avoid layoffs and "regularize" employment, just as workers' compensation worked to prevent accidents and promote industrial safety. His views were embodied in legislative proposals in Wisconsin and elsewhere and had strong influence on the development of the unemployment insurance system that was eventually adopted for the United States.

Besides alleviation of hardship and prevention of unemployment, other objectives were advanced for unemployment insurance. One was to eliminate for unemployed workers the social stigma and humiliation of needs-tested relief by substituting the "earned rights" basis of insurance. By associating unemployment insurance with public employment offices and requiring recipients to register and accept suitable work offers, the program was seen as serving the objective of reemployment. Its role in limiting economic decline through the maintenance of purchasing power was another aim stressed by some proponents. The significance of all of these objectives was contested in the debate about unemployment insurance that intensified as the depression deepened in the early 1930s. Most of all, however, the objectives of alleviation and prevention vied for primacy since each carried different implications for the design of unemployment insurance, especially of its financing.

Much of the debate of the period was over the relative importance to be assigned to these objectives. Those stressing prevention included students of Commons—Elizabeth Brandeis, Harold Groves, Paul A. Raushenbush—and others of the so-called Wisconsin school of thought.[1] A model unemployment insurance bill advanced by the American Labor Legislation Association emphasized prevention by establishing individual employer reserves to finance compensation, as Commons had proposed in Wisconsin, rather than a pooling of funds. The enactment of the first law in Wisconsin in 1932 gave great weight to this approach. The opposing viewpoint, which stressed alleviation, urged pooled funds as a means of broader financing to assure adequate benefits. The principal advocates of this position included Professor

---

1. All were members of the economics faculty at the University of Wisconsin and helped draft the bill that became the first state unemployment compensation law in the nation. Groves, also a member of the legislature, introduced the bill. Raushenbush became the Executive Director of the Wisconsin program.

William Leiserson of Antioch College and Dr. Rubinow, who were mainly responsible for the Report of the Ohio Commission on Unemployment Insurance in 1931-32. That report provided specific and strongly reasoned proposals along with impressive research support and cost estimates. Others who generally supported the so-called Ohio school of thought included Professor Paul Douglas of the University of Chicago and Abraham Epstein.[2] The Ohio report also carried great weight.

In transmitting to Congress the recommendations of his Committee on Economic Security, which led eventually to the Social Security Act of 1935, President Roosevelt reiterated his frequently expressed support of the prevention objective: "An unemployment compensation system should be constructed in such a way as to afford every practicable aid and incentive toward the larger purpose of employment stabilization."[3]

While the Social Security Act contained no statement of purposes or objectives of unemployment insurance, the first state unemployment insurance laws generally included a "declaration of policy" that usually used or adapted the following language suggested by the U.S. Social Security Board in 1936, which reflected the various purposes seen for unemployment insurance:

> Economic insecurity due to unemployment is a serious menace to the health, morals and welfare of the people of this state. Involuntary unemployment is therefore a subject of general interest and concern which requires appropriate action by the legislature to prevent its spread and to lighten its burden which now so often falls with crushing force upon the unemployed worker and his family. The achievement of social security requires protection against this greatest hazard of our economic life. This can be provided by encouraging employers to provide more stable employment and by the systematic accumulation of funds during periods of employment to provide benefits for periods of unemployment, thus maintaining purchasing power and limiting the serious social consequences of poor relief assistance (Social Security Board 1936, p. 1).

---

2. Epstein was the Executive Secretary of the Fraternal Order of Eagles and a strong proponent of old-age pensions and of the pooled-fund principle in unemployment insurance.

3. As cited in Witte (1962, p. 128).

Later Renditions of Objectives

In the early 1950s, various efforts were made to formulate broad statements of unemployment insurance purposes.[4] The statements produced were not always in close agreement.

Several broad purposes of unemployment insurance were succinctly set forth in a statement issued by the United States Department of Labor in 1955:

> Unemployment insurance is a program—established under Federal and State law—for income maintenance during periods of involuntary unemployment due to lack of work, which provides partial compensation for wage loss as a matter of right, with dignity and dispatch, to eligible individuals. It helps to maintain purchasing power and to stabilize the economy. It helps to prevent the dispersal of the employers' trained work force, the sacrifice of skills, and the breakdown of labor standards during temporary unemployment (USDOL, Bureau of Employment Security 1955).

The 1955 statement was the last official federal expression of the program's overall objectives.

A restatement of program purposes was developed in 1968-1969 by a group of authorities in unemployment insurance and related fields. They distinguished between primary objectives, which are designed for "assisting the individual unemployed worker," and secondary objectives, which aim at "promoting economic efficiency and stability." The primary objectives included: assuring adequate cash compensation of wage-loss to help sustain, "to a substantial degree," the unemployed worker's current living standard; allowing the worker "the time needed to locate or regain employment that takes full advantage of his skills and experience"; and, through coordinated employment services, helping the worker find a job and, if necessary, achieve vocational readjustment. Secondary objectives included: fuller and better use of the labor supply, by facilitating rapid and suitable reemployment; support of consumer purchasing power in the face of wage

---

4. These included, for example, work of a Joint Legislative Committee on Unemployment Insurance in New York, work of the Committee on Employment Security Objectives of the Interstate Conference of Employment Security Agencies, and a statement of the National Association of Manufacturers (see "Unemployment Compensation in a Free Economy," July 1952).

income declines in economic recessions; distribution of the social costs of unemployment among employers in some relation to their layoff experience "to improve resource allocation"; motivation of more stable use of labor by employers; and retention by employers of their skilled and experienced workers during short periods of reduced operations.[5]

The National Commission on Unemployment Compensation of 1978-80 provided no statement of broad program purposes. In his introduction to the Commission's *Final Report,* Chairman Wilbur J. Cohen wrote: "It is significant that employer, employee, and public representatives on the Commission endorse the principle that a public system of insurance against the hazards of unemployment is a logical and necessary institution in a free-enterprise economy. The controversy now shifts to the pros and cons of specific proposals" (National Commission on Unemployment Compensation 1980, p. x). The phrase "insurance against the hazards of unemployment," while not a statement of purpose, may in effect cover several of the various objectives advanced over the years, especially in their broadest terms. In turn, "controversy over specific proposals" may include disagreement about some objectives with respect to their contemporary significance or the means for their achievement.

The objectives of unemployment insurance are next considered under three main headings: alleviation of hardship, prevention of unemployment, and promotion of reemployment. The program can be said to serve all three types of goals. A few other objectives are also noted.

Alleviation of Hardship

Although motivating employers to avoid layoffs was pressed early as a primary purpose for unemployment insurance, it seems fair to say that relieving or forestalling financial hardship for the unemployed worker by partial replacement of wage loss is the central aim of the program. Unemployment insurance can and does serve other valuable

---

5. Committee on Unemployment Insurance Objectives (1969, pp. 2-3). The Committee was chaired by Professor William Haber and included Saul J. Blaustein and Merrill G. Murray.

ends; if alleviation of hardship were not the focal objective, however, it is difficult to imagine the program's existence based wholly on other purposes. It is, of course, possible to approach the hardship problems of the unemployed through a relief program based on a test of individual need or low income rather than through unemployment insurance. Negative aspects of relief emerged clearly in the early 1930s, however, providing strong impetus for the insurance approach.

Relief Problems During the Great Depression

Unemployment insurance was enacted in the 1930s after five years of bitter experience with the difficulties and inadequacies of relief as a means of easing the hardships of unemployment. It is difficult for anyone who did not live through the period to appreciate how unprepared the nation was for the large-scale unemployment of the time and how much the unemployed suffered as a result.

There was little or no public provision for the unemployed at the beginning of the depression. Unemployment relief was left normally to charity. Through communitywide campaigns, various organizations made efforts to raise additional private relief funds. In most places, local public relief was poorly organized and pitifully inadequate. It was often offered in the form of soup kitchens or, at best, in the form of food parcels which the unemployed had to seek and carry home in the full view of their neighbors. The following description of one type of relief administration is taken from the report of an investigation published in 1931 in Wisconsin:

> One of the most deplorable situations was found in one of our medium-sized cities where each applicant for relief was compelled to appear before the monthly meeting of the poor committee composed of the mayor and aldermen and be cross-examined by these 8 or 9 city officials. This winter when so many were needing help, the meeting sometimes lasted until 2 or 3 o'clock in the morning. One can imagine how much sympathetic consideration an applicant, after waiting for 8 hours to be heard, would get at 2:30 a.m. (Lescohier and Peterson 1931, p. 35).

After graphically relating his experience as Mayor of Youngstown, Ohio in struggling with the problem of providing relief for the unemployed in 1930-31, Joseph L. Heffernan gave this description of what happens to the unemployed who must go on relief:

> With quiet desperation they will bear hunger and mental anguish until every resource is exhausted. Then comes the ultimate struggle with heartache and an overwhelming sense of disgrace, they have to make the shame-faced journey to the door of public charity. This is the last straw. Their self-respect is destroyed; they undergo an insidious metamorphosis, and sink down to spiritless despondency.
>
> This descent from respectability, frequent enough in the best of times, has been hastened immeasurably by 2 years of business paralysis, and the people who have been affected in this manner must be numbered in millions. This is what we have accomplished with our breadlines and soup kitchens. I know, because I have seen thousands of these defeated, discouraged, hopeless men and women, cringing and fawning as they come to ask for public aid (Heffernan 1932).

As unemployment increased, the traditional methods of providing unemployment relief through private charities and local public poor relief became more and more inadequate. The exhaustion of resources for relief in cities that faced bankruptcy because of local tax delinquencies gradually led the state governments to take over the responsibility, often through the appointment of state emergency relief commissions. In turn, state resources also became overstrained or exhausted and the federal government had to take over the burden, first through loans to the states from the Reconstruction Finance Corporation, and then through the direct financing of relief by the Federal Emergency Relief Administration.

As the state and the federal governments assumed the major responsibility for financing unemployment relief, the methods of administration and the kind of relief provided gradually improved during the 1930s. Staffs were trained and relief was granted under less humiliating circumstances. Cash relief became the rule, and public work programs were developed for the unemployed.

Unemployment Insurance as a Preferred Alternative

Although it had been proposed for a generation and tried out on a limited scale by some unions and employers, unemployment insurance was not seriously considered in this country until the inadequacies of relief as a means of providing for the unemployed became widely apparent in the 1930s. The superiority of unemployment insurance over relief was stated eloquently in 1931 as follows:

> The alternatives before us, then, are reliance on the hastily devised machinery for the distribution of doles during the time of crisis, or systematic provision for unemployment compensation out of reserves set aside for this purpose in advance. ...Our present method reduces a multitude into breadlines and soup kitchens, and reduces to starvation those self-respecting and timid workingmen who prefer hunger and cold to the ministrations of eleemosynary agencies. The second alternative, wisely conceived and expertly managed, represents...a decent and far-sighted approach to the problem of protecting the standards of living of American employees which are our proud boast (Wolman 1931).

One of the values of unemployment insurance, as compared with public relief, is that it not only prevents destitution but enables those drawing unemployment compensation to maintain their self-respect. The basic difference between the two methods is that relief is granted only on the basis of proven need, whereas unemployment insurance is made available without regard to the applicant's need. It is provided if the claimant has worked for a substantial period in employment covered by unemployment insurance and is able and available for work. The unemployed worker does not have to wait until savings and resources are exhausted in order to be eligible for it. Instead, unemployment insurance is designed to prevent poverty by immediately providing a cash payment to help the worker sustain some of the financial objectives normally supported by the lost wage income.

Although unemployment insurance in this country has many shortcomings, the program is accepted as the best method of alleviating the strains and stresses of unemployment, short of reemployment. There may be a widespread feeling that many recipients of unemployment insurance are not genuinely unemployed and available for work, but few would abolish the system. It is generally recognized that some unemployment is unavoidable in a dynamic and free industrial society and that most workers do not have adequate resources to tide themselves over temporary spells of unemployment without some hardship.

The Reemergence of the Insurance-Relief Issue

Unemployment insurance triumphed as the preferred means for alleviating unemployment. At the outset, with its limited duration of benefits and restricted coverage, the new program was not intended to be responsive to the mass, long-term unemployment of the period. Most of the unemployed then in need of income were expected to find it through public work programs, such as those sponsored and funded by the Works Progress Administration. Need remained the main criterion of eligibility for public work relief, but the labor expended in exchange for the cash received made the latter earned income and thereby helped to reduce the indignity associated with relief; it yielded, as well, some useful productive results. Cash relief that remained was reorganized and expanded under a new federal-state welfare system for needy persons who were not able to work—the aged, the blind, the disabled, and dependent children in fatherless families. Only in some states or local jurisdictions was meager general assistance made available for some needy employable persons.

Public work relief programs disappeared in the early 1940s as war manpower needs essentially eliminated unemployment. In time, unemployment insurance expanded its coverage and benefit duration so that it insured most of the unemployment of experienced workers. Many of the insured unemployed, however, exhaust their benefits and continue jobless, especially during recession periods. The later temporary extensions of unemployment insurance for longer and longer periods, especially during recession, have raised again the issue of whether insurance or welfare is the appropriate method of alleviation, this time in the case of long-term unemployment.

The issue's revival has been helped along by the improvements made in welfare over the years. Compared with the gross inadequacies and painful, often chaotic treatment of applicants that characterized relief in the 1930s, the present welfare system, even with its serious shortcomings, offers a stark contrast. Among the improvements are higher levels of cash assistance and the addition of in-kind assistance, such as food stamps, Medicaid, and housing subsidies, although there was some slippage in the adequacy of assistance levels during the 1980s. Needy families with unemployed fathers not eligible for or no longer receiving unemployment insurance benefits who were previously excluded from Aid to Families with Dependent Children may now receive such support as long as the unemployed father is available for and seeking work. The means or income tests that applicants must pass to qualify for welfare are not so restrictive as they were much earlier. Nor are the methods used to investigate the applicant's eligibility as harsh and demeaning. Administration of welfare is more systematic and professional. Going on welfare still is not an agreeable prospect, but it is a far cry from the fearful agonies of relief during the Great Depression. The latter image no longer inhibits as much as it once did the contemplation by some policymakers of treating the needs of the long-term unemployed through welfare rather than social insurance.

A new generation has grown up with no recollection or direct knowledge of the painful stigma that attached to relief for the millions unable to find work during the Great Depression. To many in this new generation, the value of the insurance approach over welfare is not so clear. A national survey conducted in early 1980 found that 59 percent of all respondents regarded unemployment compensation as "earned insurance," while 32 percent saw it as "part of our welfare system." Younger respondents were somewhat more likely to view it as welfare, as were respondents from households which had not experienced unemployment (Curtin and Pouza 1980, pp. 766-67).

Need for Support Among the Unemployed

During the Great Depression, with its massive and prolonged unemployment and so many eventually having to seek public relief, there was no question that most of the unemployed could not live on their own resources. By contrast, unemployment has been far less massive or prolonged in later decades. Most workers today have steadier employment and earn significantly higher real wages than did their counterparts of fifty to sixty years earlier. Moreover, the multiearner household has become more common than the previously typical single-earner family. Given these favorable conditions, some people believe that workers generally should be able to accumulate sufficient savings to tide them over relatively limited periods of unemployment. Others hold that large numbers of the unemployed do not need unemployment compensation because someone else in the family is working, especially if it is the spouse of the unemployed worker.

In recent times, the worker and his or her family have been subject to heavy pressures to spend, not to save. With high-powered advertising backed by the encouragement of "easy" credit installment buying, making regular payments to reduce substantial debt incurred to purchase homes, furniture, automobiles, or other durable goods has become a way of life for the typical worker family. Some workers do manage to save while employed, even as they incur and pay off debt. A long-range goal is often the motivation for saving—a down payment on a house, college education for children, additional funds for retirement.

When unemployment interrupts the normal flow of a household's wage income, financial problems can arise quickly. How quickly and how serious they become depends on a number of factors. Studies of insured unemployed workers conducted between the mid-1950s and mid-1970s show a range of wage-loss impacts, but all indicate some degree of spending cutback by most surveyed households even with the use of accumulated savings and the support provided by unemployment insurance. At this point, only a few findings from two of the studies are cited to give some idea of the need for income support by unemployed workers generally.

A study in New York in 1972-74 of unemployment insurance recipients unemployed for eight weeks or more showed that about 35 percent withdrew savings during their unemployment. Yet, 90 percent reduced spending and about 27 percent postponed payment of bills for goods and services previously obtained (Entes 1977, pp. 8-9). A 1975-76 study in Arizona showed that two-thirds of unemployment insurance recipients unemployed for thirteen weeks had reduced their spending on "necessary and obligated expenses" from preunemployment levels, most of them by at least 20 percent. About 62 percent had some savings when job loss occurred and 76 percent of this group drew on their savings during unemployment (Burgess and Kingston 1978, pp. 20-21 and 33). Even with unemployment insurance and savings to draw from, retrenchment was still the rule, to say nothing about forgone or postponed savings goals. Without unemployment insurance, retrenchment would have been deeper and financial difficulties more widespread.

Except those from multiearner households, relatively few insured unemployed workers have much income from sources other than unemployment insurance. A large proportion of benefit recipients are sole earners in their households, including one-person households. The 1972-74 New York study found that half of all beneficiaries surveyed had no other earners in their households—57 percent of the men and 40 percent of the women. Among married beneficiaries, only 35 percent of the men had an employed spouse compared with 80 percent of the married women (Entes 1977, p. 82). The 1975-76 Arizona study found that two-thirds of the beneficiaries surveyed were the sole earners of their households—about 75 percent of the men and 55 percent of the women (Burgess and Kingston 1978, p. 25).

Questions are frequently raised as to whether working wives need benefits when they become unemployed if their husbands are working. When employed, the average working wife contributes significantly to family income. Half of all wives employed full time in 1987 accounted for about 40 percent or more of total family income.[6] Most employed wives usually do work full time, especially those who can qualify for unemployment insurance when unemployed. Loss of a wife's wage earnings because of unemployment often translates into financial stringency for the family even though the husband continues working. In 1990, for example, weekly wage and salary earnings were down to $443 or less for half of all husband-wife families in which the wife was unemployed and only the husband was working (*E&E* 1/91, table 53). Unemployment insurance benefits received by unemployed wives thus do help make up for a critical loss of income in many families.

To emphasize the role of unemployment insurance in alleviating the hardship that can result from the loss of income during unemployment, one might consider the potential effects of the absence of unemployment insurance. Few insured unemployed workers can qualify for welfare at the start of their unemployment. Without unemployment insurance, many probably could get by for a while on savings, on other household earnings, by postponing debt payments, by cutbacks on spending, or by incurring new debt. Even with unemployment insurance, past studies have shown that most benefit recipients resort to one or more of these other sources of support or adjustments; only part of the wage loss is compensated, but the net loss is limited and therefore

---

6. Unpublished data on marital and family characteristics supplied by the Bureau of Labor Statistics' Current Population Survey taken in March 1988.

more manageable. Some unemployed workers have few, if any, of these alternatives to fall back on except for reduced spending. As unemployment continues without compensation for several weeks or for a couple of months or so, more and more of them become financially squeezed, encountering strain and hardship. Those managing to stay afloat may nevertheless see serious damage done to the level of living their earnings went to support, including the loss of cars or other assets not fully paid for, and the surrender of long-term plans.

Not until the unemployed are financially drained would those with dependent children be potential candidates for welfare under existing rules. Without unemployment insurance, the sense and reality of economic insecurity would likely spread among the experienced workforce as the harsh effects of unemployment became manifest. Although the trauma of the Great Depression is no longer a personal memory of pain and anguish for most Americans, it remains a deep scar on the national psyche. It is doubtful, therefore, that the nation would abandon unemployment insurance and risk exposing workers to the threat of financial ruin and hardship because of a period of involuntary unemployment.

Prevention of Unemployment

Two objectives served by unemployment insurance are considered under this heading. One concerns the program's motivation of employers to avoid layoffs of their employees in the first place through the design for financing of unemployment benefits. The other relates to the program's role in sustaining consumer purchasing power through its compensation of the wage loss suffered by workers laid off during business downturns, thereby helping to retard or halt further worsening of business and unemployment.

Employer Incentive to Stabilize Employment

By emphasizing employer financing of unemployment insurance and by applying experience rating principles for lowering unemployment tax rates, employers are expected to be motivated to "regularize" their employment of labor and to minimize layoffs. This objective, urged quite frequently at the beginning of the program, was not mentioned as much after the first few decades.

Considerable effort was put into promoting the idea of stabilization of employment through experience rating of unemployment insurance taxes. Whether or not the attraction of reduced tax rates actually induces employers to avoid layoffs is very difficult to determine empirically, given the complexity of reasons for variations in a firm's employment level. Three interview studies, two made early in Wisconsin (1937-38) and Indiana (1941-42), and one in Connecticut (1968), sought to elicit from employers the degree to which they were influenced by the experience rating incentive. The study findings were generally similar: about one-fourth of employers indicated an appreciable degree of influence, a minority of the remainder, only a slight degree, and the majority indicated no effect at all. After reviewing the findings and emphasizing their similarity among the studies but also the uncertainties of such results, Joseph M. Becker, a leading authority on experience rating, observed:

> The general result of the three studies...provides the basis for a cautious acceptance of the proposition that while it would be false to assign major (incentive) influence to the unemployment insurance tax, it would be equally erroneous to write off the effect as insignificant" (Becker 1972a, p. 37).

In Wisconsin, it appeared that the initial impact of unemployment insurance taxes soon wore off, and experience rating did not induce much additional employment stabilization (Meyers 1945, pp. 337-54).

A major reason for the lessened impact of experience rating on stabilization over the years is that the effective differentials in tax rates assigned through experience rating have become so diminished as to lose the force of their inducement to employers to stabilize. Significant proportions of benefits paid are not charged to individual employers or exceed what some employers' taxes can finance and therefore are pooled and shared equally among all employers. Relatively high minimum and low maximum tax rates may appreciably restrict the range for assigning rates in between on the basis of experience, so as to make rate differences less effective in motivating employers. The long-term failure of the taxable wage base to keep pace with rising wage levels has shrunk the proportion of payrolls subject to the tax rates, further compressing the range of rates when viewed on the basis of total payrolls. These are program elements that can be changed to reverse the erosion of the employment stabilization incentive effect of experience rated taxes.[7] Economic factors, however, are not so controllable, and thereby limit the ability of many, perhaps most, employers to avoid layoffs even if a lower unemployment tax rate is highly desired. It should be noted that other arguments are advanced in support of experience rating in addition to motivating employers to avoid layoffs.

Stabilization of the Economy

Another preventive aim of unemployment insurance is to help minimize the spread and depth of recessions through the maintenance of purchasing power. This objective has been emphasized over the years. It was included in early statements of the purposes of unemployment insurance. The Bureau of Employment Security elaborated on this objective in 1950 as follows: "By maintaining essential consumer purchasing power, on which production plans are based, the program provides a brake on down-turns in business activity, helps to stabilize employment, and lessens the momentum of deflation during periods of recession" (USDOL, Bureau of Employment Security 1950b, p. 1).

This objective of unemployment insurance was referred to in both the majority and minority versions of the "Report of the Senate Special Committee on Unemployment Problems" in 1960. The majority report stated that "the payment of unemployment benefits has the secondary effect of maintaining purchasing power and cushioning the shock of unemployment to the community and to the national economy" (U.S. Congress, Senate, 1960, p. 87).

The minority report of the Committee made an even stronger statement: "In regard to cyclical unemployment, unemployment compensation payments have constituted an important antirecessionary measure available to the Federal government...of all the countermeasures—the so-called built-in stabilizers—which have served to sustain buying

---

7. After analyzing the results of a study of the effects of state unemployment insurance taxes on layoffs by individual employers in the mid-1970s, Robert Topel (1984) concluded that despite experience rating, the typically rated employer paid directly for only about 75 percent of the costs of the benefits drawn by workers laid off by that employer, and that even a modest reduction in the degree of subsidization of those costs by other employers would substantially improve the employment stabilization effect of unemployment insurance taxes.

power and cushion recessions, this is the most important single measure" (U.S. Congress, Senate, 1960, pp. 165-66).

On a number of occasions, the President's Council of Economic Advisers has also cited the countercyclical role of unemployment insurance as an important factor in economic stabilization. In its 1965 annual report, for example, after offering some quantitative measure of the countercyclical effects of increased unemployment benefit outlays during the 1960-61 recession, the Council concluded:

> Strengthening the unemployment compensation system deserves high priority among possible steps to increase the automatic resistance of the economy to recessions. The most important reasons for improving the system are to increase individual security and reduce the unnecessary human costs of unemployment. But a strengthened system would also sustain consumer purchasing power more effectively, thereby reducing the amount of unemployment as well (*Economic Report of the President Together with the Annual Report of the Council of Economic Advisers* 1965, pp. 101-02.).

The 1969 report of the Upjohn Institute's Committee on Unemployment Insurance Objectives, in referring to the program's capacity to "counter deflationary effects of unemployment on national and local economies," pointed out:

> Moreover, increased benefits are dispensed at just the right time, in just the right places, and among those who tend to need them the most. This happens quickly and automatically, and the process is precisely reversible at all the appropriate times and places. These effects take place as needed whether locally or nationally. They are seen most dramatically at times of national recessions, but they are also important in local downturns and, in fact, help in those circumstances to prevent local slumps from spreading (Committee on Unemployment Insurance Objectives 1969, p. 20).

After a review of a number of studies made between 1962 and 1976 to quantify the countercyclical effects of unemployment insurance, Professor Daniel S. Hamermesh of Michigan State University concluded that the postwar recessions would have been about 10 to 20 percent worse without the program. He further concludes that "unemployment benefits...must be paid automatically if we are to avoid substantially greater hardships during the recessions of the kind that have prevailed since the 1940s" (Hamermesh 1977, pp. 62-64).

A study made to estimate the impact of unemployment insurance on a local economy during the 1975-76 recession revealed a number of specific effects. The study employed an econometric model of the Tucson, Arizona metropolitan area economy to simulate effects on such key variables as employment, unemployment, income, and sales. The analysis indicated that without the benefits paid in the area, unemployment levels would have been 5 to 10 percent higher than they were in 1975-76. Each dollar of benefits paid in 1975 was estimated to have generated about $3 in disposable personal income over the two-year period. Alternative estimates of sales induced by the added income varied widely, but the bulk of them concentrated in the construction, trade, and service sectors as did the additional employment produced. The study report describes certain methodological limitations that tend to restrict the impact results.[8] This study was subsequently extended to estimate similar effects for the Phoenix, Arizona area during the same recession period. Moreover, the model was expanded to measure the effects in the two local economies of total unemployment benefits paid throughout the nation, in addition to the effects of those paid locally. The result was a larger impact than that produced by local benefits alone. Phoenix, with a broader and more cyclically sensitive manufacturing base than Tucson, exhibited a stronger impact. Overall, however, both areas showed modest benefit-induced gains in employment and income and reductions in unemployment (Oaxaca and Taylor 1986).

The extent to which unemployment insurance can help stabilize the economy by maintaining purchasing power during recessions is limited. Nevertheless, it is not insignificant and, therefore, economic stabilization can legitimately be considered as one of the objectives of unemployment insurance.

---

8. Danzau, Oaxaca, and Taylor (1979). The study did not include extended and other federally financed unemployment benefits paid in the area.

The Reemployment Objective

Return to work is the foremost concern of the unemployed worker. By itself, of course, the payment of a weekly benefit does not bring about speedy reemployment. Indeed, it may tend to delay return to work if the recipient's preference for leisure is at least temporarily strong and not overcome by the attraction of the potentially larger income from wages and other attributes of a job. The staying power provided by unemployment insurance, on the other hand, does enable the job seeker to search longer for a suitable job that is in line with previous earnings and experience. In this way, the program helps workers preserve the use of their skills through a reasonable period of job search.

The unemployment insurance program contributes to the reemployment objective in two ways. One is to keep down the disincentive to work, the preference for leisure, by placing limits on the weekly amount and duration of unemployment benefits paid. Only a portion, usually about half of the weekly wage loss, is compensated, and less if the maximum is paid. Some financial pressure thus remains on the recipient to regain employment and full wage income. The pressure builds up over time as the uncompensated wage loss accumulates, forcing more difficult adjustment; the prospect becomes especially acute as the benefit duration limit nears, usually at twenty-six weeks. The question of how restrictive these limits should be is balanced against the question of how adequate benefits should be to enable the program to achieve its other objectives.

The other way the program contributes to reemployment consists of its job search and availability-for-work requirements and the way they are administered. Eligibility for benefits requires unemployment insurance claimants to be available for work and reasonably active in searching for work. Most states specify a minimum amount of work search activity by the claimant. The program's association with the public employment service, at which most of the insured unemployed must register for work, the degree of care and effort taken in diagnosing the unemployed worker's employment prospects and needs, and the quality of counseling and job search assistance supplied and the extent and intensity of independent job search urged are all important factors that can be drawn together in the administration of unemployment insurance. Properly organized and applied, they can be brought to bear positively on the reemployment objective. The claimant's failure to cooperate with these efforts, as well as failure to register and be available for work are grounds for denial of benefits.

Unemployment insurance's positive role in pursuing the reemployment goal has received inadequate emphasis in the past. The program has tended to concentrate instead on negative considerations—tests of eligibility and detection of malingering. A few efforts have been made to address the positive side. These include, for example, the required continued payment of benefits to the unemployed while in approved training, and more insistence on independent job search. The former, however, has had little impact because of limited promotion and opportunity for training. The latter has generally taken the form of arbitrary uniform job search requirements often applied with little or no thought for the variability in the search approaches appropriate for different types of jobs, different labor market conditions, or different worker search capabilities and needs. The program's ability to contribute positively to the reemployment of its beneficiaries remains in need of development and strengthening; the objective is an important one.[9]

Other Objectives

Several other objectives served by unemployment insurance should be noted. One is to provide an orderly method of meeting the cost of unemployment since financing large scale public unemployment relief during times of great need has always been difficult and unsatisfactory. Not only is there a reluctance to appropriate adequate funds, but the costs of unemployment relief fall heavily on the most impacted states and local communities during periods of low business activity at a time when their tax revenues have fallen. Unemployment insurance, on the other hand, is a system for building up reserves in good times which are automatically available for the increased payment of benefits in bad

---

9. For a discussion of how unemployment insurance can be organized to play a more positive role in this regard, see Blaustein (1981).

times. To the extent that the program follows this reserve policy, it eases the management of unemployment costs.

The payment of unemployment compensation to employees placed on short layoffs is of advantage to an employer. The compensation tends to preserve the workforce intact, with its particular skills, training, and experience, until it can be recalled. Laid-off workers are not forced to scatter in search of jobs, at least during short layoffs. Indeed, the development in the late 1970s and 1980s of short-time compensation by a number of states within their unemployment insurance programs is a further step towards accommodating this objective.[10] While this support of workforce retention may somewhat restrict the mobility of labor, it is of value to the employer, as well as to the worker and the community.

Not usually mentioned but worth noting is another broad goal served by having available a program of unemployment insurance. It is "to preserve flexibility and freedom of choice for private and public economic policy," and further elaborated as follows:

> In a broad sense, unemployment insurance helps to support this nation's adherence to a system that emphasizes free economic choice and individual initiative by mitigating the effects of imperfections in that system. These imperfections, at times, produce involuntary unemployment for individual workers. Unemployment insurance enables the work force to endure those circumstances while enjoying the benefits of the system.

> Similarly, the program helps to cushion the effects of changes in governmental policies with regard to such matters as taxes, spending, foreign trade, and defense production and procurement—all of which could produce manpower dislocations and unemployment. It may be worth considering how the absence of unemployment insurance might affect public policies or private decisions (Blaustein 1968, p. 12).

This does not exhaust the list of objectives or values of unemployment insurance. Others have been set forth from time to time, but the

---

10. Short-time compensation provides to workers placed temporarily on reduced workweek schedules unemployment compensation for the lost work-time and its earnings, appropriately prorated.

objectives we have discussed are those which have most influenced the character of the program.

Concluding Observations

Alleviation of unemployment's hardships, prevention of unemployment, and promotion of reemployment are the major objectives of unemployment insurance discussed in this chapter. A few others have also been noted. While alleviation is here regarded as the most fundamental purpose of the program, the others are not insignificant; they are well worth pursuing.

In a multipurpose program as large and as extensive as unemployment insurance, it is not surprising that its various objectives engender debate over their comparative importance. In fact, their simultaneous pursuit can involve conflicting policies, such as adequate benefits to assure adequate alleviation and limited benefits to restrain work disincentives, thereby promoting reemployment. The problem is to find the appropriate balance among objectives.

To a large degree, the appropriate balance should be the result of a collective value judgment, but one that is enlightened by sound knowledge about benefits and costs, about experience and the effects of changing conditions, and many other kinds of information. The policy choices are made politically, and properly so in the American system, but in the best sense of that process. Regardless of the debate, however, the discussion of the various objectives of unemployment insurance makes clear that this program is a key component in the nation's system of social and economic security.

3

The Insurance Character of Unemployment Insurance

When proposals to establish unemployment insurance were debated in the early 1930s, some individuals argued that unemployment might be too unpredictable to be insurable. In the midst of the worst depression in history, unemployment had reached heights never before experienced. Critics pointed to the heavy debt incurred by the British unemployment insurance program during the 1920s and subsequent years to show that such a scheme could not be kept on a solvent basis. Fears of insolvency led to very conservative beginnings for unemployment insurance in the United States based on estimates that called for substantial payroll tax rates and limited benefits. As the years went by, especially after the accumulation of large benefit reserves during World War II, much greater confidence developed in the program's soundness and in the insurability of the unemployment risk. Payroll tax rates generally declined and benefits were improved. Except for a few state funds, the system encountered no serious financial problems until the 1970s. The more extensive insolvency experienced then and in the 1980s among state funds generated efforts to improve financing and restrict benefits, but no demands to abandon the insurance approach. Despite its higher costs since 1970, the unemployment insurance system as a whole still operates well within the 3 percent of total payroll level originally thought necessary and adopted by the system in 1935. The problems of serious insolvency so far have concerned about a dozen individual states rather than the total system.[1]

Experience has shown that the risk of unemployment meets the tests of insurability. Unemployment insurance no longer needs to be

---

1. A total of fourteen states, including the District of Columbia, Puerto Rico, and the Virgin Islands, had insolvent benefit reserve funds for seven or more years during the 1970s and 1980s; these were the only states with negative year-end fund balances which often exceeded 1 percent of total payrolls in the state. See discussion of the funding crisis of these years in the section "State Benefit Financing" in chapter 10.

defended on these grounds. It is nevertheless desirable to review the insurance principles and the tests of insurability that apply to both private and social insurance to gain a better understanding of unemployment insurance, especially in view of widespread misunderstandings about the nature of private and social insurance.

Another matter that needs discussion at the outset is whether unemployment insurance can meet its social objectives and yet maintain its insurance character. Unemployment insurance is social insurance and so has some features that would not be written into a private insurance policy. Why such social features do not destroy the insurance character" of the system needs to be explained and understood.

Pressures almost always exist to introduce features or administrative practices into the unemployment insurance system to safeguard it against abuse, since there is some "moral hazard" in compensating for unemployment.[2] Some of these proposals would undermine the insurance character of the system making it more of a welfare system rather than an insurance program.[3] They tend to destroy one of the chief values of unemployment insurance—that compensation can be claimed as a matter of earned right without any loss of self-respect by the claimant. It is, after all, this value that is a principal justification for the use of the insurance approach in the first place and which remains of central importance to workers who bear the risk of unemployment.

This chapter, then, is designed to do three things: (1) show that unemployment is an insurable risk; (2) discuss some of the features that make the program "social insurance"; and (3) indicate how adopting certain features or practices would tend to make unemployment insurance a welfare rather than an insurance program.

---

2. Moral hazard is common to all insurance plans, whether private or social, since they run the risk that the insured person may claim compensation on the basis of contrived conditions or false representation usually difficult and costly to detect.

3. The definition of welfare varies among those using the term. As used here, it means benefits conditioned on the applicant's income and assets. Benefits are either denied if such income or assets exceed a specified amount, or paid in amounts that vary inversely with the level of income or assets.

Comparison of Social and Private Insurance

Social insurance and private or contractual insurance have certain distinctly different features, yet both are "insurance" in that they contain common elements which reflect basic insurance concepts. As described by one observer, these elements include: "a widespread pooling of the risks against which protection is provided; specific, and generally complete, descriptions of all conditions pertaining to coverage, benefits, and financing; precise mathematical calculations of benefit eligibility and amounts; and specific tax or contribution (premium) rates that are computed to meet the estimated costs of the system" (Myers 1981, p. 12).

It is also useful at this point to list elements which generally distinguish private from social insurance, as noted by the same author:

1. Private insurance must be based on individual equity. Social insurance...must generally contain a considerable degree of emphasis on social adequacy principles.

2. Private insurance is on a voluntary basis as to participation....Social insurance almost invariably is based on compulsory participation.

3. Private insurance involves complete contractual rights between the two parties (the insured and the insurer)...; social insurance does not involve a strictly contractual relationship, although the benefits involve a statutory right (but the statutory provisions can be changed...by the legislature).

4. Private individual insurance must be fully funded so that the rights of the insureds are protected....Social insurance, because of its compulsory and statutory nature, need not be fully funded—in fact, it is generally thought that from an economic standpoint, full funding is undesirable (Myers 1981, p. 13).

Concerning the first point, "individual equity" means that the insured individual is entitled to compensation, should the insured contingency occur, which relates directly to the amount of premium the individual paid for the protection. Social insurance departs from that principle by imposing minimum or maximum compensation levels or by varying the compensation-premium relationship in other ways[4] in order to achieve more adequate support of some standard of living so

---

4. In unemployment insurance, for example, these include paying low-wage earners a higher proportion of wage-loss compensation, and higher benefits to claimants with dependents.

as to alleviate hardship, i.e., social adequacy. The degree to which a particular program of social insurance pursues the goal of social adequacy is a controversial matter.[5]

The Unemployment Risk and Its Insurability

There are three types of risk against which insurance is issued: (1) personal loss, (2) property loss, and (3) liability for damage to a third person. Unemployment insurance is primarily insurance against the risk of personal loss (wage loss) due to unemployment.

Some difficulties have resulted from the mixture of liability and personal loss concepts in state unemployment insurance laws. In formulating an unemployment insurance program, one school of thought put the emphasis on the third type of risk, i.e., the liability of the employer for the damage done to workers by laying them off, and sought to confine the insured risk only to unemployment for which the employer is directly responsible. Others, concerned with the personal wage loss of the unemployed worker, focused on compensating involuntary unemployment, whatever its economic cause. Organized labor, for example, has stressed wage-loss insurance; employers generally have tended to stress the liability insurance concept.

In order for a risk to be insurable, it must meet the following six tests. Essentially, the risk of unemployment does meet these tests.

1. The Risk is Genuine, Involuntary
The risk must be real or actual, not speculative or created by the insured. In other words, insurance should cover only a genuine risk that already exists, and not an artificial risk that may be created, as, for example, a gambling loss. In order to be sure that the risk of unemploy-

---

5. In unemployment insurance, for example, opponents of dependent allowances have argued that these added benefits are unrelated to wages and discriminate among the insured unemployed on the basis of need, albeit presumed need, thereby injecting too much of a welfare element into the program and weakening the "earned right" basis. On the other hand, the program has been criticized for overly restrictive qualifying requirements and harsh application of other eligibility rules which result in denying benefits to many poor, marginal, or disadvantaged unemployed workers lacking any other means of support, thus limiting too severely the program's pursuit of its social adequacy objectives.

ment being insured against is actual and not created by the insured, the state laws generally provide that benefits be paid only when the unemployment is involuntary. No question is raised when the worker is laid off for lack of work—the risk of so being laid off always exists.

Questions arise, however, in cases where unemployment may have been caused, or contributed to, by the worker's own actions. Unemployment insurance generally restricts benefits in such cases, or denies them entirely. Unemployment insurance may depart somewhat from this principle by paying benefits when certain types of voluntary or quasi-voluntary action result in unemployment. An example is when a worker voluntarily quits a job for "good cause," such as compelling family reasons. As will be discussed later, this position can be justified in a social insurance program.

2. An Economic Loss is Involved

A second test of insurability of a risk is that an economic loss is involved. Unemployment involves wage loss. Therefore, there appears to be no problem in unemployment meeting this test. Questions occasionally arise in some cases, but each goes to the basic issue of whether or not the individual worker is involuntarily unemployed and is able to work and available and looking for work. For example, a student who is laid off at the end of a summer vacation and returns to or starts school full time in the fall is deemed not to have suffered an economic loss. The reason is that the student is occupied fully with attending school and thus is not available for work. Suppose a woman, however, has worked for some years at a cannery though only during the canning season and has otherwise been occupied as a homemaker. When she is laid off by the cannery at the season's end, has she suffered a wage loss? If more employment were available, would she continue working? In this example, the answer is more difficult to determine. Such cases do occur and require careful judgment; the issue centers on whether the individual wants to work and is available for work. The majority of workers who are laid off would have kept on working if their jobs were not discontinued and thus they do suffer an economic loss. Their unemployment, therefore, meets the second test of insurability.

3. The Risk is Verifiable

Still another test is whether the occurrence of the risk—in this case involuntary unemployment—is verifiable. In other types of insurance, such as accident or life or old-age insurance, a high degree of objectivity is possible in verifying the occurrence of the hazard insured against. There is normally no difficulty in proving that a person is dead, although even life insurance companies at times have problems in verifying whether an insured person has actually died, as, for example, in a drowning when the body may not be recovered. In unemployment insurance, the reason given by a worker for the job separation that caused his or her unemployment can be verified through a report from the employer. But there still may be difficulty in determining whether the worker was separated for a reason that makes the unemployment compensatory. If the worker quit, was it for a good reason or good cause, such as sexual harassment? If the separation was involuntary, was it for misconduct on the job, or was the worker fired for poor performance in the job?

Even more difficult is the problem of verifying whether an individual claiming unemployment insurance (a claimant) is still unemployed. Various techniques have been developed to determine whether a claimant is working on another job. Difficulties also arise in determining whether the claimant who is not working is really available for work. For example, is the claimant genuinely looking for work or, in effect, taking a vacation?

It is true that a moral hazard may exist whereby a claimant misrepresents his or her situation to obstruct or falsify verification. Reasonable administrative measures need to be applied to minimize the number of cases in which the hazard materializes. Moral hazard exists in all insurance; fires may be started by the insured in order to collect fire insurance, and even life insurance is sometimes taken out by a beneficiary with the intent of killing the insured to collect the insurance. More akin to moral hazard in unemployment insurance, however, is the moral hazard in workers' compensation that an individual drawing compensation may malinger. Doctors will admit that it is often very difficult to determine whether an injured individual is able to return to work. It may be no more difficult to verify unemployment in borderline cases than it is to verify the occurrence of other risks in equally ambiguous situations. In the large majority of situations, however, the genuineness of the claimant's unemployment can be easily verified.[6]

4. The Law of Large Numbers

A fourth test is that the risk of unemployment must be subject to the Law of Large Numbers.[7] This law holds that when a particular event or phenomenon occurs at random, its frequency or rate of occurrence will tend to conform with that expected in accordance with the theory of probability if the number of cases or observations among which the event may occur is large enough. The theory of probability is popularly illustrated by the random tossing of a coin. The probability is that "heads" will come up 50 percent of the times the coin is tossed. There is no certainty that this precise result will occur. But the larger the number of times the coin is tossed, the greater is the probability that the expected percentage will occur, and that the Law of Large Numbers will apply. This law can be applied to random human contingencies if enough cases are involved. Mortality tables have been constructed periodically based on the actual experience of a large number of deaths at given ages so that it can be predicted with considerable accuracy what proportion of 100,000 people can be expected to die at each year of age.

The rate of occurrence of unemployment can easily meet the Law of Large Numbers, since a sufficiently large number of workers are covered under every state unemployment insurance law to make the laws of probability operative. Even the Virgin Islands, the jurisdiction with the smallest labor force, averaged about 42,000 workers in covered employment in 1990, a much larger number than is necessary to meet the Law of Large Numbers. This law is also met in that, as a whole, the workers covered represent a random rather than a biased selection of all workers in terms of the contingency covered. Since some classes of workers experience a higher- and other classes experience lower-than-average risk of unemployment, limiting coverage to some classes might result in a distortion of the random quality of the

---

6. How to verify continued unemployment and identify improper claims are controversial subjects. Research on these problem areas in the 1980s has shed some light, and some statutory and administrative improvements have ensued to better control improper claims.

7. See Malisoff (1961, chapter 2). Dr. Malisoff also discusses other aspects of the insurability of unemployment in a somewhat different manner than is done in this chapter.

risk being insured against. The random nature of the insured group improves as employment is more broadly covered under the system, since the employment covered becomes more highly diversified.[8]

5. Only a Limited Part is Unemployed at One Time

Another test of insurability is that the contingency happens to only a portion of the insured population at any one time, so that the cost burden of compensating for the loss is not excessive or unmanageable when spread across all the insured. A large proportion of the labor force never or rarely experiences any unemployment, and although a sizable number of workers may have some unemployment during a recession, only a limited proportion of all workers is unemployed at any one time. As already indicated, there were fears in the 1930s that unemployment was not insurable because of the unexpected and unprecedented large numbers of unemployed workers at that time. Since then, however, relative unemployment levels have been only a fraction of those in the Great Depression.

In the period 1947 through 1990, average weekly insured unemployment in the nation exceeded 6 percent of covered employment in only three years, and exceeded 8 percent in some months of those years, but such peak figures are not significant from the point of view of insurability. More important is the level of unemployment over a period of time. Average insured unemployment over several years of a business cycle tends to be considerably lower than peak monthly or yearly levels. Although the proportion in some states is higher than in others, unemployment still affects only a limited proportion of workers. Only in a few states has the annual average rate of insured unemployment sometimes exceeded 7 or 8 percent, usually in severe recession years.[9] Puerto Rico is an exception, with a rate that averaged from 10 to over 15 percent in most of the 1970s.[10] But even in states with the worst experience, unemployment meets the test that the risk happens to only a small portion of the covered workforce at any one time. Moreover, policy tendencies and cyclical safeguards built into

---

8. About 97 percent of all wage and salary jobs are now covered by unemployment insurance.

9. Based on statistics for post-World War II recession years in *Unemployment Insurance Financial Data,* 1938-1982 and annual supplements.

10. See table for Puerto Rico in *Unemployment Insurance Financial Data, 1938-1982.*

the economy foster a fair degree of confidence that a depression such as that of the 1930s is unlikely to repeat.

It should be noted that the larger the base for pooling, (per the Law of Large Numbers), the more likely it is that the proportion experiencing unemployment will range within narrower limits. While the insured unemployment rates of a few states have exceeded 8 percent in the worst recessions, other state rates were quite low. Long-term unemployment extending beyond the regular duration limits of state laws is compensated during recessions, or high unemployment periods, through a 50-50 cost sharing arrangement—half from the state and half from the federal government unemployment insurance funds. This sharing provides added manageability to the burden when heaviest and makes longer-term protection against the risk more acceptable at such times. Thus, state insured unemployment rates, including the unemployed receiving extended benefits, are even higher than those indicated above, yet still reflect a limited proportion of the covered population and well within insurable bounds.

The limited rate of occurrence of the risk and the pooling of its compensation costs make unemployment insurable by this test. Winston Churchill, with his remarkable ability to translate complex ideas into more simple understandable terms, once characterized social insurance as "bringing the magic of the averages to the rescue of the millions" (Czarnowski 1957, p. 22).

6. Unemployment is Predictable

The final and most important test of insurability is whether the rate of occurrence of the contingency (in this case unemployment) among the covered population can be predicted within reasonable limits. This test is critical since predictability is key to planning a sound financial arrangement to cover future needs for insurance outlays.

The pattern of unemployment during most of the last 50 years has also been sufficiently regular as to assure confidence in predictions of its incidence within a reasonable margin of error. That confidence was shaken somewhat by the severe unemployment experience of the mid-1970s and early 1980s. With perhaps some adjustment of the range of error, the predictability of unemployment nevertheless still remains reasonably reliable for insurance funding purposes.

A vast amount of information on the characteristics and behavior of unemployment has accumulated as a by-product of the operation of state unemployment insurance programs. Detailed studies of individual state economies support projections of employment and unemployment trends. Techniques for estimating the cost of unemployment insurance have developed and are constantly improved. Given such data, research, and increasingly sophisticated methodology, the costs of unemployment insurance over a period of time can be predicted with sufficient accuracy so that the benefit reserve funds can be kept solvent, provided that the predictions are translated into appropriate and adequate financing policies.

The insolvency of many state funds in the 1970s was in part a failure to build sufficient reserves to cover projected needs. In part, however, the benefit cost experience of the 1970s also contained unusual elements for some states that may not have been reasonably predictable based on past trends and experience. Such unusual cost can be contained within the range of insurability by a broadening of the insurance base, for example through some form of reinsurance.

As the basis for future cost estimates, predictions of insured unemployment must be made over a period of years. Unemployment's fluctuation with the business cycle does not invalidate the insurability of unemployment. Allowances must be made for recessions by making the estimates cover a long enough period of time to include at least one business cycle.

Unlike the case for private insurance, the rights to benefits can be changed in social insurance without the consent of the insured or of those who finance the program. If unemployment changes so that the estimates of fund needs do not work out, contributions or taxes can be increased or benefit entitlement reduced to take care of the changed situation. Nearly all of the states have provisions for automatic tax rate increases when reserves fall below a stated level. If these automatic measures prove inadequate, the state legislatures can increase the unemployment taxes. In this respect, social insurance has an advantage over private insurance which risks the loss of business if it raises rates. Unemployment insurance has a "captive" group of contributors whose only way of avoiding a necessary tax rate increase is by pressure on the state legislature or the Congress not to take such action or to reduce benefits instead. In the final analysis, the real test of the insurability of unemployment is whether the legislative bodies will make changes in the unemployment insurance statutes when increased cost necessitate such changes.

Pursuit of Social Objectives
Effect On Insurance Character

Many features in the unemployment insurance program would not be written into a conventional private insurance contract. In private insurance, the emphasis must be on individual equity, and benefit protection must be directly related to the amount of contributions or premiums paid. In a social insurance program, emphasis is on "social adequacy," that is, on providing the insured with benefits related to their presumed needs. In the case of unemployment insurance, certain features applicable to setting the weekly benefit amount may be used to increase the likelihood of this result. Several examples illustrate the practice, but it should be understood that they represent exceptions from the usual pattern whereby most claimants receive weekly benefit amounts designed to replace a uniform percentage of their prior weekly wages, up to a weekly benefit ceiling. In some states, minimum weekly benefit amounts are set at levels that give insured unemployed workers with the lowest earnings (usually part-time workers) a higher proportion of their former earnings than higher-paid workers receive.[11] Also weekly benefit formulas of some states "weight" benefits at the lower end of the wage scale, i.e., pay as a benefit a higher percentage of low wages than of high wages. All states set ceilings on their weekly benefit amounts; unemployed workers with wages high enough to place them at the benefit ceiling receive a progressively lower percentage of wage replacement, the higher the wage level. Such variations from private insurance practice are justified on the basis of the presumed relative needs of lower- and higher-paid workers. The presump-

---

11. Other states coordinate the minimum qualifying wage requirements with their minimum benefit amounts so that the same percentage of wage replacement results at that level as at higher wage levels.

tion is that persons with low incomes must spend the higher proportion on necessities than do those with higher incomes.

Some states depart further from private insurance principles by adding dependent allowances to basic benefits, with no differentiation in premiums. But dependent allowances are justified as serving a social purpose in providing more adequate benefits where there are more mouths to feed and, presumably, the need is greater. The Actuary for the Metropolitan Life Insurance Company in the 1930s wrote: "Just as considerations of equity of benefits form a natural and vital part of operating private insurance, so should considerations of adequacy of benefits control the pattern of social insurance" (Hohaus 1948, p. 77). Not all unemployment insurance proponents agree fully with this viewpoint and worry instead about the program's tendencies to resemble welfare more than insurance, an issue discussed in the next section.

Another variation from private insurance principles is the payment of benefits under certain circumstances for unemployment that is created by the claimants' own actions. For example, benefits may be paid for unemployment which follows the voluntary quitting of a job if the claimant can establish a "good cause" for leaving.[12] A further difference from private insurance occurs when an unemployed worker who quit *without* good cause, or was discharged for misconduct, is allowed to draw benefits after a period of disqualification. The justification given for such benefit payments is that after a certain period following separation from a job, unemployment becomes involuntary if the claimant has been unsuccessful in genuine attempts to find a job. Few states now follow this practice.

Despite these differences, it must be noted that private insurance available in the areas of workers' compensation, health insurance, and automobile insurance does compensate for wage loss and medical costs in accidents caused by the insured. It may be said that with the spread of no-fault policies, private insurance has been evolving toward a form of social insurance. The contrasts between the two sometimes are not as sharp as theory may assume.

Except for the benefit amount ceiling, the variations from private insurance principles cited above for unemployment insurance are on

---

12. "Good cause" in most states has been restricted to causes attributable to the employer or connected with the work.

the lenient side, that is, expansive of claimant benefits and entitlement. Certain departures, however are restrictive in nature. For example, most state laws vary the duration of benefits payable in proportion to the claimant's previous employment or earnings on which payroll tax contributions have been paid. In practically all types of private insurance, the amount of indemnity is not limited by the length of time the contributor has been paying premiums; the full amount of insurance becomes effective from the moment the insured signs the insurance contract. In some forms of private insurance, however, the amount of indemnity payable may decline over time (decreasing term life insurance), or the cash value of the insurance policy may increase with time (whole life insurance).

Another type of restriction not found in conventional private insurance is that unemployment benefits are paid only to workers who have had a minimum amount of qualifying employment or earnings even though whatever employment or earnings they had was covered and subject to the unemployment tax. The minimum is required in order to establish evidence that the claimant has been genuinely and substantially attached to the labor market. Such a test is more necessary than in other types of insurance because the fact of unemployment cannot be established as objectively as, for example, the fact of an accident or a death. Nevertheless, it must be recognized that such a qualifying requirement is not entirely unique to social insurance. Some kinds of private insurance specify a similar type of limitation, such as health insurance policies which exclude for a period of time coverage of previous health conditions of the insured, or life insurance policies which exclude coverage of suicide until the policy has been in force for a specified duration.

The important point about all these variations is that it is not legitimate to fault unemployment insurance simply for departing from "pure" conventional private insurance principles or practices. For *social* insurance, such variations are necessary to achieve certain social purposes which are not pertinent to private insurance. Yet, the departures must not be so extensive as to impair the insurance character of the program.

One other fairly widely held view of the program's insurance character concerns its source of financing of benefit costs. That view holds that if any general government revenues are allocated to finance benefits in place of revenues from specific taxes imposed for the purpose on the wages of covered workers, then the program becomes more of a welfare than an insurance plan. Unemployed workers derive the sense that they receive benefits on the basis of "earned rights" from the fact that they (or their employers) have paid for them. Technically speaking, the payment of insurance costs or premiums by persons or organizations other than the insured does not invalidate the insurance character of the plan or policy. In other countries, contributions from government general revenues into social insurance funds are fairly typical. To the extent that general revenues do finance most or all benefit costs, however, the sense of "earned rights" may be diminished.

Does Unemployment Insurance Differ Enough From Welfare?

The concern of the insured unemployed may be whether there is much difference between unemployment insurance and welfare programs, not whether unemployment insurance departs from private insurance principles. One of the principal advantages of unemployment insurance is that the unemployed worker is not subject to a test of need such as is applied to a welfare applicant. It was to remove the indignity of the required proof by the unemployed of their need for support that in large part accounted for the acceptance of unemployment insurance in the first place. The application of a means test, as one writer has put it, is the "watershed" dividing social insurance from public assistance (Carlson 1962, p. 7). Objections to references to need, even to "presumed need," in relation to unemployment insurance is therefore understandable in this context, although such objections cannot obscure the fact that "presumed need" is an inherent characteristic of social insurance. Care must be taken to avoid a stance that comes close to investigating individual need when the benefit provision varies compensation among the unemployed by some measure of presumed need, such as dependents, especially if that measure calls for personal information from the claimant.

A related advantage put forward for unemployment insurance over welfare is that unemployed workers feel that their benefits are paid "as a matter of right." But even this "right" may be undermined, as Professor Harry Malisoff (1961, pp. 25-27) pointed out, if the questions asked of an unemployment insurance claimant are so detailed or personal that the claimant feels his or her private life is invaded. The personal questioning about the economic needs of public welfare applicants is one of the reasons that some needy people avoid applying for relief. In the same way, some unemployed workers do not file for unemployment compensation where the practice of extensive personal questioning makes them feel that unemployment insurance is no better or no different from relief in this regard. As noted earlier in chapter 2, a substantial proportion of the public erroneously regards unemployment insurance as part of the welfare system. A fair number of eligible unemployed workers delay or avoid filing for unemployment benefits because of this perception.

That perception may be reenforced by local office harassment of claimants concerning the validity of their claims. Reasonable monitoring of a claimant's availability for work and job search to confirm claims of current unemployment is a legitimate function of unemployment insurance administration. Close scrutiny may be justified if grounds exist to suspect malingering. All kinds of insurance, including private insurance, investigate questionable claims. Social insurance is probably more sensitive to public criticism of improper benefit payments, claimant abuse of the rules, and fraud, whether real or alleged. Unemployment insurance programs therefore apply certain measures to monitor claims more effectively. For example, they may concentrate greater attention on types of claimants who experience has shown tend to file higher-than-average proportions of improper or invalid claims. It is important, however, to avoid treating all claimants so typed as guilty of filing improper claims and then subjecting them to close, personal, and adversarial questioning to establish the evidence. Many eligible claimants are likely to retreat under these intimidating tactics and forgo filing further claims to avoid the discomfort and indignity of such interrogation.[13] For these unemployed workers, turning to unemployment insurance is as painful as resorting to welfare.

---

13. One study has estimated that during the years 1982 to 1987, less than 70 percent of persons unemployed and eligible for unemployment insurance benefits collected them, a lower proportion than in earlier years. Among various reasons that can be advanced for this result are stiffened eligibility requirements and more rigorous administration in this period (Blank and Card 1991).

Welfare is intended to be restrictive, confined to those actually in need. Unemployment insurance applies to a very broad population subject to the insured risk and presumes that most need the insurance support if the risk is incurred. The unemployment insurance system covers nearly all wage and salary workers; it is compulsory and it is universal since the risk is universal. By the same token, benefits are payable to all workers who incur the risk. Eligibility should not be so restrictive as to unreasonably diminish or eliminate benefit rights. To be sure, there are problems in assuring that the unemployment is insurable and real. Still, an overly restrictive stance by the program with respect to eligibility blurs the insurance-welfare distinction.

4

Foreign Experience with Unemployment Insurance

There was considerable European experience to draw upon when unemployment insurance began to be considered seriously in the United States. Before 1935, seventeen European nations had some provision for unemployment insurance (table 4.1). Seven had national compulsory programs, while ten provided for government subsidies to voluntary plans, which in most cases were organized and operated by trade unions and other private associations. Most of the latter group of countries have since adopted national compulsory schemes. Another three countries operated unemployment assistance programs, rather than unemployment insurance, before 1935.[1] As of 1989, there were thirty-four countries with national compulsory unemployment insurance schemes and three countries with subsidized voluntary programs; 5 countries provided unemployment assistance only (table 4.2).

The early subsidy programs for voluntary unemployment insurance were of interest to American planners in the 1930s mainly regarding the degree of national control over local plans and the methods of national assistance used. The experience under the compulsory systems of Great Britain and Germany was of most value in planning early federal and state legislation in the United States.[2]

---

1. A report on foreign experience was prepared for President Roosevelt's Committee on Economic Security as it developed its recommendation for unemployment insurance in 1934. See Social Security Board (1937).

2. This information, as of 1989, does not, of course, reflect the enormous political and economic transformations which began that year to reshape Central and Eastern Europe. By 1992, some changes had already altered the picture presented by table 4.2, most notably the unification of East (Democratic Republic) and West (Federal Republic) Germany and the breakup of Yugoslavia. New national unemployment insurance or assistance schemes are likely to emerge in these regions in ensuing years.

Table 4.1   Nations with Public Unemployment Benefit Programs Before 1935

Type of program	Nation[a]	Date of first law
National compulsory unemployment insurance scheme[b]	United Kingdom	1911
	Ireland	1911[c]
	Italy	1919
	Austria	1920
	Poland	1924
	Bulgaria	1925
	Germany	1927
Subsidies to voluntary unemployment insurance plans	France	1906
	Norway	1906
	Denmark	1907
	Netherlands	1916
	Finland	1917
	Spain	1919
	Belgium	1920
	Czechoslovakia	1924
	Switzerland[d]	1924
	Sweden	1934
Unemployment assistance[e]	Luxembourg	1921
	Yugoslavia	1927
	New Zealand	1930

SOURCE: Industrial Relations Counselors (1934); USDOL, Bureau of Labor Statistics (1931); International Labour Office (1955); Blaustein and Craig (1977); U.S. Department of Health and Human Services, Social Security Administration (1990).

a. Within "type of program" category, listed in order of date of first law.

b. Not listed is the Soviet Union, which had a provision in its Labor Code for unemployment insurance from 1921 to 1930.

c. In 1922, after it gained independence from Great Britain (thereafter the United Kingdom), Ireland took over the insurance program in its own territory, based on the British National Insurance Act of 1911, as amended.

d. Also subsidized compulsory cantonal schemes.

e. Nations listed provided unemployment assistance only; others with unemployment insurance provisions may have also provided unemployment assistance.

Table 4.2   Nations with Public Unemployment Benefit Programs, 1989

National compulsory unemployment insurance schemes (34 nations)			
Argentina[a]	Cyprus	Hong Kong	Netherlands
Austria	Ecuador	Iceland	Norway
Barbados	Egypt	Iran[b]	Portugal
Belgium	France	Ireland	South Africa
Brazil	Germany, Federal	Israel	Spain
Bulgaria	Republic	Italy	Switzerland
Canada	Ghana	Japan	United Kingdom
Chile	Greece	Luxembourg	United States
China, People's		Malta	Uruguay
Republic			

Subsidies to voluntary unemployment insurance plans (3 nations)		
Denmark	Finland	Sweden

Unemployment assistance (5 nations)[c]			
Australia	New Zealand	Tunisia	Yugoslavia
Hungary			

SOURCE: U.S. Department of Health and Human Services (1990).
a. Confined to construction workers only.
b. Implemented for three years on an experimental basis starting July 1987.
c. Nations listed provide unemployment assistance only; others with unemployment insurance provisions may also provide unemployment assistance.

Foreign Voluntary Plans

The first unemployment insurance plan appeared in Basel Town, Switzerland in 1789, but it lasted only a few years. Apparently there were no further attempts to create a public unemployment insurance plan during the next century. About the middle of the nineteenth century, some trade unions began to pay benefits to their unemployed members and some mutual benefit or fraternal societies also operated unemployment benefit plans. Starting with Dijon, France in 1896, municipalities began to subsidize trade union funds for the purpose of increasing their benefits. Subsidies were granted annually on the basis of benefits paid the preceding year. This system of municipal subsidies, which became known as the "Ghent" plan, spread widely.[3] In the early part of the twentieth century, many provinces (and cantons in Switzerland) began to add their subsidies to those of the cities, and some national governments added grants. In only three countries with solely voluntary plans did employers make any contributions. In two of these, Switzerland and Spain, employers contributed to joint employer-employee plans; in Denmark, in 1921, employers were required to contribute to a central fund to provide emergency benefits to those who had exhausted trade union benefits. Some communal voluntary plans were also established, notably in Switzerland, where they were subsidized first by the cantons and eventually by the federal government. Where government subsidies were provided, government control varied from practically none in Belgium and the other countries which used the Ghent system, to very detailed requirements and controls in Switzerland. In Belgium, during the depression of the 1930s, administration became so loose that in 1933 the national government introduced rigid controls, defining membership, contributions, and benefit requirements on a uniform basis.[4]

---

3. With some modifications, the Ghent plan was emulated by other municipalities in Belgium, Denmark, Finland, France, Germany, Great Britain, Italy, the Netherlands, Norway, and Switzerland.
4. The Belgian experience was studied in detail by Kiehl (1932), and the Swiss experience by Spates and Rabinovitch (1931).

Foreign Compulsory Programs

The first attempt at a compulsory unemployment insurance system in the nineteenth century was made in the Swiss commune of St. Gall in 1894, but it ceased to function in 1897 after workers with stable employment began moving to other towns to avoid paying contributions. The first *national* compulsory system was enacted in Great Britain in 1911. The second was established eight years later in Italy, followed by compulsory systems legislated in several other countries during the 1920s.[5] The German law of 1927 was the latest compulsory plan before the Social Security Act was passed in the United States in 1935. Since the British and German systems were both the largest and most intensively studied and publicized, they had the most influence on the development of the American system. Their structure and experience therefore are described in some detail.[6]

The British Experience

The original British unemployment insurance law was passed in 1911. For about seventy-five years prior to this event, unemployed workers in Great Britain were treated largely under the reformed Poor Laws adopted in 1834. This system, which was operated locally, distinguished sharply between the able-bodied poor and those unable to work. The former were made "less eligible" for relief and subjected to the "workhouse test." If relief applicants could work but did not, they were required to accept institutionalization under harsh and punitive workhouse conditions, usually involving the breakup of families. Increasingly, urban industrial poverty towards the end of the nineteenth century made more apparent the severity of the Poor Laws and their inadequacy for dealing with the unemployed. Voluntary charities seek-

---

5. Besides those listed in table 4.1, there were compulsory subnational plans in 13 cantons in Switzerland and in Queensland, Australia.

6. For a description of foreign systems prior to the Social Security Act, see Industrial Relations Counselors (1934); USDOL, Bureau of Labor Statistics (1931). For later information, see International Labour Office (1955); Blaustein and Craig (1977); and U.S. Department of Health and Human Services (1990).

ing to offer an alternative to the workhouse were also inadequate to cope with the growing problem, as were the out-of-work benefit funds of the trade unions which covered only a small proportion of the labor force. Political unrest stirred as the socialist and labor movements focused heavily on the problem. It was the era of social critics and reformers who challenged the view underlying the Poor Law system that the able-bodied unemployed were responsible for their own destitution, the result of their personal inadequacies. The emerging counterview was that they were, instead, the victims of industrial and social insufficiency and, therefore, the responsibility of industry and society. In 1909, William H. Beveridge, publishing a summary of lectures he gave on the subject at Cambridge University, used the title "Unemployment: A Problem of Industry," thereby emphasizing the new viewpoint.[7]

Appointed in 1906 to review the Poor Laws, a Royal Commission recommended reforms which responded to some of the new thinking ("Report of the Royal Commission on the Poor Laws and Relief of Distress" 1909). Its Majority Report urged more vocational-oriented education, a public labor (employment) exchange system, and the promotion of regularization of employment in industry. For the unemployed who were unable to find work, the Majority Report urged "public assistance" benefits, instead of "Poor Law" relief, contingent on daily labor in work relief projects. The Majority Report recommended the establishment of some form of unemployment insurance, especially among unskilled and unorganized labor. It recommended, however, that this be accomplished through encouragement of voluntary schemes by government subsidy.

A Minority Report, representing mainly the views of Beatrice and Sidney Webb, had a more profound impact on the "break-up of the poor law."[8] It stressed prevention rather than relief of unemployment. The report urged a labor exchange system, plans for countercyclical public works, and restrictions on child labor, excessive work hours, and employment of mothers with young children. It argued against

---

7. For the treatment of the unemployed in Great Britain before 1911 and the criticism of that treatment, see de Schweinitz, (1943) and Lubove (1966).

8. Webb and Webb (1929). Prominent among social reformers of the period, the Webbs were the leading critics of the Poor Law system.

national compulsory unemployment insurance because the problems of "repeaters" and "bad risks" were thought to make such a scheme financially hazardous. An unemployment insurance program might work for selected categories of workers, but that would not relieve much of the unemployment problem. If tried, it would be essential to have a labor exchange to apply a work test, in accordance with a definition of "suitable work" to prevent downgrading of workers. The Webbs did encourage government subsidies for trade union jobless benefit funds. For the hard-core unemployed, they recommended case-by-case treatment emphasizing restorative remedies—training, medical treatment, and other forms of rehabilitation. While the views of the Webbs and the Minority Report of the Royal Commission greatly influenced the course of Poor Law reform, they were less significant for unemployment insurance developments.

William Beveridge (1930) also favored a public employment exchange to help bring about the "de-casualization" of labor and the readjustment of work patterns and earnings to make unattractive and unprofitable the use of the unemployed as a reserve pool of casual workers for limited labor needs. Since he believed that not all unemployment could be prevented, he urged the adoption of unemployment insurance. Beveridge was a towering figure in unemployment insurance in Britain during the first half of the 20th century. He left an enduring mark on the way modern industrial societies cope with involuntary unemployment.[9]

Many of the proposals in the reports of the Royal Commission found their way into law. A system of public labor exchanges was adopted in 1909. The government went further, however, by enacting the first national compulsory unemployment insurance program as part of the National Insurance Act of 1911 which also included sickness insurance. The unemployment insurance scheme was developed in the Board of Trade, then headed by Winston Churchill who, with his colleague, David Lloyd George, then Chancellor of the Exchequer, saw the legislation through Parliament. Hubert Llewellyn Smith, in collaboration with William Beveridge, worked out the structure and details of the program. The chief elements of unemployment insurance were

---

9. For an account of his life and work, see his autobiography, *Power and Influence* (Beveridge 1953).

described by Smith in a speech in 1910 which, Beveridge noted, contained an expression of "historical importance, as a record of the hopes, anxieties and purposes with which unemployment insurance came into the world" (Beveridge 1930, pp. 264-65). The heart of Mr. Smith's remarks are given in an appendix to this chapter.

The Original Law

The unemployment insurance portion of the 1911 Act covered only about 2.5 million workers in half a dozen industries that had a high incidence of unemployment.[10] These industries were building and construction, shipbuilding, foundries, machine shops, construction of vehicles, and sawmilling. Seasonal industries, such as cotton manufacturing and coal mining, were excluded. The program was limited in coverage because it was considered to be experimental in nature.

The original program was also quite limited as to benefits. A modest flat-rate weekly benefit was payable. The duration of benefits was limited to a maximum of fifteen weeks in a twelve-month period and payable on the basis of one week of benefit for each five weeks of contributions. The minimum requirement to qualify for any benefits was ten weeks of paid-up contributions. The insured worker had to be capable of work. Disqualification from benefits was imposed for six weeks if the worker lost a job because of misconduct or left work voluntarily without "just cause. Refusal of suitable work was also disqualifying and not imposed if the job refused was vacant because of a labor dispute, or was less favorable in wages or other conditions than the worker "habitually obtained in his usual employment." These statutory conditions were applied in a process that provided for appeals of initial judgments by local administrative officers. Employers and workers contributed equal amounts, with a government contribution equal to one-fourth of the system's total revenue. Refunds of the surplus of contributions over benefits received were to be made to workers at age 60 who had made 500 contributions, and used for rebates to employers with good employment records.

The law also provided subsidies for voluntary plans covering workers outside the insured trades. This provision induced very few new

---

10. For detailed information on the British experience under the national program prior to 1935, see Burns (1941) and Gilson (1931).

plans. Plans already in existence covering workers in the insured trades were allowed to continue with a subsidy of one-sixth of benefit costs, and these plans expanded considerably.

The program was extended in 1916 to munitions workers (among whom unemployment was expected after the war) and to workers in certain other industries including the chemical, leather, metal, and rubber industries. This extension enlarged the coverage to above 3.7 million workers. The program was extended further in 1920, bringing most wage earners under its coverage.

Up to 1920, the program was financially solvent. In fact, with the low unemployment during World War I, a substantial surplus had accumulated in the unemployment insurance fund by mid-1919. The 1920s saw a reversal of this favorable condition.

The 1920 Amendments

In 1920, coverage was extended to all workers between age 16 and 65 except those in agriculture (covered by a separate scheme in 1936), and domestic service, civil servants, railway and public utility employees, and white-collar workers earning over a specified amount in a year. The flat weekly benefit amount was increased for men and a lower benefit was set for women. Insured unemployed workers under age 18 were paid at half these amounts. In 1921, dependents allowances were added to the regular benefit amounts. One week of benefit was allowed for each six weeks, instead of five weeks, of contributions. Maximum duration remained at fifteen weeks. Contributions were increased.

Although the 1920 amendments were enacted in a favorable economic climate, unemployment began to rise almost immediately after they took effect. By December 1920, the unemployment rate was 7.8 percent; it rose to an average of 16.6 percent in the following year. During the next 10 years, the rate averaged 12.7 percent and fell below 10 percent only in 1927. In 1931 it rose to 21.1 percent.

Early Relaxation of Eligibility Requirements

The British thus faced a continuing large volume of unemployment during the 1920s, with only local relief as an alternative to unemployment insurance to provide income for the unemployed. With a duration limit of fifteen weeks, many of the unemployed exhausted their insurance benefits and remained jobless or unable to obtain sufficient work to qualify for further unemployment insurance. The conditions for receipt of local relief were onerous and the local governments were unable to finance it for the large numbers who were unemployed and uninsured. With constant hope that employment conditions would improve, the British temporarily but repeatedly expanded the unemployment insurance system to provide for the unemployed who were not eligible for insurance benefits or who had exhausted their entitlement. The result was a bewildering succession of relaxations of the conditions for benefits and extensions of the duration of "covenanted" and "uncovenanted" benefits. Surging unemployment led to such actions almost immediately after the expansion of coverage under the 1920 amendments. Even that legislation had provided that, for a temporary period, a worker could draw eight weeks of uncovenanted benefits if contributions had been paid for only four weeks instead of the higher normal minimum of ten weeks required for covenanted benefits. Because increasing unemployment prevented many from meeting even this mild qualification, the law was again changed in the following month so that a worker could qualify for eight weeks of benefits with ten weeks of work after 1919, provided that such work would have been "insurable employment" if the 1920 amendments had been in force throughout 1920, or with four such weeks after July 4, 1920.

Standard Benefits

In July 1921, the minimum eligibility requirements for standard or covenanted benefits were tightened to twenty weeks of contributions since the beginning of the last benefit year preceding the current year. Yet, this requirement was waived if it could be shown that the claimant was normally in insured employment and genuinely seeking full-time employment. By the Unemployment Insurance Act (No. 2) of 1924, the minimum qualifying requirements were further tightened to thirty weeks of contributions since the beginning of the second benefit year preceding the current one and twenty weeks in the immediately preceding benefit year. However, the Minister of Labor was authorized to waive the new condition of thirty contributions, first until October 1925, and then, by two further authorizations, until the end of 1927. To complicate matters even more, the waiver rules issued by the Minister were progressively relaxed until, beginning in February 1925, a claimant could qualify for standard benefits with eight contributions in the last two preceding insurance years or thirty contributions at any time. The statutory conditions for standard benefits were changed again by the Unemployment Insurance Act of 1927, effective in April 1928, by having only one requirement, namely, thirty contributions in the two years preceding application for benefit.

The maximum duration of standard benefits varied from fifteen to sixteen weeks in a benefit year until November 1922, when it was changed to twenty-six weeks. From April 19, 1928, to November 11, 1931, there was no statutory limitation on the duration of standard benefits. The rule of one week of benefit for each six weeks of contributions had also been relaxed in various ways and then abolished by the Act of 1927, effective April 1928. The unrestricted duration of benefits was recommended by the so-called Blanesburgh Committee which took the position that the unemployed should draw benefits for an unlimited period provided that they were genuinely seeking work.

Concern about malingering led in 1924 to the application of a genuinely-seeking-work requirement to claimants of standard benefits; it had applied for uncovenanted benefits since 1921. Much controversy surrounded this provision—its interpretation, the verification procedures required for evidencing job search, and its value or effectiveness when little or no employment was available. In March 1930, on the recommendation of the Morris Committee, the genuinely-seeking-work provision was replaced by one disqualifying a worker for failure or refusal to apply for or accept suitable work or failure to carry out the written directions of the public employment office. This later requirement was ineffective because of the limited number of job openings available. As a result, the number of persons drawing benefits increased considerably.

Uncovenanted Benefits

Even with the temporary relaxation of requirements for standard benefits in the early 1920s, large numbers of the unemployed could not meet the contributory rules. Additional benefits, called uncovenanted benefits (1921-24), "extended" benefits (1924-28), and "transitional" benefits (1928-31) were therefore paid to unemployed persons who could not meet the contribution conditions provided they met certain alternative conditions. The latter included proof that the claimant normally worked in insured employment and was genuinely seeking work on a full-time basis. For a time, such benefits were paid at the discretion of the Minister of Labor when he deemed it in the public interest. The Minister used this discretion to exclude certain classes of the unemployed for whom the benefits were deemed unnecessary in view of their other resources, that is, by a rough test of need. This discretion was abolished by the Act of 1924 but later restored by the succeeding Conservative government. The Act of 1927 aimed to abolish uncovenanted or extended benefits. However, because large numbers of workers could not meet the contributory conditions for unemployment insurance (thirty contributions in the two preceding years) and unemployment was still serious, transitional payments were provided. Only eight contributions in the preceding two years were required for such transitional payments, but even this requirement was repealed by the Act of 1930.

The maximum duration of uncovenanted benefits was first set at twenty-two weeks, but this was increased to forty-four in November 1922, and then reduced to forty-one in October 1923. During this period, no benefits were paid during temporary gaps of from one to three weeks after benefits had been paid for specified periods. Workers who exhausted their standard or covenanted benefits were able to draw uncovenanted benefits for additional weeks to bring their combined benefits up to the statutory limits for uncovenanted benefits. Beginning August 1924, when the term uncovenanted benefits was changed to extended benefits, there was no statutory limit on their duration.

Retrenchment in 1931

The combination of extensions of benefits and other liberalizations in the program kept the unemployment insurance fund in financial difficulties. The surplus built up in the ten years preceding the expansion of the program in November 1920 was exhausted by the following July, when the Treasury was authorized to make interest-bearing loans to the fund. During the next ten years, expenditures exceeded receipts in all but two fiscal years. The debt rose especially rapidly beginning with the fiscal year 1930-31. During that year alone it practically doubled. Six months later the debt rose by nearly 50 percent more. This occurred despite the payment of the entire cost of transitional benefits by the Treasury directly, instead of by the insurance fund, during fiscal years 1930 and 1931.

The heavy drains that unemployment insurance made on the Treasury led to drastic revision of the unemployment insurance system in 1931. Actions taken under the National Economy Act of 1931 increased contributions, decreased the weekly benefit amount, limited the duration of standard benefits to twenty-six weeks and introduced a requalifying requirement after exhaustion of benefits. Transitional benefits were terminated and replaced by transitional payments based on need. These payments were restricted to those unemployed who had exhausted standard benefits and would have been eligible for benefits under the 1927 qualifying requirements. Determination of need was to be made by the local assistance authorities. These changes resulted in drastic reductions in insurance fund expenditures. Although operating deficits were not entirely eliminated right away, the insurance operation showed an annual surplus after June 1933, and the debt began to decline.

The Unemployment Act of 1934

The British provisions for the unemployed were drastically changed by the Unemployment Act of 1934. The transitional payment system was abolished and an Unemployment Assistance Scheme substituted to provide support for the unemployed who were not drawing unemployment insurance and were in need. This scheme was nationally financed and administered. The unemployment insurance program was liberalized by providing that all insured workers with at least thirty weeks of work (or contributions) in the prior two years would be eligible for twenty-six weeks of benefits in a year and that up to an additional twenty-six weeks of benefits would be paid to those with a good record of employment in the last five years. Weekly benefit amounts were increased considerably, so that most beneficiaries would not need supplementary relief. Financing was equally divided among employees, employers, and the government. The insurance fund was relieved of its outstanding debt, but with provision for its repayment out of current contribution income at the rate of £5 million annually. After the reforms, the unemployment insurance system was kept on a sound financial basis and the debt was fully repaid.

Later Reforms[11]

Following World War II, the 1946 National Insurance Act unified all types of social insurance in the United Kingdom into a comprehensive scheme.[12] In 1948, unemployment assistance was absorbed into a new national public assistance program by the National Assistance Act, which evolved further into a general supplementary benefit system in 1966. The National Insurance scheme was subsequently restructured by the Social Security Act of 1975.

Unemployment insurance (as of 1989) covers all workers who earn at least £41 a week and are not self-employed, except that coverage is optional for married women and widows. Benefits are financed through an over-all wage-related contribution for all types of social insurance, payable by employers and workers, and supplemented by a government contribution. The minimum qualifying requirement for benefits calls for contributions paid on earnings equal to at least twenty-five times the minimum weekly earnings limit (£41) in one of the last two years and contributions on earnings equal to at least fifty times the minimum weekly earnings limit in the last two years. To be eligible, the unemployed worker must also register at the employment office and be available for and seeking work. Benefit disqualifications apply for up to six weeks for voluntary leaving of work, discharge for misconduct, and for refusal of suitable work or training opportunity. The weekly benefit amount is no longer varied by sex or age. In 1989, it consisted of a flat amount of £32.75 a week plus £20.20 for a dependent spouse.[13] Benefits are payable after a three-day waiting period for up to a maximum of fifty-two weeks. An income-tested supplementary

---

11. This section is based on Blaustein and Craig (1977, pp. 224-234), and U.S. Department of Health and Human Services (1990).

12. The basis for the consolidation of all social insurance programs, including unemployment insurance, into a unified comprehensive system was the Beveridge Report (1942), a review and analysis of the experience under preexisting schemes, with recommendations.

13. Based on exchange rates in 1992 before the British pound began to fall, the U.S. dollar equivalents for the weekly benefit and dependent spouse addition were about $60 and $37, respectively.

benefit is payable to those in need, financed entirely by the government.

Lessons from the British Experience

The British record of unemployment insurance was no argument for action in the United States in 1935. In fact, the British experience from 1921 to 1931 was fully exploited by those opposed to legislation in this country. The British retrenchment of 1931, and the revamping of the system in 1934, did not have much counter-influence in the United States before the Social Security Act was passed. So far as the influence of the British plan on contemporary American opinion was concerned, the story ended with the heavy debt built up by the unemployment insurance fund before the British National Economy Act of 1931. This record was cited by American opponents of unemployment insurance as proof that such a program could not be kept solvent. Moreover, the payment of benefits for ten years to large numbers of persons who had never contributed, or had a very tenuous attachment to the unemployment insurance program was cited as an example of how an insurance system could deteriorate into a "dole."

Actually, the image of the British system as a dole, as opposed to an insurance program, developed because about one-fourth of its beneficiaries in the ten years ending in 1931 had paid little or nothing in insurance contributions. About three-fourths of the beneficiaries during this period were eligible for and received standard benefits. It has been estimated that if there had been no changes in the 1920 Act, the system would have remained solvent. The estimated cost of uncovenanted, extended, and transitional benefits accounted for over 90 percent of the debt accumulated by mid-1931 (Burns 1941, p. 70). As for the continued extensions of benefits to those who had exhausted standard benefits and to those who could not meet the qualifying conditions, the British experience constituted a warning of the political pressures that develop if an alternative method of caring for the unemployed who exhaust their unemployment insurance benefits is not available. The English local Poor Law system was harsh and antiquated and the British government sought to minimize the use of it for the unemployed. Also, if it had been used to care for those unable to qualify for standard unemployment benefits, the local governments that administered poor relief would have been bankrupted.

American planners of unemployment insurance legislation learned a great deal from the British experience. First, they were careful to propose strict qualifying requirements and definite limitations on the duration of benefits in order to avoid any charges that they were proposing a dole for all the unemployed. Second, they were extremely prudent, and perhaps too conservative, in the benefits proposed in order to assure a solvent system. Finally, the British legislation, being the best known, was the most closely copied in drafting the detailed provisions of legislative proposals with respect to qualifying and disqualifying provisions and administrative arrangements.

The German System

The program established by the German Unemployment Insurance Act of 1927 differed markedly from the British scheme.[14] The experts who designed the German system had studied the British experience and endeavored to profit from its mistakes. Nevertheless, the German system had as hard going from 1929 on as did the British program after 1920, and was subject to as frequent changes. The adaptations to heavy unemployment, however, were generally in the opposite direction from those taken by the British. Instead of using the unemployment insurance system to provide for the great bulk of the unemployed as the British did, the Germans in most respects progressively restricted their program and changed it more and more into a relief system.

In spite of being the first country to establish a general social insurance system (in 1889), Germany was late among European countries in adopting unemployment insurance. It had had experience, however, with national unemployment relief for almost ten years. Immediately after the end of World War I, a national emergency relief system was created. Although it was first enacted as a temporary measure, it was

---

14. For detailed information on the German experience prior to 1935, see Carroll (1930); National Industrial Conference Board (1932); and briefer and later accounts in the studies of foreign systems listed in footnote 6.

continued up to the time the unemployment insurance law was enacted. In fact, by that time it had taken on some of the characteristics of unemployment insurance. Beginning October 1923, employers and workers contributed to relief financing. Administrative control had also gradually shifted from communal relief agencies to the employment exchanges.

Unemployment Insurance Law of 1927

This relief system was entirely superseded by the German unemployment insurance law, enacted in July and made effective in October 1927. The new law provided for a three-tier system of assistance to the unemployed. The top tier was an unemployment insurance program financed through employer and employee contributions. The second tier provided emergency benefits, based on a moderate needs test and financed four-fifths by the federal government and one-fifth by the local governments. The bottom tier consisted of local poor relief, which was originally intended to be financed exclusively by local governments, but which was given substantial federal aid during the 1929-33 depression. The provision of emergency benefits recognized the fact that ordinary benefits would not give sufficient protection during depressions. It was planned as an intermediate stage between unemployment insurance and poor relief, to be restricted or expanded according to economic conditions, with a needs test less severe than that required for poor relief. It was to be administered by the same organization as that paying regular unemployment insurance benefits.

Instead of flat-rate contributions and benefits, as under the British program, the German unemployment insurance law created 11 wage classes, both for contributions and benefits. The benefit amounts were proportionately varied by wage class so that relatively more generous amounts were payable to the lower wage workers. Dependents' allowances were also provided. Duration of benefits was the same as under the British Act of 1927—up to twenty-six weeks—with a qualifying requirement of twenty-six weeks of employment in the last year. Coverage was almost universal from the start. Manual workers, between the school-leaving age and 65, and salaried workers, earning no more than a specified amount in a year, were covered. Only agricultural workers and domestic household workers were excluded from the system.

The emergency unemployment benefits were payable for a maximum of 26 weeks during periods of exceptional unemployment, except that nonmanual workers over age 40 could receive such benefits for thirty-nine weeks. The benefits were payable to those who had exhausted regular insurance benefits or were unable to qualify for them. At first, the weekly rates of emergency benefits were the same as those for regular benefits, but the emergency benefit rates were lowered in late 1930.

Changes to Meet Heavy Unemployment

The German law of 1927 was enacted in a period of relative prosperity, but severe unemployment set in shortly thereafter. Beginning in 1928, unemployment increased and, except for seasonal improvements, continued to grow, until it reached a peak of 6 million workers in 1932. This represented almost half the workforce covered by unemployment insurance. Although the system built up a surplus during its first six months of operation, large federal loans had to be made to the insurance fund in 1928 and 1929. Contributions were increased three times during 1930, more than doubling the original combined rate (3 percent of wages) on employers and workers. Thereafter, the insurance fund had an annual surplus, even though in the fiscal year 1932-33 there was a substantial transfer to the relief fund (Metropolitan Life Insurance Company 1935, p. 39). Unemployment insurance had been cut back so drastically by then, both in the weekly amount payable and in the number of persons eligible, that the fund still had a surplus. Besides the steep increase in contributions, a whole series of new laws and presidential decrees were adopted beginning November 1929 in order to keep the insurance fund solvent. These laws and decrees adjusted coverage, extended the waiting period before benefits were payable, tightened the law against abuse, increased the eligibility requirements, and cut benefit amounts. In October 1931, the duration of benefits was reduced to twenty weeks and in June 1932, a needs test was imposed after the first six weeks of benefits. At the same time, regular weekly benefit amounts were reduced 23 percent.

In contrast to the constant changes in extended benefits made by the British, major changes were made only twice in the German emergency benefit scheme. In November 1930, insured unemployed persons in all occupations other than manual workers in agriculture, domestic servants, and persons under 21 were made eligible for emergency benefits, provided that they lived in places of 10,000 population or over and could satisfy the general conditions required for standard insurance benefits. On the other hand, the emergency benefit amount was reduced, and the duration shortened from thirty-nine to thirty-two weeks for nonmanual workers over 40 years of age, with extension in exceptional cases to forty-five weeks. A stricter proof of need was also required.

In October 1932, supplementary emergency benefits were made payable to persons with dependents, and benefits were continued for those who otherwise would have exhausted their duration entitlement. Intended as a temporary measure, these changes were continued indefinitely in March 1933. Beginning in May 1933, the cost of emergency benefits was paid out of the contributory unemployment insurance fund. It is interesting that the British took the opposite course the following year, when they separated the financing of insurance benefits and unemployment assistance.

The proportion of the unemployed who drew insurance benefits was at a peak of over 80 percent in January 1929, and dropped almost to 30 percent in January 1932. This decrease was probably due in large part to the exhaustion of benefits by an increasing number of the unemployed. The peak number drawing unemployment insurance was almost 2.5 million in February 1932. In June 1932, when insurance benefits without a needs test were restricted to six weeks, the number receiving such benefits fell to below 1 million, or about 17 percent of the unemployed. A year later, in June 1933, only about 400,000 drew such benefits, although unemployment still hovered around 5 million. Figures after that date are not comparable.[15]

The number drawing emergency benefits naturally increased as the depression wore on and workers exhausted regular benefits. In January

---

15. The only change made by the Nazi regime up to then was to exclude domestic servants in May 1933. Other restrictions later imposed were to withdraw protection from agricultural workers and all non-Aryans.

1929, a total of 145,000, or only about 5 percent of the unemployed drew emergency benefits. The number increased steadily except for seasonal fluctuations until it reached a peak of 1.7 million, or about 29 percent of the unemployed in March 1932. Thereafter, the number of emergency benefit recipients declined somewhat to 1.3 million in June 1933.

Local relief had to take care of an increasing proportion of the unemployed. Comparable figures are not available before August 1930, but in that month 450,000, or nearly 16 percent of the unemployed received local relief. The number grew to 2.4 million, or about 42 percent of the unemployed in December 1932. About 22 percent of the unemployed drew neither benefits or relief in December 1932 (Industrial Relations Counselors 1934, pp. 278-81).

Post-War Changes

After World War II, the Allies froze all German government funds and, in connection with currency reform, wiped out accumulated funds so that a fresh start had to be made in accumulating insurance reserves.[16] A new unemployment insurance law was enacted in the western zones in October 1947.[17] The Federal Republic of Germany, 1952, set up a new Federal Institution for Placement and Unemployment Insurance to administer unemployment insurance—the pattern of administration used before the war for all of Germany. The 1947 law was amended in 1952, 1953, and 1956, and completely replaced by the Employment Promotion Act of 1969.

The program's structure, based on the 1969 law, is similar to the original law of 1927. It is administered by the somewhat autonomous Federal Employment Institution (or Institute for Labor). Based on provisions effective in 1989, coverage is practically universal. Employers and workers each pay contributions at an equal rate (2.15 percent) on

---

16. This section is based on Blaustein and Craig (1977, pp. 190-199), and U.S. Department of Health and Human Services, Social Security Administration (1990, pp. 94-95).

17. An attempt was made in the Allied Control Council to develop a comprehensive social insurance system for all of Germany, but while it was being negotiated, the Russians issued an ordinance providing for a unified social insurance system, including unemployment insurance, for East Germany. The three western Allied powers then decided to let the West Germans develop a revised unemployment insurance law, subject to the approval of the occupying powers. Unemployment insurance in East Germany continued until 1977 when it was abolished.

wages up to a taxable wage ceiling (73,000DM);[18] employers, however, pay the worker share of contributions for employees earning less than 10 percent of the ceiling. The government makes up any deficit in financing insurance benefits. The minimum qualifying requirement is 360 days of insured work (180 days for seasonal workers) in the three years prior to filing for benefits. In addition, the unemployed worker must register at the employment office and be available for work. Benefit disqualification is imposed for up to twelve weeks for leaving work voluntarily, for a misconduct discharge, and for refusing an offer of a suitable job or training. Benefits are payable with no waiting period for up to sixteen to fifty-two weeks, depending on the amount of insured employment (for up to twenty-eight weeks for those over age 49). The wage-related weekly benefit amount is 68 percent of the worker's after-tax earnings (63 percent for single workers). Weekly unemployment assistance, subject to a means test, is payable after exhaustion of regular benefits at the rate of 58 percent of after-tax earnings (56 percent for single workers). The federal government finances unemployment assistance costs.

German reunification after 1989 has produced some major unemployment as an effect of the difficult process of economic integration, especially in the East. Years of transition may lie ahead for coping adequately with the industrial dislocations in the former Democratic Republic. Meanwhile, the integrity of the unemployment insurance program appears protected by the government's legal obligation to underwrite any deficits that arise because of heavy benefit outlays, and by the availability of unemployment assistance.

Lessons from the German Experience

While the British badly damaged their unemployment insurance system before 1934 by using all sorts of devices to keep the unemployed on the benefit rolls, thereby putting the program heavily in debt, the Germans almost destroyed their program by progressively restricting it in order to keep it solvent. While Germany kept unemployment insurance self-supporting, and also eventually supported emergency

---

18. Based on exchange rates in 1992, the U.S. dollar equivalent of the taxable wage base was about $46,000.

benefits out of unemployment insurance income, practically all benefits (except for the first six weeks) were placed on a needs basis.

The experience of the German system was also used by opponents of legislation in the United States to demonstrate that unemployment insurance could not meet the needs of a depression. There is little evidence that much consideration was given to the German scheme during the framing of the Social Security Act. The rather favorable experience with emergency benefits might well have been considered, in view of the very modest program of unemployment insurance proposed in this country. The German system provided somewhat of a model for varying contributions and benefits with wages. Contributions by both employers and workers, as in Germany, were adopted at first by only ten states; employee contributions now exist in only a few states. This is largely due to the emphasis that has been placed in this country on employer responsibility for unemployment costs and experience rating. While the British briefly considered experience rating at the outset of their program, the Germans never have. It has remained an exclusively American practice in financing unemployment insurance.

Concluding Observations

Knowledge about European experience with unemployment insurance prior to the passage of the Social Security Act was available in the United States and well noted by American protagonists on the subject. The smaller countries had largely relied on government subsidies of trade union plans, which were much more highly developed than in this country. Of the few countries that had compulsory unemployment insurance systems, the British and German schemes received the most attention.

That both these systems were tested and strained by heavy unemployment in the 1920s and early 1930s was of particular interest to Americans during the depression in this country. The harshness and inadequacies of the English Poor Laws in coping with industrial unemployment had so discredited such relief that governments felt politically compelled to stretch the new unemployment insurance system very far to avoid throwing unemployed workers on to local poor relief when their benefits ran out and sufficient employment could not be obtained to qualify for more benefits. Progressive relaxation of qualifying conditions and repeated additions to or extensions of the durations of covenanted, uncovenanted and transitional benefits undermined and badly damaged the program's integrity with respect to both its basic principles and its financial solvency. American reaction to inadequate and demeaning local relief in the early 1930s also contributed strongly to broadened public preference for the insurance approach to deal with unemployment. Opponents of this approach, however, pointed tellingly to the instability and disarray of the British system, to its fiscal morass, and to its image as a dole. As already noted, the response was to design a very conservative program for the United States.

German experience with unemployment insurance carried less influence in this country. Negative associations lingered from the American encounter with Germany in World War I. Because of a common language and closer cultural ties, Americans generally could identify more readily with British experience, thus giving that country's program more weight in the debate and design of unemployment insurance in the United States. By 1934 and 1935, the character of the Nazi regime in Germany had become more widely evident, casting a shadow on anything that was German. Nevertheless, for what it was worth, opponents of the insurance approach could also point to the failure of the German system to meet its objectives as further evidence that unemployment insurance could not work.

The key question about the feasibility of unemployment insurance as posed by the British and German experience was whether a program could navigate the turbulence of a massive and prolonged depression, a question perhaps less clear to those living in the middle of such a period. It was apparent that the limited program cautiously designed for the nation in the mid-1930s could not relieve much of the depression unemployment of the time. The national work relief programs then in place would continue to deal with the larger problem until the economy finally recovered. There was, however, no provision made at the time for a backup plan to cope with the burden of excessive long-term unemployment if and when it should again develop in the future. The British solution of 1934 was a national unemployment assistance program, finally overcoming its aversion to relief as practiced under the Poor Laws. This move came too late to offer any useful lessons for American planners of economic and Social Security in 1934 and 1935.

The German approach had been to resort more and more to relief and even to needs-tested unemployment insurance, thereby compromising basic insurance principles. The concept of relief payments as a back-up program to help cope in times of heavy prolonged unemployment was a lesson that might have been useful to learn from the foreign experience. Decades later, the American unemployment insurance system was to confront that problem without such a backup program in place. The system's multiple extension of duration, frequent changes, and heavy costs leading to widespread state fund insolvency were reminiscent of the British struggles with the problem a half century earlier.

APPENDIX

Excerpt from Speech in 1910 by Hubert Llewellyn Smith
(In this speech, Smith set forth the basis for unemployment insurance in Great Britain, the first national compulsory system ever adopted.)

The crucial question from a practical point of view is, therefore, whether it is possible to devise a scheme of insurance which, while nominally covering unemployment due to all causes other than those which can be definitely excluded, shall automatically discriminate as between the classes of unemployment for which insurance is or is not an appropriate remedy.

We can advance a step towards answering this crucial question by enumerating some of the essential characteristics of any unemployment insurance scheme which seem to follow directly or by necessary implication from the conditions of the problem as here laid down.

1. The scheme must be compulsory; otherwise the bad personal risks against which we must always be on our guard would be certain to predominate.

2. The scheme must be contributory, for only by exacting rigorously as a necessary qualification for benefit that a sufficient number of weeks' contributions shall have been paid by each recipient can we possibly hope to put limits on the exceptionally bad risks.

3. With the same object in view there must be a maximum limit to the amount of benefit which can be drawn, both absolutely and in relation to the amount of contribution paid; or, in other words, we must in some way or other secure that the number of weeks for which a workman contributes should bear some relation to his claim upon the fund. Armed with this double weapon of a maximum limit to benefit and of a minimum contribution, the operation of the scheme itself will automatically exclude the loafer.

4. The scheme must avoid encouraging unemployment, and for this purpose it is essential that the rate of unemployment benefit payable shall be relatively low. It would be fatal to any scheme to offer compensation for unemployment at a rate approximating to that of ordinary wages.

5. For the same reason it is essential to enlist the interest of all those engaged in the insured trades, whether as employers or as workmen, in reducing unemployment, by associating them with the scheme both as regards contribution and management.

6. As it appears on examination that some trades are more suitable to be dealt with by insurance than others, either because the unemployment in these trades contains a large insurable element, or because it takes the form of total discharge rather than short time, or for other reasons, it follows that, for the

scheme to have the best chance of success, it should be based upon the trade group, and should at the outset be partial in operation.

7. The group of trades to which the scheme is to be applied must, however, be a large one, and must extend throughout the United Kingdom, as it is essential that industrial mobility as between occupations and districts should not be unduly checked.

8. A State subvention and guarantee will be necessary, in addition to contributions from the trades affected, in order to give the necessary stability and security, and also in order to justify the amount of State control that will be necessary.

9. The scheme must aim at encouraging the regular employer and workman, and discriminating against casual engagements. Otherwise it will be subject to the criticism of placing an undue burden on the regular for the benefit of the irregular members of the trade.

10. The scheme must not act as a discouragement to voluntary provision for unemployment, and for that purpose some well-devised plan of co-operation is essential between the State organisation and the voluntary associations which at present provide unemployment benefit for their members.

Our analysis, therefore, leads us step by step to the contemplation of a national contributory scheme of insurance universal in its operation within the limits of a large group of trades—a group so far as possible self-contained and carefully selected as favourable for the experiment, the funds being derived from compulsory contributions from all those engaged in these trades, with a subsidy and guarantee from the State, and the rules relating to benefit being so devised as to discriminate effectively against unemployment which is mainly due to personal defects, while giving a substantial allowance to those whose unemployment results from industrial causes beyond the control of the individual (Beveridge 1930, pp. 265-66).

5

American Forerunners
and Early Attempts
at Legislation

The United States did not entirely lack exposure to unemployment insurance before the wave of legislation in the mid-1930s. Discussion and debate about the subject began some thirty years earlier, ranging over a wide variety of issues including the need for such a program, its role, form, philosophy, and locus of responsibility. Some practical experience with voluntary unemployment benefit schemes had accumulated through private trade union plans, joint agreement (employer-employee) plans, and company plans. Attempts to enact state unemployment insurance legislation date back to 1916. As the depression of the 1930s deepened, an increasing number of progressive reformers and representatives sensitive to worker interests were elected to governorships and state legislatures. During this period, a number of state commissions were created to study unemployment insurance and many bills were introduced at the state level. One state, Wisconsin, enacted a law as early as 1932. Some study of the question was also made in Congress and a few bills were introduced there as well. Reports of the state commissions, the resulting debates in state legislatures, and these early bills greatly influenced the character of the legislation that eventually passed.[1]

This chapter briefly reviews the American experience with voluntary unemployment insurance schemes and traces the history of legislative activity prior to the passage by Congress of the Social Security Act in 1935.[2]

---

1. Nelson, (1969) provides a comprehensive treatment of this historic background for unemployment insurance in the United States. Other details may also be found in Raushenbush and Raushenbush (1979).

2. For a more detailed description of American voluntary plans up to 1930, see Stewart (1930).

American Voluntary Plans

Private voluntary schemes of cash support for workers during periods of unemployment never became widespread in the United States. A limited number of plans of various types developed prior to 1935 through initiatives taken by trade unions, employers, or jointly by workers and employers. Several business leaders urged the voluntary approach, partly to forestall the need for compulsory government programs, but also in recognition of some employer responsibility for treating with the involuntary unemployment of their workers. Some trade unions viewed such plans as an appropriate element for collective bargaining. Few of the plans that developed before 1935 survived the early years of the Great Depression. Although voluntary plans did not become a major factor, the experience they provided and some of the individuals who designed and promoted them carried some influence in the discussions that shaped the unemployment insurance system that finally emerged.

Trade Union Plans

Unlike the experience in Europe, trade unions in this country developed very few formal unemployment benefit plans. The earliest known plan was established in 1831. During times of depression in the late 1800s and the early part of the 1900s, practically all trade unions gave assistance to their unemployed members and many unemployment benefit or relief plans sprang up, only to be discontinued when employment conditions improved. In 1931, the Bureau of Labor Statistics could report only three national unions and forty-five local unions that had unemployment benefit plans of a more or less permanent and systematic character (USDOL, Bureau of Labor Statistics 1931). Of the local plans, eight had been established after the stock market crash of September 1929 when the depression began.

The three national unions with unemployment benefit plans had a total membership of only about 1,000. The oldest, the Deutsch-Amerikanishe Typographia, started its plan in 1884, and the other two, siderographers and diamond cutters, in 1910 and 1912, respectively. The forty-five local unions with plans in 1931 had a total membership of about 45,000. They included: bookbinders; lithographers; electrotypers; photoengravers; pressmen and press assistants; typographical workers; bakery workers; lace operatives; brewery, flour, cereal, and soft drink workers; and wood carvers.

The plans varied widely both as to type and amount of contributions, which were paid entirely by union members. Contributions in some plans equaled a percentage of earnings (10 percent in one); in others a flat daily, weekly, or monthly amount was contributed (in several plans as high as $2 a week per member); and in still others, assessments were paid as needed. Benefits also varied widely. As reported in 1931, the three national union plans, perhaps because they were started in a day of lower wages, paid only $5, $6, and $9 a week, but for maximum periods varying from 16 to 26 weeks of unemployment. The local union plans paid from $5.50 to $30 a week, with the highest amount being paid by the photoengravers and electrotypers. The duration limits of weekly benefit payments ranged from eight to thirty-two weeks, with ten plans having indefinite or unlimited duration. During 1933, the latest year for which figures are available, trade union plans paid out a total of $3,700,000 in benefits, of which $2,150,000 was paid by the electrotypers and photoengravers (Metropolitan Life Insurance Company 1935, p. 67).

Joint Agreement Plans

In 1931, thirteen unemployment benefit and three guaranteed employment plans, worked out by joint agreement between unions and management, covered over 65,000 workers. All were established in the 1920s, except the wallpaper industry guaranteed employment plan which started in 1894. The thirteen benefit plans were all in the needle trades. These included the plans of the Amalgamated Clothing Workers in Chicago, New York City, and Rochester, New York, totaling 33,000 workers, and the American Federation of Full-Fashioned Hosiery Workers, with 15,000 members. The guaranteed employment plans applied to workers in the women's clothing industry in Cleveland, to the wallpaper workers, and to equipment maintenance employees of the Seaboard Airline Railway (USDOL, Bureau of Labor Statistics 1931, pp. 14-19). By 1931, a few of the plans, including that of the wallpaper industry, had been suspended or abandoned (Industrial Relations Counselors 1934, p. 66).

Employer contributions alone supported five of the unemployment benefit plans and joint contributions the other eight plans. Contributions were usually expressed as a percentage of payrolls, or wages, the highest being the Amalgamated Clothing Workers plan in Chicago with a 3 percent employer and 1-1/2 percent employee contribution. Benefits were more limited than in the plans financed by trade unions, and they usually aimed at compensating seasonal unemployment. For example, the Chicago plan of the Amalgamated provided for a maximum duration of three-and-three-quarter weeks of benefits in two seasons. The weekly benefit was equal to 30 percent of wages up to a maximum of $15 a week. The International Ladies' Garment Workers' Union plan in Cleveland guaranteed thirty-eight weeks of employment. The Seaboard plan guaranteed employment for a whole year for a minimum number of workers. The United Wall Paper Crafts plan guaranteed forty-five weeks a year at full pay.

Statistics are not available as to amounts paid out under these plans, except for the three Amalgamated Clothing Workers plans. Those plans disbursed a total of about $884,000 during the five years from April 1929 to March 1934 (Metropolitan Life Insurance Company 1935, p. 69).

Company Plans

Beginning with the Dennison Manufacturing Company in 1917, thirty-eight firms provided for some protection against unemployment through nineteen unemployment benefit plans, savings plans, or employment guarantee plans at some time between 1917 and 1933. When the BLS made its survey of voluntary plans in 1931, fifteen plans, including the fourteen-firm "Rochester Plan," had been adopted or were in operation[3]. They covered about 80,000 workers. By the end of 1933, four new plans had been adopted, but four others had suspended or ended operations. In addition, seven of the fourteen firms had withdrawn from the Rochester Plan (Industrial Relations Counselors 1934, pp. 67-70 and appendix V; USDOL, Bureau of Labor Statis-

---

3. A dismissal payment plan of the Delaware and Hudson Railroad, which the BLS did not consider as an unemployment benefit plan, was also reported in Metropolitan Life Insurance Company (1935).

tics 1931 pp. 7-13; Metropolitan Life Insurance Company 1935, pp. 69-75).

The best known of the guaranteed employment plans was Procter and Gamble's. When started in 1923, it guaranteed forty-eight weeks of employment at full pay for hourly employees whose annual earnings were less than $2,000, who were participants in the company's profit-sharing plan, and who had six months of service with the firm. Beginning 1933, membership in the profit-sharing plan was no longer required, but one year of service was mandatory.

Typical of an individual savings plans was that of the J. I. Case Company of Racine, Wisconsin, which contributed an amount equal to 5 percent of each employee's earnings, matched by a similar employee contribution until one year's earnings accrued in a savings account. During periods of depression, a laid-off employee could (after a ninety-day waiting period) withdraw 40 percent of his earnings up to a maximum of $40 for each semi-monthly period.

The General Electric Company, by far the largest employer to provide unemployment protection for its workers, put two types of plans in effect in 1930 and 1931: a guaranteed employment plan for 8,000 electric light bulb employees in Schenectady, New York; and an unemployment benefit plan for 40,000 out of 70,000 employees in the balance of the company's plants. Under the benefit plan, employer and employee contributions, each equal to 1 percent of earnings, were to be paid for three years. The original plan provided for a weekly benefit amount equal to 50 percent of an employee's normal full-time weekly earnings up to a maximum of $20 a week for up to 10 weeks in a twelve-month period. The plan was modified several times in the first three years of operation, but not fundamentally changed. Between 1931 and 1934, the plan raised about $5 million in contributions and disbursed over $3.6 million in benefits (Nelson 1969, p. 61).

The Rochester Plan also merits a brief description. This plan was uniform for the participating companies, but each company administered its own fund to which it contributed 2 percent of payrolls until the fund reached a total equal to five years of contributions. If the fund proved inadequate after January 1, 1933, all employees of the company would be required to contribute 1 percent of their pay and the company would add an additional amount. Originally, weekly benefits were to be 60 percent of earnings, up to a weekly maximum of $22.50, payable to laid-off employees with a year or more of service and earnings not exceeding $50 a week. A two-week waiting period was required, with maximum benefit duration varying from 6 to 13 weeks for employees with from one to five years of service. In November 1932, weekly benefits were temporarily reduced to 50 percent of average weekly earnings, up to a maximum of $18.75.

It is interesting that officials of eight of the company plans testified favorably at one or more hearings on state and federal legislation. Their experience convinced them that unemployment benefits should be generally available, by legislation if necessary. As Marion B. Folsom, Treasurer of the Eastman Kodak Company and a member of the Rochester Plan, testified with respect to the unemployment insurance provisions of the Social Security bill: "The employers who are on this Advisory Council—you will recall they are Mr. Teagle, Mr. Swope, Mr. Lewisohn, Mr. Leeds, besides myself—reached the conclusion that you must have legislation in order to provide security for the workers in general, which many companies are already providing, because voluntary action would be too slow."[4]

Early State Legislative Activity

Although the idea of government-supported unemployment insurance in the United States was discussed in the early 1900s, there were no attempts at state legislation until 1916. The earliest known formal treatment of the subject was a paper on the "Ghent system" by Professor Henry R. Seager of Columbia University at the first annual meeting of the American Association for Labor Legislation (AALL) in 1907. Adoption of social insurance by Great Britain in 1911 to provide workers with old-age and unemployment benefits had a profound effect in the United States on social reformers and others concerned with the problems of workers in this country. The AALL's annual meeting in 1911 included a discussion of the new British unemployment insurance

---

4. U.S. Congress, Senate (1935, p. 555). The Advisory Council referred to was that appointed by the President as advisory to the Committee on Economic Security. Mr. Swope was president of General Electric Company and Mr. Leeds of Leeds-Northrup Company, both of which had private plans.

law and a Committee on Unemployment was appointed to consider the problem. In 1913, the Association held the first American Conference on Social Insurance at which unemployment insurance was urged in the United States.

There was more widespread interest in unemployment insurance during the depression of 1914-15. In 1914, the American Association for Labor Legislation and its affiliated American Association on Unemployment held two national conferences on unemployment. At the second meeting, a tentative draft was presented, "A Practical Program for the Prevention of Unemployment," principally authored by John B. Andrews, executive secretary of the AALL. This program included unemployment insurance, as well as expansion of public employment offices, countercyclical planning and construction of public works, and greater efforts by employers to regularize employment. It was endorsed by the conference and supported by several emergency commissions on unemployment appointed during the depression.

The AALL program's emphasis on prevention rather than on relief of unemployment reflected in large measure the influence of Professor John R. Commons of the University of Wisconsin. Commons was a pioneer in applying academic study and knowledge to practical purposes in the fields of labor problems and social reform. Assisted by some of his students, he was the principal designer of the 1911 workers' compensation law in Wisconsin and became its first administrator. Noting that workplace safety improved after compensation costs were made the clear responsibility of individual employers, Commons reasoned that similar treatment of unemployment compensation costs would induce more stable employment. This view guided the thinking and efforts of many of his students in subsequent years with regard to unemployment insurance, or unemployment *compensation* as they preferred to call it. The "Wisconsin school" became a major influence in the evolution of unemployment insurance in this country that has left its imprint on the American system in ways that make it unique.[5]

John Andrews, who had been a student of Commons, carried the concept into the AALL's "Practical Program" of 1914. While some aspects of the British law of 1911 were adapted for the unemployment

---

5. For an account of Commons' life and career, see *Myself, the Autobiography of John R. Commons* (1963).

insurance section of the program, Andrews asserted that "of crowning importance in the movement toward regularization of industry is the careful development of this form of insurance with its continuous pressure toward the prevention of unemployment" (as quoted in Nelson 1969, p. 16). Interest in the Association's program, and in unemployment insurance in general, waned after 1915 as boom replaced depression.[6]

The first bill proposed to establish unemployment insurance was introduced in the Massachusetts legislature in 1916. In general, it copied the British law, with financing based on contributions by employers, workers, and the government. In 1921, a similar bill was proposed in New York by the Socialist Party. In the same year, a bill of quite a different character was introduced in Wisconsin.

The Huber Bill in Wisconsin

In February 1921, State Senator Henry A. Huber of Wisconsin introduced a bill with the unique feature of varying employers' contributions according to the regularity of their employment of workers. The principal author of this bill was John Commons. Industries covered under the Huber bill were to be classified, and premium rates established according to their experience with unemployment. The entire cost of the compensation paid to the unemployed would be borne by employers, who would be required to insure their liability for payments with a mutual insurance company controlled by the State Compensation Insurance Board.

Although the Huber bill had the support of the Wisconsin State Federation of Labor and several employers with unemployment insurance plans of their own, there was a formidable list of employers in opposition to it. The bill was defeated in the Senate by a vote of nineteen to ten. However, the Huber measure was reintroduced in each succeeding session of the Wisconsin legislature through 1929, with different sponsors from 1925 on. In 1923, it lost by one vote in the Wisconsin Senate. Although several modifications were made in the bill in succeeding years, its essential features remained intact.[7]

---

6. Most of the above information is drawn from Witte (1945, pp. 22-23), and Nelson (1969, pp. 10-17).

7. For a detailed discussion and history of the Huber bill and its successors, see Ewing (1933).

Other State Legislative Proposals

The Huber bill formed the pattern for bills introduced in other State legislatures during the 1920s. These included proposals in Connecticut, Minnesota, and Pennsylvania. Altogether, twenty-two bills in seven states were introduced in the 1920s, including bills in five states in 1929 (Industrial Relations Counselors 1934, pp. 72-73).

Interest in unemployment insurance legislation during the 1920s, however, was weak. It was a period largely of prosperity and "normalcy." Moreover, news of how poorly unemployment insurance fared in Great Britain in this decade of heavy unemployment, and in Germany under its 1927 law, did nothing to encourage support. Whatever interest there was in combating unemployment in the United States centered at this time on the efforts of some businessmen to prevent it in the first place by applying "scientific management" to their operations thereby "regularizing" employment. It was in this period that most of the company or joint employer-employee plans for unemployment benefits or guaranteed employment appeared on the scene. The emphasis was on private, voluntary actions, not on public compulsory measures, an emphasis supported by the principal national leaders of organized labor as well, given their distrust of usually unfriendly government authorities.

Increased Legislative Activity in Depression

Interest in unemployment insurance revived with the onset of the depression of the 1930s and its mounting unemployment. Private voluntary efforts, limited as they were, fell far short of the need. Some compulsory measure now seemed more and more appropriate.

The Wisconsin Act

In 1931, two bills were introduced in Wisconsin that were quite different from the Huber bill. One was based on a bill called "An American Plan for Unemployment Reserves,"[8] brought out by the American

---

8. For the text, see "Senate Passes Unemployment Bills" (1930).

Association for Labor Legislation in 1930. This bill differed from the Huber bill in that it provided for a state fund with flat contributions of 1.5 percent of payroll by employers. Provision was also made for insurance by industry and industry funds as an alternative to statewide pooling. This bill appealed to J. J. Handley and Henry Ohl, Jr., officers of the Wisconsin Federation of Labor, and they urged Robert Nixon, who had introduced the Huber bill in 1929, to use the Association draft. Early in 1931, Mr. Nixon introduced a bill in the Wisconsin legislature following the Association plan in providing for a state fund, but including the principle of experience rating of contributions.

Professor Harold M. Groves (who had been elected to the state legislature), with the assistance of Professors Paul Raushenbush and Elizabeth Brandeis and others (all from the University and most of them former students of Commons), also drafted a bill with important differences from the Huber bill. The most important change was the provision of a state fund with individual employer reserve accounts to be financed through contributions by the employer. Benefits would be paid to an employee only from the employer's account and benefits were to be reduced or stopped if the employer's reserve was inadequate. This bill was introduced in February 1931.

Following hearings held jointly on the Nixon and Groves bills, the legislature authorized an interim committee to study unemployment insurance, and to report at a special session of the legislature in the fall. At the fall session, the majority of the committee recommended enactment of an unemployment compensation bill with features quite similar to an amended bill that Groves had introduced later in the 1931 regular session. Mr. Handley, Secretary of the Wisconsin Federation of Labor, who had encouraged the Nixon bill, signed the report ("Report of the Wisconsin Legislative Interim Committee on Unemployment" 1931).

The American Association for Labor Legislation joined forces with the supporters of the Groves bill. Governor Phil LaFollette, in his opening address at the special session of the legislature in November 1931, disarmed much of the opposition by proposing that the unemployment compensation bill would take effect "conditional upon industry's failure to establish a fair voluntary system in Wisconsin within a reasonable time (i.e., a year and a half)." When the Groves bill was reintroduced, it provided that the Act would not take effect if employers of at least 200,000 workers had adopted systems of unemployment reserves that met stated requirements within the time limit. The bill passed the Legislature by large majorities and was signed by the Governor on January 29, 1932.[9] The main provisions of the Wisconsin Unemployment Compensation Act as passed were as follows:[10]

1. A state fund with individual employer accounts, funds to be invested in government securities by the State Investment Board.

2. Contributions equal to 2 percent of payroll during first two years and thereafter until employer's account averages $55 an employee; thereafter 1 percent if the account is more than $55 but less than $75; no contributions if more than $75. An additional 0.2 percent from all employers for administrative expenses and employment offices.

3. Coverage of employers with ten or more employees for four months or more in a year. Exemptions of farm workers, railroad employees in interstate commerce, logging workers, government employees and employees receiving more than $1,500 a year.

4. Benefits, after two weeks waiting period, equal to 50 percent of weekly wages with a minimum of $5 and a maximum of $10. Benefits to be reduced $1 a week for each $5 that employer's reserve account is below $50 per employee. Benefits to be paid for a maximum of ten weeks in the proportion of one week of benefits for each four weeks of employment in the last year. Each company's liability limited to the amount in its reserve fund. Benefits of a worker employed by several companies would be charged to last employer first and then in inverse order to other employers.

5. Disqualifications from benefits in cases of discharge for misconduct, voluntary leaving not attributable to the employer, refusal of suitable work, leaving employment because of a

---

9. It is of interest to note that Merrill G. Murray, a co-author of the 1966 forerunner of this book, traveled about the state in 1931 to explain the bill and develop support for it. Wilbur J. Cohen, a contributing author of this present work, was then a student of Paul Raushenbush at the University of Wisconsin and attended the debate on the bill in the Wisconsin Assembly.

10. For an authoritative contemporary discussion of the Act, see Raushenbush (1931).

labor dispute, unemployment due to an act of God, unemployment by student if he worked only during vacations.

6. Qualifying requirements: two years' residence in the state and forty weeks of employment during the period.

The minimum number of employees required to be covered under private voluntary plans adopted by their employers in order to prevent implementation of the law was reduced to 139,000, but relatively few employers adopted voluntary plans. The law took effect July 1, 1934 with respect to contributions. Benefits became payable July 1, 1936, twenty years after the first state unemployment insurance bill was introduced in Massachusetts.

Legislative Activity in Other States

In the meantime, efforts were stepped up in other states to pass unemployment insurance legislation. Altogether, fifty-two bills were introduced in seventeen states in 1931.[11] In addition to the interim committee in Wisconsin, study commissions were appointed in California, Connecticut, Massachusetts, New York, and Ohio. Four of them reported favorably regarding unemployment insurance.

Also in 1931, Governor Franklin D. Roosevelt of New York invited the governors of six other states to meet with him to explore the possibilities of simultaneous action by the states.[12] As Governor Roosevelt put it in his opening talk to the governors, "All must act, or there will be no action." His remark indicated how a state's reluctance to place its industries at a competitive disadvantage inhibited the state from adopting employer-financed unemployment insurance without assurance of similar action elsewhere. As a result of the conference, an Interstate Commission on Unemployment Insurance was created, to which each of the governors appointed a member. Members included Professor

---

11. For a state-by-state tabulation of bills from 1916-33, see Industrial Relations Counselors (1934, pp. 72-73). A bill authorizing private insurance companies to sell private plans of unemployment insurance was passed by the New York Legislature in 1931, but vetoed by Governor Franklin D. Roosevelt.

12. Represented at the conference were Connecticut, Massachusetts, New Jersey, New York, Ohio, Pennsylvania, and Rhode Island. New York Labor Commissioner, Frances Perkins, later to be President Roosevelt's Secretary of Labor, planned the conference with the assistance of, among others, Professor Paul Douglas of the University of Chicago and later U.S. Senator from Illinois.

Leo Wolman of Columbia University as chairman; A. Lincoln Filene, a large retail employer of Boston, who strongly supported unemployment prevention as the prime rationale for unemployment insurance; and Professor William M. Leiserson of Antioch College, who favored pooling of funds as better assurance of relief.[13] This Commission issued its report in February 1932, unanimously recommending compulsory legislation of the individual employer reserves type, very similar to the Wisconsin law that had just been passed.[14]

Of the state study commission reports, the one made by the Ohio Commission in 1932 was the most significant because of the wide attention it received in proposing a different type of plan than that passed in Wisconsin.[15] The Commission recommended a state pooled fund, rather than individual employer reserves. Employees were to contribute 1 percent of their earnings, and employers 2 percent of their payrolls, although provision was made for variation of employer contribution rates based on experience. All workers who qualified for any benefits would be entitled to receive payments while unemployed for up to a flat or uniform duration limit of sixteen weeks, regardless of the amount of their prior employment. The weekly benefit amount recommended was half the wage up to a maximum of $15, benefits to begin after a three-week waiting period designed to cut out many seasonally unemployed workers. I. M. Rubinow, a long-time advocate of social insurance and a member of the Commission, was mainly responsible for the estimate that a combined 3 percent contribution rate would be sufficient to finance such a benefit program over a period of years which included an occasional mild recession and a more severe depression about once a decade. The Ohio plan received substantial acclaim and became a model for a number of bills introduced in other state legislatures.

---

13. The other members were Charles R. Blunt, Commissioner of Labor, New Jersey; Charles A. Kulp, University of Pennsylvania; and W. J. Couper, Deputy Commissioner of Labor, Connecticut.

14. Professor Leiserson, although he signed the report, took "exception to any implication in it that an insurance system with pooling of contributions may not be better than a plan of separate plant reserves."

15. Ohio Commission on Unemployment Insurance (1932). Professor William Leiserson, who eventually chaired the Commission, asserted effective leadership in producing this favorable report.

The plan gave significant stature to a point of view about unemployment insurance that contrasted sharply with the unemployment prevention focus so strongly established by the Wisconsin school. Much of the intellectual base for the suggested approach was provided by Professor Douglas out of a study of unemployment begun at Swarthmore College in 1930. Douglas and his associate, Aaron Director, reviewed the European unemployment insurance plans, the voluntary plans in the United States, and the Commons approach embodied in the Huber bills in Wisconsin. From this review, along with their analysis of the causes and effects of unemployment, especially the effects on workers, they concluded that the only feasible means for dealing with the effects of the problem was through a pooled insurance fund. They saw alleviation of individual distress and countercyclical support of purchasing power as the key objectives for unemployment insurance. Only a genuine funded, pooled insurance plan, not individual employer reserves, could provide assured and adequate compensation for wage loss. They believed that, by and large, unemployment was beyond the control of individual employers. While experience rating of employer contributions might encourage some prevention of unemployment, "...it is probable that its efficacy has in the past been overstressed by advocates of unemployment insurance. There are already strong financial incentives to regularize and it may be argued that a saving of some 2 percent on the payroll may not be decisive" (Douglas and Director 1931, p. 489).

Since 1932 was an "off" legislative year (most legislatures did not meet in even-numbered years), bills were introduced in only five states. High hopes were entertained, however, for state legislation in 1933, given the favorable interstate and state commission reports. Altogether, 68 bills were introduced that year in twenty-five states, with several types of bills being introduced in some state legislatures. According to a tabulation of the American Association for Labor Legislation, its American Plan (for a state fund but with funds by industry and dividends to employers) was introduced in sixteen states and in Congress.[16] Bills for individual employer reserves, such as the Wis-

16. In June 1933, the Association brought out a new model bill providing for individual employer accounts in a state fund, but providing also for pooling by industry when the administrator finds this desirable to safeguard the reserves. Senator Robert Wagner introduced a bill (S. 1943) for the District of Columbia embodying this new model bill with minor modifications.

consin Act, were proposed in twelve state legislatures and bills for industry pools in six state legislatures. The Ohio plan for a single state pooled fund was introduced in sixteen states. No state passed a law in 1933, but a bill passed one house in seven states. Of these seven states, four passed bills for a state pooled fund, one for individual employer reserves, one for industry funds, and one for both establishment funds and industry pooled funds.[17]

Of eleven state study commissions appointed in 1933 and 1934, ten made favorable reports (Witte 1936, p. 158). Most of these commissions recommended either the Wisconsin or Ohio type of laws. The Virginia Commission recommended individual employer reserves, but with a part of each employer's contribution going to a state guaranteed fund. The Connecticut Commission recommended a dismissal wage. Although no laws besides Wisconsin's were passed until 1935, these state commissions no doubt influenced the legislation eventually passed in their states. Despite the lack of legislative success in the years prior to 1935, the efforts made in the states had served to educate the public and illuminate the issues. The major result was to elevate the objective of relief of unemployment distress over that of unemployment prevention, as exemplified in the employer reserves-type program of Wisconsin. Labor had clearly moved to support those proposals most designed to achieve the former purpose. Support for the conservative prevention approach eroded in the gloom of the depression and general disillusion with business leadership.

Federal Studies and Proposals

Early Considerations

The federal government gave very little attention to unemployment insurance until shortly before the depression of the 1930s. The earliest known official recommendation was that of the United States Commission on Industrial Relations, appointed by President Woodrow Wilson in 1913 to investigate labor unrest. In its final report, the Commission

---

17. Memorandum prepared by the American Association for Labor Legislation, published in U.S. Congress, House (1934, pp. 102-6).

recommended the study and preparation of plans for insurance against unemployment "in such trades and industries as may seem desirable."[18]

In February 1916, Representative Meyer London of New York, a Socialist, introduced a resolution in the House of Representatives for the establishment of a national commission to study social insurance and develop proposals for public programs. The House Committee on Labor held hearings in April. Although there were favorable witnesses representing insurance, social legislation, and research organizations, labor opposed action. Samuel Gompers, president of the American Federation of Labor, took a stand against the proposal, but said that if a commission was established: "I would have them investigate the subject of social insurance of a voluntary character and how far it can be established in the United States with such aid as the Government can give. I am more concerned, as I have tried to indicate, with the fundamental principles of human liberty and refusal to surrender rights to government agencies, than I am with social insurance" (U.S. Congress, House 1916, p. 172). This remained his position and the official position of the American Federation of Labor until 1932. The London bill was killed in Committee, but it aroused considerable interest.

In 1921, President Warren Harding called a national conference on unemployment, under the chairmanship of Secretary of Commerce Herbert Hoover. In his opening statement, Mr. Hoover spoke of "direct doles" to individuals as "the most vicious of solutions" and hoped the conferees would find solutions that do not "come within the range of charity." After reviewing private plans in this country, the Economic Advisory Committee on Unemployment and Depression Insurance, appointed at the conference, said that "any form of unemployment insurance which would create an economic motive to regularize employment is worthy of consideration." It recommended that reserve funds be created and used in depressions, not to pay unemployment compensation to idle workers but to keep them employed in such activities as making repairs or improvements on equipment and facilities,

---

18. U.S. Congress, Senate (1916, Vol. 2, p. 1160). It is interesting to note that the research staff of the Commission included a number of economists from the University of Wisconsin, associates or students of John Commons who was a member of the Commission.

and to continue production for inventory ("Business Cycles and Unemployment" 1923).

In 1928, the first federal unemployment insurance bill (H.R. 12205) was introduced in Congress by Representative Victor Berger. It received no attention, but in May 1928 the Senate adopted Senate Resolution 219, introduced by Senator James Couzens of Michigan, "providing for an analysis and appraisal of reports on unemployment and systems for prevention and relief thereof." The Senate Committee on Education and Labor held hearings on the subject. Professor Commons, one of the principal witnesses, testified at length on how unemployment compensation could serve to stabilize employment. Other testimony covered voluntary benefit plans, employment exchanges, and European unemployment insurance. In its report the Committee thought that government should encourage private industry in its responsibility to stabilize employment. Its second recommendation was that: "Insurance plans against unemployment should be confined to the industry itself as much as possible. There is no necessity and no place for Federal interference in such efforts at this time. If any public insurance scheme is considered, it should be left to the State legislatures to study the problem" (U.S. Congress, Senate 1929, p. xv).

As the depression deepened in the early 1930s, Senator Robert F. Wagner, a liberal Democrat from New York, obtained the adoption of Senate Resolution 483 in February 1931, providing for the appointment of a Select Committee on Unemployment Insurance. Senator Wagner had been asserting increasing leadership in pressing for government action in the crisis. He was the prime sponsor of legislation calling for a strong public employment service, public works planning, improved unemployment statistics, and study of unemployment insurance. His Employment Exchange bill finally passed in February 1931, only to be vetoed by President Hoover. His employment services bill did become law in June 1933 (the Wagner-Peyser Act). The system of employment offices created by this law was to provide the vital framework for the federal-state unemployment insurance program that emerged from the Social Security Act of 1935.

Senator Felix Hebert of Rhode Island was appointed chairman of the Select Committee, and Senator Otis F. Glenn of Illinois and Senator Wagner were the other two members of the Committee. Hearings were held in April and the last three months of 1931. The Committee obtained the services of Hugh S. Hanna of the Bureau of Labor Statistics who supplied members with extensive information on foreign systems and American plans. In a rather comprehensive report, Senators Hebert and Glenn, both conservative Republicans, took the position that a federal system of unemployment insurance would be unconstitutional and undesirable. Although they favored voluntary plans, they recognized that these were being established so slowly that state compulsory legislation might be necessary. They suggested (as was done in the Wisconsin law) that state legislation fix a period during which employers could formulate their own plans. Their only recommendation for federal action was that "the Federal Government contribute to such systems of private unemployment reserves to the extent of permitting employers who maintain them to deduct some portion, if not all, of the contributions thereto out of their income for tax purposes" (U.S. Congress, Senate 1932b, pp. 51-52).

In a minority report, Senator Wagner concluded that "unemployment insurance or wage reserves, to be successful, should be inaugurated under compulsory State legislation and be supervised by State authority"; that "each system should be organized to provide incentives to the stabilization of employment"; and that the federal government should allow employers to deduct from income tax their payments into unemployment reserves or insurance plans (U.S. Congress, Senate 1932a, p. 26). He differed from the majority in recommending that 30 percent of such payments be deductible directly from the tax itself, rather than from gross income. Senator Wagner introduced his income tax credit proposal in the same session of Congress.[19]

Besides these bills, Senator Wagner also introduced a bill in January 1931 (S. 5634), to apportion $100 million among the states in proportion to each state's contributions to unemployment reserves. In 1933, two bills on unemployment insurance were introduced in Congress and four bills were introduced the following year. Of these, the identical bills introduced by Senator Wagner and Congressman David J. Lewis of Maryland are discussed below in detail because of their influence on the unemployment insurance features of the Social Security Act.[20]

---

19. S.J. Res. 26, 72d Cong. In December 1930, Senator Wagner had introduced a bill (S. 5350), 71st Cong., which was similar to the recommendations of the majority of the Select Committee.

The Wagner-Lewis Bill

The failure of any state to enact an unemployment insurance law in 1933, despite the widespread and intensive effort in the states, pointed to the necessity of federal action.[21] The strongest obstacle to state action was the argument that legislation by individual states would place industry in such states at a competitive disadvantage with industry in states without legislation. It should also be noted that conservative forces, especially business groups, vehemently opposed governmental programs of this type as being in gross conflict with basic American values of individual liberty and free private enterprise. Unemployment insurance was often represented as a manifestation of socialism. This treatment proved quite effective in discouraging support for that approach, particularly at the state level.[22]

A type of federal legislation that would induce state action was suggested by Supreme Court Justice Louis D. Brandeis while his daughter, Elizabeth, and her husband, Paul Raushenbush, of Wisconsin were visiting him on Cape Cod during the summer of 1933. His idea was to apply the method used in the Federal Estate Tax Act of 1926. The State of Florida had been encouraging wealthy persons to move to the state by publicizing that it had no inheritance tax law. The Federal Estate Tax Act imposed a federal inheritance tax, but with a provision that 80 percent credit would be given for taxes paid under a state inheritance tax law. Although the federal estate tax was passed in order to induce Florida to pass a similar law and thus remove its competitive advantage with other states, raising thereby some question of the federal law's constitutionality, the Supreme Court of the United State unanimously declared the federal law to be constitutional.[23]

---

20. These bills, H.R. 7659 and S. 2616, were introduced on February 5, 1934. Lewis had also introduced one of the bills proposed in 1933.

21. In fact, during 1933, resolutions were introduced in the Maine, Minnesota, Montana, and Wisconsin legislatures calling upon Congress to enact unemployment insurance legislation.

22. William Haber, a contributing author of this book, recalled his experience of speaking publicly at various locations in Michigan during the early 1930s to advocate unemployment insurance legislation, always to be opposed on the spot by a spokesman of the state manufacturers' association who lumped together proponents of unemployment insurance as "Communists and college professors."

23. *Florida v. Mellon*, 273 U.S. 12.

Justice Brandeis' suggestion that the estate tax credit approach might serve as a model for federal unemployment insurance legislation was discussed in early January 1934 in Washington with several key individuals, including Senator Wagner and Secretary of Labor, Frances Perkins, who responded favorably to the idea. Secretary Perkins then assigned Thomas H. Eliot, Associate Solicitor of the Department of Labor, to work with Paul Raushenbush to draft a bill along the lines of the Federal Estate Tax Act. The bill was introduced early in 1934 by Senator Wagner and Congressman Lewis.[24]

The Wagner-Lewis bill, as it came to be called, imposed a federal excise tax of 5 percent of payrolls on employers similar to those types covered by the Wisconsin Act. An employer covered by the federal act could receive 100 percent credit against the federal tax for contributing into a state unemployment insurance fund or reserves as required by a state law that met prescribed conditions, even if the contributions were lower than the federal tax because of favorable unemployment experience. It is significant to note that the bill had minimum benefit standards. In order for its employers to receive federal tax credit, a state law would have to provide compensation of not less than $7 a week or not less than average earnings for twenty hours of work. Partial benefits would have to be paid to supplement actual earnings of partially unemployed workers up to the weekly benefit amount for total unemployment. Benefits would have to be payable for a maximum duration of at least ten weeks in a year or, if paid in proportion to previous weeks worked, for a maximum of at least fifteen weeks. The state law could not deny workers benefits for refusing to accept new work if (1) it was made available because of a labor dispute; (2) it provided substandard wages, hours, or working conditions; or (3) it would require joining a company union, or interfere with joining or retaining membership in a *bona fide* labor organization.[25] Under the Wagner-Lewis bill, a state could choose either the pooled fund or the employer reserves approach, a difference heatedly contested between adherents of the Ohio and Wisconsin schools.

---

24. The story of the origin of the federal tax credit approach idea for unemployment insurance and its development into the Wagner-Lewis bill is told in Raushenbush and Raushenbush (1979).

25. This last provision was the only standard regarding benefit rights that was contained in the Social Security Act when it was passed the following year.

At hearings held on the Lewis bill (H.R. 7659) in March 1934 by a subcommittee of the House Committee on Ways and Means, an impressive array of witnesses, including several employers, testified in favor of the bill. Opposition was voiced mainly by employer organizations. The bill also had the blessing of the administration, with President Roosevelt writing a letter of endorsement and Labor Secretary Perkins serving as the leading witness. Nevertheless, no action was taken on the bill. The opposition, which came mainly from employers, had grown stronger than had appeared at the hearings on the bill. In addition, various people apparently had approached the President to point out weaknesses in the Wagner-Lewis bill and urge that it be given further study. The President was particularly impressed by the argument that the large unemployment reserves that would accumulate might increase the severity of the depression unless the reserves were under federal control. He was also not completely satisfied with a bill providing for subsidies of state old-age pensions, which had passed the House. Accordingly, during May 1934, the President informed a number of supporters of these two bills that he thought it best to delay action and prepare a comprehensive program for presentation at the beginning of the first session of the next Congress (Witte 1962, pp. 4-5). In June 1934, the President sent Congress his special message on economic security and soon after created his Committee on Economic Security.

Concluding Observations

The development of private unemployment benefit plans in the United States was too limited to spread the unemployment insurance concept very broadly or build much of a base of support for it. Perhaps the major contribution the plans made was to demonstrate that such voluntary action was unlikely to respond adequately to the needs of the unemployed, given the dimensions of the problem. A few of the employers who did establish plans became important advocates of a public program despite the vigorous and widespread opposition of their fellow employers. They provided useful input into the evolution of the system that eventually did emerge.

The negative position of organized labor prior to 1932 regarding public unemployment insurance may seem strange, looking back from the post-New Deal era. It is understandable, however, considering the largely hostile attitudes of government towards unions before and during the first third of the twentieth century. As the depression took hold and worsened, the political climate changed; labor sensed a growing responsiveness by government to worker needs and interests. Organized labor reversed its stand and placed its support behind a compulsory unemployment insurance program.

The character of the program, its basic purposes and form, became issues of wider concern as legislative hearings and study commissions on the subject proliferated in the early 1930s. Previously, these matters were mainly of interest in academic circles, particularly at the University of Wisconsin where the subject received early and creative attention. Its long lead helped give the approach developed by the Wisconsin school considerable influence in ensuing national developments, influence especially strengthened when its views became embodied in the first state unemployment insurance law in Wisconsin years before successful action elsewhere. The Wisconsin emphasis on individualizing employer responsibility for unemployment benefit costs has had a lasting and profound impact on the American unemployment insurance system through its experience rating method of financing. Different viewpoints, articulated most cogently in the Ohio Study Commission's report of 1932, did contend for attention. These stressed assurance of adequate benefit payments from pooled funds combining contributions of all employers and employees. The Ohio and Wisconsin ideas were central in the creation process that led to the national unemployment insurance proposals of 1935.

One other factor had to be recognized in order to engage that process energetically at the federal level. The perceived threat of competitive disadvantage was proving an effective barrier to individual state action on unemployment insurance, leaving unfulfilled the hopes and expectations raised by the accelerated efforts at that level in the early 1930s. Beginning in 1933, the focus shifted increasingly to Washington, where a new administration and a new Congress took charge of the federal government with a willingness to use its power and resources to deal with the huge problems of the depression. How to encourage and help the states overcome their inhibitions to act on unemployment insurance was still the main concern of congressional legislative proposals. The Wagner-Lewis bill of 1934, utilizing the tax-credit concept suggested by Justice Brandeis, appeared to be the likely vehicle to accomplish that end. While the administration supported this approach, it adopted a strategy to carefully plan and assemble a broad program of economic and Social Security, including unemployment insurance that would deal comprehensively with the nation's problems.

6

The Social Security Act of 1935
Breakthrough

By 1934, it had become clear that few, if any, states would adopt unemployment insurance laws unless federal action occurred first. High hopes had been entertained for the 1934 Wagner-Lewis bill, passage of which would have stimulated the enactment of state legislation. While disappointed that the bill did not pass, the supporters of unemployment insurance had their hopes revived when the President appointed the Committee on Economic Security in June 1934. The discussions and debates on the Wagner-Lewis bill, including the congressional hearings, went far towards illuminating the issues and widening the understanding of unemployment insurance. This result was important as preparation for the next phase, since very few people in the United States were truly knowledgeable about unemployment insurance at the time. Also of great significance was the increasingly evident commitment by President Roosevelt to federal legislation to bring about unemployment insurance, a commitment he had reached while governor of New York.

Soon after the Committee on Economic Security began its deliberations, strong differences emerged among proponents of legislation as to what directions a federal law should take regarding the kind of system to establish for unemployment insurance in the country. Foremost among these were whether the proposed arrangement should be a wholly national or a joint federal-state system. If it were to be the latter, there was controversy as to the federal role in the system. These disagreements stemmed from conflicting views about the extent of federal control that should be provided and the political and constitutional implications of different plans. The particular federal-state arrangement chosen at the outset was critical, and it has continued as a central issue during much of the program's development.[1]

---

1. For a comprehensive treatment of that arrangement and how it has evolved, see Rubin (1983).

The alternatives presented to the Committee on Economic Security by its Technical Board, Advisory Council, and staff, and the process by which decisions were reached are described in some detail in this chapter. The chapter also highlights the congressional considerations of the unemployment insurance proposals and the changes made as those proposals were fashioned into law.

Deliberations of the Committee on Economic Security

On June 8, 1934, in a special message to the Congress, President Roosevelt listed what he considered to be the unfinished legislative goals of his administration. Among these were the "furthering of the security of the citizen and his family through social insurance." He held that the various types of social insurance were interrelated and difficult to solve piecemeal. "Hence, I am looking for a sound means ...to provide at once security against several of the great disturbing factors in life—especially those which relate to unemployment and old age" (H. Doc. No. 397, 73d Cong., 2d sess. 1934).

Formation of the Committee

The President followed this message with an Executive Order (No. 6757) on June 29, creating the Committee on Economic Security. The Order directed the Committee to "study problems relating to the economic security of individuals." It was clearly understood that these problems would include unemployment and insecurity in old age, and that social insurance would be the major approach for dealing with them.

The Committee on Economic Security consisted of the Secretary of Labor (Frances Perkins), the Secretary of the Treasury (Henry Morgenthau, Jr.), the Attorney General (Homer Cummings), the Secretary of Agriculture (Henry Wallace), and the Federal Emergency Relief Administrator (Harry Hopkins). Secretary Perkins was designated to chair the Committee. The Executive Order also provided for an Advisory Council, a Technical Board of qualified representatives from federal agencies, and an executive director of the Committee.

A 23-member Advisory Council was chaired by Frank P. Graham, president of the University of North Carolina and later elected a U.S. Senator. High-ranking representatives of labor and management were appointed to the Council, as were other national figures from interested groups. Dr. Arthur J. Altmeyer, then second Assistant Secretary of Labor and subsequently Commissioner of Social Security, was named chairman of the Technical Board, which consisted of 21 members. Dr. Edwin E. Witte, professor of economics at the University of Wisconsin, was appointed executive director.[2] A staff of experts in many fields was assembled, including Dr. Bryce M. Stewart, research director of Industrial Relations Counselors, Inc., who was appointed director of the Committee's unemployment insurance staff.[3]

Proposals for National and Federal-State Systems

Soon after the Technical Board and Committee staff began their work, disagreement became evident as to what type of unemployment insurance program should be recommended. The President had stated his views in his congressional message of June 8, but they were rather general:

> I believe there should be a maximum of cooperation between States and the Federal Government. I believe that the funds necessary to provide this insurance should be raised by contribution rather than by an increase in general taxation. Above all, I am convinced that social insurance should be national in scope, although the several States should meet at least a large portion of the cost of management, leaving to the Federal Government the responsibility of investing, maintaining and safeguarding the funds constituting the necessary insurance reserves (H. Doc. No. 397, 73d Cong., 2d sess. 1934).

This language implied that the President was thinking in terms of a federal-state system.

---

2. Altmeyer was also from Wisconsin. Both he and Witte had been students of John Commons and had served in administrative positions in the Wisconsin Industrial Commission. Wilbur J. Cohen, a contributing author of this book, was chosen by Witte from among the young recent graduates at the University to come to Washington as his research assistant.

3. One of the authors of the 1966 forerunner of this book, Dr. Merrill G. Murray, another University of Wisconsin alumnus, was appointed associate director of the unemployment insurance staff. The other members of the staff are listed in Social Security Board (1937, p. 521).

Dr. Witte reported that late in August 1934, the President "expressed decided preferences for state administration of unemployment insurance, but again stressed that the reserve funds must be handled by the federal government; also, that unemployment insurance should be set up to give encouragement to the regularization of employment" (Witte 1962, p. 18). However, Witte said the President did not insist that the Committee necessarily recommend his ideas.

Despite the President's views, Dr. Stewart, director of the unemployment insurance staff, made a preliminary report in September recommending a uniform national system because of his belief that most unemployment was due to national rather than local causes. The plan he recommended, however, would have permitted entire industries and, perhaps, large nationwide employers to have their own funds. This report was presented to the Technical Board, together with recommendations by Witte for a federal-state plan along the lines suggested by the President.

The arguments for a national system that were put forward in Stewart's report and in subsequent discussions included the following: (1) it would provide uniformity of protection to all covered employees throughout the country exposed to the same risk of unemployment; (2) it would provide an easy and uniform method of handling the problem of employees who worked in more than one state; (3) it would also avoid burdening employers who operated across state lines with having to pay taxes and make reports under a multiplicity of state laws and regulations, as would occur under a federal-state system; (4) it would permit the pooling of reserves on a national basis, with a lower reserve fund level required for adequate financing than that required for separate state reserves in the aggregate; and (5) it would provide a superior basis for actuarial estimates, since state statistics on unemployment were practically nonexistent.

On the other hand, the arguments of those who favored a federal-state system included the following: (1) a national system would be cumbersome to operate, and centralization of administration might paralyze action; (2) a national system would require immediate decisions on such controversial issues as employee contributions, methods of experience rating, and variable versus uniform duration of benefits, whereas under a federal-state system these could be left for discussion and decision by individual states; (3) a federal-state system would permit wide latitude for experimentation by the states which would be desirable in the absence of experience with unemployment insurance in the United State; and (4) if mistakes were made in individual states in their legislation, they would not have as serious repercussion in a federal-state system as mistakes made in legislation for a national system.

The Technical Board set up an unemployment insurance committee, to which it referred the question of whether a national or federal-state system should be recommended.[4] This committee reported to the executive committee of the Technical Board a few days later in favor of a national system, differing in some details from Dr. Stewart's plan. In October, the executive committee, in turn, presented a statement of principles regarding unemployment insurance to the Committee on Economic Security. One of these principles read: "If constitutional, a nationally administered system of unemployment insurance is to be preferred to a State system, but the Committee should be satisfied that a nationally administered system is constitutional before commitments in favor of such a system are made to the public" (Witte 1962, p. 114). Eventually, however, the Technical Board's unemployment insurance committee reversed its position and voted unanimously for a federal-state plan similar to that in the Wagner-Lewis bill of 1934.

Subsidy or Tax Credit for Federal-State System

The Wagner-Lewis bill provided for a Federal Unemployment Tax against which tax credits could be taken for contributions paid under a state unemployment insurance law. The executive committee of the Technical Board, however, was divided on what type of plan to recommend. During the Technical Board's discussions in October, a "subsidy plan" was suggested under which a federal tax would be collected from employers, with proceeds from each state to be returned to that state if it met federally prescribed standards for unemployment compensation.[5] This subsidy plan would have met the conditions laid down by

---

4. This committee included Alvin H. Hansen, Chief Economic Advisor, Department of State, as chairman; William M. Leiserson, Chairman of the National Mediation Board; Jacob Viner, Assistant to the Secretary, Treasury Department; Thomas Eliot, Associate Solicitor, Department of Labor; and E. Willard Jensen, Executive Secretary, Business Advisory Council, Department of Commerce.

5. According to Dr. Witte's recollection, this approach was suggested by Mr. Emerson Ross of the Federal Emergency Relief Administration (Witte 1962, p. 115).

President Roosevelt and was the second choice of those who favored a wholly national system. The subsidy plan was seen as having the advantages of a national plan in that it would permit the writing of definite standards on benefits into the federal law without endangering its constitutionality. The lawyers feared that if federal standards were put in a tax-credit type of law, its constitutionality would be endangered. The subsidy plan was opposed, however, by some members of the staff and Technical Board who did not think it wise, without practical experience, to prescribe standards for the state laws.

A report made to the Committee on Economic Security on November 9, 1934 set forth the pros and cons for the three alternatives: a national system, a federal-state system based on a tax-credit plan of the Wagner-Lewis type, or a federal-state subsidy plan. The Committee voted unanimously to cease further consideration of a national plan, but reached no conclusions on the relative merits of a tax-credit or subsidy plan for a federal-state system.

The Committee's decision for a federal-state system was conveyed to the President. A few days later, a National Conference on Economic Security was held, attended by about 150 experts and representatives of various interests. In his address to this conference, President Roosevelt said that in the program recommended to Congress, unemployment insurance would be proposed as "a cooperative federal-state undertaking," but he was no more specific than this. The alternatives of a tax-credit plan, such as that of the Wagner-Lewis bill, or a subsidy plan continued to be discussed.[6]

Advisory Council Views

The Advisory Council held its first meeting on November 15 and 16, immediately following the National Conference on Economic Security. The Council's discussion was taken up entirely with unemployment insurance at this meeting. In view of the President's announcement that unemployment insurance would be on a federal-state basis, discussion of the type of system was confined to the tax-credit and subsidy plans. The Advisory Council appointed a committee to consider this issue and

---

6. The Conference provided an airing of many, often conflicting ideas. It was not expected to reach any conclusions or offer recommendations, and did not do so (Witte 1962, pp. 41-47).

other questions discussed at its meeting.[7] This committee held several meetings during the next month but made no formal report to the Council. Instead, it presented individual views and a mass of other material. The Council voted nine to seven in favor of the subsidy plan, but since six members were absent or did not vote, it indicated that the vote represented individual views, that the tax-credit and subsidy plans each had their good features, and that the issue should be decided by the Committee on Economic Security. The Advisory Council completed its report on December 15.

The Committee Adopts Tax-Credit Plan

The Committee on Economic Security, worried about the delays in reaching decisions on unemployment insurance, had gone ahead with final consideration of its recommendations. By the time it made its final decisions, it had the report of the Advisory Council but not the report of Bryce Stewart and his unemployment insurance staff. The Committee, however, knew his views favoring a national system as a first choice and the subsidy federal-state plan as a second choice. The Committee once more thoroughly reviewed the alternatives of a subsidy or tax-credit plan and voted for the latter.

The history of the discussions regarding the three alternative approaches for establishing an unemployment insurance system has been given in some detail to show the considerable division of opinion as to the degree of participation by the federal government in the system. The decision to recommend a federal-state system was in accord with the President's own predilections, and so was reached more readily than was the decision on the type of federal-state plan to be recommended. Moreover, passage of the Wagner-Peyser Act the year before, which mandated a federal-state network of employment service offices, may have helped to set the choice of a federal-state scheme for unemployment insurance rather than a wholly national one. What tipped the scales in favor of the Wagner-Lewis type tax-credit plan over the subsidy alternative was the belief that the tax-credit approach

---

7. The members who served on the committee were Frank P. Graham, Chairman of the Advisory Council; Grace Abbott of the University of Chicago; Marion B. Folsom, assistant treasurer of Eastman Kodak Company; Morris E. Leeds, president of Leeds and Northrup Company; and William Green, president of the American Federation of Labor.

stood a better chance of being approved by the Supreme Court as constitutional. It was also recognized that a subsidy plan with federal benefit standards was likely to have a better chance with the Supreme Court than a tax-credit plan with the standards. But since the Committee had already decided to have as few standards as possible, a tax-credit plan with few standards faced little or no disadvantage in the arguments over the comparative constitutionality of the tax-credit and subsidy approaches, even though this issue remained in doubt. Moreover, under the tax-credit plan, the states would have their own self-sustaining laws that could continue even if the federal legislation was declared unconstitutional.

Political considerations also contributed to the decision. The Wagner-Lewis approach had come to be seen as a middle course between two strongly opposing camps. On one side were those who favored a limited plan of individual employer reserves with emphasis on unemployment prevention, such as embodied in the Wisconsin law. Led by Paul and Elizabeth Brandeis Raushenbush and a number of business leaders, this group wanted federal legislation to overcome the interstate competition barrier to state action, but without federal control over state policy. At one extreme, of course, were those opposed to any federal legislation—mostly employer groups. The other side favored a plan more focused on adequate compensation and more assured financing with emphasis on unemployment relief. This group, which included Paul Douglas, Abraham Epstein, William Leiserson, I. M. Rubinow, and Bryce Stewart, believed that only a program with strong uniform federal standards and multiple financing sources would suffice. It is to the credit of Witte, Altmeyer, and Secretary of Labor Perkins that they adhered to the pragmatic line in steering the Committee on Economic Security toward the Wagner-Lewis type of tax-credit approach as the only alternative that was likely to make it through the Congress as well as conform with the President's views and, by minimizing federal standards, also survive the challenge of constitutionality.[8]

---

8. For views of a much later observer on these deliberations, see Nelson (1969, pp. 204-211).

Other Issues

The Committee dealt with a number of questions relating to unemployment insurance financing. These included whether to have employee and government contributions, whether to permit the Wisconsin system of individual employer reserve accounts or to allow experience rating, and what the rate of employer contributions should be.

Employee and Government Contributions.

After extended discussion, a majority of the Advisory Council voted against employee contributions. However, four of the employer members of the Council along with a public member, Raymond Moley,[9] felt so strongly about employee contributions that they wrote a separate statement advocating them. They believed that employee contributions would make it possible to have more adequate benefits, as well as a more effective administration, since the workers would have a clearer conception of their responsibilities.[10] The consensus of the Council was that there should not be government contributions, especially in view of the large outlays being made by the government for general relief at the time.[11] In keeping with its recommendation to avoid federal standards, the Committee made no specification on these matters for the states.

Experience Rating.

The President's desire to encourage stabilization of employment through the experience rating of unemployment insurance contributions was generally accepted. The difficulty was in deciding how to do it. Bryce Stewart, who supported the subsidy plan, argued that "merit rating," as it was called then, could be accomplished under a subsidy plan through federal tax refunds to "any insurance unit" that had built up a sufficient reserve. (As insurance units, he proposed individual

---

9. Moley, a professor of public law at Columbia University and a trusted adviser of President Roosevelt, was a public member of the Advisory Council who kept in close touch with the work of the Committee on Economic Security.

10. Statement presented to U.S. House Ways and Means Committee (U.S. Congress, House 1935, pp. 873-74).

11. Paul Kellogg, editor of *The Survey* magazine and a member of the Advisory Council, felt so strongly that there should be government contributions that he urged them at every opportunity.

employers, groups of employers, or industries.) The issue of pooled funds versus individual employer reserve accounts was not settled until the final meeting of the Committee on Economic Security (Witte 1962, p. 127). Several members of the Committee were opposed to individual employer accounts, such as were provided for in the Wisconsin law, but it was finally agreed to permit state laws to have such accounts, provided the state required employers to contribute at least 1 percent of their payrolls to a central pooled fund—a recommendation of Dr. Altmeyer.

Rate of Employer Tax.

Although there was general agreement that employers should contribute, it was felt that the imposition of an employer tax should be so timed as not to impede industrial recovery. The Advisory Council thought that the tax rate of 5 percent of payrolls proposed in the Wagner-Lewis bill of 1934 was too high, and agreed to recommend a 3 percent rate.[12] The Technical Board's unemployment insurance committee recommended that the proposed rate of contributions be achieved in stages over a three-year period by steps geared to the level of the Federal Reserve Board index of industrial production to assure that increases in the tax would take effect only as business recovered. The Committee on Economic Security adopted this idea, along with the level of 3 percent for the full rate. It should be noted that this rate applied to the total payrolls of covered employers, unlike the rate for old-age insurance contributions which was to apply to the first $3,000 in wages paid to an employee during the year.

---

12. Adequate employment and unemployment statistics were not available as a sound basis for cost estimates. Some national estimates were prepared nevertheless by staff statisticians of the Committee on Economic Security under the direction of Robert Nathan. These indicated that about 5 percent of payrolls would be needed over a period of years to finance a relatively modest unemployment benefit program (Social Security Board 1937, ch. 4). These estimates were not regarded as official, and Professor Witte (1962, p. 34) believed they overstated the real unemployment problem. As noted in chapter 5, the Ohio Commission Report of 1932 had estimated that a 3 percent rate of contributions would finance a modest program in Ohio over a 10-year period.

Report of the Committee on Economic Security

In its report to the President, formally submitted January 15, 1935, the Committee stressed the need for federal legislation on unemployment insurance in order to remove the chief obstacle to state action, namely, the fear each state had that imposing a tax on its employers would place them at a competitive disadvantage with employers in other states which did not impose such a tax. The Committee recommended that this fear be removed through a uniform federal excise tax on payrolls, with a tax credit to employers for insurance contributions they made under a compulsory state unemployment insurance law. The uniform tax would remove the obstacle to state legislation, while the tax credit would encourage each state to act to enable their employers to qualify for it. The second major recommendation of the Committee was that the federal government grant the states sufficient funds for proper administration of their unemployment insurance laws. The specific legislative recommendations of the Committee were directed to these two major proposals.

Unemployment Tax, Tax Credit, and Trust Fund

The Committee recommended a federal excise tax on employers who employed four or more workers for 13 or more weeks in a year. It advised setting this tax equal to 1 percent of total payrolls in 1936 and 3 percent by 1938, with increases in the interim tied to increases in the Federal Reserve Board index of industrial production. Although the Committee recommended that no industries be exempted, it favored a separate federal system for railroad employees and maritime workers.

The Committee would allow employers credit, up to 90 percent of the federal tax, for contributions paid under a state unemployment insurance law, provided the state cooperated with the federal government in the administration of the program, deposited contributions it collected into a trust fund set up for the purpose in the federal Treasury, and used such contributions solely for paying unemployment benefits. These were the only conditions mentioned in the Committee report that a state would have to meet.

The Committee further recommended that if a state allowed employers to contribute at rates below the maximum credit allowed against the federal tax because they had stable employment, additional credit toward the federal tax be allowed for the taxes that otherwise would have been paid under the state law. The Committee urged stiff requirements for such additional credit. In states with plans based on individual employer reserve accounts, such as that adopted in Wisconsin in 1932, which would be permitted, an accumulated reserve equal to at least 15 percent of annual payrolls would be required before an employer could qualify for an additional tax credit because of a reduced rate. In addition, employers contributing to such accounts would have to contribute at least 1 percent of their payrolls to a state pooled fund.[13] Employers contributing solely to state pooled funds would not be allowed lower rates until the state law had been in operation for five years.

The Committee recommended that all money collected by the states to finance unemployment benefits be deposited in a special trust fund in the federal Treasury to be called the Unemployment Trust Fund, with an account to the credit of each state. The Secretary of the Treasury would invest the money in the trust fund as a whole. Interest on the amount in each state account should be allowed at the average rate of interest on primary obligations of the United States. Also recommended was that the collection of the Federal Unemployment Tax as well as the investment of state reserves be under the control of the Secretary of the Treasury, and that other federal aspects of the legislation be administered by a three-member social insurance board housed in the Department of Labor.

Grants to States for Administration

The other major recommendation of the Committee was for the federal government to grant the states money for administration of their laws "under conditions designed to insure competence and probity." Among these conditions, the Committee considered it vital that the selection of administrative personnel be on a merit basis, which at that

---

13. Under the Committee proposals, state could also provide an option to employers to maintain guaranteed employment accounts instead of reserve funds to pay their employees unemployment benefits, and such accounts would need to accumulate to at least 7.5 percent of annual payroll before the employer could qualify for additional tax credit. The option was provided in the Social Security Act, but apparently no one ever made use of it.

time was a practice in very few states. Another condition was that the states accept the provisions of the Wagner-Peyser Act for a federal-state employment service system and pay unemployment benefits through employment offices. It was assumed that the funds for administrative grants would be financed from the portion (10 percent) of the Federal Unemployment Tax that would be retained by the federal government after allowance of the tax credit. For constitutional reasons, however, it was not recommended that the taxes be earmarked for this purpose.

Although, in his congressional message of June 8, 1934, the President had suggested that "the several states should meet at least a large portion of the cost of management," the Committee recommended that the federal government pay the entire cost of administration. It did so, evidently, because of a fear based, in part, on workers' compensation experience that state legislatures would not provide adequate funds for administration and that standards of administration would not be high enough to insure successful operation of the program. Yet the Committee trusted the state legislatures fully with respect to providing proper benefits and benefit conditions.

State Latitude and Federal Standards

In its report, the Committee justified the proposed federal-state system on the grounds that it would permit variations in state laws "so that we can learn through variation what is best." The Committee recognized that a uniform national system would be superior in some respects, particularly in relation to workers who move from state to state. It also recognized that in other respects, "state administration may develop marked inadequacies." If experience showed that a national system was desirable, the Committee rather blithely stated: "It is always possible by subsequent legislation to establish such a system." Against this possibility, the Committee recommended that the states be required to include in their laws a reservation of power to modify or repeal the law and that the federal law contain a similar reservation.

With respect to its choice of the tax-credit type of federal-state legislation in preference to the subsidy type, the Committee said:

> We prefer a tax credit device to one in which the tax would be
> wholly collected and then remitted, as grants-in-aid, to the States,
> because under the latter system the States would not have self-
> supporting laws of their own, and as with all compensation having
> its source in Federal grants there would be great and constant
> pressure for larger grants exceeding the money raised by the tax,
> with a subsequent confusion of compensation and relief ("Report
> to the President of the Committee on Economic Security" 1935, p.
> 17).

The prevailing position of the Committee was thus to allow the states considerable leeway in evolving the kind of unemployment insurance programs they deemed appropriate. As noted earlier, very few federal standards were recommended, in keeping with this position. Those recommended dealt with the control and use of state benefit funds, with matters relating to administration, and with requirements to qualify employers given reduced tax rates by their state for additional federal tax credit. No standards were recommended regarding how much of a benefit a state should pay to unemployed workers, or for how long, or what the requirements should be for benefit eligibility.

The Committee recommendations were incorporated in a bill to be sent to the Congress along with the Committee's final report. Not mentioned in the Committee report, but included in the bill was the so-called "labor standards" provision that would have to be included in the state law in order for it to be approved for tax-credit purposes. This standard was designed to protect claimants from benefit disqualification for refusing to accept offers of work that entailed certain employment conditions disadvantageous to themselves or to their labor union.[14] It was the only standard relating to benefit rights included in the bill. Although any standard as specific as this might be construed to give the tax a regulatory purpose and thus endanger the constitutionality of the law, it was included to allay labor's fear that unemployment insurance might be used to break unions or weaken labor standards. It was chiefly this fear that had caused the American Federation of Labor to oppose compulsory unemployment insurance until its convention of

---

14. The standard was included in the Social Security Act. See condition (5) for approval of state laws under "Title IX" given in the appendix to this chapter.

1932. Inclusion of the standard helped to produce strong labor support for the measure in 1935.

Congressional Consideration of Proposals

The Committee on Economic Security's report was promptly submitted to the Congress with a special message in which the President urged that legislation "should be brought forward with a minimum of delay." The hope was that Congress would pass the legislation in time for the states to act in their 1935 legislative sessions, since only a few states would hold sessions in 1936. Congress proceeded, however, with what might be termed deliberate speed. Practically all of the state legislatures had gone home by the time a bill was passed.

The Legislative Process

A bill had been drafted by Thomas Eliot, Associate Solicitor of Labor, which was immediately introduced as the Economic Security Act in the Senate by Senator Wagner, and in the House by Congressman Lewis and Congressman Robert L. Doughton of North Carolina.[15] Since Doughton was chairman of the House Committee on Ways and Means, the hearings were conducted on his bill (H.R. 4120). The bill was referred to his Committee and to the Senate Finance Committee because of its tax provisions.[16] The bill contained titles on a number of other measures besides unemployment insurance, including

---

15. Although Lewis had been a chief sponsor of the 1934 Wagner-Lewis bill, Doughton was accorded that honor for the 1935 bill because he was chairman of the key committee and because he was from the South where opposition to the proposed legislation was expected to be the heaviest. He became an influential supporter of the bill and of Social Security legislation in later years. Senator Pat Harrison of Mississippi, Senate Finance Committee chairman, similarly lent his influence with southern colleagues to help bring about passage of the bill.

16. The chairman of the House Labor Committee, Congressman William P. Connery, Jr., tried to get the bill referred to his Committee. When this was not done, his Committee held hearings on the "Lundeen bill" (H.R. 2827) which provided for unemployment compensation equal to the difference between earnings, if any, and average local wages for as long as a person ab le and willing to work was unemployed or underemployed. Such benefits were to be paid out of federal general funds, to be increased if necessary through increases in inheritance and income taxes. This bill was reported favorably by the Labor Committee but was never acted upon by the House.

old-age insurance; public assistance for the aged, dependent children and the blind; other child care services; and public health measures. As a result, only a fraction of the time was devoted to unemployment insurance. In fact, during the entire congressional consideration of the bill, major attention was given to the old-age assistance and old-age insurance titles of the bill.

Both committees promptly began hearings on the bill in January.[17] The House Ways and Means Committee hearings continued almost daily until February 12. Most of the next two months was occupied with executive sessions of the Committee and meticulous work by its legislative counsel, Middleton Beaman, and his staff in redrafting parts of the bill, with much consultation with Thomas Eliot.[18] The Committee reported out a revised bill in early April retitled as the Social Security Act. The House passed it two weeks later by the overwhelming vote of 371 to 33.

The Senate Finance Committee's hearings on the Wagner bill (S. 1130) ran for about a month beginning in January. After the Social Security bill passed the House, the Finance Committee reviewed it thoroughly and made a number of changes. The Committee reported the bill to the Senate on May 20. About a month later, after some delay due to the precedence of other bills on the calendar and several days of debate, the Senate passed it also by an overwhelming vote of 77 to 6.

Differences between the two bills remained to be reconciled by a Conference Committee of the House and Senate. Because of a controversial amendment added in the Senate to the old-age insurance provisions of the bill, the Conference Committee was deadlocked for weeks.[19] The Conference finally reached agreement and reported its bill. Congress approved it shortly thereafter early in August. The bill was signed into law by the President on August 14, 1935 in a signing

---

17. The extensive hearings held by the two committees were published and included all testimony, supporting materials, and written statements that were submitted. They reflected the broad range of viewpoints held at the time by representatives of all segments of society throughout the nation regarding unemployment insurance, as well as other programs included in the proposed legislation. See: U.S. Congress, House (1935); and U.S. Congress, Senate (1935).

18. An amusing but informative account of his participation in the drafting of the bill was given by Eliot (1960).

19. The impasse was over the so-called "Clark amendment," which would have exempted workers under employer pension plans from coverage under the old-age insurance program if those plans met certain standards.

ceremony in the White House with the congressional leaders and Labor Secretary Perkins in attendance. The provisions of the 1935 Social Security Act relating to unemployment insurance are summarized in an appendix to this chapter.

Congressional Modifications of Administration Proposals

The principal change made by the House in the Federal Unemployment Tax part of the bill was to strike out the provisions for additional credit to employers paying state tax rates that were lowered because of experience rating. During the hearings of the Committee on Ways and Means, Congressman Jere Cooper had perceived the inconsistency between the proposal for a uniform federal tax on all covered employers throughout the country in order to meet the problem of interstate competition posed by unequal state tax costs and the proposal to permit variation of contributions in the states through experience rating, which would eliminate such uniformity. He was able to persuade the Committee to report the bill without the additional credit provisions.

At the Senate Finance Committee hearings, employer witnesses had strongly advocated the additional credit provisions in the bill, stressing the desirability of permitting experience rating in state laws.[20] These provisions were subsequently restored by the Senate Committee through an amendment proposed by Senator Robert LaFollette, Jr., of Wisconsin. The amendment was accepted by the Senate without much debate and agreed to in the House-Senate conference. In the process, the requirement in the bill, as introduced in the House, of a minimum contribution of 1 percent of payroll to a state pooled fund was eliminated. Moreover, the requirements for experience rating under individual reserve accounts and state pooled funds were eased. The proposal to tie the increase in the federal tax from 1 to 3 percent of payroll to increases in the index of industrial production was eliminated, and increases to 2 percent for 1937 and to 3 percent beginning in 1938 were substituted.

The bill emerged from Congress with much more restricted unemployment insurance coverage than that proposed by the administration.

---

20. See especially the testimony of Marion B. Folsom, representing the employer members of the Advisory Council to the Committee on Economic Security in U.S. Congress, House (1935, p. 557 ff).

The Committee on Ways and Means had changed coverage to employers with ten or more employees in twenty weeks. The Senate changed it back to the original bill's coverage of employers with four or more employees in thirteen weeks. The Conference Committee agreed to a compromise coverage of eight or more in twenty weeks. The Committee on Ways and Means also restricted unemployment insurance coverage by excluding agricultural workers, domestic servants, employees of nonprofit organizations, members of the immediate family of the employer, and government workers. These exclusions remained in the bill finally adopted. The Committee on Economic Security's recommendation that railroad workers and maritime workers be covered by a separate system was not followed. Maritime workers employed on the navigable waters of the United States were exempted, but railroad workers were covered.

Finally, although one of the principal objectives of the Committee on Economic Security in providing for federal administrative grants to the states was to be able to require the employment of state personnel on a merit basis, Congress specifically excepted the "selection, tenure of office, and compensation of personnel" from the methods of administration that the Social Security Board could require of the states.[21]

Although these and a few other changes were made by Congress in the unemployment insurance features of the Social Security Act, the basic structure followed the recommendations of the Committee on Economic Security and the administration. The labor standards provision included by the administration in the bill sent to Congress was retained in the Act. While there were many witnesses critical of the proposals, according to Dr. Witte (1945, pp. 31-32): "the members of Congress throughout took it for granted that if anything was to be done about unemployment insurance, the Administration's proposals would have to be approved."

---

21. This provision was amended in 1939 to give the Board authority to require merit-based employment within prescribed limits, as described in the next chapter.

Concluding Observations

The passage of the Social Security Act with its unemployment insurance provisions was the key step toward the establishment of a system in the United States. Action by the states remained to complete the structure and bring it to life. Despite vigorously contested and often closely divided viewpoints on several basic issues within the Committee on Economic Security and its supporting components and staff, and among various interest groups, conflicts that were thoroughly aired in both House and Senate Committee hearings, the Social Security Act was approved in the Congress by very wide margins. In the congressional debate, more controversy seemed to focus on issues in old-age insurance than in unemployment insurance. The solid result is a tribute to the political skills of administration and legislative leaders, and to the broad appreciation accumulated over prior years of the need for unemployment insurance and for its value, concepts, and alternative designs.

Although decided in 1935, the critical question of a national or a federal-state system was to fester for many years. The idea of a federal subsidy to the states instead of the tax credit approach soon faded, but the relative roles of the two levels of government within the system was to be a major and evolving element affecting the program's development and operation. Nor was the issue of experience rating put to rest in 1935, a subject yet to develop at the state level and to attract persistent argument, pro and con. Unemployment insurance began in controversy; it was never to be free of controversy. For a vital program of considerable magnitude that was to become firmly imbedded in the nation's social and economic fabric, that condition should be neither surprising or unwelcome.

It is worth noting that strong early initiatives, under the right circumstances, can carry a large idea to fruition many years later while still reflecting much of the influence of its first proponents. The intellectual force of Wisconsin professor John Commons, both directly and through his students, clearly led the way to a particular formulation of unemployment insurance which materialized in the first American law to establish a program, that in Wisconsin, several years before the Social Security Act. That success added further weight to this source of influence as it contributed heavily to help shape the program to be provided for the nation. It was not accidental that individuals from Wisconsin were prominent among the people responsible for designing the unemployment insurance provisions of the Social Security Act. To be sure, others also contributed significantly to the process. But the Wisconsin imprint was unmistakable and lasting.

APPENDIX
Unemployment Insurance Provisions
of Social Security Act of 1935

The Social Security Act as passed contained two titles regarding unemployment insurance: Title IX providing for the Federal Unemployment Tax and its related provisions; and Title III providing for federal administrative grants. A summary of these titles follows:

Title IX

Title IX provided for an excise tax on employment by employers of eight or more persons in twenty or more weeks in a year. The tax would be equal to 1 percent of total payroll in 1936; 2 percent in 1937; and 3 percent in 1938.

Employment excluded from the tax were:

(1) agricultural labor;

(2) domestic service in a private home;

(3) services by the crews of vessels on navigable waters of the United States;

(4) service by specified immediate members of the family of the employer;

(5) service for the federal government or federal instrumentalities;

(6) service for state and local governments and instrumentalities;

(7) service for nonprofit organizations of a religious, charitable, scientific, literary, or educational nature or for the prevention of cruelty to children or animals.

Employers making contributions to approved state unemployment compensation laws could receive credit for such contributions up to 90 percent of the federal tax, if the state law met the following conditions:

(1) All compensation is to be paid through public employment offices or such other agencies as the Social Security Board (established by the Act) might approve.

(2) No compensation is to be paid for two years after contributions commence.

(3) All money received in the state unemployment fund is to be immediately deposited in the Federal Unemployment Trust Fund created by the Act, (to be credited to the state's account in the fund).

151

(4) All money withdrawn from the Trust Fund is to be used solely in the payment of unemployment compensation.

(5) Compensation will not be denied to any otherwise eligible unemployed worker for refusing to accept new work under any of the following conditions:

    (A) if the position offered is vacant due directly to a strike, lockout, or other labor dispute;

    (B) if the wages, hours, or other conditions of the work offered are substantially less favorable to the individual than those prevailing for similar work in the locality;

    (C) if as a condition of being employed the individual would be required to join a company union or to resign from or refrain from joining any bona fide labor organization.

(6) All the rights, privileges and immunities created by the state law are subject to the power of the legislature to amend or repeal the law at any time.

"Additional credit" would be given against the federal tax for state contributions not made because of a lower experience rate under the following conditions:

(1) If the employer was contributing to a state pooled fund, he has had three full years of "compensation experience";

(2) if he is contributing to a guaranteed employment account, he has fulfilled the guarantee (at least thirty hours of wages for at least forty weeks in the preceding year) and his account equals at least 7-1/2 percent of his total payroll in the preceding year; or

(3) if he is contributing to a separate reserve account in the state fund for one or more employers,

    (A) compensation was payable from the account throughout the preceding year;

    (B) the account is not less than five times the largest amount of compensation paid out of the account in any of the last three preceding years;

    (C) the account is equal to 7-1/2 percent of total wages payable in the preceding year.

The Unemployment Trust Fund was created in the Treasury of the United States. The act provided that deposits in the fund must be invested in federal securities that would yield the average rate of interest paid on all federal securities. It also provided that funds could be invested in special obligations issued to the Trust Fund that yielded such average rate of interest.

Title IX would be administered by the Treasury Department, except that the Social Security Board would determine whether the state unemployment compensation laws met and continued to meet the prescribed conditions. The Board was required to give reasonable notice and a fair hearing to the state before it refused to certify a state that did not meet the conditions.

Title III

Grants were authorized to be made to each state in such amounts as the Social Security Board determined to be necessary for the proper administration of its unemployment compensation law. The Board's determination was to be based on (1) the population of the state; (2) an estimate of the number of persons covered by the state law and of the cost of proper administration of such law; and (3) such other factors as the Board found relevant. Dollar limitations were placed on the amounts that could be granted—not more than $4 million for the fiscal year ending June 30, 1936, and not more than $49 million in any fiscal year thereafter.

In order for a state to receive administrative grants, its law had to be approved under Title IX, and also had to include provisions for:

(1) Such methods of administration (other than those relating to selection, tenure of office, and compensation of personnel) as were found by the Board to be reasonably calculated to pay benefits when due;

(2) an opportunity for a fair hearing, before an impartial tribunal, for unemployed workers whose claims for benefits were denied;

(3) the making of such reports as the Social Security Board might require; and

(4) making available upon the request of any federal agency charged with public works or assistance through public employment information under the state law.

In addition to these conditions, the first three conditions listed above for approval under Title IX were also included in Title III.

The state law not only had to meet these conditions but a state could also be denied administrative grants if the Board after reasonable notice and opportunity for hearing found that the state had failed to comply substantially with the specified conditions or had denied compensation in a substantial number of cases to persons entitled to it.

7

Beginnings
The System Takes Shape

Following adoption of the Social Security Act, efforts concentrated on obtaining passage of state unemployment insurance legislation that met the conditions laid down in the federal law. These efforts and their successful results are described in this chapter, along with the composition of the first state laws and the early experience under them. The nation's conversion to a wartime footing in the early 1940s completely altered the economic atmosphere with profound and unexpected effects on the unemployment insurance system. These developments, worries about reversion to depression conditions after the war, and the relatively quick and easy reconversion of the economy to a civilian peacetime basis by 1947 are also traced in this chapter.

The Social Security Board

In accordance with the Social Security Act, the President appointed a bipartisan three-member Board to administer its provisions.[1] The Board was established and staffed quickly. John G. Winant, a Republican and former governor of New Hampshire, was named its first chairman. Arthur J. Altmeyer, one of the other two members—who were both Democrats—was appointed to the Board in 1935 and succeeded Winant as chairman in 1936; he was to head the Board, later the Social Security Administration, until 1953. A number of bureaus were formed, including the Bureau of Unemployment Compensation.[2]

---

1. For an authoritative account of the establishment and early operation of the Social Security Board, see Altmeyer (1966, ch. 2).

2. The Bureau was headed by R. Gordon Wagonet, who remained in charge of unemployment insurance in the federal government for about twenty-five years. Wilbur J. Cohen and Merrill G. Murray were members of the original staff of the Bureau of Unemployment Compensation.

A major function of the Social Security Board was to provide technical assistance to the states in developing appropriate unemployment insurance legislation. Although some states had given considerable thought and study to the subject, particularly those that had study commissions, most states were ill-prepared for the task. The Committee on Economic Security anticipated this problem and in its report had suggested some considerations the states should take into account. The Committee provided various actuarial cost estimates for several combinations of benefit provisions under different assumptions about unemployment. It emphasized the importance of requiring adequate reserves in the accounts of individual employers before experience rating was permitted, so as to assure that benefit liabilities could be met. The Committee also had draft bills prepared setting forth alternative provisions under pooled fund and individual employer reserve account laws.[3] Social Security Board staff subsequently revised these model bills. They were used extensively by the states, in some cases with on-site assistance by Board staff in adapting them to particular state needs. As a result, most of the early laws were very similar in language, although there was nevertheless substantial variation in content. Board staff also assisted states in setting up administrative machinery.[4]

The Board, operating through its Bureau of Unemployment Compensation, assumed and carried out its responsibilities for reviewing state unemployment insurance laws to determine their conformity with federal requirements, for examining state administrative budgets as the basis for allocating federal administrative grants, and for setting policies and procedures designed to assure proper state program administration. In the latter category, for example, the Board decided at the outset to approve payment of unemployment benefits only through public employment offices that were affiliated with the United States Employment Service. Since the federal authority and responsibility for the employment service system was then located in the U.S. Department of Labor, the Board and the Department agreed formally, in 1937,

---

3. These draft bills were prepared by Merrill G. Murray with the assistance of Arthur J. Altmeyer and Paul A. Raushenbush. They were printed in U.S. Congress, Senate (1935, pp. 591-632).

4. In a few states, such recognized authorities as Professor William Haber of the University of Michigan drafted or helped to draft the initial laws. An example of Social Security Board assistance was the participation by Wilbur J. Cohen in the drafting of the District of Columbia and North Carolina laws.

to coordinate and integrate their activities insofar as these involved both unemployment insurance and employment service matters. In most states, the responsibility for both functions was joined in a single agency.

Constitutionality of Unemployment Insurance Laws Upheld

A major concern overhanging the unemployment insurance provisions of the federal law was that they might be ruled invalid by the courts, as had been the fate of some other New Deal legislation (U.S. Congress, Senate (1937). The critical choices of a federal tax offset approach to bring about state action and of a federal-state system with as few federal requirements as possible were, in large measure, dictated by that concern. Whether the new program could withstand the constitutional challenges that were sure to be made was a question confronted soon enough.

The challenges came at both the state and federal levels. Tests of state laws appeared in a number of states. One of these involved the Alabama unemployment insurance statute. The case was carried eventually to the U.S. Supreme Court, as was a challenge of the federal law. The Court handed down its decisions on both these cases on the same day—May 24, 1937. In both, the Court affirmed the validity of the laws.

In the test of the federal law, specifically of Titles III and IX of the 1935 Social Security Act, the arguments made against these provisions covered a number of points. Perhaps the most significant of these was that the purpose of the Federal Unemployment Tax with its tax credit provision and conditions was not to raise revenue but rather to force state action. As such, the tax constituted an unlawful invasion of reserved state powers, and the states unlawfully surrendered their responsible functions by yielding to that coercive tax. In delivering the opinion of the Court, Justice Cardozo rejected this argument by indicating that a state enacting a law which met the prescribed conditions and thereby reaped a federal tax advantage for its employers was not acting under duress but exercising a choice it was free to make and unmake.[5]

In the case involving the Alabama law, the principal constitutional arguments made against the statute were that it violated the due process and equal treatment clauses of the Fourteenth Amendment, and that it represented an invalid surrender of state power to the federal government induced by a coercive federal tax imposed for the purpose. Justice Stone, in delivering the Court's opinion, referred to the Court's decision that day regarding the challenge to the federal law which disposed of the latter argument also made against the validity of the federal tax. The fact that the state tax applied only to employers with eight or more workers and excluded many categories, as was true of the federal tax, was not seen as infringement of the due process and equal treatment clauses of the Fourteenth Amendment. Taxes were frequently imposed in this way for good reasons that were not at all capricious, arbitrary, or unreasonable. Administrative factors were noted as prominent in the restrictions on coverage; it was not for the Court to question the reasonableness of the specific exemptions made by the state legislature.[6]

With these decisions, the constitutionality of the unemployment insurance system itself and of the right of the states to establish a program within it were no longer in doubt. In anticipating the kinds of basic legal issues that would be raised, the designers of the system had framed it well.

Adoption of State Laws

Although all the states, the District of Columbia, and the Territories of Alaska and Hawaii had unemployment insurance laws by July 1937, this result was not achieved without some heel-dragging. Besides Wisconsin, four states had adopted unemployment insurance laws (all in 1935) before the Social Security Act passed: California, New Hamp-

---

5. *Stewart Machine Co. v. Davis*, 301 U.S. 548 (1937). The Court ruled 5 to 4 to validate the federal law.

6. *Carmichael v. Southern Coal and Coke Co.*, 301 U.S. 495 (1937). The Court's decision was 5 to 4 to uphold the Alabama law.

shire, New York, and Utah. Late in 1935, four more states—Alabama, Massachusetts, Oregon, and Washington—enacted legislation, and Congress passed a law for the District of Columbia.[7]

During the first 11 months of 1936, only nine more states adopted unemployment insurance laws. Few state legislatures had regular sessions that year. It was an election year with the Social Security Act as a center of political controversy in the presidential and many congressional campaigns; governors were thus reluctant to call special sessions. The first Federal Unemployment Tax payment was due January 31, 1937 on 1936 wages, and only states with unemployment insurance laws approved by the end of 1936 could qualify their employers for the 90 percent tax credit. The Social Security Board indicated late in 1936 that it could not extend the time for approval. As a result, there was a great flurry of legislative activity after the general election in November as many states called special sessions to pass the required legislation in order to "get it under the wire." A total of eighteen state unemployment insurance laws passed in December 1936. By the close of the year, the Board had approved thirty-six state laws for the tax credit offset. Congress subsequently authorized tax offset refunds credited to the accounts of the remaining states which passed their first laws after the deadline. A few states had continued to hold out in the hope that the federal law would be ruled unconstitutional. After the Supreme Court handed down its decisions in May 1937, upholding both the federal law and the Alabama unemployment insurance law, the remaining states passed the required legislation. Illinois was the last to do so, its law being signed on June 30, 1937.

Content of Early Laws

Since most states made use of the model draft bills and other technical assistance provided by the Social Security Board in developing their legislation, the laws enacted at the outset were probably more

---

7. The Washington law was invalidated by that state's Supreme Court and had to be reenacted later. Congress enacted the law for the District of Columbia, as well as all its subsequent amendments, since the District had no self-governing legislative authority.

alike than at any other time. The principal differences were in the funding and financing provisions, for which the model bills offered some options.[8]

Type of Fund

The most hotly contested issue in the formation of the original state laws was whether to have the Wisconsin type of individual employer reserves or a completely pooled fund. It was argued that individual employer reserves gave maximum incentive to stabilization of employment. The pooled-fund advocates, on the other hand, maintained that individual reserve accounts could easily be exhausted; they urged pooling of funds to give maximum protection to the worker. Many of the pooled-fund proponents also opposed experience rating. The model draft bills offered compromises between the two extremes. One bill provided for individual employer reserve accounts within the state unemployment insurance fund, but with a partial pooling of contributions. The other bill provided for a completely pooled fund, but with experience rating of contributions of individual employers. Both bills proposed a reduction of the contribution rate from 2.7 percent to 1.8 percent if the accumulated surplus of contributions by an employer over benefits paid to former employees exceeded 7.5 percent of annual payroll, and a reduction of the rate to 0.9 percent if the surplus was 10 percent or more of payroll.[9] Experience rating methods for adjusting the unemployment insurance tax rates of individual employers may use other approaches for the purpose as long as the method applied reflects in some way the unemployment experience of the employer's former workers. (State experience rating provisions are described more fully in chapter 8.)

Despite the early example of the Wisconsin law, only six other states adopted the individual employer reserves approach, of which two provided for partial pooling of contributions. The remaining jurisdictions established fully pooled funds, all but eleven of them with experience rating of employer contributions; nine of these eleven made provision

---

8. Information about early state provisions is drawn primarily from: Federal Security Agency (1940); and Federal Security Agency (1947).

9. The rate of 2.7 percent was generally regarded as the "standard" rate; it represented the maximum credit allowed against the federal tax.

to study experience rating. Four states also allowed for guaranteed employment plans and three for "contracting out" of employers who provided benefits equal to or larger than those provided by the state law. There is no record of these latter provisions ever having been used, and they were subsequently repealed. Eventually, all states adopted completely pooled funds with experience rating.[10]

Contributions

From the beginning, every state required contributions from employers to finance benefits since employers, subject to the Federal Unemployment Tax, would otherwise lose the possibility for tax credits and have to pay the full federal tax. Except for five states in 1937, the standard rate at which employers contributed (that applicable before experience rating took effect) was equal to the maximum tax credit allowed—90 percent of the federal tax rate of 3.0 percent. In the five states, it equaled the full federal rate.[11]

Only nine states adopted employee contributions at the outset. New Jersey joined this group in 1938, but three states repealed employee contributions that year. The contribution rates which applied at the time ranged between 0.5 and 1.5 percent. Except for New Jersey, all the other states that had them have since abandoned worker contributions. Alaska adopted employee contributions beginning in 1955, and Pennsylvania and West Virginia did so in the 1980s, making four states in all as of 1990. The original District of Columbia law was the only one that provided for a government contribution to the state fund. Appropriations of $100,000 were made in 1936 and $125,000 in 1937. The provision was repealed thereafter.

With few exceptions, all contribution rates, both federal and state, applied to total wages paid in the first few years of the program.[12] A federal taxable wage base limit was not imposed for unemployment insurance until a 1939 amendment specified one, to become effective January 1, 1940.

---

10. Puerto Rico, which entered the federal-state system in 1961, did not authorize experience rating until 1992.

11. By 1940, only Michigan, New York, and the District of Columbia continued to apply the full 3.0 percent as the standard rate, rather than 2.7 percent which was standard elsewhere.

12. In Michigan, New York, and South Carolina (in 1939), contribution rates applied to the first $3,000 paid.

Coverage

The federal law spelled out the extent of coverage indicating employment subject to the Federal Unemployment Tax and the specific exemptions from that coverage. State laws did the same with regard to state unemployment insurance contributions. There would be little or no purpose served if a state did not cover employment covered by the federal tax, since no tax credit could be taken. States may, however, be more extensive in their coverage if they so choose, and many have been. A small majority of the state laws originally covered the same size of firms as was covered by the Federal Unemployment Tax— employers with eight or more employees at some time in each of twenty or more weeks in a year. The District of Columbia law went the whole way in covering employers with one or more at any time, while nine other states covered employers of one or more in twenty weeks. Coverage in the other states scattered between these extremes, with a small concentration of states covering employers of four or more, the level recommended originally by the Committee on Economic Security. As experience was gained in administering the collection of contributions, additional states covered smaller employers, many covering employers of one or more workers.

By and large, the original state laws matched the other coverage provisions of the federal law. These mostly concerned certain specified exclusions, such as agricultural labor, domestic service, maritime employment, service for relatives, government employment, and service for nonprofit organizations. Apart from the intent to widen coverage, as with the coverage of small firms in many states, several state laws deviated somewhat from federal exclusion specifications or in their definitions of employment. In time, these deviations tended to increase and proliferate, leading occasionally to problems of disputed interpretation. Many were addressed by amendments of the federal law to alter or clarify the coverage provisions.

Benefit Entitlement Provisions

Most of the original state unemployment insurance laws specified qualifying requirements and methods for determining the weekly amounts and duration of benefits payable in ways which were soon recognized as administratively unfeasible. The aim of qualifying requirements, which all states have, is to confine eligibility to only those individuals claiming benefits who have had substantial attachment to the labor market and to exclude those who have worked only casually or intermittently. Many of the earliest laws generally required a minimum number of weeks of employment in a base period—one or two years preceding the first claim—to qualify. The weekly benefit amount was usually set at half the claimant's full-time weekly wage up to a $15 maximum,[13] and the number of weeks payable was most commonly figured on the basis of one week of benefit for four weeks of work during the base period up to a maximum of sixteen weeks of benefits.

Obtaining and maintaining information from employers about weeks of work and weekly earnings of their employees, in addition to handling data from the quarterly earnings reports employers had to file with their contributions, proved too cumbersome for most state agencies in those days long before the general use of automatic data processing equipment, let alone electronic computers. It was also burdensome for employers.[14] "Full-time weekly wage" was often a vague measure difficult to develop for workers with variable work and pay patterns. As a result, efforts turned toward simplification of these first provisions. Within a short period, most states adopted formulas for these three key elements—the qualifying requirement, the weekly benefit amount, and duration—which were closely interrelated. The formulas were based on quarterly and annual earnings rather than on direct measures of employment or the weekly wage. The objective of the new formulas was to produce results that were reasonably equivalent to those based on direct measures of employment and the weekly wage. The first change many states made before they began paying benefits was to set the weekly benefit amount as a fraction of high-quarter earnings, that quarter of the base period in which the claimant earned the most, instead of trying to measure the full-time weekly wage more directly. The high-quarter formula usually specified half of one-thirteenth of the earnings of that quarter, assuming that those earn-

---

13. The District of Columbia provided only 40 percent of the weekly wage, but added dependents' allowances; until 1945, it was the only law to provide dependents' allowances.

14. Wisconsin eased this problem by requesting employers to supply the additional required information for only those employees who had filed a claim for benefits.

ings reflected thirteen weeks of employment, or one-twenty-sixth of the quarterly earnings total. Some states used a fraction somewhat larger than one-twenty-sixth so as to allow for workers with a little less than thirteen weeks of employment in the high quarter.

Given this change for calculating the weekly benefit, the qualifying requirement was generally converted from a direct measure of weeks of employment to a measure of total base-period earnings by specifying the requirement in terms of the latter as a minimum multiple of the weekly benefit amount. Thus, for example, a requirement that total earnings equal at least thirty times the weekly benefit would be equivalent to fifteen weeks of work if the high-quarter weekly benefit formula produced an amount equal to half the claimant's weekly wage.

The method of calculating the duration of benefits allowed was also changed by many states to a formula using base-period earnings instead of weeks of work. The formula usually provided a fraction of total earnings as the dollar limit for the total amount of benefits payable during the period of eligibility (benefit year), with the fraction specified as a third or less in the first applications of this approach. By dividing the weekly benefit amount into the resulting total allowed, the number of weeks payable could be determined, but always subject to an overall maximum number of weeks. Some states substituted a uniform number of weeks allowed for all eligible claimants in place of one that varied by prior employment or earnings. The uniform duration concept, however, was more than a matter of simplifying administration; for many, it became a desired feature of unemployment insurance as a means of assuring adequate protection. Ohio had adopted a uniform duration provision at the outset; by October 1940, another ten states had joined this category.

Some states went much further in their drive to simplify administration of these aspects of the law. A number of them adopted a minimum flat base-period earnings qualifying requirement, making no attempt to approximate length of employment. Several states calculated the weekly benefit amount as a fraction of total base-period wages, abandoning entirely the concept of relating the benefit to the weekly wage. By March 1940, fifteen states required simply a flat amount of earnings in a year to qualify, and four of these states also used a schedule based on a fraction of annual wages to set the weekly benefit amount.[15] State provisions specify limits on the weekly amount as well as for the duration of benefits payable. At the end of 1937, all but two states set $15 as the maximum weekly benefit amount.[16] Maximum duration at that time ranged from twelve to twenty weeks among the states, with most at sixteen weeks.[17] All states also imposed waiting periods—certified weeks of unemployment which were not compensated—before benefits became payable. The original laws generally provided three- or four-week waiting periods; by 1940, most states specified two weeks. The waiting period allowed time to process the claim, assemble the necessary information, and determine the entitlement. It also conserved benefit funds. The cost estimates provided to the states by the Social Security Board along with the draft bill benefit provisions used the number of waiting weeks as well as duration allowed as key variables for alternative combinations of provisions likely to be supportable at given contribution rates.

At the beginning, all but six states provided benefits for partial unemployment during a period of less than full-time work. In such cases, the benefit normally paid for a week of total unemployment is reduced by earnings in partial employment. Partial benefits are paid to motivate a claimant to accept minor or temporary low-paid or part-time jobs by disregarding some of the wages earned when they are used to reduce the full weekly benefit amount.

---

15. At this date, a dozen states also specified a uniform base period for all claimants as the calendar year preceding the first claim regardless of when filed, as opposed to individual base periods which varied by when the first claim was filed and which reflected more recent experience. All but one of these states also applied a uniform, rather than individual, benefit year during which the benefits allowed could be drawn, in many cases severely curtailing the time available for drawing these benefits.

16. The draft bills recommended this level for the maximum weekly benefit, which was about 60 percent of the average weekly covered wage in the United States in 1938. The weekly maximum was $16 in Michigan and $18 in Wyoming.

17. Five states also provided additional weeks of benefits based on a past record of long-term employment which had not been used previously to establish entitlement to benefits. Such a provision was suggested by the Social Security Board to allow one added week of benefit for every two weeks of work in the prior five years. These provisions were repealed, however, before they could be used.

Eligibility Rules and Disqualifications

To be eligible for benefits, claimants are required to be unemployed involuntarily and to be able and available for work. These conditions have been imposed by all states from the beginning; failure to satisfy them results in benefit denial or disqualification. Several reasons for disqualification relate to separation from the previous employer. These include voluntary leaving of work without good cause, discharge from a job for work-connected misconduct, and involvement in a labor dispute. Other reasons unrelated to the job separation include refusal to apply for or accept a suitable job, and fraudulent misrepresentation to obtain benefits. Claimants who initially qualify for benefits may later be denied benefits because of failure to meet the continuing eligibility requirements. If they are unable to work or are not available for work, they are denied benefits as long as the restricting circumstances continue. States require claimants, with certain exceptions, to register for work at the local employment office as evidence of their availability, and to expose them to job openings which employers may list—this process is part of the so-called "work test".

The majority of the original laws generally followed the provisions recommended on these matters in the draft bills, but there was a fair amount of variation in some of the details. For example, "good cause" in the case of leaving work originally appeared in the laws as a general term and was interpreted to include good personal causes for leaving which therefore were not disqualifying. A few states, however, specifically restricted good cause to circumstances attributable to the employer or connected with the work. Leaving a job for any other cause, however reasonable or understandable, was disqualifying in these states. By 1940, this group had grown to seven states. Over half the states, in keeping with the Social Security Board's draft bills, began with disqualification for voluntary leaving that postponed the payment of benefits for the week during which the claimant left work and from one to five weeks (plus the waiting period) thereafter; other states postponed benefits for longer periods.[18] Only Wisconsin, in addition, cancelled benefit rights. In 1940, a larger number of states postponed benefits for less than six weeks, usually not including the waiting

---

18. New York had no disqualification for voluntary leaving.

period, but five states denied benefits to disqualified claimants for the duration of their unemployment and 12 states also reduced or cancelled benefit rights.

Discharge for misconduct was usually interpreted as meaning misconduct "connected with the work," although this wording was not originally included in the draft bills. The disqualification period of benefit postponement suggested for a misconduct discharge was longer—nine weeks—than was recommended for voluntary leaving. Most states, however, considered nine weeks too severe; only seventeen states adopted this period. Some states (eleven) used the same one-to-five-week period as for voluntary quits, while most of the others ranged between five and nine weeks of postponement. Washington applied a duration-of-unemployment disqualification, and Wisconsin cancelled benefit rights. By 1940, a dozen states reduced or cancelled benefit rights of claimants disqualified for misconduct discharges.

Issues regarding disqualifications for refusal of suitable work without good cause often turn on what is meant by "suitable work." The Social Security Act specified certain conditions (the so-called labor standards) under which a state, in order for its law to be approved, cannot disqualify a claimant for refusal of new work.[19] These conditions are designed to enable a worker to refuse a job where a labor dispute exists; where wages, hours, or working conditions are substandard; or where the right to join a *bona fide* labor union would be restricted. All state laws contain such conditions. In addition, state laws may also list certain criteria for testing the suitability of the work. These usually include the degree of risk to the claimant's health, safety, or morals; the claimant's physical fitness for the work; and prior training, experience, and earnings. Some states take into consideration the length of the claimant's unemployment and, after a certain period, may require acceptance of a less suitable job than previously held. Some states specify that the claimant's prospects of obtaining local work in a customary occupation and the distance of available work from home must be taken into consideration in determining suitability. These factors entered into many of the early state laws.

---

19. Title IX of the Social Security Act. For the wording of this provision, see the appendix to chapter 6, Condition (five) among conditions state laws must meet to enable employers to receive federal tax credit.

The draft bills suggested the same period of benefit postponement when disqualification was for refusal of suitable work as for voluntary quitting without good cause—from one to five weeks plus the waiting period. Thirty-one states followed this recommendation while most of the other states postponed benefits for shorter periods. Four states disqualified claimants who refused suitable work for the duration of their unemployment, and two states cancelled all benefit rights. By 1940, there were eight states with duration disqualifications for refusals and 11 states that reduced or cancelled benefit rights.

It is generally agreed that a worker idled by and a party to a labor dispute should not receive benefits during that dispute. All but three states originally disqualified workers for any week of unemployment due to a labor dispute in which they were involved. The three states that were exceptions disqualified for a stated period: New York for ten weeks, Rhode Island for eight weeks, and Pennsylvania for three weeks. By 1940, three more states had adopted a limited period disqualification: Tennessee for four weeks, Alaska for six weeks, and Louisiana for ten weeks.[20] Most states did not disqualify workers unable to work because of a labor dispute if they were not involved in the dispute in any way, such as through participation, financing, or direct interest. How these details were specified in the law grew increasingly complex and varied over time.

Originally, all but four of the states relied upon criminal prosecution in cases of fraudulent misrepresentation to obtain benefits. The range of fines and maximum periods of imprisonment were specified in the laws. Convictions and penalties were so difficult or took so long to obtain that states added statutory benefit disqualifications. By 1940, such provisions existed in fourteen states. These disqualifications did not free the claimant from repayment of the benefits unlawfully obtained or absolve the claimant from possible fine and imprisonment if convicted.

Forty-five of the states originally followed the draft bills' recommendations, with minor variations, for reducing benefits by the amount of income a claimant received in the form of wages in lieu of advance

---

20. In time, all of these states repealed their limited period disqualification provisions except New York which, as of 1990, remained the only state that paid benefits, after a disqualification period of seven weeks.

notice of separation, workers' compensation for temporary partial disability, or old-age insurance benefits paid under the Social Security Act. By 1940, the number of states that counted one or more of such types of income as disqualifying had declined to thirty. Most reduced the unemployment benefit payable by the amount of income received; several applied total benefit disqualification regardless of the income amount.

None of the original state laws contained specific disqualifications aimed at individuals who left work because of family obligations, the need to accompany a spouse to another location, or because of pregnancy. However, if the separation occurred for one of these reasons, the claimant could be denied benefits on the ground of being unable to work or unavailable for work, and often were. By 1940, one state had adopted a pregnancy disqualification provision and four had specified marital or family circumstances as the basis for benefit denial. In time, such discriminatory provisions were to spread, although some were eventually struck down by the courts.

Determinations of eligibility in cases involving issues raised under any of the rules or disqualification provisions discussed above depend on adequate development of the facts and appropriate decisions based on the facts. Not all cases are clear-cut, and some result in contested decisions. This area of administration was and remains a major function of the administrative agency. It requires considerable care, skill, and fairness on the part of the assigned personnel. From the outset, all states provided for appeals from initial determinations with procedures that assure fair hearings, as required by federal law. Questions relating to eligibility rules and disqualifications have been, since the beginning, among the most complicated and controversial that the unemployment insurance program has had to encounter.

Early Experience

After enacting its unemployment insurance law, each state had to establish administrative machinery to carry it out. Staff had to be recruited, supervision assigned, premises obtained and equipped, procedures developed, forms prepared, and personnel trained for specific functions. With no experience in hand, and little or no time to plan or prepare, beginning operations were bound to be rough, even chaotic in some locations. In time, the state agencies took increasing hold of their functions, learned from their experience, by adjusting quickly and continually improving their procedures. Regular day-to-day operations became reasonably smooth and efficient for the most part.

Contributions and Benefit Operations

Certain aspects of the program came into play right away, others not until later. The first program function to be undertaken was the collection of contributions from employers, and employee contributions where applicable. Wisconsin began collecting contributions in July 1934, most states in 1936, and the rest in 1937. The Federal Unemployment Tax first applied to 1936 covered payrolls and was payable by January 31, 1937. Employers in states with federally-approved unemployment insurance laws in 1936 could offset the state contributions they paid that year against the federal tax up to the allowed 90 percent limit of that tax.[21]

Total covered wages were subject to the federal tax until 1940, as was the case for state tax contributions in almost all states. The states usually adopted as their standard employer contribution rate 90 percent of the federal rate, the level of the full tax credit[22]. Benefits were not payable until at least two years after contributions began, as required by federal law, allowing state funds to accumulate some reserves beforehand. The first benefit payment was made in Wisconsin in July 1936. Other states did not begin paying benefits until 1938 or 1939; over twenty states did so in January 1938.

The prolonged depression continued throughout the 1930s with some variation in its severity, but the nation never satisfactorily overcame its serious unemployment problem in this period. Some economic recovery occurred about the middle of the decade, enabling many workers to gain employment in jobs covered by the new unem-

---

21. The total Federal Unemployment Tax rate for 1936 was 1.0 percent (2.0 percent for 1937); after the maximum offset, the net federal tax payable came to 0.1 percent of payrolls for 1936 (0.2 percent for 1937). Beginning in 1938, the federal tax rate was 3.0 percent and the net rate payable was 0.3 percent after the full 90 percent offset was taken.

22. The District of Columbia, Michigan, and New York set their rates equal to the full federal tax rate of 3.0 percent. Wisconsin's standard rate was 2 percent in 1936 and 1937 and 2.7 in 1938.

ployment insurance program. Recovery faltered, however, during the last half of 1937 as the first large group of states was preparing to start their benefit operations. When many states opened claim offices for business in January 1938, a full flood of recently laid-off workers immediately overwhelmed the staff and facilities in many locations. With difficulty and some temporary disarray, the program's machinery managed to function through these first hectic months. As the year progressed, business conditions improved and unemployment subsided. States that began paying benefits later in 1938 and in 1939 generally faced an easier task of establishing their claims and benefit payment operations.

This early experience led quickly to two major conclusions. One was to confirm doubts about the feasibility of administering the original benefit entitlement provisions enacted by the states. Many had already begun to simplify their formulas, as described above, even before benefits became payable. The move to simplification quickened as the result of actual experience, with many more states acting in 1939.

The other conclusion was that revenues produced by the standard contribution rates substantially exceeded benefit costs in most states even after taking account of the heavy unemployment experience of 1938. Unemployment benefits were paid throughout that year in twenty-three states; in only five of them did benefit costs amount to 3 percent or more of covered payrolls. With unemployment and benefit outlays down in 1939, the reserve funds grew rapidly. By the end of that year, they totaled more than $1.5 billion, about 5.3 percent of covered payrolls or nearly twice the level of contributions for the year. Pressures were building to reduce contributions or to improve benefits, or both. A major focus at the state level was on experience rating which required at least three years of benefit experience for pooled funds before it could take effect.

Interstate Cooperation

Beginning late in 1935, representatives of some of the states that had already enacted unemployment insurance laws held occasional informal meetings with each other and Social Security Board staff to discuss common problems. Representation at these meetings expanded as more states adopted legislation. Most of the discussion naturally centered on technical and administrative problems at the time. With the system becoming increasingly universal, a permanent organization of state agency directors formed under the title of Interstate Conference of Employment Security Agencies. Its first official annual meeting was held in October 1937. Federal staff cooperated with the Interstate Conference, and the Board officially participated in its activities by supplying an executive secretary. The Conference became an important factor in the future development of unemployment insurance as well as the employment service.

A major early contribution of the Interstate Conference was its development of a plan under which an unemployed worker who moves away from the state where previously employed can still file for unemployment benefits after the move based on the wages earned before the move. Under the plan, the state to which the worker moves, acting as an agent for the state liable for the benefits, takes the claim and forwards it to the liable state. Eventually, all states agreed to this plan. The Interstate Conference also developed other interstate plans to coordinate or combine qualifying wages and employment so as to produce the appropriate benefit entitlement for a claimant who has worked on jobs in more than one state. Many years later, the federal law was amended to require all states to participate in these plans.

Early Federal Legislative Changes

Besides being subject to change through state legislation, the federal-state unemployment insurance system has also been modified by amendments to the federal law. Several important federal changes occurred in 1938 and 1939.

Railroad Unemployment Insurance

Although the Committee on Economic Security had recommended that railroad workers be covered by a separate federal program, they were originally covered under the federal-state system. In 1938, however, a federal railroad unemployment insurance program was created under a bill worked out jointly between the railroads and the railroad unions, with the assistance of Murray W. Latimer, chairman of the Railroad Retirement Board. The new program became effective in 1939 (P.L. 75-722). It is administered in conjunction with a pension program by the Railroad Retirement Board. Since all the states had covered railroad workers, the 1938 Act provided for the transfer to a new unemployment insurance account in the Unemployment Trust Fund of the excess of contributions by the railroads over benefits paid to railroad workers from the state funds. All the states passed the necessary legislation to implement the Act.

The 1938 Railroad Unemployment Insurance Act was less liberal than most state laws, but by subsequent amendments became much more liberal in time, at least until the 1970s. The basic principles of the 1938 Act, however, have been retained. Because railroad employment operates on a full seven-day-a-week basis, the benefit provisions of the Railroad Unemployment Insurance Act are considerably different from those of state unemployment insurance laws. Railroad unemployment benefits are figured on a daily basis and paid biweekly. The daily benefit rate is based on annual earnings in railroad employment in the base year. Benefit duration allowed is uniform for 130 days (twenty-six weeks) in a year.[23] Employer contributions finance railroad unemployment insurance. Unlike the state programs, however, there was no experience rating until some financing reforms were made in the 1980s. The original contribution rate was 3 percent of the first $300 of monthly earnings, which paid for both benefits and administration. Sickness benefits were added later, along with extended long-term unemployment benefits; these additions required raising the contribution rate. The taxable wage base also increased.

Social Security Amendments of 1939

Many significant changes were made in 1939 in the old age insurance provisions of the Social Security Act, but only a few changes were made affecting unemployment insurance. One proposed unemployment insurance amendment passed one house but not the other; it evoked some stormy controversy concerning federal minimum benefit standards, an issue that continued to beset the program over the years.

---

23. Additional benefits were provided later for workers in railroad employment for ten or more years.

The two most important changes regarding unemployment insurance were setting a $3,000 limit on the covered wages paid in a year to an employee that were subject to the Federal Unemployment Tax, and adding the requirement that states use the merit system for staffing their agencies. Other amendments clarified coverage exclusions relating to agricultural labor, nonprofit organizations, and certain salesmen and other agents who worked on a commission basis. The federal tax provisions in Title IX of the Social Security Act were replaced by the Federal Unemployment Tax Act which incorporated those provisions in the Internal Revenue Code.

The Federal Unemployment Tax base was changed from total payrolls to the first $3,000 paid each employee in order to match the tax base used for the old age insurance contributions, thereby simplifying federal employer tax collections for both programs. It also simplified tax payment procedures for employers covered by both programs. At the time, the change was not considered to be important, aside from the increased convenience, since it reduced the total of covered wages subject to the unemployment tax by only about 8 percent. No one, of course, could foresee the dramatic increase in wages which would develop in later years, reducing significantly the proportion of payrolls taxable under the $3,000 limit. Employers strongly supported the change; no opposition was in evidence. The $3,000 limit had been applied for old age insurance from the beginning because that program's benefits were based on earnings up to that level, and with employees also contributing, it was thought that the tax and benefit base should be the same.

The added merit system requirement for staff selection applied for state personnel administering unemployment insurance and public assistance. Recommended originally by the Committee on Economic Security and urged strongly by the Social Security Board, this standard was not popular with those who favored the political patronage system for the appointment of public office holders. Support by state program administrators, who emphasized the need for the most highly qualified staff possible to handle the difficult, technical work involved, was an important factor in gaining approval for this amendment.

The House of Representatives adopted an amendment proposed by Congressman John McCormack of Massachusetts to permit states to reduce their contribution rates below the 2.7 percent level, without loss of federal tax credit, sooner than allowed by the minimum of three years delay required by the existing experience rating provisions in the federal law. His proposal was a response to the current rapid accumulation of reserves in many states. To lower rates sooner, however, or to allow its average rate to fall below 2.7 percent, a state would have to adhere to certain benefit standards and a reserve solvency standard. The latter would require a state fund equal to at least 1.5 times the highest annual benefit outlay of the last ten years. The benefit standards specified floors for weekly benefit maximum ($15) and minimum ($5) amounts, and for maximum duration (sixteen weeks), and a ceiling for a waiting period (two weeks).[24] Considerable opposition to the McCormack amendment surfaced at the Senate Finance Committee hearings, chiefly from employer representatives and state agency administrators. The former mainly opposed any weakening or qualifying of the experience rating concept. The latter opposed the addition of standards that would further circumscribe state discretion in the program. The Senate Committee eliminated the amendment and the House accepted this deletion. Thus ended the first attempt to establish federal benefit and fund solvency standards.[25]

Employment Service-Unemployment Insurance Merger

Despite efforts to coordinate actions and policies at the federal level, the states continued to experience difficulties in dealing with two separate federal agencies on unemployment insurance and employment service matters. Recommendations by the states and by others to merge the two were finally realized in 1939. The President's Reorganization Plan No. 1 of 1939 established the Federal Security Agency, a new broad grouping of a number of independent federal units that had emerged in preceding years, including the Social Security Board.[26] As

---

24. Social Security Board Chairman Altmeyer had objected to McCormack's original proposal simply to allow states to lower rates in 1940 rather than wait another year or two. He objected because of the lack of state experience and suggested at least adding such standards as a condition, although the benefit standards adopted by the House were more modest than he had in mind. See Altmeyer (1966, p. 104).

25. Altmeyer (1966, p. 104) reluctantly agreed to the elimination of the McCormack amendment because of the possibility that the minimum benefit standards might become the maximum provisions in state laws.

26. Other components included were the U.S. Public Health Service, Office of Education, National Youth Administration, and Civilian Conservation Corps.

part of this reorganization, the United States Employment Service was transferred to the Board from the Department of Labor. There it was joined with the Bureau of Unemployment Compensation to form a new Bureau of Employment Security.[27]

War and Reconversion

The year 1940 was the first in which the unemployment insurance system was fully operational throughout the year in all states. Most states had amended their original laws to make their provisions easier to administer. The $3,000 taxable wage base took effect in 1940 for the federal tax rate, and for state rates in all but eight states.[28] Experience rating was applied in five states that year, all of them individual employer reserve systems; thirty-four other states had experience rating provisions scheduled to take effect during the next few years. Revenues exceeded benefit outlays in 1940 by wide margins in most states, despite high levels of unemployment. Benefits in 1940 totaled 1.6 percent of total covered payrolls, a benefit cost rate equaled or exceeded by the system as a whole in only five of the next fifty years.[29] By the end of 1940, reserves aggregated $1.8 billion, about 5.6 percent of total covered payrolls that year.

The War Years (1940-1945)

During 1940, the economy began its increasing conversion to military production. As time went on, especially after the U.S. entry into World War II in December 1941, unemployment almost disappeared and was replaced by labor shortages. Conversion to a war economy produced some temporary dislocations and short-term unemployment.

---

27. Altmeyer coined the name "employment security" to embrace the two programs; many states adopted it for their agencies in ensuing years.

28. By 1941, only Idaho and Nevada continued to tax total payrolls; Idaho adopted the $3,000 limit in 1943 and Nevada in 1945.

29. Includes benefits paid under the regular state unemployment insurance program only; if the extended benefits that were provided later are included, the combined benefit cost rate may have reached 1.6 percent or more in one or two additional years. See *Unemployment Insurance Financial Data, 1938-1982,* and annual supplements.

To help replace the millions of young men drawn into the armed forces, large numbers of women and older persons entered the civilian labor force. In January 1942, the state employment services were federalized for the duration of the war to concentrate on the task of nationwide manpower mobilization and allocation.

During the war years, the unemployment insurance program shrank sharply in terms of its benefit operations. From a peak of $519 million in 1940, aggregate annual benefit outlays declined to $62 million by 1944 (table 7.1). In no state did benefits paid exceed 0.2 percent of payrolls in 1944. With expanding employment and payrolls, contribution revenues rose until 1943 and continued high despite the spreading application of lower rates through experience rating and the limitation of the taxable wage base. The total of all state reserves grew to $6.1 billion by the end of 1944 and to $6.9 billion by the end of 1945, equal to more than 10 percent of total covered payrolls in the latter year. At no other time has the year-end reserve ratio been even close to this high level.

Several factors influenced the course of state and federal unemployment insurance legislation during the war period. The sizable accumulation of reserves accelerated the spread of experience rating to forty-five states by the end of 1945. For an approach as controversial as experience rating to become almost universal within a few years was surely due, in large measure, to the huge reserve buildup and to the fact that it was the only way permitted to reduce unemployment insurance taxes.[30] The drive to lower taxes through experience rating overcame arguments for keeping taxes up as a counterinflationary measure and as a means of strengthening reserves to meet heavy benefit liabilities which many anticipated would become payable after the war ended.

High reserves also supported demands to improve benefits, and several states did move in this direction. The most important gains came in reductions of waiting periods, rising weekly benefit ceilings, and increased duration of benefits (table 7.2). More states also extended coverage to smaller firms. On the other hand, disqualification provisions became more restrictive and severe in many states, reflecting

---

30. Except for Wisconsin, no state could begin experience rating before 1941. During the years after the war when wage levels rose rapidly, the maintenance of the taxable wage limit at $3,000 also served to keep taxes lower.

Table 7.1   Selected Unemployment Insurance Statistics, United States, Selected Years 1940-1947

Item	1940	1944	1945	1946	1947
Average monthly covered employment (millions)	23.1	30.0	28.4	30.2	32.3
Total covered payrolls (billions)	$32.4	$69.1	$66.6	$73.4	$86.6
Total taxable payrolls (billions)	$30.1	$60.6	$58.5	$63.7	$73.0
Ratio of taxable to total payrolls	.93	.88	.88	.87	.84
Average state UI tax rate (percent)[a]	2.7	1.9	1.7	1.4	1.4
Total state UI taxes collected (millions)	$854	$1,317	$1,162	$912	$1,096
Total benefit outlays (millions)	$519	$62	$446	$1,095	$775
Benefit outlays as percent of total payrolls	1.6	0.1	0.7	1.5	0.9
Total state reserves at year end (billions)	$1.8	$6.1	$6.9	$6.9	$7.3
Reserves as percent of total payrolls[b]	5.6	8.8	10.4	9.4	8.4
Average weekly covered wage	$27.02	$44.25	$45.11	$46.69	$51.59
Average weekly benefit paid[c]	$10.56	$15.90	$18.77	$18.50	$17.83
Number of first payments (millions)	5.2	0.5	2.8	4.5	4.0
Average actual duration of benefits (weeks)	9.8	7.7	8.5	13.4	11.1
Estimated exhaustion ratio[d]	50.6	20.2	18.1	38.7	30.7

SOURCES: *Unemployment Insurance Financial Data, 1938-1982* and annual supplements.
a. Applicable to taxable wages.
b. Also known as reserve ratio.
c. For week of total unemployment.
d. Total number exhausting benefits during the year as a percent of total first payments during the twelve months ending September 30 of that year.

stiffening attitudes toward claimant behavior that raised doubts about ready availability for work when the need for full productive effort was so great. The increased employment of women also led to more specific benefit eligibility restrictions in many state laws applicable to periods of pregnancy, to wives who quit jobs to follow their husbands transferred elsewhere, and to working mothers who limited their availability for work to certain shifts or locations because of child-care problems. Becoming increasingly sensitive to benefit charges as experience rating took greater hold, employers mounted more pressure for wider adoption of provisions to suspend benefits of disqualified claimants for the duration of their unemployment and to reduce or cancel their benefit rights. By the end of 1945, there were fourteen states that imposed a duration disqualification and twenty-six states that reduced or cancelled benefit rights for one or more of the three major reasons for disqualifications—voluntary leaving, misconduct discharge, and refusal of suitable work (Federal Security Agency 1947).

During the war, national considerations overrode state concerns. The momentum created by New Deal era programs and by the vast machinery of the federal government assembled during the early 1940s to direct the nation's war efforts seemed to encourage tendencies to seek comprehensive national solutions for most problems. The federalization of the state employment services was the most prominent effect of this orientation on employment security.[31] The Social Security Board moved far in the direction of supporting a national unemployment insurance system. In a report issued in 1942, the Board stated that it "is convinced that nothing less than a national uniformly operated employment service, sustained by an adequate and soundly financed Federal unemployment insurance system will meet the needs of the period immediately following the war and the longer-range objectives of Social Security."[32]

In January 1942, the administration proposed a national war displacement benefits program to supplement state unemployment insurance benefits. Opponents suspected that the proposal was aimed at federalization of the state programs. Hearings were held on a bill covering a version of this proposal, but the bill died in the House Ways and

---

31. The employment services were restored to state control in 1946.
32. Social Security Board (1942, p. 17). The Board reiterated this position in succeeding years.

Means Committee. State employment security administrators effectively organized opposition to such proposals. In the process, considerable friction developed between state and federal officials which had long-lasting effects on federal-state relationships in the system.

Table 7.2   Distribution of States by Selected Unemployment Insurance Coverage and Benefit Provisions October 1940 and December 1945

	Number of states	
Provision	October 1940	December 1945
Total	51	51
Size of firm covered (no. of workers)		
8 or more	25	22
4-7 or more	12	10
2-3 or more	3	3
1 or more	11	16
Waiting period (no. of weeks)		
3	3	0
2	27	13
1	21	37
0	0	1
Maximum weekly benefit amount		
$15	41	10
$16-$19	10	14
$20-$24	0	22
$25 or more	0	5
Maximum duration[a] (no. of weeks)		
12-15	13 (4)	2 (1)
16	29 (7)	12 (5)
17-19	3	5
20	5	21 (6)
21-25	0	6 (1)
26	1	5 (1)

SOURCE: Federal Security Agency (1947, pp. 18, 20, 29, and 40).

a. Counts of states include the number (shown parenthetically) of states with uniform duration— a total of eleven in October 1940 and fourteen in December 1945.

Other recommendations emerged for a comprehensive federal Social Security system which incorporated unemployment insurance.[33] Legislation introduced in the Congress from 1942 to 1945 was designed to establish such a system.[34] Though supported by the Social Security Board and by organized labor, these bills never received any serious consideration by the Congress.

Postwar Planning

As the war's outlook turned favorable for the Allies in 1943 and 1944, more attention focused on planning for the postwar period. The principal expectation, and fear, was that the economy would slide back into its prewar depressed state once the stimulus of military production was gone. Simultaneous demobilization of the armed forces and reconversion of industry to civilian production would presumably raise unemployment to massive proportions. Various states appointed study commissions to consider the potential impact of such postwar dislocations and the possible remedies. It was widely held that these problems were likely to be so severe and widespread that the individual states would be unable to cope with them entirely on their own. A dozen states did enact provisions for special "war-risk" contributions to supplement the regular unemployment insurance contributions. They were applicable, in most cases, to large employers who had experienced substantial increases in payrolls during the war. These provisions resulted in rates higher than those yielded by the regular experience rating schedules or in an added flat rate on "excess" payrolls. Overall, taxable payrolls rose from about $30 billion in 1940 to over $60 billion in 1944 (table 7.1).

In 1944, Congress moved to deal with some of the anticipated postwar problems. The Servicemen's Readjustment Act of 1944 (the GI Bill) was enacted in June. Title V provided federal servicemen's readjustment allowances (SRA) for World War II veterans unemployed after discharge. SRA was paid at a uniform weekly rate of $20 for up to

---

33. These included recommendations contained in "Security, Work, and Relief Policies," a report issued in 1942 by the Committee on Long-Range Work and Relief Policies of the National Resources Planning Board. William Haber was Chairman of the Committee.

34. Most prominent among these were the Wagner-Murray-Dingell bills of 1943 and 1945; in the latter year, S. 1161 and H.R. 2861, 78th Cong., 1st sess.

fifty-two weeks. State weekly unemployment insurance payments in 1944 averaged only $16, and over half the states that year still limited duration to less than twenty weeks. Although the SRA program was administered nationally by the Veterans Administration, the state employment security agencies paid the benefits as agents of the federal government. The program lasted from 1944 to 1950. It was criticized in some quarters as the "52-20 club," because many veterans returning to their small home towns received the benefits for fifty-two weeks without a strict enforcement of the work test to assure current availability for work.

Later, as part of the Social Security Amendments of 1946, Congress also provided a temporary program of readjustment benefits for seamen on ships controlled by the War Shipping Administration. After the war, unemployment was heavy among seamen formerly employed on such vessels. The federal-state unemployment insurance system had not covered maritime workers prior to the 1946 Act. The temporary program provided benefits under the terms of the law of the state where the seaman filed a claim, but the federal government paid the cost. This special program continued until 1950.

Various federal proposals emerged in 1944 to provide special unemployment benefit protection for employees engaged in war production on federal jobs, such as those in shipyards, munitions plants, and atomic energy facilities, as well as for maritime workers, or to expand the regular unemployment insurance program to cover them. Other approaches were suggested to supplement state benefit provisions to make them more adequate, or to impose federal minimum benefit standards on the state programs. Some proposals offered federal financial backing to cover the expected added costs of unemployment benefits through reinsurance or loans. Special provisions for retraining and relocation of the unemployed were also advanced. All these measures were designed to be temporary to help get the country through the reconversion period.

In the end, Congress took only limited action in these areas. By and large, it decided that the major responsibility for unemployment insurance during the reconversion period rested with the states. Moreover, the prevailing congressional view regarded the administration's gloomy predictions of the reconversion problem as overdrawn. The result was the passage of the War Mobilization and Reconversion Act of 1944.[35]

The Act's chief feature with regard to unemployment insurance was the provision for interest-free federal loans to state funds that fell below specified levels. The loans would cover benefit costs exceeding 2.7 percent of taxable payrolls in a calendar quarter. They would be financed by appropriations to a new loan fund account in the Unemployment Trust Fund from excess revenues of the Federal Unemployment Tax that were not used for administrative grants. Loans were to be available through 1947. The provision was extended twice, but allowed to expire March 1952. During its life, no appropriation was ever made to the loan fund, nor was any application ever made for a loan. Other provisions in the Act included those for retraining and reemployment of workers laid off because of war production cutbacks, but no others that significantly affected unemployment insurance.

One other action taken by Congress in this period should be noted, although it did not relate directly to the unemployment insurance system. In 1945 and 1946, Congress debated and finally passed legislation designed to commit the government to an annual review of the nation's economy (P.L. 304) The bill originally introduced in 1945 was more specific in its aim—a guarantee of full employment, mainly through federal fiscal policies if the rest of the economy failed to achieve it. Congress backed away from that firm a commitment because of concerns raised over difficulties in defining the full employment goal in measurable terms, controversy about the efficacy of fiscal policy manipulations, worry about potential inflation, and general resistance by many to deliberate government interference in the economy. The Employment Act of 1946, however, did retain emphasis on unemployment as a major problem to be avoided or minimized as much as possible. It called for the President to report annually on the state of the economy and to recommend actions to keep it in good health or restore it if faltering. The Act established a Council of Economic Advisers to assist the President in this task. To the extent that the exercise of this function has contributed to the prevention of serious mass unemploy-

---

35. Known as the George bill, after Senator Walter George, chairman of the Senate Finance Committee; the bill became law in October 1944. The unemployment insurance loan fund provided by this law became known as the "George Fund."

ment of the dimensions of the depression years, it has helped the unemployment insurance system operate within a feasible range.

Reconversion (1945-1947)

Demobilization and the termination of war production following the end of hostilities in 1945 did lead to high levels of unemployment soon afterwards and during 1946. Unemployment benefit outlays rose sharply, reaching to over $400 million in 1945 and over $1 billion in 1946 (table 7.1).[36] The latter year was the first in which the federal-state system overall operated at a current deficit, although the interest earned by the reserves closed most of the gap. Compared with the previous high unemployment year of 1940 when the number of new beneficiaries (first payments on table 7.1) was even higher, the average weekly benefit paid in 1946 was almost 80 percent larger and payments lasted three-and-six-tenths weeks longer, on average. Improved benefit provisions in state laws, as well as higher wages and steady base-period employment contributed to the higher amounts and longer protection in 1946.

The unemployment insurance system had weathered a fairly severe test. In 1947, unemployment headed downward and employment reached new peaks even exceeding wartime levels. No state had experienced any financial difficulty. None had need to resort to federal loans. By mid-1947, the economy was well through its reconversion to a civilian peacetime economy.

Yet, despite statutory gains made since 1940, program inadequacies were evident with regard to coverage and benefits. As of September 1947, about half the states still only covered firms with eight or more workers. Few states covered other major excluded employment categories. All but four states had higher maximum weekly benefit levels than in 1940, but wage levels generally were rising rapidly, so that claimants were less likely to be compensated for half their wage loss. About 70 percent of all benefit payments in 1946 were made at the statutory ceilings. Gains in duration provisions had been notable. Forty states paid up to twenty or more weeks of benefits as of September 1947,

---

36. In addition, readjustment allowances totaling about $1.5 billion were paid out of federal general revenues in 1946 to more than 5 million veterans under the Servicemen's Readjustment Act of 1944 (the GI Bill).

compared with only six states in 1940. The number providing uniform duration had increased from eleven to fifteen. Even so, the average potential duration (the average number of weeks for which claimants qualified) in 1947, was less than twenty weeks in about thirty-five states and below sixteen weeks in almost half of them.[37]

Criticisms leveled at the unemployment insurance program and at the broader Social Security system, along with a need for a general evaluation, led the House of Representatives, in 1945, to authorize a technical staff to investigate and review problems and issues in Social Security programs. Staff findings were expected to guide the House Ways and Means Committee considerations of proposed Social Security amendments. With respect to unemployment insurance, the 1946 staff report covered much of the historical background, objectives, experience, and program issues, but avoided making any evaluations or recommendations.[38] The Ways and Means Committee held extensive hearings on the subject during the first half of 1946 which again revealed the conflicting positions on unemployment insurance of employers, labor, the Social Security Board, and state employment security agency officials. The Social Security Amendments enacted that year made no basic changes in unemployment insurance. Under the Amendments,[39] Congress formally authorized the states to cover maritime workers employed on American vessels operating on navigable waters within or without the United States, with the proviso that they would receive equal treatment with other workers covered by state laws. Employment of maritime workers was covered by the Federal Unemployment Tax, but Congress exempted employment on fishing vessels, unless they were fishing for salmon or halibut, or were vessels weighing more than 10 net tons. Congress also exempted service by crews of foreign vessels while in ports of the United States. Except for this provision and the temporary program of readjustment benefits for seamen employed in war shipping, described above, no other provisions applied to unemployment insurance.

---

37. These data are from Federal Security Agency (1947).

38. *Issues in Social Security*, a report to the Committee by its Social Security Technical staff, established pursuant to H. Res. 204, 79th Cong., 1st sess., 1946. The study was directed by Leonard J. Calhoun, a former assistant to Senator Pat Harrison of Mississippi.

39. P. L. 79-719, *Social Security Amendments of 1946*, Public Law 79-719, Title III, approved August 10, 1946.

Concluding Observations

The federal-state unemployment insurance system came through its first decade of operations well established and in good working order. It also appeared to have gained the general acceptance of employers, workers, and the public as a whole. The fundamental objections to the very concept of unemployment insurance and its feasibility, raised primarily by employers prior to 1937, were heard no longer. No political leaders urged repeal or major changes in the philosophy or structure of the system. Unemployment insurance had become an essential part of the American economy.

Considering that the program had to weather depression conditions at the outset and the economic gyrations of war and reconversion, its solid position in 1947 spoke well of the wisdom and strength of the design adopted in 1935 and of the conservative approach pursued at the start. At no time during the first decade did the overall system, or any individual state program for that matter, experience any financial strain. Indeed, reserve funds were far more than ample, and as experience rating spread and took hold, contribution rates declined steadily. The shadows cast by the earlier financial fiascos of the British and German unemployment insurance programs on the prospects for unemployment insurance in the United States were long gone by 1947.

To be sure, it was the combination of minimal benefit outlays of the war years and the high levels of contribution income that swelled reserves so greatly, not simply the initial conservative approach. Since experience rating was the only means for reducing employer rates, the standard rate (usually 2.7 percent) tended to become the maximum rate in state tax schedules, as long as reserves continued high. Moreover, with the taxable wage base fixed at $3,000, rising wages worked year by year to reduce the proportion of total payrolls subject to the tax. Again, with reserves high, no inclination developed to increase the tax base. The benefit cost experience of 1940 and 1946, the heaviest years of unemployment and claims encountered by the program in the first decade, gave indication that the initial cost estimate for unemployment insurance of 3 percent of total payrolls was much too high.

The conservative approach recommended to the states also led them to adopt modest benefit provisions in their first laws. The early cost experience and rapid reserve accumulation supported some improvements, particularly in the duration of benefits allowed by the states, and reduced waiting periods. Weekly benefit amounts, on the other hand, began to lose ground as legislative adjustments of benefit ceilings tended to lag behind the pace of rising wage levels. The adequacy of weekly benefit protection was lacking in the eyes of some critics who urged stronger efforts to improve state provisions or federal minimum benefit standards to assure that end. While more states were gradually extending their program's coverage to employment in smaller firms, few had broadened protection to include other major categories of employment exempted from coverage under the federal tax.

With the employment services restored to the states after World War II, the state employment security agencies were in a firm and settled position by 1947 to carry on the normal operations of their programs. The agency was one of the most important elements in the state government, and the program often attracted major attention and contention in the state legislature. Within this framework, employers and, in many states, labor unions were usually organized to advance their interests regarding the program. The Social Security Board continued to offer guidance to the states in further development of program policies, extending the active role it played at the outset in helping to set up their laws. By 1947, however, the states had accumulated their own experience and expertise, and points of view as well, which did not always coincide with federal positions. Conflict was sometimes the result. States generally resented and resisted federal efforts to control or dominate the program and usually succeeded in avoiding legislation designed to foster such control, as in the case of proposed federal benefit standards. The federal-state system had become a more equal and mature partnership which would require reasonable working relations to maintain a proper balance.

8

Growth
The System Develops
(1947-1969)

The 1950s and 1960s constituted a period of unprecedented expansion of the American economy. Several temporary setbacks (recessions) occasionally slowed this long climb of the nation's output and income. Here and there, a few pockets of stagnation remained, residues of the tides of structural economic change. Overall, however, the American scene was one of strong growth, widening affluence, and rising confidence in the nation's ability to overcome such problems as poverty, discrimination, declining industries and regions, and possibly even the business cycle.

Throughout this time, the unemployment insurance program served its function of tiding workers over periods of temporary unemployment. It drew most attention and was most used during economic recessions, of which there were four between 1947 and 1969. Table 8.1 provides an idea of how the economic trends of the times affected the program, and some perspective against which to view the unemployment insurance legislation of the period. The table shows the same kind of aggregated data given for earlier years in table 7.1. Added here are insured unemployment rates, which were not available before 1947, and total unemployment rates. The data are presented for two groups of selected years: (A) three prerecession years when unemployment rates were relatively low, and two other low unemployment years in the 1960s; and (B) the four recession years of the period. It should be noted that at no time during the entire period covered, even in the worst recession years, were the overall unemployment rates close to the range of about 15 to 25 percent of the labor force estimated for rates in the depression years prior to World War II.[1]

---

1. Estimates of unemployment rates for the years 1931 through 1940 range from 14.3 to 24.9 percent of the civilian labor force, as published in Statistical Abstract of the United States, 1954.

Table 8.1 Selected Unemployment Insurance Statistics, United States, Selected Years: 1948-1969

Item	(A) Low unemployment years				
	1948	1953	1957	1965	1969
Total unemployment rate[a] (percent)	3.8	2.9	4.3	4.5	3.5
Insured unemployment rate (percent)	3.0	2.7	3.6	2.9	2.1
Average monthly covered employment (millions)	33.1	36.7	39.7	45.1	52.4
Total covered payrolls (billions)	$96.1	$139.2	$173.6	$257.9	$365.7
Total taxable payrolls (billions)	$78.5	$99.6	$112.8	$144.0	$181.8
Ratio of taxable to total payrolls	.82	.72	.65	.56	.50
Average employer UI tax rate (percent)[b]	1.2	1.3	1.3	2.1	1.4
Total state UI taxes collected (millions)	$1,000	$1,348	$1,544	$3,054	$2,545
Collections as percent of total payrolls	1.0	1.0	.9	1.2	.7
Total benefit outlays (millions)	$790	$962	$1,734	$2,166	$2,126
Benefit outlays as percent of total payrolls	.8	.7	1.0	.8	.6
Total state reserves at year end (billions)[c]	$7.6	$8.9	$8.7	$8.2	$12.6
Reserves as percent of total payrolls[d]	7.9	6.4	5.0	3.2	3.5
Average weekly covered wage	$55.85	$72.98	$84.18	$109.99	$134.31
Average weekly benefit paid[e]	$19.03	$23.58	$28.17	$37.19	$46.17
Number of first payments (millions)	4.0	4.2	5.6	4.8	4.2
Average actual duration of benefits (weeks)	10.7	10.1	11.5	12.2	11.4
Estimated exhaustion ratio[f]	27.5	20.8	22.7	21.5	19.8

Item	(B) Recession years			
	1949	1954	1958	1961
Total unemployment rate[b] (percent)	5.9	5.5	6.8	6.7
Insured unemployment rate (percent)	6.2	5.2	6.5	5.7

Average monthly covered employment (millions)	31.7	35.4	38.1	40.1
Total covered payrolls (billions)	$93.9	$137.1	$171.4	$199.0
Total taxable payrolls (billions)	$76.3	$96.5	$109.2	$119.3
Ratio of taxable to total payrolls	.81	.70	.64	.60
Average employer UI tax rate (percent)[c]	1.3	1.1	1.3	2.1
Total state UI taxes collected (millions)	$987	$1,136	$1,471	$2,450
Collections as percent of total payrolls	1.1	.8	.9	1.2
Total benefit outlays (millions)	$1,736	$2,027	$3,513	$3,423
Benefit outlays as percent of total payrolls	1.8	1.5	2.0	1.7
Total state reserves at year end (billions)[d]	$7.0	$8.2	$6.8	$5.6
Reserves as percent of total payrolls[e]	7.5	6.0	4.0	2.8
Average weekly covered wage	$56.95	$74.52	$86.49	$95.53
Average weekly benefit paid[f]	$20.48	$24.93	$30.54	$33.80
Number of first payments (millions)	7.4	6.6	7.8	7.1
Average actual duration of benefits (weeks)	11.8	12.8	14.8	14.7
Estimated exhaustion ratio[g]	29.1	26.8	31.0	30.4

SOURCES: *Unemployment Insurance Financial Data, 1938-1982* and annual supplements.

NOTE: Unemployment insurance data reflect state programs only; they exclude federal programs for railroad workers, veterans, ex-servicemen, federal employees, and extended benefits. Figures shown for covered employment, payrolls, tax collections, regular benefit outlays, average weekly covered wage, and average weekly benefit paid relate to taxable employers and exclude data for reimbursable employers.

a. From chapter 1, table 1.1.

b. Applicable to taxable wages.

c. Net of outstanding loans.

d. Also known as reserve ratio.

e. For week of total unemployment.

f. Total number exhausting benefits during the year as a percent of total first payments during the twelve months ending September 30 of that year for ratios through 1959, and thereafter as a percent of first payments during the 12 months ending June 30.

Employment covered by the state unemployment insurance programs rose by about 60 percent from 1948 to 1969, while payrolls
nearly quadrupled. Average weekly covered wage levels were up
almost 150 percent, outstripping the approximately 50 percent rise in
the Consumer Price Index over this period. Taxable payrolls increased
much less than total payrolls because of the continued wage base limitation at $3,000 in most states.[2] By 1969, only about half of all wages
were taxable. While employer tax rates averaged between 1.1 and 1.5
percent of taxable wages in most of the 1950s, and higher through
much of the 1960s, the revenues collected were a considerably smaller
proportion of total payrolls, averaging 1.0 percent over the whole
period. The difference between recession and low unemployment years
can be seen most in the levels of benefit outlays and the numbers of
unemployed workers who received first benefit payments. The aggregate of state reserve funds, as a percentage of total payrolls, continued
a steady decline from high war-time levels, reaching to less than 3 percent in the early 1960s. Several states experienced financial problems
during the 1950s. The average duration of benefits paid to claimants
and benefit exhaustion ratios also reflect the impact of recessions.
Widespread benefit exhaustion was a problem that drew much legislative attention in this period.

Both federal and state legislation contributed to the system's development and shaped its responses to the challenges of the times. This
chapter reviews the major federal legislative actions of the period
through 1969; the following chapter carries that review through the
next two decades. State unemployment insurance legislation is the subject of chapter 10. Federal unemployment insurance laws enacted
between 1947 and 1969 concerned chiefly the areas of coverage, benefit duration, and financing. Other legislation, especially in the 1960s,
centered on manpower policy and the role of the employment service,
which also had effects on the unemployment insurance program. Some
proposals to establish federal minimum benefit and solvency standards
had promising prospects in Congress but, in the end, were rejected or
pigeonholed.

---

2. Beginning in 1954, an increasing number of states applied higher taxable wage bases, ranging
by 1969 from $3,300 to $3,600 in sixteen states and higher in six.

Before reviewing the federal legislation of the period, a brief account is provided of how the federal responsibilities for unemployment insurance were managed during this time.

Federal Administration of Unemployment Insurance Functions

Soon after World War II ended, the United States Employment Service (USES) was transferred back to the Department of Labor from the dissolved War Manpower Commission, which had operated it as a federal service during the war period. It was from the Labor Department that the USES had been shifted to the Federal Security Agency in 1939 to merge with the Bureau of Unemployment Compensation of the Social Security Board to form the Bureau of Employment Security. The USES continued at the Labor Department until July 1948, when the Congress transferred it back to the Federal Security Agency to be again part of the Bureau of Employment Security. In 1949, the President's Reorganization Plan No. 2 transferred the entire Bureau of Employment Security, including both its unemployment insurance and employment service components, to the Department of Labor where those operations have remained.[3] The frequent shifting and subsequent reorganizations of the USES were not without unsettling effects on its staff and functional capacities at the national level.

The Unemployment Insurance Service component of the Bureau of Employment Security continued to carry out the federal responsibilities of the federal-state system, other than the collection of the Federal Unemployment Tax and the maintenance of the Unemployment Trust Fund. The latter functions have been carried out by the U.S. Treasury Department.

Technical assistance to the states with respect to unemployment insurance legislation and review of state laws for their conformity with

---

3. Robert C. Goodwin became director of the Bureau of Employment Security in 1948 and continued to head the Bureau after its transfer to the Labor Department until a reorganization that occurred about twenty-five years later. Prior to this appointment, Goodwin had held regional positions in Ohio for the Social Security Board before World War II, then served with the War Manpower Commission, and was director of the USES after the war.

federal law remained major activities of the federal Unemployment Insurance Service. Although the states became increasingly more self-sufficient in this regard and the recipients of advice from various interest groups, federal advice was still welcome by and large. The earlier model bills were revised from time to time; the last was issued in 1950 and continued to be useful to the states (USDOL, Bureau of Employment Security 1950a). Amendments of the federal law required changes in state laws, and Bureau guidance in these areas was helpful. The Bureau issued various legislative policy guides as statements, usually in the form of program letters to all states, or as manuals.[4] Federal staff review of state legislation generally sought to forestall conformity problems. Such problems occasionally did materialize, however, leading to negotiations and, if necessary, to formal hearings and rulings by the Secretary of Labor. These cases represented the ultimate testing of the federal-state relationship in the system and sometimes became sources of serious friction.[5]

The Unemployment Insurance Service also supplied assistance to states on technical administrative matters. Drawing on state experience, federal staff (some of them former state agency employees) sought to distill and spread those practices that exhibited merit and success in application. The emphasis was on cooperation with the states in developing the best procedures and the most efficient and economical operations possible. Bureau staff worked closely with committees of the Interstate Conference of Employment Security Agencies on these matters, held regional meetings with state technicians, and consulted directly with individual states on specific problems to the extent staff resources permitted. The Bureau maintained technical manuals and issued other types of written materials for the states. It operated a network of regional offices through which it kept in close touch with the states on these as well as other matters. Review of state agency administrative budget requests as part of the annual federal

---

4. For example, in 1947 the Bureau of Employment Security issued "Unemployment Insurance Legislative Policy, 1947," *Supplement to Manual of State Employment Security Legislation* (1947), and USDOL, Bureau of Employment Security 1962.

5. For a description of the types of conformity cases that arose during the first 45 years of the program and of the legislative review functions of the Unemployment Insurance Service, see Rubin (1983).

grants process has been a powerful control in federal hands and a source of contention, putting strains on the federal-state relationship.

Special federal unemployment compensation programs came into being over the years, some temporary and a few permanent. These include programs providing benefit protection for unemployed war veterans and federal civilian employees, and temporary extensions of benefits. Although the state agencies operated these programs as agents for the federal government, the Unemployment Insurance Service had to assume additional administrative responsibilities of a more direct nature with respect to them than it did for the state unemployment insurance programs.

The Unemployment Insurance Service also carried out research and actuarial activities to meet needs at the national level and assisted the states in such activities at their level. A system of statistical reporting developed whereby data compiled by the states on their program operations and finances flowed regularly to the national office where they were summarized and published. These data provided a source of vital intelligence about insured unemployment and the workings of the state programs that permitted significant analyses and evaluations in support of national legislative policy developments. As financial problems began to emerge in a few state programs, analyses of financial statistics and actuarial methods for estimating costs and revenue needs assumed increasing importance at both the federal and state levels. The Bureau provided for special training in such work for state technicians.[6] It also supported and helped to develop special studies in particular problem areas, such as the adequacy of weekly benefits and experience of claimants after exhaustion of benefits.[7]

In 1949, a new Federal Advisory Council on Employment Security was organized to make recommendations to the Secretary of Labor

---

6. For example, under contract with the Department of Labor, Professor William Haber helped to organize and stage a number of training programs at the University of Michigan during the 1960s for state personnel on actuarial and financial analysis, as well as on other aspects of unemployment insurance.

7. From 1955 to 1967, Saul J. Blaustein was heavily involved in much of the program research activity of the Unemployment Insurance Service and headed up this work in the last half of that period.

regarding unemployment insurance and the employment service.[8] It was constituted as a tripartite body with members representing employers, labor, and the public. The members were appointed by the Secretary and served for a period of two years, but were often reappointed. The Council usually met two or more times a year to review program developments and problem areas, with the assistance of Bureau staff reports. Various committees were also formed to study and report on specific aspects of the employment security program.[9]

Unemployment Insurance Service staff provided significant input and supporting material in the process of developing federal legislative proposals for the administration. During the course of congressional consideration of proposed unemployment insurance bills, staff assembled available and relevant material to assist the legislative process at that stage as well. The staff also assisted by supplying materials to technical and advisory groups authorized by congressional committees to study and report on unemployment insurance policy issues. The first of these (the Calhoun report) was made to the House Committee on Ways and Means in 1946, as already noted in chapter 7. The second report was made in 1949 to the Senate Finance Committee by the Advisory Council on Social Security (U.S. Congress, Senate 1950, pp. 137-80). Neither of these reports played any significant role in subsequent unemployment insurance legislative proposals or congressional debates.

Coverage Legislation

Most of the significant federal extensions of unemployment insurance coverage did not take place until after 1969. Those changes are discussed in the next chapter. Several important amendments of the

---

8. Before 1949, the Federal Advisory Council had a checkered history as a statutory body. It was provided originally by the Wagner-Peyser Act of 1933 to deal with employment service matters. Its scope was widened in 1939 to include unemployment insurance, but because of frequent shiftings of the USES, the Council did not function effectively or regularly.

9. William Haber was chairman of the Council from 1948 to 1954 and served on it in later years. Merrill G. Murray was for many years the Council's executive secretary.

federal law were enacted in the 1947-1969 period, however, and these
did broaden the coverage and scope of the federal-state system.

Smaller Firms

A major advance in coverage through federal law came in 1954
when Congress extended the application of the Federal Unemployment
Tax from employers of eight or more to employers of four or more
employees in any twenty weeks in a year, effective January 1956 (P.L.
83-767). Thus, it took twenty years after the federal tax first applied to
reduce the size of firms covered. Many states had already covered
employers of four or more workers, and even smaller firms. Still, about
1.4 million additional jobs became covered under state laws as a result
of the amendment.

Definition of Employee

Another coverage matter that received some, though inconclusive,
legislative attention was the meaning of "employee" for purposes of
the Federal Unemployment Tax, a term not defined in the 1935 act. The
problem concerns workers who fall between the clear status of a wage
or salaried employee and that of a self-employed person or independent contractor. These include, for example, outside salesmen or agents
who work on a commission basis; barbers, beauticians, taxi and truck
drivers who own their own equipment; and home workers of various
kinds.[10] Early federal regulations had applied a narrow construction to
the term based on the common-law "master-servant" relationship. In
1947, the Supreme Court ruled that the language of the 1935 act permitted a broader interpretation, which meant that "employee" could
include a wider range of workers than as construed under the common-
law rule.[11] Congress then passed a "status quo" amendment in 1948 to
confine the definition to the common-law rule.[12] Although many states
had adopted a broader definition of employee for their own laws, several hundred thousand workers were excluded by the 1948 *status quo*

---

10. The problem also related to the Social Security tax, since its application and rates also vary
between employees and the self-employed.

11. *U.S. v. Silk*, 331 U.S. 704, 712-14 (1947).

12. P.L. 80-642. This law was passed over President Truman's veto. See Cohen and Calhoun
(1948). Cohen helped to draft the veto message.

amendment in those states with laws that followed the federal definition.

Federal Civilian Employees

One of the largest expansions of the system occurred in 1954, when federal civilian employees obtained coverage.[13] Beginning January 1955, a separate federal program was provided for them in a new title (Title XV) of the Social Security Act. Although financed entirely by the federal government out of general revenues, the benefits were to be paid in accordance with the law of the state in which the federal employee last worked. Federal employee unions objected strongly to this feature because it meant different levels of protection in different states for employees with identical salaries and employment records. The unions, however, accepted and supported the legislation when it became clear that they could get nothing better. The legislation provided for the states to pay the benefits under agreements with the Secretary of Labor. The law covers service in the employ of the United States or its wholly owned instrumentalities, with certain specified exceptions, principally elected officials and aliens working for the government outside the United States. A total of almost 2.2 million federal civilian jobs were covered under the new program in 1955, a number which rose in later years as federal employment expanded. Only a small percentage of federal employees filed claims for benefits, averaging about 25,000 to 30,000 insured unemployed weekly during the new program's first 10 years (USDOL, Manpower Administration 1968, pp. 97 and 127).

Ex-Servicemen

Workers who have withdrawn from the civilian labor force for a period of military service often have a difficult time finding civilian work upon their return. This is particularly true of the young person who may never have had a civilian job. Congress took action on several occasions to meet this problem. The first was the Servicemen's Readjustment Allowances (SRA) program provided under the G.I. Bill of Rights enacted in 1944 for World War II veterans (described in

---

13. P. L. 83-767, the same legislation that extended coverage to smaller firms.

chapter 7). The next program, also temporary, provided unemployment compensation for veterans of the Korean war period. Finally, Congress adopted a permanent program for persons discharged from the armed forces at any time.

Unemployment Compensation for Veterans

In 1952, a program of Unemployment Compensation for Veterans (UCV) was enacted for veterans of the Korean conflict.[14] This program was more closely coordinated with state unemployment insurance than was the earlier SRA program. UCV provided benefit payments of $26 a week for up to twenty-six weeks, a maximum total of $676. However, if a veteran qualified for other unemployment benefits under either federal or state law, these were subtracted from the UCV entitlement. While the 1944 law set its own eligibility and disqualification provisions for SRA, the 1952 act specified the application of such provisions in the law of the state in which the veteran was drawing benefits. The only exception was that if the state law cancelled all benefit rights under a disqualification provision, this provision would not apply to claimants under the UCV program. The program terminated at the end of January 1960. UCV claims peaked in 1954 when they averaged about 80,000 weekly. A total of nearly $108 million was paid out in UCV benefits that year (USDOL, Manpower Administration 1968, pp. 129 and 142).

Unemployment Compensation for Ex-Servicemen

In 1958, while the UCV program was still in existence, Congress passed the Ex-Servicemen's Unemployment Act (P.L. 85-848). The Act amended Title XV of the Social Security Act, the title created four years earlier to establish unemployment compensation for federal civilian employees. The 1958 amendment provided the same protection for ex-servicemen. The new program was adopted because it had become evident that for the indefinite future, large numbers of persons would serve a period of military service and many of them would face unemployment after discharge. Benefits are paid according to the law of the state in which the ex-serviceman files a claim.[15] The weekly benefit amount payable is based on the claimant's military pay grade

---

14. Title IV, Veterans' Readjustment Assistance Act of 1952, P. L. 82-550.

and a schedule of remuneration provided to the state agencies by the federal government. Costs are federally financed out of general revenues. The armed forces covered by the new program numbered about 2.6 million at the time it took effect. Claims for benefits averaged about 55,000 per week during the first years of the program (USDOL, Manpower Administration 1968, pp. 98 and 128).

Puerto Rico

The inclusion of Puerto Rico as a "state" in the federal-state system is noted here, although this act was more than an extension of coverage. Puerto Rico enacted an unemployment insurance law in June 1956. The government of this Commonwealth wanted its law to come under the federal-state system, but Congress did not give it this status until 1960 (P.L. 86-778). In 1961, its first year in the system, Puerto Rico's average monthly covered employment was larger than that of fifteen other states. Its average weekly covered wage level has been lower than that of any other state and its insured unemployment rate is usually at or near the highest among the states. Until 1992, Puerto Rico was the only "state" in the system that did not provide for experience rating.

Temporary Extended Benefit Programs

State benefit duration provisions were improving from their modest beginnings as experience made clear that longer protection was financially feasible. Maximum duration of twenty-six weeks of benefits, for example, became more common among the states in the 1950s. Nevertheless, recession experience demonstrated that unemployment at such times lasted so much longer for so many laid-off workers that even the more liberal duration provisions could not forestall large-scale and widespread exhaustion of benefits with the mounting hardships that entailed. The principal remedy that developed was to extend tempo-

---

15. Changes adopted in the 1980s specified more federal rules to govern what benefits would be paid, for example, reducing the duration of benefits payable to some ex-servicemen as compared with other claimants in the same state (see chapter 9).

rarily the usual or regular duration of benefits during recession periods. State response to the problem was limited. Pressures rose for action at the federal level.

Temporary Unemployment Compensation Act of 1958

The recession of 1958 resulted in an unprecedented number of insured unemployed workers exhausting their benefits. To respond to this urgent problem, Congress enacted a temporary program of extended benefits which was signed into law in June 1958 (P.L. 85-441). The legislation provided that federal funds would be advanced to those states that entered into agreements with the Secretary of Labor to pay extended benefits to unemployed workers who had exhausted their regular benefits. Extended benefits would be payable up to a maximum duration equal to one-half the duration of the regular benefits paid each exhaustee. The extended benefits would be reduced by the amount of any temporary extended benefits payable to an individual under a state law.[16] The weekly benefit amount would be the same as that paid for regular benefits. Any unemployed worker in a participating state who had exhausted regular benefits after June 1957 would be eligible for extended benefits for unemployment occurring after the program took effect. Payments of extended benefits could be made for weeks of unemployment beginning fifteen or more days after enactment of the legislation and not later than the end of March 1959.[17]

The extended benefits were financed by advances out of federal general revenues, but a state agreeing to pay such benefits would have to restore these advances to the United State Treasury either by a transfer from its Unemployment Trust Fund account or out of other state funds. If such restoration was not made by November 10, 1963, the full credit of 2.7 percent allowed against the Federal Unemployment Tax paid by employers in the state would be reduced progressively each year beginning in 1963 until the full amount advanced to the state for

---

16. Several states had adopted temporary extended benefit provisions of their own about the same time.

17. The program was extended in 1959 so that persons who had filed claims before April 1959, but had not used up all the extended benefits to which they were entitled, would have until the end of June 1959 to draw them (P. L. 86-7, approved March 31, 1959).

extended benefits was restored.[18] No interest was charged on the advances.

State participation in the program was voluntary. Only seventeen states chose to enter it fully. Another five states had adopted similar programs of their own and decided to remain independent of the federal program. Together, these twenty-two states accounted for about 70 percent of all claimants who exhausted their regular benefits during the period of the program.[19] Throughout this time (June 1958 through June 1959), about two million persons received a total of $600 million in extended benefits in the twenty-two states. They drew, on average, a benefit of $30 per week for nearly ten weeks. About 60 percent exhausted their extended benefits as well (USDOL Bureau of Employment Security 1959).

Temporary Extended Unemployment
Compensation Act of 1961

When President Kennedy took office in January 1961, a recession had been under way for some months and exhaustions of regular benefits were again on the rise. Within three weeks, he transmitted a bill to Congress for another federal temporary extension program. A bill was passed and signed into law only seven weeks later (P.L. 87-6).

In many respects the new act was similar to the 1958 act. Unemployed workers who had exhausted regular benefits after June 1960 were eligible for extended benefits. The extended weekly benefit amount was the same as for regular benefits. Extended benefits were payable for up to one-half the duration of regular benefits, except this time the extended duration was limited to a maximum of thirteen weeks, and the combined maximum duration of regular and extended benefits was thirty-nine weeks. These limitations were made because nine states were then paying regular benefits in excess of twenty-six

---

18. The tax credit was reduced to 2.55 percent in 1963, to 2.4 in 1964, and then was to decline to 2.25 in 1965, and so on. P. L. 88-173, approved November 7, 1963, amended this arrangement by providing that the reduced tax credit shall continue to be 2.4 percent each year after 1964 until the advance was repaid.

19. Some of the other states agreed at least to provide the extended benefits to unemployed veterans or former federal employees, or both, who had drawn regular benefits under the separate federal programs described earlier since the states incurred no liability for these wholly federally-financed benefits.

weeks; without the thirty-nine-week limitation it was thought that regular plus extended benefits might be unnecessarily long in those states. The new act provided for termination of the program on April 1, 1962, except for those who began receiving extended benefits before that date; the latter were allowed another three months to draw on their remaining entitlement. Again, the benefits were to be administered by the states under agreements with the Secretary of Labor.

The principal change from the 1958 approach was in the method of financing. The new act called for payment of the entire cost of the extended benefits by the federal government rather than by the individual states through repayment of federal advances, as provided in the 1958 act. The costs were to be covered by a temporary increase in the Federal Unemployment Tax. The proceeds of this increase were pooled nationally and used to finance the extended benefits wherever they were paid. Thus, there would be a truly federal program of extended benefits, although the states would administer it.

The national pooling of these added funds was not accepted without a struggle. The bill, as it passed the House, provided for a Federal Unemployment Tax addition of 0.4 percent of taxable payrolls for the calendar years 1962 and 1963.[20] The bill was amended by the Senate Finance Committee to allocate the tax increase instead to the states in accordance with their shares of all taxable wages. At the end of the program, any excess of the tax increase allocated to a state over extended benefits paid by that state would be transferred to the state's account in the Unemployment Trust Fund. On the other hand, if a state paid out more in extended benefits than its allocated federal tax increase, that state's employers would have to make up the deficit through future reductions in their federal tax credits. Thus, the Senate Finance Committee's bill, in effect, called for individual state financing of the proposed program. When the bill came before the Senate, the biggest battle was waged over this amendment, which was narrowly defeated by a vote of 46 to 44. The House version for financing the program prevailed.

---

20. Since it became evident that the 0.4 percent federal tax increase for 1962 and 1963 would leave a surplus estimated at $172 million over the costs of the program, Congress in 1963 reduced the 1963 increase from 0.4 percent to 0.25 percent (P. L. 88-31, approved May 29, 1963).

Since benefits were to be financed on a nationwide basis, another important difference from the 1958 act was to provide for state reimbursement of benefit payments in excess of twenty-six weeks in any state paying more than twenty-six weeks in benefits under its own law, whether regular or state-extended benefits.[21] It was considered only fair to do so to avoid penalizing states that were more generous than most in their duration provisions.

Another feature of the 1961 law was to reduce the claimant's extended weekly benefit by the amount received as a pension if the pension was provided or contributed to by the claimant's base-period employer (Social Security pensions were excluded). Thus a federal standard of a negative character regarding receipt of pension was added to the bill. In all other respects, however, benefits were to be paid according to state law.

Finally, because charges were made that a large portion of the benefits would go to "secondary" workers, that is to nonheads of families who allegedly did not need them, an amendment was added by the Senate Finance Committee requiring each state to collect data, on a sample basis, on the personal and family characteristics, employment background, and benefit experience of those who drew extended benefits under the act. The amendment's primary purpose was to furnish ammunition for those who might wish to restrict extended benefits in any future program. The amendment resulted in the collection of the most comprehensive statistics on the long-term insured unemployed ever obtained up to that time.[22]

In view of the method adopted for financing the new program, it was a foregone conclusion that all states would enter into agreements to pay the benefits—the principal objective of the financial arrangements. Only a minority of states had participated fully under the 1958 temporary extension act. A total of 2.8 million persons drew extended benefits under the 1961-62 program, averaging about $31 a week for nine weeks. Extended benefit outlays aggregated about $800 million. Approximately 60 percent of those who drew these benefits exhausted them. The special sample surveys conducted during the life of the pro-

---

21. Besides the nine states with a maximum duration for regular benefits of more than 26 weeks, six states provided for their own temporary extensions.

22. For a more detailed history of the passage of this act, see Booth, (1961, pp. 909-21).

gram indicated that the majority (over 60 percent) of the claimants were the primary or sole earners of their families or lived alone, about 75 percent had been in the labor force for at least thirty-six months prior to filing for extended benefits, and about 60 percent were in their prime working years—age 25 to 54. Overall, the surveys did not reveal any serious or extreme distortions in patterns of characteristics, as compared with workers generally, except that the extended benefit claimants had been unemployed for a long time.[23]

Aborted Proposals for Extended Benefits

During the mid-1960s, two competing proposals for permanent extended benefit programs were considered. One, advanced by the Johnson administration, was introduced in 1965 as part of a broad set of unemployment insurance reforms and termed Federal Unemployment Adjustment Benefits.[24] It would provide up to twenty-six weeks of added benefits with an overall maximum of fifty-two weeks of regular and extended benefits. The federal government would finance the entire cost of the extended benefits partly out of an increase in the Federal Unemployment Tax and partly by a government contribution from general revenues. The extended benefits would be payable at all times, not only during recessions. They would be payable to claimants who exhausted regular state benefits and who had at least twenty-six weeks of employment in the base period and seventy-eight weeks in the three years preceding the regular benefit year (or the equivalent in earnings). A claimant could be disqualified for refusing to attend or make satisfactory progress in a retraining program to which he or she had been directed. In other respects, state unemployment insurance provisions would apply.

The rival proposal, developed by the Interstate Conference of Employment Security Agencies was also introduced in 1965 (H.R. 7476 and H.R. 7477). It provided for federal financing of half the cost of any benefits paid by a state in excess of twenty-six weeks during a "state recession period." Such a period would begin, or "trigger on"

23. Data about the program and claimant characteristics from a report on a study of claimants under the Temporary Extended Unemployment Compensation Program of 1961-1962 (USDOL Bureau of Employment Security (1963).

24. Contained in H.R. 8282; these reform proposals are described more fully below.

when the state's insured unemployment rate, averaged over thirteen successive weeks, was at least 120 percent of the average for the corresponding weeks of the two prior years, and "trigger off" when it fell below that level. Provision for payment of benefits beyond twenty-six weeks would be optional: a state could pay such benefits on a regular basis, or as a temporary extension in recession periods, or not at all. The federal sharing of cost would be limited to thirteen weeks of benefits. An additional 0.1 percent Federal Unemployment Tax would finance the federal share.

The House Committee on Ways and Means, after lengthy hearings, discussion, and debate, reported out a comprehensive unemployment insurance bill in 1966 that included an extended benefit program in which all states would have to participate. The federal government would cover half the cost of such benefits. They would be payable during high unemployment periods triggered on and off on a national and state basis. Extended benefits would trigger on nationally when the seasonally adjusted national rate of insured unemployment was at least 5 percent for three consecutive months and the number of claimants exhausting their benefits during those months totaled at least 1 percent of covered employment. The national extension would end when either of these two conditions was no longer satisfied. A state extended benefit period would trigger on when the state's insured unemployment rate for thirteen weeks averaged 3 percent or more and was at least 120 percent of the corresponding rate averaged for the two prior years. The state extension would trigger off when either requirement was no longer met. Extended benefits would be paid for up to half the claimant's regular benefit duration not to exceed thirteen weeks and with a combined maximum of thirty-nine weeks for regular and extended benefits. All other state provisions would apply. An additional 0.2 percent Federal Unemployment Tax would finance the federal share of the cost of extended benefits.

The bill containing this program passed both the House and Senate but with differences affecting, mostly, other provisions; there was essential agreement on the extended benefit provisions. A conference committee failed to reach agreement on other disputed features of the bill resulting in the demise of the entire bill. An extended benefit program similar to that contained in this bill was enacted in 1970 and is described in the next chapter.

Changes in Financing

The basic financial structure of the federal-state unemployment insurance system was not changed in any fundamental way during the period under review in this chapter. The only important addition to it during this time was the permanent provision for advances to states from a federal loan fund. Several changes were made affecting federal standards on experience rating, and some action was taken with respect to administrative financing arrangements. A few other proposals addressing problems of fund solvency and experience rating were advanced and debated, but rejected.

Prior to 1947, the only significant change in the federal tax provisions was the adoption of the $3,000 taxable wage base limit in 1939, which remained unaltered through 1971. As can be seen in table 8.1, this limit had become increasingly restrictive as wage levels rose steadily, so that by 1969 only half of all payrolls were subject to the tax even though some states had raised their own tax bases somewhat. None of the increases proposed before 1970 for the federal tax base was adopted despite the erosion.

Experience Rating

Only minor changes were made in the "additional credit" (experience rating) provisions of the Federal Unemployment Tax before 1954. One, for example, came in 1947, when an amendment permitted states to take account of voluntary contributions made by employers to their accounts so as to promote the computation of reduced rates (P.L. 80-226).

In 1954, a more important change was made affecting experience rating. Until then, the federal law required that an employer must have had at least three years of unemployment experience before being eligible for a lower state tax rate with full credit against the federal tax based on that experience. The change in 1954 permitted a state to shorten the experience period to one year. It was applicable not only to newly covered employers, but also to new employers just starting in business.[25] The change was not mandatory for the states and some states did not take advantage of it.

State experience rating provisions have been among the most troublesome from the point of view of conformity with federal requirements. They tend to be very technical and detailed. Their review, the conformity questions they evoke, and the resolution of those questions have occupied a disproportionate amount of time of the federal staff assigned to the process. They have also been a source of friction between the federal and state agencies. In 1965, the administration proposed to alleviate this problem by deleting from the law all federal requirements pertaining to experience rating and allowing the states complete freedom to set their taxes as they chose.[26] The idea was strongly opposed by those who favored experience rating and who feared that some states would abandon it without the federal requirements that did not permit reduced rates on any other basis. The suggested change was eliminated from consideration.

Federal Loan Fund

In 1944, as described in chapter 7, Congress established a special Federal Unemployment Account (the so-called George Fund) in the Unemployment Trust Fund from which loans could be made to states with reserves almost depleted because of heavy benefit outlays which were widely expected to follow World War II. The loan provisions were temporary; after two extensions they were allowed to expire in March 1952. During their existence, no appropriation was ever made to the loan account and no state ever applied for a loan.

Discussion continued, however, concerning ways of assisting states in financial distress. Besides loans, the concept of reinsurance grants had been considered through the years, even by the Committee on Economic Security. One factor that influenced the discussion was the growing surplus of Federal Unemployment Tax revenues over the amounts appropriated to cover the administrative costs of the system.

---

25. P. L. 83-767. The same act extended federal coverage to smaller firms with four or more employees.

26. The proposal was part of the comprehensive package of unemployment insurance reforms introduced into the Congress as H.R. 8282.

A portion of this surplus, it was suggested, could be used to finance grants or loans to states needing financial help.

As part of the Employment Security Administrative Financing Act of 1954 (The Reed Act), the federal loan fund was reactivated and a new permanent set of loan provisions adopted.[27] The new law called for the automatic appropriation of the receipts of the Federal Unemployment Tax to the Unemployment Trust Fund. The excess of Federal Unemployment Tax receipts over federal and state administrative expenses was to be placed in the Federal Unemployment Account (loan fund) until it reached $200 million. From this account, an interest-free federal advance could be made to a state reserve account if at the end of any calendar quarter the state's account had a balance that was less than the state's total benefit payments over the preceding four calendar quarters. The amount of the advance might not exceed the state's highest benefit expenditures in any of the four preceding calendar quarters. Since it was assumed that a state would normally need an advance during an economic recession, the state could delay repayments for four years. If not repaid by then, the loans would be recovered through a reduction in the Federal Unemployment Tax credits allowed to the state's employers. The reduction would equal 0.15 percent of taxable payrolls in the first year, 0.30 percent in the second year, and so on, progressively, until the loans were repaid.

Advances were made from the Reed Act loan fund to Alaska between 1955 and 1960, and to Michigan and Pennsylvania in 1958 and 1959, respectively. The latter two states exhausted the loan fund's resources of $200 million available at the time.[28] Neither actually needed the borrowed funds to pay benefits then, although Pennsylvania finally did in 1961. The three borrowing states did not fully repay their loans until the mid-1960s.

The requirements for the receipt and repayment of federal advances were tightened by amendments enacted in 1960 (P.L. 86-778). These amendments provided that a state would not be eligible for an advance unless its reserve account was so low that it could not meet the benefit

---

27. P. L. 83-567, named for Representative Daniel Reed, chairman of the House Committee on Ways and Means.

28. Pennsylvania also borrowed smaller additional amounts in 1960 and 1961. Three other states (Delaware, Oregon and West Virginia) met the requirements for loans during or soon after the 1958 recession but did not borrow.

payments estimated for the current month or the next month. Moreover, the state would be advanced only sufficient funds to carry it through the month. The advances would be repayable in two years, rather than four, before recovery through federal tax credit reductions began. The annual credit reductions would be at double the rates specified in the 1954 act. To assure that the state would increase its taxes so as to get its fund in a sounder financial position, the amendments also provided that while a state has an outstanding advance it must have average contribution rates of 2.7 percent for the third and fourth years after the advance is made; thereafter, average contribution rates must equal the state's average cost rate, or 2.7 percent, whichever is higher, until the advance is repaid. Paradoxically, at the same time the stiffened requirements seemed to eliminate the likelihood of any advances being made, the maximum size of the loan fund was increased to $550 million or 0.4 percent of all taxable wages, whichever was a greater amount. No further borrowing occurred until the 1970s.

Administrative Financing

Although the net Federal Unemployment Tax was always regarded as the source of revenue to cover the administrative costs of the program, the original Social Security Act expressed no connection between the two in order to avoid any constitutional issue that might be raised. The Reed Act of 1954, for the first time, earmarked these revenues for employment security purposes only. The funds were to be automatically deposited in the Unemployment Trust Fund and used first for administrative expenses. Tax receipts exceeded these expenses by substantial amounts at the time and during the next several years. As described above, the excess went into the federal loan fund, which was authorized to accumulate to a ceiling of $200 million, and rapidly did so. The continuing excess in these years was distributed to the states; most have used these "Reed Act" distributions to finance the construction of new offices.

By 1960, however, the federal loan fund was depleted by the advances drawn by Michigan and Pennsylvania. Moreover, administrative costs had increased in the states to where the margin of tax receipts over such costs was narrowing rapidly. Taking both these factors into account, Congress in 1960 raised the Federal Unemployment Tax rate from 3.0 to 3.1 percent, but kept the maximum credit allowed employers against the tax at 2.7 percent, thus increasing the federal share from 0.3 to 0.4 percent of taxable payrolls.[29] At the same time, a ceiling of $350 million was placed on annual grants to the states for administrative costs. In 1963, this ceiling was replaced by a flexible limit of 95 percent of estimated receipts from the net Federal Unemployment Tax (exclusive of the temporary increases in the tax for 1962 and 1963 to finance the Temporary Extended Unemployment Compensation program) (P.L. 88-31). The combination of the persistent rise in state administrative costs and the ever heavier restraint that the constant $3000 taxable wage base placed on federal tax revenues produced chronic strains and problems for financing administrative costs.

Legislative Efforts of 1965-1966

Several allusions have already been made to proposals for unemployment insurance reforms in 1965 and 1966, including those for a permanent program of extended benefits. A general description of the legislative efforts that took place appears appropriate, since they centered on the most extensive set of proposals to be made for unemployment insurance since passage of the Social Security Act. Much of what was proposed did pass in 1970.

In 1965, the Johnson administration submitted its unemployment insurance proposals, introduced as H.R. 8282 in the House and S. 1991 in the Senate. Their scope was comprehensive. Included were provisions to extend coverage to employers with one or more employees, to nonprofit organizations, to large farm employers, and other excluded groups. Provision for a program of Federal Unemployment Adjustment Benefits for workers who exhaust regular benefits was described above, along with a rival proposal for a triggered extended benefits program for state recession periods.

The most controversial proposals in H.R. 8282 were for minimum benefit standards, particularly as applied to the weekly benefit amount.

---

29. P. L. 86-778, which also increased the loan fund ceiling and stiffened lending and repayment provisions.

To qualify its employers for the full federal tax credit, a state would have to provide a weekly benefit amount of no less than half the claimant's weekly wage up to a maximum equal to at least two-thirds of the state's average weekly wage in covered employment. It was the latter requirement that created the most reaction; except for Hawaii, no state at the time came close to meeting it. The proposal would allow states to reach the required ceiling in stages over a period of years. The required weekly benefit maximum was deemed necessary to assure that the great majority of insured workers would be able to receive a weekly benefit of half their weekly wage if unemployed. Another proposed standard would require each state to provide up to at least twenty-six weeks of benefits to every claimant with twenty or more weeks of base-period employment. If a state failed to meet these benefit amount and duration standards, its employers would be eligible for a tax credit equal to its average annual benefit cost rate of the last four years, or 2.7 percent, of their taxable payrolls, whichever was lower. Other proposals would prohibit states from imposing very long disqualifications or from reducing or cancelling benefit rights because of disqualification.

To strengthen financing, the Johnson administration urged increases in the taxable wage base, in two steps, to $6,600 by 1971. It also proposed a new program of federal grants to high-cost states covering two-thirds of a state's benefit costs in excess of 2 percent of total payrolls, regardless of the financial condition of that state's fund. The state would have to meet the benefit standards to be eligible. The grants would be financed by funds raised from the Federal Unemployment Tax and allocated from general revenues.

These were the principal proposals advanced by the administration in 1965.[30] The House Committee on Ways and Means held extensive hearings on them throughout the month of August that year (U.S. Congress, House 1965). The Committee met again the following March to hear additional testimony from representatives of the Interstate Conference.[31] The Interstate Conference had met in January 1966 to discuss these and other proposals and had polled its members with respect to them. The majority of the state agencies favored the coverage exten-

---

30. For a full description and discussion of the proposals, see Murray (1966).

31. These hearings, held solely for Interstate Conference recommendations and testimony, were published as a sixth volume of U.S. Congress, House (1965).

sions with some modifications; opposed the administration's Federal Unemployment Adjustment Benefits proposal and favored the triggered federally shared state extended benefits in state recession periods; and opposed the benefit standards and requirements specified in H.R. 8282. The majority did accept a recommendation for a federal requirement that the state weekly benefit ceiling be at least half of the statewide average weekly covered wage. The majority opposed the idea of federal grants to states for excess costs, but favored increasing the taxable wage base to $3,900 and then setting it at 70 percent of the annual average wage.

In June 1966, the Ways and Means Committee reported out a bill (H.R. 15119) which included the proposed coverage extensions (somewhat modified), a federally shared extended benefits program for periods of high unemployment triggered on a national or state basis, and a two-stage increase in the taxable wage base to $4,200 by 1972, as well as several other amendments. None of the proposed minimum benefit standards or federal grants for excess costs was included. The House passed the bill and sent it to the Senate.

The Senate Finance Committee held hearings on the bill in July 1966 at which administration officials urged amendments to restore some of the original proposals, particularly for the higher taxable wage base and benefit standards (U.S. Congress, Senate 1966). The Senate did adopt a bill with the benefit standards, although in a form different from that proposed.[32] At the ensuing House-Senate conference in October, House conferees refused to accept the benefit standards provisions. Administration and other proponents of standards felt so strongly about this issue that they opposed giving up standards in order to assure passage of the rest of the legislation. As a result, no agreement was reached, and Congress adjourned shortly thereafter. It is ironic, perhaps, that several important provisions that could have been enacted in 1966—extensions of coverage, a triggered federal-state extended benefits program, and a taxable wage base increase—were adopted four years later, without benefit standards.

---

32. The Senate Finance Committee recommended that states be required to set their maximum weekly benefit amounts at 50 percent of the state average covered weekly wages or, as an alternative, at a level that assured 65 percent of covered workers half their weekly wage if unemployed.

Other Federal Legislation

Additional legislative actions took place in the 1960s which did not focus on unemployment insurance but which affected the program to one degree or another, especially with respect to its relationships with other programs. Some of the laws enacted are noted briefly so as to provide a more complete account of the federal legislative background of this period.

Manpower Training and Retraining

Several acts of the early 1960s addressed the problems of persistent unemployment associated with technological and other structural changes, depressed areas, and import competition. The first to pass was the Area Redevelopment Act of 1961, followed by the Manpower Development and Training Act of 1962 and the Trade Expansion Act of 1962. Each of them provided for federally subsidized assistance to unemployed workers who were dislocated from jobs under certain conditions or who met specific eligibility requirements. The assistance included training or retraining and other forms of reemployment aid to help make the workers more employable in other jobs. Cash training allowances were made available for some. Under the Trade Act, weekly Trade Readjustment Allowances were payable to workers laid off by firms certified by the Tariff Commission as adversely affected by increased imports due to lowered trade barriers. The Tariff Commission, however, did not make any adverse effect certifications under the Act during the 1960s. In 1965, the Automotive Products Trade Act was passed to provide similar assistance to workers adversely affected by trade agreements with Canada relating to automotive products. Rulings of adverse effects were made the responsibility of a special board, and such certifications were issued. The Trade Readjustment Allowances paid were more generous than unemployment insurance benefits, both in weekly amount and duration.

State unemployment insurance provisions at that time generally held that claimants in school or in training were not available for work and therefore were ineligible for unemployment benefits. Those who qualified for training allowances were paid an amount equivalent to their unemployment insurance benefit. Others on training allowances received the average weekly benefit paid in the state.

These laws were passed originally as temporary measures and modestly funded. Subsequent amendments extended and expanded them until they constituted a major element in federal employment and training policy. The federal-state employment security system was involved to the extent that the employment services were given the responsibility for identifying workers eligible for assistance and counseling them with respect to their training and job search needs. The state agencies also handled the disbursement of cash allowances provided by these programs through the payment machinery established for unemployment insurance. While the allowances, training costs, and other assistance provided were financed by federal general funds and some state general funds, administrative costs were not always fully covered.

Antipoverty Program

Also in the 1960s, another stream of federal legislation aimed at reducing and eradicating poverty. A major approach emphasized efforts to enhance the employability of low-income persons disadvantaged by the lack of education and skills and by discrimination. The programs established provided for training and other job preparation assistance, usually accompanied by cash allowances. As the decade wore on, legislative amendments affecting these programs and those under the Manpower Development and Training Act shifted the priorities more and more to employment and training assistance for the poor and disadvantaged, particularly youths and minorities. Unemployment among experienced workers had been declining, reaching very low levels in the late 1960s. Increasingly, the Employment Service was drawn into broader manpower roles and then oriented more fully toward serving the low-income, unskilled and marginal members of the labor force. This shift weakened and, to a large extent, disconnected its relationship to unemployment insurance, which dealt primarily with experienced unemployed workers.

Federal Budget Reform

Prior to 1967, the official federal budget, known as the "administrative budget," did not include the transactions of the various trust funds held by the government. Those funds are not available for general purposes of the government; therefore, they were not included in the budget. They were shown separately, however, and presented with the budget as part of a statement of consolidated cash receipts from and payments to the public. In the 1960s, these trust funds, which included the Unemployment Trust Fund, as well as those of other Social Security Act programs and the interstate highway program, had grown to significant proportions, together accounting for about 25 to 30 percent of total federal receipts and outlays. Increasing attention focused on the consolidated cash statements because of their growing significance and economic impact. Discussions of different budgets led to some general confusion.

In 1967, a Commission on Budget Concepts, appointed by the President, recommended a single unified budget as the official budget of the federal government. The unified budget would include the transactions of the trust funds. This approach was adopted beginning with the budget for the fiscal year 1969. The inclusion of the Unemployment Trust Fund meant not only that the federal accounts in this Fund (for administrative expenses and the loan fund account) would be part of the federal budget, but the state benefit reserve accounts as well even though the latter reflect tax and benefit provisions of state laws.[33]

At the time the change was made, little or no objection was raised. Trust funds were then generating surpluses which had the overall effect of offsetting some of the heavy military expenditures on the Vietnam war, and, thus, were politically welcome for that reason. The change, however had very different impacts years later when trust fund surpluses disappeared and turned into deficits and when unified budget deficits grew so large despite trust fund surpluses.

---

33. For a full account of the change described here, see Henle (1980).

9

The System Under Financial Strain
(1970-1990)

As the 1960s ended, so did the era of strong postwar growth and spreading prosperity. The closing years of that decade represented a high peak of economic expansion and relatively full employment. Yet, signs of a change appeared as 1970 loomed ahead. A new administration took hold in Washington in 1969 and pressed for restraints on federal spending, especially for military procurement. The resulting sharp cutbacks in aerospace and other defense industries helped to precipitate a recession soon after the 1970s opened. Inflation became a serious problem in that decade, reflecting some of the effects of deficit financing in the Viet Nam War build-up of the 1960s. The Arab oil embargo of late 1973 and the subsequent skyrocketing of fuel prices sent shock waves through the national and world economies.

The recession of the early 1970s was followed by the more severe recession of the mid-1970s. Recovery from each was slow and faltering. Youngsters from the maturing postwar baby boom generation flooded into the labor market at a time of curtailed expansion of job opportunities. Continued growth in the rate of labor force participation by women, and reduction in the armed forces following the phasedown of military activity in Viet Nam also swelled the supply of labor. The recessions and limping recoveries combined further to raise unemployment to well over usual post-World War II levels and rates. At the same time inflation persisted—even worsened—despite sluggish business, prompting the use of the term "stagflation" to describe the condition of the economy.

Some improvement took place in the late 1970s. Before that decade closed, however, deterioration began again and recession conditions returned by 1980. This slump was more confined to a few areas of the country and appeared to be ending in 1981. In 1982, recession became full-blown and nationwide. Unemployment rose to the highest levels seen, both in number and rate, since the depression years of the 1930s and 1940.

Insured unemployment reflected the changing economic scene, especially the impact of recessions and long-term unemployment. The 1960s had concluded with about seven consecutive years of relatively moderate-to-low levels of unemployment insurance claims and benefit outlays, which encouraged a certain amount of complacency about reserves and financing. With the recessions of the early and mid-1970s, many of the state funds became insolvent and were forced to borrow from the federal loan fund.[1] After a few years of some recovery, the successive and deep recessions of the early 1980s did more damage to state unemployment insurance funds. By mid-1983, the majority were insolvent. For the first time, the entire federal-state system was in a net negative balance position with regard to the aggregate of all state and federal unemployment insurance trust funds. When 1983 closed, twenty-three state funds owed a total of $13.4 billion.

Table 9.1 presents data which convey some idea of how the unemployment insurance system reacted to the changed economic picture after 1970. The data are comparable to those provided previously for earlier periods (see tables 7.1 and 8.1). Sharp increases in covered employment levels after 1971 and 1975 reflected mostly the significant coverage extensions provided by federal laws. Total covered payrolls also rose for this reason and because of wage inflation as well, especially after 1975.[2] State taxable wage base increases expanded taxable payrolls substantially in 1972, 1978, and 1983 because of increases in the federal taxable wage base in those years.[3] These gains, however, were soon eroded in the 1980s, as seen in the falling ratio of taxable to total payrolls. Regular benefit outlays far exceeded tax revenues in

---

1. It is possible too that since advances were available from the federal loan fund without interest at the time, some states were inclined to avoid the hard policies required to prevent insolvency or to restore depleted reserves quickly. Noting this behavior may in turn have weakened the resolve of other hard-pressed states that were striving to maintain solvency.

2. Besides the covered employment and payrolls of taxable employers shown on table 9.1, additional employment and wages were covered representing payrolls of reimbursing employers brought under the program by the coverage extensions in the 1970s to state and local government and nonprofit employers most of whom cover 19 million in average employment and $418 billion in total wages, but only about $564 million in benefit outlays.

3. State taxable wage bases, if lower, rose to at least the level of the federal taxable base when the latter rose from $3000 to $4200 in 1972, to $6000 in 1978, and to $7000 in 1983.

some years, resulting in the widespread insolvency and debt already noted. Despite the rapid increase in wages, average weekly benefit amount levels more or less kept pace throughout this period. What is also noteworthy is the persistently high average duration of regular benefits and the high exhaustion ratios in most of these years. The new federal-state extended benefit program came into play in these two decades, supplying important added income support during high unemployment periods. Not shown in table 9.1 are outlays under the temporary federal emergency and supplemental benefit programs which added further long-term support during these times.[4]

Following the recession of 1982-83, the economy began a slow, gradual recovery that continued for the rest of the decade. Unemployment rates declined to pre-1974 levels, reaching 5.2 percent of the civilian labor force by 1989. Insured unemployment rates fell even more sharply, precipitating a debate over reasons for the significantly lower proportions of insured-to-total unemployment in the 1980s compared with those of the 1970s.[5] The long recovery period enabled the states to pay off their debts and restore their funds to solvency. By the end of 1988, no state fund was insolvent. (One state, Michigan, still owed some old interest-free loans, but had more than enough reserves to repay them.)[6] The level of reserves, however, did not appear adequate in most cases to withstand the impact of a severe recession and avoid the need to borrow.

Financial crisis was the dominating element in unemployment insurance since about 1975. Federal legislation concerned itself repeatedly with this problem. Provision of extended benefit support beyond the duration limits of state laws also prominently occupied the attention of the federal partner in the system during recession periods and their aftermaths. Legislation in 1970 and 1976 broadened the coverage

---

4. The additional benefits are not reported in table 9.1, since they were funded entirely by the federal government rather than from state reserve funds. These benefits totaled over $500 million in 1972, over $6 billion in 1975-77, about $6.3 billion in 1982-83, and about $3 billion in 1984-85. These temporary programs are discussed in a later section in this chapter.

5. See the discussion of this issue in chapter 1 in the section on "The Insured Unemployed."

6. These loans dated back to before 1981 and were being repaid from reserves each year in amounts equal to the aggregate of the reductions in Federal Unemployment Tax credits that would have otherwise occurred for Michigan employers, an optional means of repayment provided by federal loan repayment provisions. The absence of any interest burden on this debt gave Michigan no incentive to repay it faster.

Table 9.1　Selected Unemployment Insurance Statistics, United States, Selected Years: 1970-1989

(A) From the 1970s

Item	1971	1973	1975	1978
Total unemployment rate[a] (percent)	5.9	4.9	8.5	6.0
Insured unemployment rate (percent)	4.1	2.5	6.1	2.8
Average monthly covered employment (millions)	52.1	59.9	58.6	68.5
Total covered payrolls (billions)	$403.4	$510.0	$579.5	$830.0
Total taxable payrolls (billions)[b]	$182.8	$254.9	$261.9	$411.9
Ratio of taxable to total payrolls	.45	.50	.45	.50
Average state UI tax rate (percent)[c]	1.4	2.0	2.0	2.8
Total state UI taxes collected (millions)	$2,637	$4,996	$5,211	$11,212
Collections as percent of total payrolls	.7	1.0	.9	1.4
Total regular benefit outlays (millions)	$4,952	$4,006	$11,754	$7,710
Regular outlays as percent of total payrolls	1.2	.8	2.0	.9
Total state reserves at year end (billions)[d]	$9.7	$10.9	$3.1	$4.6
Reserves as a percent of total payrolls[e]	2.4	2.1	.5	.6
Average weekly covered wage	$148.96	$163.71	$190.28	$232.90
Average weekly benefit paid[f]	$54.35	$59.00	$70.23	$83.67
Number of first payments (millions)	6.6	5.3	11.2	7.6
Average actual duration of benefits (weeks)	14.4	13.4	15.7	13.3
Estimated exhaustion ratio[g]	30.5	27.6	37.8	26.8
Total extended benefit outlays (millions)[b]	$664	$143	$2,494	$692

(B) From the 1980s

Item	1980	1982	1985	1989
Total unemployment rate[a] (percent)	7.1	9.5	7.1	5.2
Insured unemployment rate (percent	3.9	4.7	2.8	2.1
Average monthly covered employment (millions)	71.3	70.7	77.8	86.2
Total covered payrolls (billions)	$1,026.0	$1,183.9	$1,477.3	$1,918.0
Total taxable payrolls (billions)[b]	$458.6	$479.1	$613.2	$738.5
Ratio of taxable to total payrolls	.45	.40	.42	.38
Average state UI tax rate (percent)[c]	2.4	2.5	3.1	2.2
Total state UI taxes collected (millions)	$11,415	$12,112	$19,258	$16,452
Collections as percent of total payrolls	1.1	1.0	1.3	.9
Total regular benefit outlays (millions)	$13,768	$20,358	$14,101	$13,642
Regular outlays as percent of total payrolls	1.3	1.7	1.0	.7
Total state reserves at year end (billions)[d]	$6.6	-$2.6	$10.1	$36.9
Reserves as a percent of total payrolls[e]	.6	--	.7	1.9
Average weekly covered wage	$276.89	$321.95	$365.38	$428.03
Average weekly benefit paid[f]	$98.95	$119.34	$128.23	$151.76
Number of first payments (millions)	10.0	11.6	9.4	7.4
Average actual duration of benefits (weeks)	14.9	15.9	14.3	13.2
Estimated exhaustion ratio[g]	33.2	38.5	31.3	28.0
Total extended benefit outlays (millions)[h]	$1,763	$2,455	$75	$12

SOURCES: *Unemployment Insurance Financial Data, 1938-1982,* and annual supplements.
NOTE: Unemployment insurance data reflect state programs only; they exclude federal programs for railroad workers, veterans, ex-servicemen, federal employees, and extended benefits. Figures shown for covered employment, payrolls, tax collections, regular benefit outlays, average weekly covered wage, and average weekly benefit paid relate to taxable employers and exclude data for reimbursable employers.

Table 9.1 (continued)

a. From chapter 1, table 1.1.
b. As determined by the taxable wage bases of each state.
c. Applicable to taxable wages.
d. Net of outstanding loans.
e. Also known as reserve ratio.
f. For week of total unemployment.
g. Total number exhausting benefits during the year as a percent of total first payments during the twelve months ending June 30 of that year.
h. Paid under federal-state shared extended benefit programs, including federal share.

of the program so that almost all wage and salary workers were now included. Several other reforms were also enacted and a national commission was established to review the program comprehensively for the first time. As the financial crisis grew, federal legislation covering state borrowing and repayment rules increased in volume and detail, along with tendencies toward restrictions affecting the application of state eligibility and benefit provisions.

This chapter summarizes the principal changes produced by federal legislation enacted after 1969 as they affected major aspects of the unemployment insurance program. These include coverage, eligibility and disqualifications, benefit duration, and financing. Other relevant legislation is also reviewed.

Federal Administrative Changes

Before reviewing the legislative record, a brief account of how the federal administration of unemployment insurance evolved is in order. Some significant changes occurred during the period which affected the development of unemployment insurance policy and legislation.

The Bureau of Employment Security, which combined the unemployment insurance and employment service functions, had operated continuously as a combined unit since 1948, and as part of the Department of Labor since 1949. Programs stemming from the Manpower Development and Training Act greatly expanded the responsibilities of the Department in the 1960s. Some of these affected the Bureau of Employment Security, especially its employment service component. A separate Manpower Administration was established to coordinate most of these new functions, which soon grew in size and scope. In 1966, the Manpower Administrator was elevated to the position of Assistant Secretary of Labor for Manpower Administration. The following year, the various related functions were more tightly organized under that position, including those of the Bureau of Employment Security. At this stage, the regional offices of the component units were consolidated, with emphasis on decentralization of authority to the new regional administrators.

In a subsequent reorganization of the Manpower Administration in 1969, the Bureau of Employment Security was abolished, and the Unemployment Insurance Service was kept as a separate unit headed by an Associate Manpower Administrator. Increasingly, policy and legislative matters relating to unemployment insurance came under the influence of officials outside the group that had been more directly involved in the program's administration at the federal level for many years. Moreover, after long careers of public service dedicated to the unemployment insurance program, many of the most experienced and able officials were ending their careers, mainly through retirement. The hold of tradition and of the authority and philosophy of the past weakened, opening the program to greater effects of such external factors as employment and training concerns and fiscal policy considerations. Another consequence of the reorganization was to further loosen the already weakened linkage between unemployment insurance and the Employment Service. Federal relations with the states with regard to unemployment insurance went less smoothly, especially as the reoriented regional offices were often more absorbed by manpower or employment and training problems and programs. National administrations of the period tended toward less federal and more state and local control in domestic programs and policies. This stance, generally termed the New Federalism, worked to reduce the vigor of the federal influence and leadership with respect to unemployment insurance matters at the state level. These changes clearly affected the nature of federal legislation as well as the program's administration.

Coverage

The major gaps in coverage that remained through the 1960s were closed, for the most part, by the legislation enacted in 1970 and 1976.[7] All but a small fraction of wage and salary employment is now protected by unemployment insurance in this country. The most important

---

7. The Employment Security Amendments of 1970 became law in August 1970 as P.L. 91-373. The Unemployment Compensation Amendments of 1976 were enacted in October 1976 as P.L. 94-566.

segments of the workforce brought under coverage by these laws were employees of small firms, nonprofit organizations, state and local government, and large farm employers. The only significant paid employment that remains uncovered is that for small farm employers and for domestic household service.

Small Firms

The size of employers subject to the Federal Unemployment Tax was reduced by the 1970 amendments from four or more to one or more employees in at least 20 weeks of the year, or with at least $1,500 in payroll in one calendar quarter. Nearly half the states had already covered employers of one or more by 1969. The extension, effective in 1972, brought an estimated 1.3 million jobs under the program.[8]

Nonprofit Organizations

Few states covered employment in nonprofit organizations before the 1970 amendments extended coverage to most employment in this category, effective 1972. The federal provision required states to cover such organizations that employ four or more workers, but continued to exclude churches, religious organizations, and primary and secondary schools. Nonprofit employers were exempted from the Federal Unemployment Tax. The coverage became a federal requirement for approval of state laws to enable other employers to qualify for the federal tax offset. The states were required to offer nonprofit employers the option of covering their unemployment benefit costs either through application of the usual state unemployment insurance tax provisions or by reimbursement of charges, i.e., self-insurance. Nonprofit employers who choose reimbursement may form groups to pool their costs and reimburse the state fund for benefit charges through their pooled funds. Over 2 million additional jobs were covered as a result of this

---

8. Estimates for 1971 indicated that 1.6 million jobs in small firms were not covered; for 1972, the estimate of noncovered employment in small firms was down to about 300,000. See USDOL, Manpower Administration (Revised 1972 and 1973, chart 1).

extension. The 1976 amendments eliminated the exclusion from coverage of nonprofit elementary and secondary school employees.[9]

State and Local Government

The largest segment of the wage and salary labor force not covered by unemployment insurance at the start of the 1970s was employed by state and local government, estimated at 9.4 million in 1971. It was also the fastest growing segment at the time. Most states provided for some coverage, but it was usually limited or spotty, some mandatory and some on an elective basis for local units.

The 1970 amendments required the states to cover all state hospitals and state institutions of higher education. Since nonprofit hospitals, colleges, and universities were also being covered, this provision equalized the treatment of employment in almost all such institutions. For constitutional reasons, the Federal Unemployment Tax cannot apply to covered state and local government payrolls. States may finance benefit costs of public employers through contributions by employing units to the state unemployment insurance reserve funds or through reimbursement of the funds by such units for benefits paid and charged. The 1970 federal provision extended coverage to about 1.5 million jobs in state hospitals and state institutions of higher education (USDOL, Manpower Administration, Revised 1972 and 1973, chart 1).

Another associated provision in the 1970 amendments prohibited eligibility for benefits of college faculty and other school professionals during the summer or between terms if they had a contract to return to work. Under certain conditions, states could exclude from coverage employment by schools of students and their spouses and the employment of patients by hospitals.

In 1976, coverage was extended to all state and local government employment, with a few minor exceptions. This provision alone increased covered employment by over 8 million. Another amendment in 1976 broadened the scope of the prohibition on benefit eligibility between terms of professional staff of higher educational institutions to

---

9. Noncovered employment by nonprofit organizations was estimated at 2.8 million for 1971 and about 600,000 for 1972. In 1975, the estimated number not covered was 700,000; by 1978, this number had been lowered to 400,000 (USDOL, Manpower Administration, Revised 1972 and 1973, chart 1, and 1978 edition).

apply it to such employees at all educational institutions, including primary and secondary schools, if the employee had a contract or reasonable assurance of employment in the coming term. States were given the option to apply the same between-terms denial conditions to nonprofessional school employees. This option was removed by a 1983 amendment which made denial of benefit mandatory in these cases.[10]

Agricultural Coverage

The 1970 amendments eliminated the federal exclusion from coverage of certain categories of agricultural processing employment. The major move in agriculture, however, came in 1976 when coverage, effective in 1978, was extended to hired farm labor of large employers—those with ten or more workers in at least twenty weeks of the year or with payrolls of at least $20,000 in a calendar quarter.[11] The provision temporarily excluded (until 1980) the employment of aliens admitted as farm labor on a limited time basis. This exclusion has been extended several times, the last by legislation adopted in 1986 continuing the exclusion until 1992. Such aliens are not eligible for benefits since they may not remain in the country legally when not employed.

Other Coverage Extensions

The 1970 amendments extended coverage to previously excluded employment of outside salesmen and agents and commission drivers. The 1976 amendments covered domestic household workers of employers who paid wages totaling at least $1,000 for such work in any calendar quarter.

The 1976 extensions became effective in 1978, including those noted above for state and local government employment and farm labor. Emergency legislation enacted at the end of 1974, however, established a Special Unemployment Assistance program to provide benefit support during the recession period ahead to jobless workers unable to draw unemployment insurance for certain reasons, including

---

10. Social Security Amendments of 1983, adopted in April 1983 as P.L. 98-21.

11. These extensions in 1970 and 1976 brought under coverage about a half million jobs in agriculture, an estimate derived from USDOL, Manpower Administration (Revised 1972 and 1973, chart 1).

their exclusion from coverage.[12] As a result, these workers were able to obtain benefits on a basis quite similar to that for unemployment insurance until 1978 when coverage became effective for many of them. The Special Unemployment Assistance benefits were financed by federal general revenues.

The 1976 amendments also admitted the Virgin Islands unemployment insurance program into the federal-state system, effective 1978. That year, covered employment in the Virgin Islands averaged only about 20,500; no other state averaged less than 100,000.

When the 1976 amendments took effect in 1978, an estimated 97 percent of all wage and salary employment was covered by unemployment insurance (USDOL, Manpower Administration 1978 ed., chart 16). The objective of universal coverage had come near full achievement.

Permanent Extended Benefit Program

As described in chapter 8, the temporary federal extensions of benefits during the recessions of 1958-59 and 1961-62 stimulated proposals during the 1960s for permanent provision of long-term benefit support. Some states had raised their regular duration limits beyond the usual twenty-six-week maximum; others established provisions to extend benefits during high unemployment periods only. The latter approach was the one finally adopted as the national policy by the 1970 amendments. The program was altered somewhat during the 1970s with respect to its trigger specifications. Many more amendments significantly modified this program in the 1980s.

The establishment of a permanent program for extended benefits when unemployment is high, carrying the combined regular and extended length of protection up to a maximum of thirty-nine weeks, did not eliminate a perceived need for even longer income support during recession periods. In the recessions of the 1970s and early 1980s, various forms of temporary emergency federal legislation provided for

---

12. Emergency Jobs and Unemployment Assistance Act, adopted December 1974 as P.L. 93-567.

supplemental benefits carrying the total duration of all unemployment benefit support during such times to, in one period, as much as sixty-five weeks.

Extended Unemployment Compensation Act of 1970

The permanent program adopted in 1970 was about the same as that agreed to as part of the 1966 legislative package which failed to pass because of the impasse on federal benefit standards. The program called for a 50 percent extension of the duration of regular benefits allowed to a claimant, up to thirteen more weeks, but not in excess of 39 weeks in all.[13] Extended benefits became available (triggered on) during periods when insured unemployment rates reached specified levels and terminated (triggered off) when the rates fell below those levels. Extensions could become payable on a statewide or nationwide basis with separate trigger specifications for each. Under the 1970 law, extended benefits were payable in a state when its insured unemployment rate averaged 4.0 percent or more over a thirteen-week period and was at least 120 percent of the average rate for the corresponding periods of the two previous years.[14] The state extended benefit period ended when its current thirteen-week average rate fell below either of these two trigger points. If the seasonally adjusted national insured unemployment rate was 4.5 percent or more for three consecutive months, extended benefits became payable in all states and remained so until the trigger-on requirement was *not* met. Once triggered on, however, an extended benefit period continued for at least thirteen weeks, and was off a minimum of thirteen weeks as well.

Claimants who exhausted their regular benefits could draw extended benefits, when payable, unless they became eligible for regular benefits in a new benefit year. Extended benefits were paid at the same weekly rate as regular benefits. All other state provisions applied at first, but later amendments specified certain departures from this rule.

---

13. This program was adopted as part of the Employment Security Amendments of 1970.

14. Weekly insured unemployment rates varied seasonally in some states, often to exceed 4.0 percent about the same period each year. Since the state rate was not then seasonally adjusted, the required increase of at least 20 percent over the levels of the two prior years was incorporated into the trigger mechanism so as to confine the extended benefit response to recession rather than to seasonal unemployment as well.

Financing provisions called for federal and state unemployment insurance funds to share extended benefit costs on a 50-50 basis.[15] The Federal Unemployment Tax was raised by 0.1 percent of taxable payrolls with proceeds to go into a new Extended Unemployment Compensation Account in the Unemployment Trust Fund, out of which the federal share is paid. A state's share is financed by its trust fund account. The state has the option of experience rating its extended benefit costs or pooling them uniformly among all covered employers. The federal fund also reimburses a state for half the cost of any regular benefits it pays a claimant beyond the twenty-sixth week during an extended benefit period, subject to the thirty-nine-week overall maximum.

The 1970 Act required all states to adopt the necessary extended benefit provisions to become effective by January 1972, but allowed them to start earlier if they chose. A total of twenty-two states did so as recession conditions emerged and spread, triggering on extended benefits, in a few cases as early as October 1970. The national trigger went on in January 1972. During 1971 and 1972, extended benefit outlays totaled over $1 billion, adding about 12 percent to total regular benefit outlays for these two years. In the recession of the mid-1970s, when benefits paid out were much heavier, extended benefits totaled about $2.5 billion in 1975 and $2.3 billion in 1976, about 22 percent of regular benefit outlays.[16] The federal extended benefit account had to borrow funds from the U.S. Treasury to help finance its share of these costs, and the Federal Unemployment Tax was increased by 0.2 percent of taxable payrolls to pay off the debt of this account.

Amendments to Relax Trigger Requirements in the 1970s

The changes made in the extended benefit program during the 1970s nearly all related to state triggers and tended to ease their restrictiveness. Those made in the 1980s were more drastic, affecting not only the triggers but also the program's basic structure and some of the conditions for benefit eligibility. These later changes served mainly to restrict the availability and outlays of benefits.

---

15. There is no federal sharing of extended benefits paid to state and local government workers as no federal tax is paid on the wages of these workers.

16. Based on data from *Unemployment Insurance Financial Data, 1938-1982.*

The first change applied to that part of the state trigger requiring that the current thirteen-week average insured unemployment rate be at least 20 percent higher than the corresponding average for the two prior years. In some states, high rates persisted well after the worst early recession months so that a year later, those early peak rates began to raise the prior two-year averages. In time, even though they continued high in many of these states, the current thirteen-week averages slipped below the 20 percent requirement and triggered off extended benefit periods. The higher two-year average base sometimes prevented extended benefits from triggering on when unemployment levels turned up again. To avoid these effects, Congress acted repeatedly to suspend this requirement temporarily, or to ease the combination of the two state trigger requirements. The first such action came in October 1972 and permitted the states to suspend the 120 percent requirement for triggering off until June 30, 1973.[17] Congress then allowed the states to continue that suspension for triggering both on and off until the end of 1973, but the state's current thirteen-week rate had to be at least 4.5 percent to trigger on. Congress continued the suspension through 1974 but dropped the required thirteen-week current rate back to the 4.0 percent minimum. This temporary suspension was renewed by Congress several times until late 1976. Beginning 1975, the states were also permitted to pay extended benefits if the national insured unemployment rate was 4.0 percent or more (P.L. 92-572). Finally, in October 1976, a permanent change was made allowing states to suspend the 120 percent requirement if their current thirteen-week average rate was at least 5.0 percent (P.L. 94-566). Most states adopted this option.

The October 1976 amendments also changed the basis of the national trigger from a 4.5 percent insured unemployment rate (seasonally adjusted) for three consecutive months to a current thirteen-week average, also seasonally adjusted, so as to coincide with the basis for the state trigger rate. The minimum off period of thirteen weeks under the national trigger was eliminated.

---

17. The first suspension of the 120 percent requirement came in P.L. 92-599 (October 1972).

Restrictive Amendments of 1980-1981

A number of changes made in 1980 restricted the outlays for extended benefits under certain circumstances. One limitation was to deny federal sharing of the first week of extended benefits if the claimant had not served a noncompensable waiting week for regular benefits (P.L. 96-499). Most states did apply a waiting week, but some had eliminated it; the amendment served as an incentive for the latter states to reestablish one.

Another restrictive approach taken was to impose federal standards to require the states to deny extended benefits to certain claimants. One prohibits payment of extended benefits, after the first two weeks, to a claimant who has filed an interstate claim from a state not currently in an extended benefit period (P.L. 96-364). Other standards require states to deny extended benefits to claimants who do not actively seek work, or who refuse to apply for or accept suitable work offers or referrals, provided that the refused job offer or referral is in writing or listed with the employment service (P.L. 96-499). Under the amendment, unless the claimant has good prospects for obtaining customary employment reasonably soon, "suitable work" means any work within the claimant's capabilities that pays at least the legal minimum wage or more than the weekly benefit amount. To avoid disqualification for failure to seek work, the claimant must furnish tangible evidence of a systematic and sustained effort to seek work each week for which a claim is made for extended benefits. This requirement is more demanding than the usual state work search rules for regular benefits. The disqualification for extended benefits for job refusal and failure to seek work applies for the duration of the claimant's unemployment and until the claimant has been reemployed at least four weeks, with earnings of at least four times the weekly benefit amount, and is again unemployed under qualifying conditions.

Another federal standard called for by the 1980 amendments requires states to deny extended benefits to claimants disqualified and denied regular benefits for voluntary leaving, misconduct discharge, or suitable work refusal if they had not disqualified such claimants for the duration of their unemployment and required them to satisfy a minimum reemployment test (P.L. 96-499). Most states had adopted the latter type of disqualification for regular benefits, but some still imposed a temporary suspension instead. After 1980, more states moved toward the duration disqualification in their regular benefit provisions. Claimants denied benefits for the same reasons while drawing extended benefits are also subject to the duration disqualification and a reemployment test.

Several amendments adopted in 1981 went much further in restricting the availability of extended benefits by modifications of the trigger requirements and calculations (P.L. 97-35). The most significant change was to eliminate provisions to pay extended benefits on a nationwide basis. Since August 1981, only state triggers have controlled the start and termination of extended benefit periods. In addition, the count of the insured unemployed used in determining each state's trigger rate was revised so that it no longer included, as it had previously, claimants filing for extended and supplemental unemployment benefits. The effect of their exclusion from the calculation was a lower rate, especially after extended benefit periods had begun, tending to terminate such periods sooner. Only claimants of regular benefits are counted. Another change raised the trigger points needed to begin and terminate a state extended benefit period. The thirteen-week average insured unemployment rate required to trigger on extended benefits was increased from a 4.0 percent minimum to a 5.0 percent minimum. The option to disregard the comparison between the current and the prior two-year rates was made to depend on a 6.0 percent minimum current rate rather than 5.0 percent. The effect was to begin extended benefit periods later and terminate them sooner, or to fall short of triggering on at all.

Yet another amendment adopted in 1981 set a separate federal minimum qualifying requirement for extended benefits at twenty weeks of base-period employment, or the equivalent in a minimum base-period earnings measure (forty times the weekly benefit amount or one-and-one-half times high-quarter earnings). Previously, state qualifying requirements applied, many of which were less stringent. This amendment took effect in September 1982.

Most, though not all of these changes and restrictions were fully implemented throughout 1982; by 1983, all were in effect. Some idea of how these changes affected extended benefit experience may be gained from data in table 9.2, which compares such experience for 1975 and 1976 with that for 1982 and 1983. Both 1975 and 1982 were

Table 9.2   Comparison of Extended Benefit Experience in 1975-1976 and 1982-1983, United States

Item	1975	1976	Percent change 1975 to 1976	1982	1983	Percent change 1982 to 1983
Total unemployment rate (percent)	8.3	7.7	-7	9.5	9.5	0
Insured unemployment rate (percent)	6.1	4.4	-28	4.7	3.9	-17
Benefit outlays (millions)						
Regular benefits	$11,754	$8,973	-24	$20,358	$17,720	-13
Extended benefits	2,494	2,298	-8	2,455	1,767	-28
Average extended weekly benefit amount	$66	$70	6	$121	$129	7
Exhaustions of regular benefits (thousands)	4,195	3,270	-22	4,175	4,180	a
Extended benefit first payments (thousands)	4,012	3,253	-19	2,193	1,402	-36

SOURCES: *Unemployment Insurance Financial Data, 1938-1982*, and annual supplement for 1983.
a. Less than 0.5 percent increase.

severe recession years. Total unemployment showed some improvement in 1976 but not in 1983; insured unemployment was down in both these years from previous year highs. The major contrast between the two recession periods is seen in extended benefit outlays and first payments. While the number exhausting regular benefits was about 4.2 million in 1975 and 1982, the number who began drawing extended benefits in 1982 was only a little more than half the exhaustee count compared with over 95 percent in 1975. Extended benefit outlays in 1982 were somewhat below 1975 levels, even though the average weekly amount paid was 83 percent higher in the later year. Extended benefit first payments and outlays fell off substantially more, in proportion, from 1982 to 1983 than from 1975 to 1976 even as regular benefit exhaustions totaled about the same in each of the two later years, compared with a 22 percent decline from 1975 to 1976. The statutory changes adopted in the early 1980s had cut back the extended benefit program significantly.

Federal Supplementation
of Unemployment Benefits

Since the enactment of the federal-state extended benefit program in 1970, each recession except that in 1980 has been the occasion for the provision of additional weeks of benefit support through temporary emergency federal programs. The heavy long-term unemployment at such times resulted in hundreds of thousands of jobless workers exhausting both their regular and extended benefits, many with little or no further means of financial assistance available. Simply waiting for a recovery of uncertain strength and timing to solve the problem was generally unacceptable. Each of the three supplemental programs adopted during these years had significant differences from one another, but all had certain features in common. They were temporary, wholly federally financed, provided compensation for weeks of unemployment beyond the thirty-ninth week, and were tied in one way or another to state insured unemployment rates as triggers. The states administered the programs as agents for the federal government and, except as specified otherwise in the federal law, the regular state eligibility and benefit provisions applied.

Emergency Unemployment Compensation Act of 1971

With extended benefits triggered on in almost half the states during 1971, exhaustions of these benefits began to mount late in the year spurring the enactment of the emergency legislation (P.L. 92-224). The Act provided another 50 percent of the individual's regular benefit entitlement up to thirteen more weeks for an overall maximum of fifty-two weeks for all benefits. These added benefits became payable when a state's specially computed unemployment rate averaged 6.5 percent or more over a thirteen-week period. This rate was calculated by adding together the state's insured unemployment rate, as computed for the federal-state extended benefit program, and an exhaustion rate, representing one-fourth of the total number exhausting regular benefits in the state during the last twelve calendar months taken as a percent of the state's average monthly covered employment. Originally planned to operate for only the first half of 1972, the program was extended through March 1973 (P.L. 92-329). The added benefits were to be financed out of the federal Extended Unemployment Compensation Account with U.S. Treasury advances to that account providing the necessary funds. When the program was extended beyond June 1972, an increase of 0.08 percent of 1973 taxable payrolls was added to the Federal Unemployment Tax to pay for the resulting further costs of the temporary compensation.

A varying number of states paid the temporary emergency compensation at different times during 1972 and early 1973—up to nineteen states in late June 1972. Because of differences between the triggers used for extended benefits and the emergency compensation, some states had triggered off extended benefits because their trigger rates failed to meet the 120 percent requirement, but they did pay the emergency compensation to claimants who exhausted their regular benefits. More than one million claimants drew over $500 million in these added benefits during 1972, more than paid out in extended benefits that year and equal to about 10 percent of all regular benefits paid in 1972.[18]

Federal Supplemental Benefits, 1975-1977

Recession, long-term unemployment, and benefit exhaustions reemerged as serious problems in late 1974 prompting Congress to pass another Emergency Unemployment Compensation Act at the end of that year (P.L. 93-572). Like its predecessor, this Act also provided for added benefits up to 50 percent of regular entitlement, with a thirteen-week limit and an overall fifty-two-week maximum. Unlike the earlier program, the supplemental benefits were payable only to exhaustees of both regular and extended benefits, and only when extended benefits were payable. Federal Treasury advances to the Extended Unemployment Compensation Account provided the funds needed. The advances were to be repaid out of future unemployment tax revenue allocations. The program was to run through March 1977.

Amendments changed the program several times before it finally expired. One amendment, adopted in March 1975 (P.L. 94-12), doubled the duration of supplemental benefits by allowing up to twenty-six added weeks and sixty-five weeks in all. This increase, applicable at first only for the next six months, was extended for the rest of 1975 by further legislation enacted in June (P.L. 94-45). That amendment also specified an added state trigger requirement for federal supplemental benefits starting in 1976. The state trigger rate had to be at least 5.0 percent; if it was less than 6.0 percent, up to thirteen weeks of supplemental benefits were payable; if 6.0 percent or more, up to twenty-six weeks were payable. In April 1977, a last-minute extension passed to continue the program through January 1978, but it reduced the maximum from twenty-six to thirteen weeks of supplemental benefits (P.L. 95-10). Moreover, all remaining costs incurred under the program were financed directly by general revenues and not by the Unemployment Trust Fund. These amendments also established special job search and disqualification rules applicable to claimants of federal supplemental benefits so that failure to actively seek work or refusal of suitable

---

18. For a summary of the experience under the temporary emergency unemployment compensation program of 1971, see Murray (1974, pp. 37-39).

work, as defined for the purpose, would discontinue eligibility for these benefits.

The federal supplemental benefits program paid out over $6 billion during the 1975-77 period, almost as much as paid out by the extended benefit program in these years. They accounted for about 15 percent of all benefit outlays of the regular, extended, and supplemental programs combined for this period. Over 2 million claimants began drawing supplemental benefits in each of the first two years, and about 1.2 million did so in 1977.[19]

Federal Supplemental Compensation, 1982-1985

No supplemental program was adopted during the brief and less widespread recession of 1980. The 1982 recession period was well advanced before another temporary program of added benefits was enacted in September 1982 (P.L. 97-248). The Federal Supplemental Compensation program established then was quite different from its predecessors. It was more complex in design, circumscribed by more special eligibility requirements, and it was to be amended much more often. Its costs were financed entirely by federal general revenues.

At the outset, supplemental compensation was payable for up to six, eight, or ten additional weeks, depending on the level of the state's extended benefit trigger rate. Half of a claimant's regular duration, but only up to ten weeks, could be paid to claimants who exhausted their benefits in states that triggered on extended benefits any time after May 1982. The minimum rate to trigger on extended benefits was 5.0 percent by then. In other states, up to eight weeks of supplemental benefits were payable if the state's extended benefit trigger rate was at least 3.5 percent for three consecutive weeks, and six weeks of benefits were payable elsewhere. Thus, some federal supplemental compensation was payable everywhere, regardless of whether extended benefits were also payable.

The changes made in the federal-state shared extended benefit program with regard to how the insured unemployment rate was calculated and to eligibility rules applied here as well. To be eligible for federal supplemental compensation, a claimant must have worked for

---

19. Based on data in National Commission on Unemployment Compensation (1980, pp. 60-61, tables 2 and 3).

at least twenty weeks during the base period, or had the equivalent in earnings. Similarly, the requirements adopted in 1981 for extended benefits relating to active job search and refusal of suitable work offers or referrals were applied to supplemental compensation, as were the disqualifications imposed. The program, as first enacted, was to run through March 1983. As with the previous federal supplemental benefit programs, subsequent amendments extended its life well beyond the original expiration date.

The first significant change made in the program came a few months after it began. An amendment adopted in December 1982 raised the amount of supplemental compensation payable from 50 percent to 65 percent of the claimant's regular benefit entitlement up to maximums ranging from eight weeks to sixteen weeks, instead of six to ten weeks (P.L. 97-424). In a state that had triggered on extended benefits, the maximum supplement could be as high as sixteen weeks if its insured unemployment trigger rate was at least 6.0 percent, making the maximum for all benefits combined a total of fifty-five weeks. In a state with no extended benefits triggered on and a rate below 3.5 percent, the maximum supplement was eight weeks, making its overall duration limit thirty-four weeks, assuming its regular duration maximum at twenty-six weeks. Three other maximum levels of supplemental compensation applied between these two extremes for intermediate trigger rate thresholds. The amended structure became effective in January 1983. No change was made in the program's March 1983 expiration date at this time.

Amendments adopted a few months later extended the program through September 1983 (P.L. 98-21). Whether a state had triggered on extended benefits was eliminated as a factor determining the maximum amount of supplemental compensation allowed; only the level of the trigger rate was to govern. The maximum level of sixteen weeks was dropped; the maximum range then ran from eight to fourteen weeks, depending on the trigger rate.

Early in October 1983, Congress extended the program for a few weeks until it could determine its final positions regarding several other changes (P.L. 98-92). It did so near the end of that month, at which time the Federal Supplemental Compensation Program was extended for a year and a half, through March 1985 (P.L. 98-135). The existing structure involving maximums of eight, ten, twelve, or fourteen weeks, depending on the level of the state extended benefit trigger rate was retained. The amendments added a new element to the design, however, based on a long-term average rate. If the state's insured unemployment rate since January 1, 1982 averaged at least 4.5 but less than 5.5 percent, the maximum supplemental weeks payable would be twelve weeks, regardless of that state's current rate. If it averaged at least 5.5 percent, the maximum would be fourteen weeks. A claimant's individual entitlement to supplemental compensation remained unchanged once established, and the maximum for a state could not change more than once every thirteen weeks. All claimants who exhausted supplemental compensation between April 1, 1983 and mid-October 1983 were eligible for five more weeks of such benefits if still unemployed, regardless of the state's trigger rate; fewer added weeks were available to previously eligible claimants who exhausted after mid-October 1983.

The program was finally allowed to expire in March 1985.[20] During its existence, it paid out a total of more than $9.3 billion in supplemental compensation. Most was disbursed ($6.7 billion) from the program's beginning in September 1982 through the end of 1983 while the nation's unemployment rate continued to range well above 8.0 percent.[21] It is ironic that as amendments restricted the permanent extended benefit program in the 1980s, federal supplemental compensation continued to be paid to exhaustees of regular benefits. During 1983, supplemental compensation outlays totaled more than three times those of extended benefits. By the closing months of 1983, only Puerto Rico and West Virginia were paying extended benefits. In 1984, the supplemental program continued to pay out a total of about $2.3 billion, while outlays of extended benefits, payable in only a few states, came to about $43 million (*Unemployment Insurance Financial Data 1938-1982*). One result of the extended benefit program restrictions and the provision of federal supplemental compensation was to

---

20. Claimants already qualified for supplemental compensation before March 31 were permitted to draw on their remaining entitlement during the three-month phaseout period ending June 30, 1985.

21. Corson, Grossman, and Nicholson (1986, p. 24, Table 113). The total of $9.3 billion cited in the text omits a small amount paid during the calendar quarter following the program's termination in March 1985 when claimants were permitted with previously established entitlement to draw remaining benefits if eligible.

shift much of the cost of long-term support from employer taxes to general revenues.

Federal Standards

The period after 1969 saw a rising number of federal requirements imposed on state unemployment insurance laws. Many of them affected their regular eligibility and disqualification provisions. Other requirements, as already noted, were added to the federal-state extended benefit program and to the later temporary federal supplemental benefit or compensation programs; they superceded regular state provisions which otherwise applied for these programs. Administration-backed federal minimum standards for the regular weekly benefit amount, similar to those advanced in the mid-1960s, were proposed in 1975 but were turned aside.

This section reviews the more significant of these new federal requirements applied to regular state laws, apart from those related to financing which are covered in the following section. The few federal program standards adopted before the 1970s or contained in the original law were designed primarily to protect the rights of claimants or to expand the protection provided against wage loss. Those adopted since have included several that are restrictive in nature, aimed at eliminating or reducing benefit entitlement in certain circumstances which came more and more to be regarded as of questionable validity or the result of abuse. These matters have been extremely controversial. An important factor that helped to overcome resistance to such restrictive standards was the cost-reduction imperative to which both state unemployment insurance fund insolvency and federal budget deficits gave increasing force in the Congress.

Coverage Standards

These were noted earlier in the section describing federal extensions of coverage. Since the Federal Unemployment Tax was not applied to nonprofit organizations or to state and local government, coverage of their employees was accomplished by making it a requirement for state law. Failure to meet the requirement would sacrifice federal approval of the law as the basis for the credit offset allowed against the Federal Unemployment Tax for all other employers in the state who are subject to it.

The other significant standard adopted in relation to coverage extension required states to deny benefits to professional school personnel between terms if they had a contract or other assurance for resuming employment in the next term. Its application was broadened as coverage of school personnel broadened. It was amended to apply for holiday and other recess periods as well as between academic terms. Finally, in 1983, the benefit-denial requirement was made mandatory for all school employees, including nonprofessional staff, a matter previously left to each state to decide for itself.[22]

Protective Standards

Several standards adopted with the 1970 amendments aimed at protecting or enhancing the unemployed worker's benefit entitlement. One of these represented an important shift of policy reflecting the growing emphasis placed on training for the unemployed throughout the previous decade. In general, an unemployment insurance claimant who entered school or a formal training program was held to be unavailable for work and denied benefits on that ground. The new federal standard prohibited states from denying benefits to claimants because they were taking training if the training was approved by the state agency.

Another standard adopted in 1970 ruled out state provisions that cancel or eliminate all benefit rights of a claimant because of a disqualifying act, except for a work misconduct discharge, fraud related to the claim, or receipt of disqualifying income. A number of states had provisions that totally cancelled benefit rights in the case of disqualifications for voluntary leaving or refusal of suitable work. Since the federal prohibition, several states have provided for cancellation of all but a minimal amount of benefits, such as one week, in these cases.

One standard from the 1970 amendments outlawed state provisions that reduce or deny benefits when claimants have filed interstate claims, and another required all states to participate in interstate plans for combining wage or employment credits of a claimant who worked

---

22. This option was restored to the states by legislation adopted by 1991 (see Epilogue).

in more than one state in a base period. These requirements eliminated discriminatory practices in several states that penalized interstate claimants and multistate workers. A standard adopted in the 1976 amendments prohibited states from denying benefits solely on the basis of pregnancy, as some state provisions did. The Supreme Court had ruled against such provisions.[23]

Restrictive Standards

The 1970 amendments included a prohibition against paying benefits in a new benefit year to a claimant who had no employment since the start of the preceding benefit year. The problem addressed was one which can arise in a state with a lag between the start of a benefit year and the end of the relevant base period. Most states have such a lag, lasting from one to two calendar quarters. Employment and wages in the lag period can be sufficient to qualify a claimant for benefits in a second benefit year without further employment. Where allowed, such cases were criticized as the "double dip." The standard required states to specify some minimum employment beyond the lag period to qualify for benefits.

Several other restrictive standards were adopted with the 1976 amendments. One required states to deny benefits to professional athletes between playing seasons if they have reasonable assurance of reemployment. Another prohibited the payment of benefits to aliens not legally admitted into the country or not legally permitted to work when admitted. The need for these two standards does not appear to have been established at the time. Considering the administrative burdens they entail for the states, if properly enforced, and the potential inequities that can result, their value is in some doubt.[24]

A third and more significant standard first specified in the 1976 amendments, and later modified, required the states to reduce a claimant's weekly benefit amount by the amount of certain pension income received, as prorated on a weekly basis. The treatment of pensions by unemployment insurance had been a longstanding issue for the pro-

---

23. *Mary Ann Turner v. Department of Employment Security and Board of Review of the Industrial Commission of Utah,* 96 S. CT. 249 (1975).

24. For a further discussion of these and other restrictive standards, see Rubin (1983, pp. 83-94).

gram, both as to whether and how to take account of them.[25] The application of this standard was postponed and then amended in 1980 before taking effect (P.L. 96-364). It requires the states, as a minimum, to reduce the weekly unemployment benefit by the prorated weekly amount of any pension received by a claimant if the pension was based on employment by a base-period employer and financed wholly or in part by that employer. While the required reduction also applies for Social Security and Railroad Retirement pensions received, the condition restricting the reduction to pensions related to base-period employers does not apply. States have the option to adjust the amount of the pension deducted from the unemployment benefit by taking account of contributions made toward the pension by the claimant.

Financing Legislation

Unemployment insurance financing was a major concern of Congress in the 1970s and 1980s, especially from 1975 on. That concern arose largely over two problems. One was the shortage of federal revenues produced by the net Federal Unemployment Tax to meet the cost responsibilities of the federal partner in the system. The other was the spreading and deepening insolvency of state benefit reserve funds and their increasing dependence on advances from the federal loan fund. Legislative proposals in these areas grew to an almost constant stream, many of them representing efforts to obtain relief for states in the most serious financial difficulty. Proposals enacted did address the federal revenue shortage, at least until the next crisis. Legislation which dealt with loan and repayment requirements blended some relief with pressure on states to initiate significant improvements of their own financial conditions. This section summarizes federal legislation enacted during the period in both these areas and a few other changes.

Federal Unemployment Tax Revenues

By the end of the 1960s, it was apparent that administrative costs of the program, swollen by inflation, were outstripping their federal

---

25. For an early treatment of this issue, see Murray (1967).

source of funding. Although the Federal Unemployment Tax rate was increased in 1960 by 0.1 percentage point to help relieve a similar strain at that time, the fixed tax base and inflation combined to renew the problem later in the decade. The adoption in 1970 of the federal-state extended benefit program added new federal cost obligations.

The 1970 amendments included an increase in both the tax rate and the taxable wage base to resolve the problem. The rate was raised from 3.1 to 3.2 percent, increasing the net federal tax retained from 0.4 to 0.5 percent of taxable payrolls. The rate increase was made effective in 1970, and its proceeds for 1970 and 1971 were allocated entirely to the new extended benefit account in the Unemployment Trust Fund. After 1971, 10 percent of net federal tax revenues were to be so allocated. The taxable wage base was raised to $4,200, effective 1972. It was the first change from the $3,000 base since 1940. The impact of this increase was also felt by state tax structures, since all but five states had wage bases for their own taxes below $4,200 in 1971, most at $3,000. In that year, only somewhat more than 45 percent of total covered payrolls were taxable by the states, a proportion that rose to almost 52 percent with the tax base increase in 1972. Between these two years, taxable payrolls expanded by about 29 percent, compared to a 13 percent increase in total payrolls.[26]

Since many states adopted and triggered on extended benefits in late 1970 and 1971, and all states were paying extended benefits in 1972, the federal extended benefit account had no chance to build up a reserve. Repayable U.S. Treasury advances from general revenues into this account were required to cover the costs of the added temporary emergency benefits, also financed from this account. In June 1972, when the emergency benefit program was extended to run beyond June and into 1973, the Federal Unemployment Tax was raised by 0.08 percent of taxable payrolls, for 1973 only, to pay for the resulting additional benefit costs (P.L. 92-329). The advances covering the temporary emergency benefits paid earlier were to be repaid out of Federal Unemployment Tax revenues if any remained after all prescribed allocations were made to the extended benefit, loan, and administration accounts, a prospect that seemed quite remote at the time.

---

26. Based on data in *Unemployment Insurance Financial Data 1938-1982.*

The continuing inflation and the recession of the mid-1970s put further strains on Federal Unemployment Tax revenues. By late 1974, the extended benefit account had accumulated some reserves, but also carried about $600 million in debt for advances made to cover emergency benefits paid earlier. The drains of extended benefits in the mid-1970s, along with the costs of another temporary federal supplemental benefit program, required substantial additional advances from general revenues into the extended benefit account. More advances were also flowing into the loan fund, which had been exhausted by the heavy borrowing by insolvent state funds. Rising administrative costs were again becoming hard to cover from existing federal tax revenue allocations.

The 1976 amendments attempted to resolve these problems by raising again both the tax rate and the taxable wage base. The rate increase was 0.2, effective 1977, with proceeds going into the extended benefit account. With this increase, the net federal tax was 0.7 percent of taxable payrolls, including 0.25 percent allocated to the extended benefit account. When all advances owed by this account were repaid, the 0.2 rate increase was to terminate. The taxable wage base was lifted from $4,200 to $6,000, effective 1978. In 1976, over half the states had a $4,200 base for their own taxes; the base was $6,000 or more in fifteen states. The ratio of taxable to total wages had declined since 1972 to about 46 percent (*Unemployment Insurance Financial Data 1938-1982*). The 1976 amendments also modified loan fund provisions, to be discussed below.

More inflation and a return of recession conditions in 1980 again eroded the adequacy of Federal Unemployment Tax revenues. The response came in 1982, with another rise in both the rate and tax base (P.L. 97-248). The rate increased by 0.1 which made the net federal tax rate 0.8 percent, including the temporary 0.2 increase adopted in 1976 for extended benefits. The taxable wage base was raised from $6,000 to $7,000. Both increases became effective in 1983. The changes also provided that 40 percent of the net federal tax be allocated to the extended benefit account. The 1982 legislation, in addition, specified a major change in the gross Federal Unemployment Tax rate and in the tax credit provisions, effective 1985. These mainly affect experience rating and are described below.

The next action affecting Federal Unemployment Tax revenues came near the close of 1987. In May of that year, the debt owed to the U.S. Treasury by the extended benefit account was finally repaid in full. The 0.2 percent addition to the federal tax, adopted in 1976 to help repay this debt, was therefore due to terminate at the end of 1987. The Budget Reconciliation Act of 1987, however, extended this tax component for three more years—through 1990 (P.L. 100-203). The continued added revenues were to bolster further the reserve accounts accumulated for extended benefits and loan funds against the potential demands of the next recession. A major motivation for retaining these revenues, however, was to help offset some of the current federal budget deficit. Besides equally dividing the revenues of the continued 0.2 percent tax component between the extended benefit and loan accounts, the Act altered the allocation of the permanent 0.6 percent net federal tax. The share going into the administration account, from which appropriations are made to cover the program's administrative costs, was raised from 60 to 90 percent; the share to the extended benefit account was reduced from 40 to 10 percent. Additionally, the ceilings on the extended benefit and loan accounts were increased substantially.[27]

Loan and Repayment Provisions

By 1969, the loan fund had built up to its current statutory ceiling of $550 million. No loans had been drawn under the revised provisions adopted in 1960, and all prior loans had been repaid. Borrowing began in 1972; the loans were interest free. Only three states drew loans before 1975, but that year a total of sixteen states did so. The loan fund was soon exhausted, but was replenished as needed by U.S. Treasury advances. Through the end of 1979, twenty-five states had borrowed more than $5.6 billion; at that time, thirteen states still owed about $3.8 billion (National Commission on Unemployment Compensation 1980, p. 96; *Unemployment Insurance Financial Data 1938-1982*).

---

27. Each account's ceiling had been set at 0.125 percent of total wages. The extended benefit account ceiling was raised to three times that level (0.375 percent), and the loan fund ceiling made five times higher (0.625 percent). Total covered payrolls in 1987 exceeded $1.7 trillion; the new ceilings thus came to about $6.4 billion and $10.6 billion, respectively, at that time.

Repayment provisions called for a reduction in the federal tax credit allowed to employers in a state that had not repaid a loan in two to three years after it was made.[28] The reduction applied each year the debt remained unpaid and the amount of the reduction was progressive—0.3 percent of taxable payrolls the first year, 0.6 the second year, 0.9 the third year, and so on. In addition, in the third and fourth years of tax credit reduction, the tax credit was to be further reduced by the amount, if any, by which the state's average tax rate fell short of the 2.7 percent level. In later years, other added tax credit reductions were to apply if the state had not stepped up its own tax rates adequately to match past cost rates. (These further reductions were later waived if the state met certain criteria.) The resulting additional federal tax paid went to reduce the state's debt.

The first tax credit reduction applied to 1974 taxable payrolls in Connecticut, which had initially borrowed in 1972. An amendment of the repayment provision in 1975 allowed a temporary three-year deferral of the tax credit reduction if the state met certain criteria prescribed by the Secretary of Labor designed to promote fund solvency.[29] The temporary deferral applied for tax credit reductions that were due for the years 1975 through 1977. In 1977, the deferral provision was extended for another two years (P.L. 95-19).

After some improvement in state benefit reserves in the late 1970s (only three states borrowed relatively small amounts in 1979), another surge in borrowing began in 1980 and continued heavily for several years. By mid-1983, twenty-nine states owed a total of more than $13 billion (USDOL, Employment and Training Administration, August 1983a, p. 12).

The temporary deferrals of tax credit reductions provided for the late 1970s had expired. A number of states in the meantime had liquidated their earlier debt from accumulated reserves. Others began repayment through reduced tax credits. In 1981, Congress amended the repayment process to offer some relief to debtor-state employers from the ever-mounting federal tax in return for greater state effort to restore

---

28. If not repaid by November 10 of the second calendar year following the year in which the loan was made, the tax credit reduction applied for that second year.

29. P.L. 94-45, adopted June 1975. To qualify for the deferral, the state's average tax rate, as a percent of total payrolls, had to exceed the average benefit cost rate of the preceding ten years, and the minimum tax rate had to be at least 1.0 percent. 58. P.L. 95-19, adopted April 1977.

solvency (P.L. 97-35). The new provision allowed a state to avert continuing larger reductions in the tax credit after the second year of reduction in any year that the state satisfied specified conditions with respect to its tax effort and debt position. A state could thus "cap" the reduction at 0.6 or at a higher level if it met those conditions. Temporary at first, this capping provision was made permanent by subsequent amendments.

Also in the 1981 legislation, loan provisions were amended so that loans made after March 1981 were subject to interest.[30] The interest rate was 10 percent, or that paid by the U.S. Treasury on positive state accounts, if less. Payment of interest may not be made directly from state benefit reserves, or indirectly through manipulation of the state's unemployment insurance tax rates. This prohibition is a federal standard with which a state must conform or lose certification of approval of its unemployment insurance law. Loans made before April 1981 remained interest-free. The repayments made through federal tax credit reductions or from state reserves in place of the credit reduction are applied first to the oldest loans outstanding.[31]

Amendments adopted in 1982 and 1983 included provisions allowing a state to defer a major part of interest due and pay it in installments. Under one provision, a state could do so if its insured unemployment rate, as used to trigger on extended benefits, averaged at least 7.5 percent for the first six months of the calendar year preceding the interest due date (P.L. 97-248). If qualified, a state can pay as little as 25 percent of the interest when due and another 25 percent in each of the next three calendar years. This provision represented a permanent change in the interest-payment rules. Other amendments added another option applicable only during fiscal years 1983, 1984, and 1985 which allowed a state to defer 80 percent of the interest due, to be paid subsequently in four equal installments, and to obtain a discounted interest rate if it undertook certain measures and achieved

---

30. No interest applied on loans made after that date if they were repaid before October 1 of the same year in which they were made, provided no further borrowing occurred during the last quarter of the year; these are so-called cash-flow loans.

31. P.L. 97-248, adopted September 1982, gave a state the option, under certain conditions, of making a repayment equivalent to the amount of the tax credit reduction out of its own reserves, including those raised through experience rated taxes, instead of through a uniform net federal tax increase.

results in improving fund solvency as specified.[32] The amendments also allowed a state, as a temporary option, to defer interest due up to nine months if its recent annual average total unemployment rate was at least 13.5 percent. The amendments of 1982 and 1983 provided, also on a temporary basis, further conditions for capping tax credit reductions or for limiting an added tax credit loss to a partial reduction; the earlier capping provisions were made permanent. Gradual recovery of the economy after 1983 and the absence of further recession during the rest of the 1980s enabled the states to liquidate their accumulated debt and to bring about some rebuilding of their reserves. Federal legislation in this area finally subsided.

Other Financing Changes

In 1970, when significant extensions of coverage were enacted, the federal requirements for experience rating were amended to allow states to assign tax rates as low as 1 percent to newly covered employers on a "reasonable basis" other than individual experience. Those initial rates apply until the employers are subject to the state law long enough to qualify for rates based on their experience.

A major change, adopted in 1982 and made effective in 1985, was to raise the gross Federal Unemployment Tax rate from 3.5 to 6.2 percent (P.L. 97-248). The maximum credit allowed for state unemployment insurance taxes, including the additional credit for experience rating reductions, was increased to 5.4 percent, doubling the previous maximum credit of 2.7 percent. The net federal tax remained at 0.8 percent, including the temporary 0.2 percent segment imposed to repay general revenue advances to the extended benefit account. With the maximum tax credit set at 5.4 percent, any state tax rate assigned to employers below that level must be set on the basis of experience rating. Thus, no maximum state tax rate may be less than 5.4 percent. As of 1983, the majority of the states could assign maximum tax rates below that level.[33] This change was made largely to force those states to raise the

---

32. P.L. 98-21, adopted April 1983. This law also made the failure to pay interest when and as due grounds for withholding approval of the state for administrative grants.

33. USDOL, Employment and Training Administration (1983b, pp. 2-39 to 2-42, Table 206). Under the most favorable tax schedules, maximum rates were under 5.4 percent in 36 states; under their least favorable schedules, maximum rates were below 5.4 percent in 27 states.

upper limits of their rate schedules and thereby encourage a potential source of added revenues for state funds. Another intended result was to broaden the application of experience rating and increase the share of the benefit cost burden borne by high-cost employers.

Authority to use surplus Federal Unemployment Tax revenues that were distributed to the states in the 1950s, as provided by the Reed Act of 1954, was scheduled to expire in the early 1970s. These funds were available to cover administrative and benefit costs. Authority for continued use of these funds was extended until 1983 by legislation adopted in 1971 and for another 10 years by 1982 legislation (P.L. 92-224 and P.L. 97-248).

Reinsurance Proposals

When financial crisis became a dominant theme in unemployment insurance in the mid-1970s, proposals for reinsurance and cost equalization schemes emerged. Because so many state funds experienced insolvency, these ideas aroused considerable debate and more serious interest than usual. A major development was a plan advanced by the Interstate Conference of Employment Security Agencies. Several other plans were put forward during the late 1970s. All of these ideas varied in their mix of reinsurance and cost equalization elements, in the degree of national pooling provided, and in the mechanisms to be applied to determine a state's eligibility for a reinsurance or equalization grant, and the amount of the grant. Some of these schemes found their way into legislative proposals.[34] None, however, attained sufficient support to be enacted. Interest in the subject waned in the early 1980s, despite the continued financial crisis.

Other Federal Legislation

Some of the changes adopted in the 1970s and 1980s affected unemployment insurance in ways different from those noted. Several of

---

34. The most prominent bills were introduced by Congressman William Brodhead of Michigan in 1977 (H.R. 8292) and 1979 (H.R. 3937) and by Senator Jacob Javits of New York, also in 1977 (S. 1853) and 1979 (S. 825).

these are significant and are summarized here more or less in the chronological order of the legislation enacted.

Judicial Review

The 1970 Employment Security Amendments allowed states to appeal to the courts a decision by the Secretary of Labor holding a state unemployment insurance law out of conformity with federal requirements. Heretofore, the Secretary's ruling was final. A state may now carry its case to the U.S. Court of Appeals and beyond to the Supreme Court.

Revised Advisory Council

The 1970 amendments also replaced the Federal Advisory Council on Employment Security by two separate councils, one on unemployment insurance and the other on the employment service. While they functioned during the 1970s, they had little or no impact on these programs. Although some new council members were appointed after the Reagan administration took office in 1981, the Council never met and, in time, simply ceased to function.

National Commission

The 1976 Unemployment Compensation Amendments authorized the establishment of a National Commission on Unemployment Compensation to review the program and make recommendations. Such a comprehensive study had been urged for many years. The Commission was appointed in 1978, some members by the President and others by the Speaker of the House of Representatives and the President Pro Tempore of the Senate. Wilbur J. Cohen served as Chairman. The Commission issued its final report in mid-1980 when a new recession had emerged. The report expressed deep concern about the current and future soundness of the state unemployment insurance reserve funds and of the federal loan fund. More generally it recommended that "government, business, and labor work cooperatively to develop and implement political, monetary, fiscal, and other economic policies that will reduce unemployment" (National Commission on Unemployment Compensation 1980, pp. xii-xiii).

Taxing Unemployment Benefits

Legislation enacted in 1978 amended the personal income tax provisions of the Internal Revenue Code to include unemployment insurance received in adjusted gross income for tax purposes if the claimant's family income was at least $25,000, or at least $20,000 if the claimant filed as a single individual (P.L. 95-600). In 1982, these income thresholds were lowered to $18,000 and $12,000, respectively (P.L. 97-248). The Tax Reform Act of 1986 eliminated the thresholds altogether (P.L. 99-514).

Deduction of Child Support

A 1981 amendment requires state unemployment insurance agencies to deduct and withhold from unemployment benefits paid to a claimant amounts owed by that individual for child support. The amounts owed are those agreed to by the claimant or specified as legally obligated by the state or local child support enforcement agency (P.L. 97-35). Withheld amounts are forwarded to that agency.

Restrictions on Unemployment Compensation for Ex-servicemembers (UCX)

As part of the move to tighten benefit eligibility and reduce benefit outlays, federal legislation adopted in 1981 and 1982 included changes affecting the UCX program. An amendment in the Omnibus Budget Reconciliation Act of 1981, adopted August 1981 (P.L. 97-35), disqualified claimants for UCX if they terminated their military service after a period of enlistment instead of reenlisting when they were eligible to do so. Such terminations were treated as equivalent to voluntary leaving without good cause. The application of this new rule, however, made clear that some service personnel who chose not to reenlist after having completed several periods of duty in order to pursue a civilian career were financially disadvantaged by the benefit denial when they needed time to find suitable civilian employment.

The next year, Congress returned to UCX with several amendments in the Miscellaneous Revenue Act of 1982, enacted October 1982 (P.L. 97-362). One amendment, in effect, eliminated the disqualification provision adopted in 1981 for UCX benefits of service personnel choosing not to reenlist. Another specified a noncompensatory waiting period of four weeks following the week in which the UCX claimant's service termination occurred. A third amendment limited the maximum duration of benefits payable to UCX claimants to thirteen weeks, including extended benefits or any federal supplemental unemployment benefits. These last two amendments were repealed nine years later (see Epilogue).

Work Sharing

A special provision enacted in 1982 undertook to encourage and assist states in adopting short-time compensation or work sharing benefits through their unemployment insurance laws (P.L. 97-248). The federal provision called for the Department of Labor to develop model legislation and otherwise assist states wishing to provide such benefits, and to evaluate experience. The objective was to augment or change existing partial benefit provisions of state laws to permit the payment of reduced weekly benefits to workers placed on reduced weekly work schedules pursuant to agreed plans designed to avoid full layoffs. The proportionate reduction in the weekly benefit amount would generally correspond with the proportionate reduction in normal weekly hours of work. Several states have adopted work sharing which is widely used in other countries. An evaluation of the experience was reported in 1986. The findings were not encouraging. The evaluation concluded that work sharing led to more, not less, unemployment, as employers used the work sharing provision to reduce further their effective workforces (Kerachsky, Nicholson, and Hershey 1986).

Health Insurance for the Unemployed

A provision, adopted in 1983, represents a very limited response to the problem of the termination of job-related health insurance of workers following layoff. Loss of such insurance by unemployed workers grows to serious proportions during recessions and generates legislative proposals to extend, preserve, or replace this important form of group protection. In many, perhaps most cases, the worker's family is also left unprotected. The lost health insurance is much more expensive to purchase on an individual basis than on a group basis. Legislative proposals made after the mid-1970s recession attracted substantial but insufficient support. They were in the forefront again with the 1982 slump. The provision enacted in 1983 merely permits states to deduct amounts from unemployment insurance benefits, as elected by claimants, to pay for health insurance premiums under plans approved by the Secretary of Labor (P.L. 98-21).

Required Reporting of Quarterly Wages

Information available in state employment security agency records about workers and unemployment insurance claimants can be useful in the administration of other federal or federally funded programs, such as Aid to Families with Dependent Children, food stamps, and other welfare programs. These programs apply income and employment criteria for eligibility. Federal law has directed that state agencies cooperate with administrators of these programs by supplying relevant information about individual welfare applicants to help check their claims and eligibility. The major source for individual worker employment and earnings data has been the quarterly wage reports most states have required employers to file for unemployment insurance purposes. By and large, these states use the data to determine claimant entitlement to benefits, applying formulas based on quarterly wages. Not all states required such reports, however; some requested needed information from employers only after claimants filed for benefits and only for the claimants, not for all employees. These states, therefore, were unable to provide the basis for the more extensive verification desired for the other entitlement programs. To remedy this shortcoming, a provision was included in the Deficit Reduction Act of 1984 (P.L. 98-369) to require all states to obtain the quarterly information. All states have complied and, as a result, more states have adopted unemployment benefit entitlement formulas based on quarterly wages.[35]

Unemployment Insurance Support for Self-Employment Experiments

Proposals are advanced occasionally for using trust fund reserves to assist the unemployed in ways other than compensating weeks of

---

35. While all states provide the required information, a few obtain the data from a source other than unemployment insurance wage reports, such as Social Security. As of 1992, only Massachusetts, Michigan, and New York still requested employers to report employment and wage data only for claimants after they filed for benefits.

insured unemployment, their only allowed use under existing federal law. It can be argued that the standard adopted in 1970 prohibiting states from denying benefits to claimants in approved training was a breach in this stance and a precedent for other deviations. The depletion or near depletion of benefit reserves in the 1970s and 1980s largely discouraged serious consideration of other uses.

One idea, however, did attract sufficient support at least for some testing of its potential and feasibility. The idea was to permit the continued payment of benefits to claimants who were trying to establish a small business or to become self-employed, rather than search for paid employment. New, especially small businesses had been shown to account for a substantial proportion of all new jobs (Birch 1981, pp. 3-14; encouraging small business for the unemployed thus offered potential multiplier effects for employment. British and French experience with such use of unemployment benefits indicated some modest though positive results, stimulating more interest in the idea in this country.[36] The provision authorizing the experiments was included in the Budget Reconciliation Act of 1987. It called for demonstrations in up to three states. The design for these projects provides a waiver of the work-search requirement for claimants participating in the demonstration who are starting their own small businesses. As of 1990, only one state, Massachusetts, had undertaken a demonstration project of this design. Another self-employment demonstration, funded separately by the U.S. Department of Labor in the State of Washington, has a somewhat different design. In that demonstration, participants are paid a lump sum equal to the remainder of their unemployment insurance entitlement once an acceptable business plan has been submitted. Each of these demonstrations offers substantial assistance, including training and counseling, to the participants in the planning and development of a small business plan.[37]

---

36. Bendick and Egan (1987, pp. 528-542). For a summary and evaluation of foreign experience with the use of unemployment insurance to encourage self-employment, see Leigh (1989, pp. 126-131).

37. Information about these demonstration projects made available by Stephen A. Wandner of the Unemployment Insurance Service (U.S. Department of Labor) from a report prepared for the Organization for Economic Cooperation and Development.

Railroad Unemployment Insurance Reforms

Ever since its separation from the federal-state system in 1939, the railroad unemployment insurance program has operated independently though in administrative association with the Railroad Retirement system.[38] Temporary disability benefits were added to the unemployment insurance program in 1946 so that railroad employees were protected against wage-loss interruption due to temporary nonwork-connected illness or injury as well as unemployment. Benefit amount, duration, and eligibility provisions generally have been more liberal than corresponding provisions of state unemployment insurance laws, except that in the 1970s, the maximum benefit amount paid to railroad workers began to slip and eventually fell below most state benefit ceilings. The equivalent maximum weekly benefit amount in the railroad program in 1984 was $125 (benefits are based on days of unemployment in a two-week period); basic benefit ceilings were lower in only three states that year. Nearly all railroad claimants received the maximum benefit, since all but a few earned more than the maximum wages taxable under the program ($600 per month), which would qualify them for it. By 1988, the *average* weekly benefit paid by the states was $145.

Since 1946, the maximum normal duration of benefits allowed has been twenty-six weeks. Since 1959, extended benefits have been payable at all times for up to thirteen or twenty-six more weeks to unemployed railroad workers with ten-to-fourteen and fifteen or more years of service, respectively. As in the federal-state system, temporary extended benefits were paid, up to thirteen weeks, during the recessions of the late 1950s and early 1960s to lower seniority railroad workers (less than ten years of service) who are more vulnerable to layoff. In 1975, a permanent program was adopted to pay extended benefits to such workers during periods of high unemployment as determined by the national trigger rate used by the federal-state extended benefit program, until the national trigger was abolished in 1981, or by the railroad unemployment rate.

Benefit and administrative costs of the railroad program are financed entirely by employer payroll taxes. A separate trust fund

---

38. Much of the description of the railroad program and its development is based on the Report of the Railroad Unemployment Compensation Committee established by the Railroad Retirement Solvency Act of 1983; the Report was issued June 21, 1984.

account is maintained for the program to handle revenues and disbursements. From the outset, employers have paid a uniform tax rate applied to taxable wages—until 1984, the first $400 paid an employee each month and since then, the first $600. The tax rate assigned, depending on the level of the fund, rose over the years from less than 1 percent before 1955 to the statutory maximum of 8 percent by 1977 where, except for two years, it remained. It should be noted that taxable wages accounted for only about 20 to 25 percent of all wages after 1984. Feeling the severe effects of the recessions of the mid-1970s and early 1980s, trust fund reserves diminished rapidly and then were depleted entirely, making necessary the sustained high tax rate as well as heavy borrowing from the Railroad Retirement fund. The latter was permitted by legislation adopted in 1959.

The financial crisis of the early 1980s, affecting both the unemployment insurance and retirement programs, grew to emergency proportions by 1983. Congress passed the Railroad Retirement Solvency Act of 1983 (P.L. 98-76) to address the immediate problem. With respect to unemployment insurance, the Act increased the monthly taxable wage base to $600 and instituted an additional tax to pay off the debt and interest owed to the retirement fund. In 1984, Congress set this repayment tax rate to begin at 4.3 percent in 1986, rising to 6.0 percent by 1988. The 1983 Act also set up a Railroad Unemployment Compensation Committee, combining railway labor and management representatives, to review the program's problems and recommend longer-range remedies.

The Committee's 1984 report offered a consensus package of reforms which it believed would restore the program to solvency and maintain its continued independent operation on a sound basis. In contrast, the Reagan administration proposed that the program be absorbed by the federal-state system. After discussion and debate, the legislation that finally emerged—the Railroad Unemployment Insurance and Retirement Improvement Act of 1988 (P.L. 100-647)—followed the Committee recommendations for unemployment insurance for the most part. The financing reforms included the introduction of experience rating, beginning 1990; extension of the loan repayment tax at the 4 percent level until all of the debt and interest were repaid; and the addition of a surcharge rate schedule geared to low fund levels and indebtedness in the future. Other changes made in the program were relatively modest.

Special Benefits Outside Unemployment Insurance

Aside from unemployment insurance payments, unemployed workers may be eligible for wage-loss compensation as well as other kinds of assistance under various programs established by federal laws. Chapter 8 noted Trade Readjustment Allowances provided by the Trade Expansion Act of 1962 for workers adversely affected by changes in national trade policies. By and large, these types of programs were adopted to compensate workers displaced from jobs because of some government action or policy, such as the urging of consolidation or reorganization of railroad and airline carriers, airline deregulation, expansion of a national park (restricting harvesting of redwood trees), among others. Most of these programs were designed for specific industries, and some were in effect for a limited period. The compensation provided usually went well beyond the levels normally paid by unemployment insurance. Assistance with the costs of relocation, job search, and training was often included as well. The approach was generally viewed as a means for indemnifying workers for damage suffered as the direct result of federal actions. It also served to reduce labor opposition to government policies likely to have those effects. The approach was applied as early as the late 1930s to accommodate consolidations promoted by the federal government in the railroad industry. Special programs of this type multiplied in the 1960s and 1970s, only a few of which were of substantial proportions.[39]

The most significant of these was the program of Trade Readjustment Allowances which, unlike the usual pattern, was not confined to a single industry. Stringent rules under the 1962 Trade Expansion Act made it virtually impossible to certify any industry or firm as adversely affected so as to enable displaced workers to qualify for the allowances. Certification rules were considerably relaxed by the Trade Act of 1974 (P.L. 93-610). Thereafter, many thousands of workers qualified for allowances, and some also received training and relocation assistance. Under the 1974 Act, the weekly allowance was 70 percent of the

---

39. See Rubin (1980, pp. 791-807).

worker's wage up to a maximum of $250, which could be drawn for twenty-six weeks or as much as fifty-two weeks if the recipient was age 60 or more or was in training. General revenue appropriations financed these benefits. The program was administered for the federal government by the state employment security agencies. In a four-year period from 1975 to 1979, total outlays exceeded $700 million (Rubin 1980, p. 804). The liberal provisions under the 1974 act were cut back in 1981 by amendments in the Omnibus Budget Reconciliation Act of that year (P.L. 97-35). The weekly amount was made the same as that paid under state unemployment insurance. Workers could not draw allowances until they had exhausted their unemployment insurance entitlement first and could not receive more than fifty-two weeks in all for unemployment insurance and trade allowances combined unless they needed more time to complete training; longer duration of allowances for older workers was eliminated. In general, the stricter eligibility rules adopted concerning job search and acceptable suitable work criteria to apply to recipients of extended unemployment insurance benefits were also to apply for trade allowance recipients. The volume of trade allowances paid declined sharply once these provisions went into effect.

Disaster Unemployment Assistance

One other program outside the unemployment insurance system was established permanently by the Disaster Relief Act of 1974 (P.L. 93-288). In case of a major natural disaster which strikes a particular area or region and which, in response to a request from the state's governor, is declared a major disaster area by the President, workers rendered unemployed as a result may receive disaster unemployment assistance if they are not eligible to receive unemployment insurance. The weekly amount payable is that payable under state unemployment insurance had the worker's wages been fully covered, or the average weekly unemployment insurance benefit amount paid under the state law, whichever is larger. The assistance is available over a twenty-six-week period beginning with the date of the disaster declaration. State agencies administer this program, which is federally financed. Since 1974, unemployment insurance coverage has become more universal, diminishing the importance of this program.

Concluding Observations

Taking a broad overview of the approximately four decades after 1947, federal unemployment insurance legislation enacted in the first half of this period differed distinctly from that of later years in its character, scope, and impact. Before 1970, Congress successfully resisted the urge to assert a more dominant federal role in the system. The states enjoyed a relatively free hand to develop their programs as they deemed appropriate, while the economy followed a pattern of long-term expansion with occasional temporary interruptions for recessions.

Extensions of coverage were among the major federal actions before 1970. The most significant of these covered workers state laws could not cover—federal employees, veterans, or military personnel. Of greater influence on the system was the federal response to the recession-spawned long-term unemployment of the late 1950s and early 1960s. Most states by then had greatly improved their benefit duration provisions, raising the maximum allowed up to twenty-six weeks. Federal action in 1958 aimed to encourage states to increase by half the duration allowed during the current recession period. Interest-free U.S. Treasury advances were offered to the states to fund the added benefits, with repayments extended over many years. All regular state provisions would apply except for the increased duration. Participation was at each state's discretion. The majority chose not to participate, although the large industrial states did and several had similar temporary extensions of their own independent of the federal program. The federal temporary extension program of 1961 was more insistent in that the added benefits were financed by an increase in the Federal Unemployment Tax; all states agreed to pay these federal benefits. Again, regular state benefit provisions applied, except that certain pension income received by claimants was subtracted from the extended benefit amount, regardless of how the state normally treated such income.

Most other federal unemployment insurance legislation adopted before 1970 was designed to ease matters for the state programs. A 1954 amendment, for example, permitted the states to experience rate newly covered firms after one year rather than three years as previously required. The federal loan fund established by 1950 legislation was protective of state programs that encountered financial difficulty. Borrowing requirements were mild, no interest applied, and repayment was easy and could be prolonged.

While state unemployment insurance programs were left generally unencumbered by federal statutory rules beyond those established at the outset in 1935, there were repeated attempts before 1970 to expand on the original requirements. All failed despite powerful advocates; the sentiment in Congress to preserve state control continued strong enough to repel these efforts, though the one in 1966 was a close call.

The Employment Security Amendments of 1970 finally overcame the resistance to federally mandated changes in the system. They included broad extensions of coverage which most states had been unable or unwilling to adopt on their own. The permanent program of federal-state shared extended benefits for high unemployment periods was created. The 1970 Amendments also established a number of new specific federal rules governing state disqualification provisions applicable to claimants in training and filing interstate claims, and limiting states in canceling or reducing all benefit rights of disqualified claimants. The Unemployment Compensation Amendments of 1976 added more federal initiatives that affected the state programs as well as the system as a whole.

Congress was now less hesitant about asserting and expanding the federal role in unemployment insurance. It tinkered repeatedly with the trigger mechanism of the federal-state extended benefit program and added temporary all-federal supplemental programs for more benefits during recessions. When financial crisis threatened the system's viability, the federal loan, interest, and repayment provisions were amended and embellished almost constantly to coax or virtually force the debtor states to alter their tax and benefit entitlement provisions so as to improve their fund positions.

In the late 1970s and in the 1980s, federal unemployment insurance legislation took a relatively new turn. Previously, the objectives of such legislation had almost always been to expand the program or to protect claimant rights. The policy that had guided federal relations with the states was throughout the years one of encouraging the states to improve their programs, to widen their scope and coverage, to pay better and longer benefits, and to avoid harsh disqualifying provisions. That policy now shifted, a change driven by financial crisis, by the need to contain the huge federal budget deficits, and by the accumulated perceptions of claimant abuse and lax administration. Federal unemployment insurance legislation became more restrictive. Eligibility rules for extended and supplemental benefits were toughened by amendments adopted in these later years, often stiffer than those applying under many state laws. Some of these states changed their regular provisions to match the stricter federal rules though they were not required to do so for regular benefits. Other federal amendments did set several restrictive standards applicable directly to regular state benefit provisions. The extended benefit program was narrowed by altering the trigger requirements so that extended benefit periods began later and ended sooner, or did not begin at all; the national trigger was eliminated entirely. The result of all this restrictive legislation was to reduce significantly the total of benefit outlays and the proportion of the unemployed receiving unemployment insurance support.

As recession abated after 1983, the financial crisis eased. Sustained economic recovery and stability throughout the rest of the decade enabled the states to repay their loans and accumulate positive reserves. New federal unemployment insurance legislation diminished accordingly; proposals for further reform were usually set aside as if Congress and the nation were weary of the subject.

The financial crisis, however, left its mark. It is unlikely that the expansiveness that characterized the federal amendments of 1970 and 1976 will return any time soon. The specter of high cost and financial nonviability that haunted the program's planners in the 1930s had shown its face again. After so many years over which the costs of the program averaged little more than 1 percent of total payrolls, the heavier costs incurred in the recession-ridden 1970s and early 1980s may have colored the nature of federal as well as state unemployment insurance legislation for years to come. It is interesting to note, however, that in only one year, 1975, did the total cost of the system as a whole, including all extended and supplemental benefit outlays, approach 3.0 percent of all payrolls, the level of tax originally estimated as needed over time to support a modest unemployment insurance program.[40]

At the end of the 1980s, all state unemployment insurance funds were solvent, but few of them met the standard formerly used as a measure of minimum fund adequacy.[41] Without significant additional fund accumulation, a new serious recession with slow recovery is likely to result in insolvency and debt in many states. Unemployment insurance would reemerge as an active subject for federal legislation.

---

40. Regular state plus extended and supplemental benefit outlays totaled $16.3 billion in 1975, equal to about 2.8 percent of total payrolls of $580 billion that year. The system's administrative costs would have raised that rate to about 2.9 percent.

41. This measure specifies that a state's reserve ratio (reserves as a percent of total payrolls) should equal at least one-and-one-half times the state's highest twelve-month benefit cost rate (total benefit outlays during a twelve-month period as a percent of total payrolls of that period). Thus, the state fund should be adequate to finance at least one-and-one-half times of its worst relative twelve-month benefit cost experience. At the end of 1989, only four states had adequate reserves by this measure; eighteen states had funds at less than half this level of adequacy including half of the 10 largest *(Unemployment Insurance Financial Data 1938-1982* and annual supplement for 1989).

10

State Laws Evolve
1948-1990

Federal law sets the basic framework and a few of the specifics of the unemployment insurance system, but it is state law that defines most of the details—the "flesh and bones." State law spells out the terms and conditions unemployed workers confront when they file for benefits, and the basis of the payroll taxes employers pay into state unemployment insurance reserve funds.

This chapter reviews patterns and trends of state statutory provisions since 1948. The review covers the program's major elements, including benefit financing, but makes no attempt to trace legislative changes over the years in any great detail. Chapter 7 described the earlier state provisions and some of the modifications made soon after the programs began. A summary of where the states stood with regard to several key provisions in 1940 and 1945 is presented in table 7.2.

In reviewing subsequent provisions, this chapter focuses chiefly on three years—1948, 1971, and 1990.[1] The first of these years, 1948, follows the first complete round of state legislative sessions after World War II and the nation's reconversion to a civilian economy. The next year, 1971, reflects the position of the state programs soon after the start of the 1970s when the long postwar economic expansion appeared to falter seriously and just prior to when the federal Employment Security Amendments of 1970 took full effect. The last year, 1990, describes state unemployment insurance provisions at the conclusion of the long period of recovery following the serious recession of the

---

1. Specific information about state provisions for these years and at other times is drawn from *Comparison of State Unemployment Insurance Laws*, published by the U.S. Department of Labor after 1948. The *Comparison* has been issued and revised or updated periodically over the years. Information for 1948 is from the *Comparison* issued by the Social Security Administration (October 1948). For 1971, it is from the *Comparison* issued by the Manpower Administration (August 1971). For 1990, it is from the *Comparison* issued by the Employment and Training Administration (January 1990).

early 1980s. Until 1960, the "states" consisted of 51 jurisdictions—the 50 states (including Alaska and Hawaii while they were still territories) and the District of Columbia. In 1960, Puerto Rico became the 52nd "state" in the system; the Virgin Islands made the total 53 in 1978.

Factors Affecting State Legislation

Before turning to a review of how state unemployment insurance provisions have evolved, some perspective on the subject may be gained by considering a few of the many factors that tend to influence the course of state legislation. The impact of federal law is an obvious and fairly direct factor. Prior discussions of federal legislation have pointed out many of these effects and need no further elaboration. Economic forces are also important influences. Chapter 1 discusses some of these, such as cyclical changes in business activity, longer term industrial developments, seasonal patterns of employment, changes in labor force composition, changes in the character of labor markets, and how these affect unemployment insurance. The discussions in Chapter 1 also cover regional and state differences with respect to a few of these factors. A state's unemployment insurance provisions will reflect to some extent certain distinctive aspects of its economy.

The Large States

How large or small a state is or, more precisely, the size of its program does not strongly affect the kind of provisions it has. Large states show about as much statutory diversity as do other states. Because they are large, however, they tend to be interested in each other's experience with respect to certain approaches; large states do share some common problems, particularly with regard to administration. The significance of the large state programs is that together, although a limited number out of all the states, they dominate the national unemployment insurance scene, and they account for a large share of the total system however it is measured.

Table 10.1 presents one measure of that concentration—the amount of employment covered by state laws. In each of three selected years during the long period under review, the table lists the ten states with

Table 10.1   Ten Largest States, by Level of Average Monthly Employment Covered by Unemployment Insurance—1948, 1971, 1990

State[a]	Average monthly covered employment (thousands)[b]		
	1948	1971	1990[c]
U.S. - total	33,084	52,080	106,333
California	2,515	5,149	12,919
New York	4,369	5,309	7,932
Texas	1,189	2,619	6,780
Florida	d	1,601	5,275
Illinois	2,383	3,134	5,078
Pennsylvania	3,103	3,298	4,906
Ohio	2,216	2,861	4,672
Michigan	1,605	2,304	3,822
New Jersey	1,305	2,046	3,476
North Carolina	e	e	3,024
Massachusetts	1,463	1,686	g
Indiana	908	f	f
Total - ten largest	21,057	30,006	57,885
(% of U.S. total)	(63.7)	(57.6)	(54.4)
Total - ten smallest	642	1,226	3,010[h]
(% of U.S. total)	(1.9)	(2.4)	(2.8)

SOURCES: *Unemployment Insurance Financial Data, 1938-1982* and annual supplements.
a. Ten largest states arrayed from largest to smallest as of 1990.
b. Excludes employment covered under federal unemployment insurance programs for railroad workers and federal civilian and military services.
c. Includes employment by nonprofit employers and by state and local governments handling benefit costs on a reimbursable basis.
d. Florida was 25th in size in 1948.
e. North Carolina was 13th in size in 1948 and 12th in 1971.
f. Indiana was 11th in size in 1971 and 14th in 1990.
g. Massachusetts was 11th in size in 1990.
h. Excludes the Virgin Islands, smallest "state" in the unemployment insurance system with average monthly covered employment in 1990 of about 42,000, much less than the next smallest, Wyoming, with about 183,000.

the highest average levels of covered employment. Although fewer than a fifth of all the states, they collectively have accounted for over half of the covered employment in the system. The degree of concentration declined over these years, ranging from about 64 percent in 1948 to about 54 percent in 1990. Except for Indiana, which Florida replaced among the "big ten" by the end of the 1960s, and North Carolina, which replaced Massachusetts in 1990, all states in this group have been the same in all years through 1990, a remarkable record of stability. Table 10.1 also shows the contrastingly small concentration of covered employment in the ten smallest states in each of these years—between about 2 and 3 percent of the total. The composition of this group has been more varied over the years.

When one applies other measures, such as the average level of insured unemployment or the total of state benefit outlays, the large state concentrations are even more pronounced. For insured unemployment in the same three years, the ten largest states accounted for 72 percent of the U.S. total in 1948, 63 percent in 1971, and 59 percent in 1990. In each year, at least eight of the ten states listed in table 10.1 were consistently among the largest by this measure as well. By amount of regular benefit outlays, a similar picture emerges with concentrations ranging from 77 percent in 1948, to 71 percent in 1971, to 66 percent in 1990. Among the states listed in table 10.1, only Florida, Indiana, North Carolina, and Texas do not appear in all three years among the ten largest when measured by insured unemployment or benefit outlays. Subsequent discussions review and analyze state unemployment insurance provisions for all states in the three focus years 1948, 1971, and 1990, and also for the ten largest states as a group as identified in table 10.1 for the same years.

The Wage Factor

Variation in wage levels among workers in a state is important for the unemployment insurance program, since its benefits are functionally related to wages. Wage levels in general differ considerably across states, as can be seen in comparisons of statewide average weekly wages in covered employment.[2] Most of the high-wage states have

---

2. These averages are calculated for each year, by state, and are published in *Unemployment Insurance Financial Data 1938-1982* and annual supplements.

been in regions where heavy industry is most concentrated—along the mid-Atlantic seaboard, the Great Lakes, and the West Coast. The states with the lowest average wages have been more prevalent in the South and in the western plain and mountain regions where industry has tended to be light and less developed, although industry expanded greatly in much of the South in later years, raising wage levels substantially.[3]

Table 10.2 gives some idea of wage-level variations and trends over the years. Five of the ten highest-wage states shown on the table were the same in each year shown. These five were also among the ten largest in each year. Because of this concentration of large states (at least six in each year), the national average weekly covered wage has exceeded the averages of most of the states. In 1948, all ten states with the lowest average weekly covered wages were in the South. The number in the South dropped to four by 1971 and to three by 1990. In the later years, western plains and mountain states replaced most of the early low-wage southern states in the bottom ten. Weekly wage developments influence unemployment insurance legislation, especially provisions applying to the weekly benefit amount formula and the qualifying requirement.

Level of Unemployment

Certainly the amount and rate of unemployment a state experiences significantly influences the character of its unemployment insurance provisions. Of particular importance is how unemployment varies over time. The way a state designs its financing provisions, for example, depends to a great extent on whether it tends to suffer severe reductions in employment when national recessions develop, and how rapidly employment rebounds during recovery periods. Some states manage to ride out most recessions with relatively little impact, a pattern suggesting a different statutory response for their programs as compared with heavily impacted states. In a number of states, seasonal

---

3. During the later 1970s, a number of western plains and mountain states (for example, Colorado, Oklahoma, Texas, and Wyoming) experienced significant expansion of employment in the oil, gas, and other energy-producing industries which tended to pay high wages, causing the average covered wage levels in these states to rise from below to above the national average by 1982, only to resume their usual below-average levels in subsequent years as the boom collapsed.

Table 10.2   Ten Highest- and Ten Lowest-Wage States, by Level of Average Weekly Wage in Covered Employment, 1948, 1971, 1990

1948		1971		1990	
State	Average weekly wage	State	Average weekly wage	State	Average weekly wage
10 highest averages[a]					
Michigan	$64.33	Michigan	$175.82	Connecticut	$561.17
Illinois	62.50	New York	169.31	New York	558.17
New York	62.44	Illinois	166.50	New Jersey	545.96
California	61.48	California	161.06	Massachusetts	512.25
New Jersey	59.68	Delaware	160.91	California	495.08
Washington	59.09	New Jersey	160.73	Michigan	491.51
Oregon	58.94	Ohio	159.76	Illinois	488.67
Nevada	58.74	Connecticut	155.36	Delaware	474.29
Ohio	58.64	Washington	155.17	Maryland	456.91
W. Virginia	58.44	Indiana	152.63	Pennsylvania	444.58
10 lowest averages[b]					
Mississippi	$37.44	Arkansas	$111.10	S. Dakota	$302.22
Arkansas	38.32	Mississippi	113.19	N. Dakota	333.06
S. Carolina	41.57	S. Dakota	113.49	Mississippi	333.43
N. Carolina	42.61	S. Carolina	117.95	Montana	335.27
Georgia	42.86	N. Carolina	120.36	Arkansas	342.07
Alabama	44.70	Maine	121.77	Nebraska	347.14
Tennessee	45.29	New Mexico	123.17	New Mexico	355.87
Louisiana	46.49	N. Dakota	123.39	Idaho	360.04
Virginia	46.66	Idaho	124.06	Iowa	363.77
Florida	47.02	Wyoming	124.13	S. Carolina	368.86
U.S. average weekly wage	$55.85		$148.96		$446.68
No. of states:[c]					
—above avg.	14		14		11
—below avg.	37		38		42

SOURCES: *Unemployment Insurance Financial Data, 1938-1982* and annual supplements.
a. States arrayed from highest to lowest for each year; excludes Alaska and the District of Columbia where, for various reasons, average wage levels are not comparable.
b. States arrayed from lowest to highest for each year; excludes Puerto Rico and the Virgin Islands where average wage levels are not comparable.
c. Includes all jurisdictions in system.

employment and unemployment are a major factor which may induce distinctive unemployment insurance provisions to deal with such patterns. A long-term decline in an important industry in a state poses other kinds of problems for its program, perhaps with statutory consequences. During the four decades under review here, individual states did not consistently experience one single pattern of unemployment throughout the entire period. Several states tended to have above-average rates of unemployment for a lengthy span of years, but then enjoyed relatively low unemployment levels. Unemployment insurance legislation in such states generally exhibited similar long-wave patterns in response, though perhaps with lags that missed key turning points. The principal legislative concerns arise when unemployment is high, especially during recessions whether national or local. At such times, worker representatives press for higher weekly benefit and duration provisions; employers worry about payroll tax effects as state reserves run down, and they resist changes that would increase costs.

While state financing provisions can be made adaptable to cyclical patterns of unemployment which offer some degree of regularity for planning reserve and tax needs, they are less sensitive to the relatively unexpected developments that can quickly swell unemployment in one state or region. The unemployment insurance programs of small states are particularly vulnerable to the sudden difficulties posed by such developments. The almost overnight fizzle in the mid-1980s of the oil and gas boom which began in the 1970s badly hurt the economies of several western and Gulf states. Major cutbacks in federal defense procurement outlays have at times hit certain states very hard after years of lucrative, high employment-generating contracts for some of their important industries. The strains on the unemployment insurance programs of these states can be extreme. Pressures mount to change provisions in different directions in response. Trying to legislate program changes in such a charged atmosphere fueled by unusually high levels of unemployment does not always result in the wisest provisions for a state unemployment insurance program.

Other Factors

State unemployment insurance laws have also been affected by various social factors and by political tendencies that make a state generally conservative or progressive in outlook. The relative strength and influence of organized labor and of business groups have made a difference, as has the degree of urban industrialization in a state. Despite growing concentrations of populations in urban areas, most state legislatures reflected a strong rural-agrarian outlook until fairly recent times. They were rural-dominated in their makeup because legislative electoral districts were drawn to keep them that way. As a result, legislative proposals to improve unemployment insurance that would mostly benefit urban workers did not usually attract strong support, perhaps helping to account for some of the program's inadequacies as perceived by many critics during the 1950s and 1960s. It took many years and a 1962 Supreme Court ruling to loosen the rural domination of the legislatures.[4] Only in more recent years has this particular barrier to unemployment insurance legislative improvements diminished significantly.

The way the legislative process is organized, the force of individual personalities, and the swings of political fortunes over time have also contributed to the nature and fate of unemployment insurance amendments at the state level. These factors, of course, have been distinctive for each state. In some, the governor largely defined the state's unemployment insurance policy. A change in party control of the executive or legislative branch often meant a change in direction for unemployment insurance, or a stalemate. Employment security agency directors in several states, by contrast, were able to establish considerable authority and influence over a long period of time, regardless of the party in power. They skillfully shaped the development of legislative change in their states and came to be relied upon by the political leaders for handling these matters. Continuity became more the exception than the rule, however. In a program that grew increasingly complex, agency staff who remained in central positions played key roles as they accumulated expertise on which top administrators and legislators came to depend.

In a few states, patterns developed over time whereby an individual or two representing a large employer or group of employers would

---

4. *Baker v. Carr*, 369 U.S. 186 (1962). This "one man-one vote" ruling by the U.S. Supreme Court eventually forced the states to redraw their electoral districts to be more evenly representative of their populations.

work out compromise proposals with a counterpart from labor, and the legislation would move through smoothly to enactment. State unemployment insurance legislation, almost always controversial, thus took different paths in different states, sometimes falling short of proposed objectives, sometimes getting through but in a form dictated by the process of the particular state.

The Broad Perspective

State unemployment insurance programs had become well established by 1948. As a result of the low unemployment during World War II, they were also well funded. During ensuing years, they developed mainly in response to amendments of federal laws and, in varying degrees, to economic and labor market developments. Some state programs changed more often and more rapidly than others. In time, differences among the states in their unemployment insurance provisions multiplied and widened. The states turned increasingly away from following the provisions recommended by the federal government as they gained more experience and confidence, and as interest groups asserted more influence at the state level. What a neighboring state did with regard to a particular provision was sometimes of greater importance. Although state provisions became more diverse, common general patterns remained recognizable.

State Program Administration

Before proceeding to a review of the patterns and trends in state legislation, a brief account is presented of the arrangements in the states for the administration of their unemployment insurance programs. State administration has been organized in several different ways. The administrative agency, which in all but a few states also operates the state employment (or job) service, may be established as an independent body in the executive branch of the government, or as a subordinate part of a broader state department. As state government has grown in size, scope, and complexity, the trend has been toward less independence for the state unemployment insurance agency.

In the late 1940s, about two-thirds of the states administered unemployment insurance through independent boards or commissions (twenty-one states), or as independent departments or bureaus of employment security (twelve states). Unemployment insurance administration operated as a subordinate division in a department of labor or industrial relations, or in an equivalent department, in sixteen states in 1948; in two other states, it was administered by the workers compensation agency. By 1971, the number of unemployment insurance agencies operating as subordinate entities of broader departments had grown to twenty-three, and to twenty-seven by 1990. The independent board or commission form declined in importance as compared with the independent department or bureau of employment security. The ten largest states exhibited about the same pattern and trend in regard to their administrative arrangements.

Almost all states provide for statewide advisory councils to assist the administrative agency in formulating policy, recommending legislation, and resolving operating problems. Council membership is usually representative of employers, labor, and the public. Many states also permit the appointment of local or other special advisory bodies. The influence of advisory councils on state program development and administration has varied a great deal among the states and over time. In a few instances, a state advisory council may have become virtually irrelevant or inoperative for a time.[5]

Federal law requires the states to provide impartial procedures for individuals to appeal denials of their claims. Each state, therefore, has appeals machinery within the program's administrative framework with subsequent right of appeal to the state judicial system. Employers as well as claimants have access to the process. All but a few states allow for at least two stages of appeal and some permit requests for redeterminations as well. The first-level appeal is usually made to a referee (or examiner) or to a referee (examiner) and two associates representing employer and worker interests. Procedures representing due process and a fair hearing apply. Appeal to a second level of review may be made from the first-stage decision. As of 1990, about half the states provided for an independent Board of Review or Board of

---

5. For a review and evaluation of state advisory councils during the first 20 years of the program, see Becker (1959).

Appeals to hear the second stage. In the remaining states, the independent boards or commissions that run the unemployment insurance agencies, or the agency heads, usually handled this function. Final administrative appeal decisions may be taken to the state courts for further review. Issues involving federal law and constitutional questions may result in appeal to the federal courts.

Coverage

Except for earlier inclusion by many states of smaller firms, almost all important expansions of unemployment insurance coverage of employment under state laws came about in response to changes in federal laws which extended the application of the Federal Unemployment Tax or required coverage of certain categories of employment by state law.

Size of Firm

In 1948 when the federal tax still applied only to employers of eight or more workers, twenty-nine states (including seven of the ten largest) covered smaller firms; seventeen of them covered employers of one or more. Following the 1954 federal extension to four or more employees in twenty weeks, all states covered firms of that size or smaller. A slow increase occurred over the ensuing years in the number of states covering employers of one or more. By 1971, shortly before the effective application of the federal amendment extending coverage to one or more, nearly half the states had already gone that far. As of 1990, twenty-three states including five of the ten largest, went beyond the existing federal requirements by covering employers of one or more employees in fewer than twenty weeks of the year or with a quarterly payroll of less than $1,500.

Agricultural Labor

By and large, state laws followed the federal definitions of agricultural labor, which generally excluded their wages from the Federal Unemployment Tax. The only notable exceptions prior to the major federal extensions to farm workers in 1976 were in Hawaii and Puerto Rico.[6]

After the federal extensions of coverage in the 1970s to previously excluded categories of agricultural labor, states amended their laws accordingly. As of 1990, eight states have gone beyond the minimum federal specifications for coverage of large farm employers—ten or more employees in at least twenty weeks of the year or a quarterly payroll of at least $20,000. The most important of these states is California, which covers any farm employer with a quarterly payroll of $100 or more—the same rule applicable to all employers. Florida and Texas, also important for farm employment, are among the eight states that exceed the federal coverage requirements.

Nonprofit Organizations

Only six states covered employment by nonprofit organizations prior to the passage of the federal amendments of 1970, which required such coverage in all states.[7] The federal requirement specifies coverage of nonprofit employers of four or more employees in twenty weeks. As of 1990, twenty-one states, including four of the largest ten, covered organizations employing one or more. Service in the employ of a religious organization for religious purposes is excluded by federal law. As required, all states allow nonprofit employers the option of self-financing their benefit costs (benefit reimbursement) in place of financing through the regular state unemployment insurance tax system.

The federal law excludes from required coverage the employment by colleges and universities of enrolled students, and nearly all states follow suit. Many states also exclude employment by these schools of the spouses of students. Student nurses and interns employed by hospitals are excluded from coverage in most states. These exclusions apply for public as well as nonprofit schools and hospitals.

---

6. Coverage in these jurisdictions applied mainly to sugarcane workers. Minnesota also had some limited coverage of agricultural employment. The District of Columbia did not exclude agricultural labor, but it was an entirely urban area.

7. The six states were Alaska, Colorado, Connecticut, District of Columbia, Hawaii, and New York. California allowed for voluntary coverage of nonprofit employers on a self-financing (benefit reimbursement) basis. Connecticut and New York also provided for such financing.

State and Local Government Employment

Most states had at least some coverage of state and local government workers before their coverage was required by the federal amendments adopted in 1970 and 1976. Such coverage has since become universal with some minor exceptions for elected or appointed officials, members of state National Guard units, and temporary emergency employees. The states provide local government entities a benefit reimbursement option for financing benefit costs, as required by federal law.

Domestic Service

The federal amendments of 1976 extended coverage to employers of domestic household workers if the cash wages paid total $1000 or more in a calendar quarter. Before this change, only three states had covered any domestic service.[8] As of 1990, four states (District of Columbia, Hawaii, New York, and the Virgin Islands) covered employers with smaller quarterly payrolls. Several other states included non-cash remuneration in applying the minimum $1000 quarterly payroll requirement.

Employer-Employee Relationship

The definition of "employee" for the purposes of coverage is left largely to state law, although federal law and federal court decisions have had a significant bearing on individual state provisions. A major problem is the determination of the employer-employee relationship. As of 1990, only six states still basically applied the common law master-servant rule. Most states use a broader concept involving one to three tests to determine if the worker is not an employee. These include (a) absence of employer control over the worker's performance, (b) performance of service outside the regular course or place of the employer's business, and (c) customary operation by the worker as an independent business or profession. In 1990, twenty-eight states applied all three tests while twelve states applied only one or two. Among the ten largest states, three applied all three tests. The pattern was about the same in earlier years. Other states relied on a contract for

---

8. Arkansas, Hawaii, and New York.

hire, whether expressed or implied. Most states specifically excluded from coverage insurance and real estate agents who work on a commission basis.

Self-employed individuals are not covered by unemployment insurance laws because such an individual's unemployment status is so difficult to determine and may be subject to the individual's control.[9]

Qualifying Requirements

To a large degree, the 1948 pattern of state base-period earnings and employment requirements to test a claimant's prior work attachment as a basis for benefit eligibility reflected the earlier trends toward simplification of qualifying and benefit formulas. A third of the states that year (including three of the ten largest) applied the simplest approach—the minimum flat annual earnings test, the one least likely to assure any specific amount of employment.[10] Most of these states held on to their flat annual requirements for many years, but their numbers gradually dwindled; more of them at least began to require earnings in more than one calendar quarter of the base period to try to assure that earnings were not limited to a small number of weeks. Only seven states, including California and Illinois, remained in this category in 1990.[11] (See table 10.3 for trends in state requirements.)

The most direct measure of past work attachment, weeks of base-period employment, was used for qualifying tests by only three states in 1948. More adopted this approach in succeeding years—as many as sixteen states by 1971, including six of the ten largest states. The number declined in the 1980s, partly because of the federal requirement that states obtain quarterly wage information about individual employees from their employers not previously collected by some states, as

---

9. California permits voluntary coverage of self-employed individuals under certain conditions.

10. Minimum annual earnings required by these states then ranged between $100 and $300; only one state required, in addition, earnings in at least two calendar quarters to increase the chances that the claimant's wages were spread over more than only a very limited period.

11. California's flat requirement in 1990 called for at least $1200 in high-quarter wages with no minimum specified for the base period, so claimants could qualify with no other earnings outside the one quarter. (See, however, footnote b on table 10.3 for alternative requirement if high-quarter wages were less than $1200.)

**Table 10.3   Distribution of States by Type and Level of Minimum
Qualifying Requirement—1948, 1971, 1990**

Type and level of requirement (base-period employment or earnings)	Number of states					
	1948		1971		1990	
Total - all states (10 largest)[a,b]	51	(10)	52	(10)	53	(10)
Weeks of employment	3	(2)	16	(6)	10	(6)
20 weeks	1	(1)	7	(3)	6	(5)
14-19 weeks	2	(1)	9	(3)	4[c]	(1)
Multiple of high-quarter wages	2	(1)	12	(1)	24	(2)
More than 1.5 times	-	-	-	-	1	(0)
1.5 times	1	(0)	9	(1)	17	(1)
Less than 1.5 times	1	(1)	3	(0)	6	(1)
Multiple of weekly benefit amount	30	(5)	15	(1)	15	(2)
40 or more times	2	(0)	2	(0)	7[d]	(0)
31-39 times	0	(0)	5	(0)	3	(1)
30 times	18	(4)	6	(0)	4	(0)
Less than 30 times	6	(1)	0	(0)	0	(0)
Varying-weighted multiples	4	(0)	2	(1)	1	(1)
Flat annual earnings	17	(3)	11	(3)	7	(2)
Less than $250	11	(2)	-	-	-	-
$250-$499	6	(1)	1	(0)	-	-
$500-$999	-	-	10	(3)	-	-
$1,000-$1,999	-	-	-	-	4	(2)
$2,000-$2,800	-	-	-	-	3	(0)

SOURCES: *Comparison of State Unemployment Insurance Laws*: for 1948, the October 1948 edition issued by the Federal Security Agency, p. 40, table 13; for 1971, the edition reflecting revisions issued August 31, 1971 by the USDOL, Manpower Administration, pp. BT-3, 4, table BT-2; for 1990, the edition reflecting revisions issued January 7, 1990, by the USDOL, Employment and Training Administration, pp. 3-27 to 3-29, table 301.

a. See table 10.1 for the ten largest states.

b. Subtotals by type add to more than the totals for all states and the ten largest since the following states are counted under two types of requirements in the same year: in 1948—California required 30 x WBA *or* 1-1/3 x HQW; in 1971—Hawaii required 15 weeks of work *and* 30 x WBA, Pennsylvania required 37-32 x WBA *but* 18 weeks of work if base-period earnings less than $600; and in 1990—California required at least $1200 in the high quarter (could be the only quarter of earnings) *but* 1-1/4 x HQW if less than $1200 and at least $900, Minnesota required 15 weeks of work *and* 1-1/4 x HQW, and Pennsylvania required 16 weeks of work to qualify for minimum duration payable *but* 40-37 WBA for maximum duration payable.

c. Includes Washington, which in 1990 required 680 hours of work in the base period (weeks not specified).

d. Includes South Dakota, which in 1990 required 30 x WBA in part of base period outside high quarter with total required multiple not specified, but since the WBA was calculated as 1/26 HQW, the total multiple required was at least 56 x WBA.

their qualifying and benefit formulas did not use quarterly wage measures. States applying a weeks-of-work test were among the latter; many requested employers to report weeks worked and wages after claimants had filed for benefits. With the new quarterly wage collection requirement, several of these states shifted to a different qualifying test. The large states, however, held on to their long-established weeks-of-work tests.

The majority of states have tested past attachment by measuring the claimant's base-period earnings as a multiple of high-quarter earnings or of the weekly benefit amount, which itself is usually based on high-quarter wages. The multiple measure is a means of approximating a level of weeks of employment. Nearly all states using these approaches in 1948 applied minimum weekly benefit amount multiples, but many later shifted to high-quarter multiples. The weekly benefit multiple proved inadequate in many states as a proxy measure for an amount of base-period employment when very large proportions of claimants qualified for relatively low weekly benefit ceilings which had not kept pace with rising wage levels. Thus, while a multiple of thirty times a weekly benefit that equaled half the claimant's prior weekly wage translated required base-period earnings into fifteen weeks of employment at that wage, thirty times the maximum weekly benefit amount (usually less than half the prior wage) could have been earned in significantly fewer than fifteen weeks in the base period. The high-quarter multiple approach avoids this deficiency. More states applied the high-quarter multiple in 1990 than any other type of requirement.

The qualifying requirement almost always specifies a minimum earnings amount for the week or high quarter or base period, along with the number of weeks or level of the multiple required. The minimum base-period earnings amount is the only element of the flat annual qualifying test except for the requirement that these wages be earned in at least two calendar quarters. In states testing by weeks of work, a minimum amount in each week, or an average weekly minimum over all weeks worked, is required. These minimums ranged from $20 to $99 a week in 1990. High-quarter and weekly benefit multiple states normally specify minimum earnings in the high quarter or the base period or both. These earnings floors are intended to screen out casual workers. Over the years, the required earnings minimums have risen, largely in response to rising wage levels. The increases have been much more substantial in some states than in others; in a number of states the minimums have remained fairly low. Minimum base-period earnings amounts required among all the states, as specified in their laws or as derived from their formulas, ranged from $150 to $900 in 1971 and from $150 to $3,640 in 1990.

A tendency, especially in later years, has been to stiffen the qualifying requirements. The shift to weeks-of-work and high-quarter multiple tests made for closer reflection of actual employment. In addition, the minimum number of weeks and the size of the multiple required increased in some states. The minimum amount of earnings required per week or in the base period also rose, in some instances more than simply to catch up or keep pace with rising wage levels. The addition in 1981 of a minimum federal qualifying requirement (twenty weeks of work, or equivalent tests of one and one-half times high-quarter wages or forty times the weekly benefit amount) for federally-shared extended benefits spurred the stiffening tendency in state requirements. The financial crisis many states faced in the 1970s and 1980s also encouraged these trends. Analysis of the state distributions across the years as compared on table 10.3 shows that the number of states requiring at least twenty weeks of work or the equivalent in multiple tests, the most demanding level of these requirements, increased from a total of four in 1948 to eighteen in 1971 and to thirty-one in 1990.

State qualifying tests also grew more complex. Some added features to their basic requirements either to screen out claimants regarded as weakly attached to the labor force who would be admitted by the basic test alone, or to avoid excluding claimants considered sufficiently attached to warrant some benefit support. An example of the former is the requirement of earnings in two or more quarters of the base period added by flat annual states and some weekly benefit multiple states. Several states have added a required minimum level of earnings outside the high quarter or in the last two quarters of the base period to assure recent attachment. Examples of features added to ease the basic test include "step-down" provisions that some weekly benefit and high-quarter multiple states have applied so that if a claimant's high-quarter earnings or the weekly benefit amount calculated as based on those earnings could not meet the test when the multiple was applied, a lower level of high-quarter wages or weekly benefit would be used to meet the multiple. Step-down provisions became less popular by 1990.

A few states have provided alternative requirements, so that claimants whose earnings and work patterns are marginal and unable to qualify under the standard test might be able to do so under another test (see footnote b on table 10.3).[12] A number of states have provided claimants with higher base-period earnings an alternative flat annual requirement in place of the basic weeks-of-work or multiple tests. Examples of such alternatives in 1990 are New Jersey's flat annual earnings of $6000 in place of twenty weeks of work, and Oklahoma's $9,500 in place of one and one-half times high-quarter wages.

By 1990 the range and diversity of state qualifying requirements had become quite wide. It should be understood that at the minimum qualifying levels, claimants are eligible for minimum benefits, both as to the weekly amount and duration, except where the duration allowed is uniform.

Eligibility Rules and Disqualifications

Voluntary leaving of work without good cause and discharge from a job for misconduct have continued to be major grounds for benefit disqualification in all states. Claimant refusal to pursue or accept suitable job offers or referrals by the public employment office is also an important reason for disqualification. Being unavailable for work, failing to search actively for work, and showing in other ways a lack of genuine participation in the labor market all can lead to benefit denial. Over the years, the terms and conditions of eligibility set forth in state laws have become more detailed and demanding, and the disqualifications imposed have grown stiffer. Beginning in 1980, new federal standards regarding eligibility and disqualifications applicable for extended benefits have reenforced these trends in state regular benefit provisions.

---

12. New York has provided a unique alternative to its twenty-weeks-of-work requirement for claimants with fewer than twenty but at least fifteen weeks in the base period. The alternative enables them to qualify if they had at least forty weeks of work in all in the base period and prior year combined.

Job Separation Issues

State laws have increasingly restricted acceptable "good cause" for voluntary leaving to causes attributable to the job or the employer, ruling out the worker's personal circumstances. In 1948, restricted good cause provisions applied in sixteen states; the number grew to twenty-six by 1971 and was thirty-seven in 1990. In 1990, most of these states did allow for one or more exceptions to this rule, such as leaving because of illness, sexual harassment, or to take another job.[13] To be disqualified, a misconduct discharge must be for misconduct related to the job.

Table 10.4 indicates how the disqualifications imposed for voluntary leaving and misconduct discharges became more severe over time. In 1948, most states postponed benefit payment for a period lasting usually under ten weeks. The period was uniform as fixed by law in some states, but more states specified a range within which the claims examiner could set the length of suspension depending on the circumstances of the job separation. Only a limited number of states suspended benefits for the duration of the disqualified claimant's unemployment— eleven states for voluntary leaving and six for misconduct discharge. Most duration disqualification states also required affected claimants to work subsequently for a minimum period of time or to earn a minimum amount before requalifying for benefits should unemployment recur. Among the ten largest states in 1948, four denied benefits for the duration of the claimant's unemployment for voluntary leaving and three for a misconduct discharge. Nearly a third of all states also reduced or canceled the claimant's benefit rights.[14]

By 1971, duration disqualifications were provided in twenty-eight states for voluntary leaving (although some of these applied only for voluntary retirement) and in twenty states for misconduct discharge. Over half of the ten largest states provided for duration disqualifications in these two categories. When states postponed benefits for a lim-

---

13. A claimant who quits one job to take another and is subsequently laid off may otherwise be disqualified for having voluntarily left the previous job without acceptable good cause.

14. A few states in 1948 canceled all benefits by canceling base-period wage credits on which the benefits were based, usually those wages from employment with the employer from whom the claimant separated; if there was no other base-period employer, the cancellation amounted to a total elimination of benefit rights for the benefit year, a harsher treatment than partial reduction of the claimant's benefits.

Table 10.4 Distribution of States by Type of Disqualification Imposed for
Voluntary Leaving of Work, Misconduct Discharge, and
Refusal of Suitable Work—1948, 1971, 1990

Reason for disqualification and year	Number of states (10 largest)[a]							
	Benefits postponed for[b]						Benefits reduced or canceled	
	Fixed number of weeks		Variable number of weeks		Duration of unemployment			
Voluntary leaving								
1948	13	(3)	28	(3)	11	(4)	16	(3)
1971	16	(2)	17	(3)	28	(7)	19	(2)
1990	2	(0)	2	(0)	50	(10)	7	(0)
Misconduct discharge[c]								
1948	11	(4)	35	(3)	6	(3)	16	(4)
1971	18	(3)	23	(3)	20	(6)	18	(2)
1990	5	(1)	8	(1)	42	(9)	13	(0)
Suitable work refusal								
1948	10	(2)	30	(4)	12	(4)	17	(4)
1971	18	(4)	17	(3)	23	(5)	16	(4)
1990	6	(2)	8	(2)	41	(7)	13	(3)

SOURCES: *Comparison of State Unemployment Insurance Laws*: for 1948, the October 1948 edition issued by the Federal Security Agency, p. 60; for 1971, the edition reflecting revisions issued August 31, 1971, USDOL, Manpower Administration, pp. ET-2 through ET-4; for 1990, the edition reflecting revisions issued January 7, 1990, by the USDOL, Employment and Training Administration, tables 401, 402, and 404.

a. Number of states shows count among all states with the count among the ten largest states shown in parentheses; see table 10.1 for ten largest states in these years.

b. Some states may be counted in more than one type of disqualification for a given reason category.

c. Count excludes disqualification for gross misconduct.

ited time, the periods of suspension tended to be longer than they were in 1948. A few more states also reduced or canceled benefit rights in 1971.

Duration disqualification became predominant by the 1980s. In 1990, this approach was used by fifty states for voluntary leaving and by forty-two states for misconduct discharge. To requalify for benefits, all these states required claimants to have a minimum amount of subsequent work or earnings. All ten of the largest states applied the duration disqualification for voluntary leaving and nine did so for misconduct discharge.[15] The practice of reducing or canceling benefit rights declined as the duration disqualification became more prevalent.

Some states have adopted provisions for designating "aggravated" or "gross" misconduct discharges as the basis for more severe disqualifications. Such misconduct may also be termed "willful," "flagrant," or "unlawful." Twelve states provided for these more serious misconduct discharges in 1948, twenty-two states in 1971, and thirty states (including six of the largest) in 1990. Most of these states canceled or reduced the claimant's benefits, besides denying benefits in the current unemployment spell.

Work Refusal

Issues relating to claimant refusal, without good cause, to pursue or accept jobs turn mostly on whether the job is considered suitable. As described in chapter 7, federal standards in the original Social Security Act prohibited benefit denials for claimant refusal to accept new work that would require surrender of certain rights with respect to union membership, or work under conditions and at wage levels substantially below certain prevailing levels. All state laws adhere to these labor standards, but they also spell out other conditions defining the suitability of work for a claimant with some variation as to details. Many provisions aim at protecting workers from requirements to accept unreasonable job demands regarding health, morals, safety, travel distance to work, and the relationship of the job to previous experience and skills. The length of an individual's unemployment has been a fac-

---

15. The federal standard, adopted in 1980, required states to impose a duration disqualification and requalifying test for most disqualifications in order for claimants to be eligible for extended benefits.

tor all states take into account in determining the degree to which the claimant's past wage and grade of work should control the range of jobs to consider as suitable. In recent years, a trend has grown towards specifying more closely the amount of reduction in wage level that would have to be accepted by the claimant after a given length of unemployment.[16] The federal standard adopted in 1980 (see chapter 9) that applies such a rule to claimants of extended benefits has been part of and, perhaps, has encouraged this trend.

The kinds of disqualifications imposed for job refusal have followed patterns and trends similar to those applied for the major job separation issues (see table 10.4).

Availability and Work Search Requirements

All states deny benefits to claimants who are unable to work and are unavailable for work in the week for which they claim benefits. Failure to register for work or to report to the employment or claims office as required are also reasons for denial. Some states—twenty-one in 1990—specify that claimants must be available for work that is suitable, or that is in their usual occupations, or for which they are reasonably fitted by training and experience. The application of these provisions can give rise to issues similar to those that may occur in job refusal cases. State provisions defining "ability" and especially "availability" have multiplied and diversified, testifying to the difficulties in applying this requirement.

Being able and available for work and registered at the employment office is not usually enough. Except for workers laid off temporarily and awaiting recall at a definite date, claimants are expected to be looking for work. Over the years, more and more states have made the work search requirement explicit in their laws, often specifying a minimum amount of search and submission of evidence of the search. While all states require claimants to be actively seeking work as appropriate to their circumstances, the number of states that have deemed it

---

16. An Iowa provision as of 1990, for example, called for lowering the level of wages considered suitable after the fifth week of unemployment from 100 percent to 75 percent of the claimant's base-period high-quarter average weekly wage, to 70 percent after the twelfth week, and to 65 percent after the eighteenth week; in no case, however, must a claimant accept less than the statutory minimum wage (USDOL, Employment and Training Administration 1990a, pp. 4-11).

important enough to require an explicit statement of work search activity has grown from fifteen in 1948 to thirty in 1971 and to forty in 1990. Among the ten largest states, the comparable numbers were three in 1948, six in 1971, and six in 1990. The rising statutory emphasis on work search rules combined with stricter enforcement has reflected the general trend toward stiffening of eligibility requirements.

Treatment of Special Groups

Application of the normal voluntary leaving and availability provisions are usually effective in denying eligibility to claimants in a wide variety of circumstances without detailed delineation of each of them in the law. In part because of negative public reactions to the payment of benefits under certain circumstances that seemed unwarranted or difficult to explain, some states have adopted special provisions that single out particular classes of individuals for automatic or more severe disqualification. These include states that deny benefits to claimants who leave work or are not available for work because of marital obligations, such as a wife moving to be with a husband, or staying home temporarily to care for domestic responsibilities. Until a federal standard was enacted prohibiting the practice, most states automatically barred benefits to pregnant women for specified periods before and after childbirth, simply assuming their unavailability for work. As many as thirty-eight states had such pregnancy rules as of 1971. That year, twenty-two states had marital obligations provisions; the number dwindled to twelve by 1990, all requiring some subsequent employment before the disqualified claimant could become eligible.

In general, students are not eligible for benefits while attending school, even though they may have prior qualifying employment. Their unavailability for work or restrictions on job search tend to disqualify them. In 1990, special provisions in twenty-two states automatically denied benefits to students even though some may have been available for work. Many of these states made exceptions for students who worked part time or had worked while attending school before becoming unemployed.

In contrast, during the 1960s when government-supported training for the unemployed became an important policy, a rising number of states adopted special provisions permitting claimants who were in approved training programs to continue drawing their benefits even though they were unavailable for work at the time. When the federal standard was passed in 1970 that prohibited benefit denial in such cases, more than half the states had provisions of this type. Under the standard, claimants may not be disqualified while in approved training because of unavailability for work, refusal to take suitable work, or failure to search for work. The standard did not stipulate the basis for state approval for training. Generally, the states have approved only vocational and basic education training. As of 1990, four states may require claimants to accept training as a condition for benefit eligibility; elsewhere, acceptance of training is voluntary.[17]

As noted earlier in connection with the extension of coverage to school personnel, federal standards prohibited the payment of benefits based on school wages to such employees between school semesters or terms, or during summer vacation or holiday periods, provided the employees have a contract or reasonable assurance for resuming employment when school resumes. The federal standard first applied only to professional staff, leaving the states free to apply the denial to nonprofessional employees if they chose, and most did choose the denial for all. In 1983, the federal standard became applicable to all school employees for all states.[18]

Another federal standard, adopted in 1976, singled out professional athletes for similar treatment. States may not pay benefits to such individuals between playing seasons if they have a contract or other assurance of employment in the next season. A 1976 federal amendment also prohibited payment of benefits to aliens who were not legally present in the country while employed or while claiming benefits.

Labor Disputes

In case of work stoppages due to labor disputes, all states suspend benefit payments to affected workers in order to maintain neutrality and to avoid heavy drains on reserve funds. Specific provisions vary a good deal with regard to the designation of the establishments affected

---

17. Massachusetts and Michigan have provided added weeks of benefits to claimants in approved training.

18. In 1991 the federal standard was changed again to restore to the states the option of paying or denying benefits to nonprofessional school employees at such times.

by the work stoppage and of the workers covered by the suspension. Some states exclude lockouts by employers from this category; the number of states that did so grew from seven in 1948 to twenty-five in 1990, including six of the ten largest states. In 1990, nine states excluded disputes resulting from failure by an employer to conform with a labor-management contract or with requirements of federal or state labor laws. Most states do not apply the disqualification to workers idled by a dispute if the workers do not participate or have a direct interest in it. In 1990, all states but one (New York) denied benefits as long as the dispute lasted or while the work stoppage was due to the dispute. New York and Rhode Island had been the only states since the mid-1940s to limit the suspension to a fixed period, after which benefits were payable. Rhode Island repealed its provision in the 1980s. If a dispute lasts beyond seven weeks plus the normal waiting week in New York, benefits become payable.

Fraudulent Misrepresentation

Originally, all but four of the states relied entirely upon court prosecution in cases of fraudulent misrepresentation to obtain benefits. Convictions were so difficult to obtain that all the states eventually adopted statutory administrative as well as criminal penalties. These disqualifications do not free the claimant from repayment of the benefits unlawfully received or from possible fine and imprisonment. Disqualification from benefits is usually up to a year although a few states vary the penalty with the number of weeks of fraudulent claims. Benefits are reduced by the number of weeks of the disqualification or are canceled entirely. If the fraud is discovered after the benefits have been paid, the fraudulent payments are recovered or deducted from future benefits. Disqualifications for fraud vary a great deal among the states and are difficult to generalize. They tend to be more severe than the usual disqualifications. All but a few states provide for reduction or cancellation of benefit rights either specifically or as the result of an extended period of disqualification that lasts throughout the benefit year or longer.

Disqualifying Income

All states reduce a claimant's weekly unemployment benefit amount by certain pensions received, on a weekly pro rata basis, as required by a federal standard that took effect in 1980. The pensions include Social Security and Railroad Retirement benefits, as well as any other pensions relating to employment for a base-period employer who helped finance the pension. At its option, a state may take account of a claimant's contributions toward financing the pension by limiting the amount of the reduction accordingly. A state may also disregard pensions based entirely on employment prior to the base period, although this option does not apply for Social Security and Railroad Retirement benefits. In 1990, thirty-five states limited the pension reduction when the employee had contributed to its financing, and twenty-four states disregarded pensions unaffected by base-period employment. Among the ten largest states, the comparable numbers were seven and three, respectively.

Prior to 1980, many states took account of pensions in more or less similar fashion. Social Security benefits were less commonly treated as disqualifying income to offset against the unemployment benefit. In 1971 for example, thirty-three states reduced the weekly benefit by employment-based pension received, including twenty states that confined such reductions to pensions involving base-period employers. Social Security old-age pensions were included by only fifteen states. Seven of the largest states treated pensions as disqualifying income in 1971. In the 1940s, when pensions were not yet a significant factor, such provisions were less developed or widespread.

As of 1990, thirty states reduced benefits by wages received in lieu of notice of job termination or by dismissal payments, or they denied benefit payment to the worker who received them. The number was down from thirty-eight states in 1971. Of the ten largest states in 1990, seven reduced or denied benefits for receipt of such pay. Many states treat dismissal pay as wages for contribution purposes, as they have been treated under the Federal Unemployment Tax Act since 1951.

Beginning in the 1950s, many labor-management agreements provided plans for the payment of supplemental unemployment benefits

(SUB) to employees placed on layoff.[19] The payment, when added to the state unemployment benefit, would equal a specified percentage of the worker's weekly wage. A ruling by the federal Internal Revenue Service held that SUB was not to be regarded as wages. Most states interpreted or amended their laws to allow the continued full payment of unemployment benefits without treating SUB as disqualifying income. As of 1990, only four states (New Mexico, Puerto Rico, South Carolina, and South Dakota) had not taken action on this question; all other states permitted receipt of SUB without disqualification or reduction of state unemployment benefits.

Workers' compensation has been specified as disqualifying income in almost half of the states as of 1990, some calling for complete benefit denial for the week it was received and others applying it to reduce the weekly unemployment benefit. The remaining states applied their able and available provisions to determine eligibility of a workers' compensation recipient. Those on partial disability compensation are the most likely to be able to work and available, but most of the states with disqualifying provisions for such income include temporary partial disability payments.

To avoid duplication of benefits, all states disqualify workers from receiving benefits if they receive or seek unemployment benefits for the same week under another state or federal law. No such disqualification is imposed if benefits are denied under the other law.

The Weekly Benefit Amount

Weekly unemployment benefits paid to insured unemployed workers deteriorated seriously in the 1940s and 1950s as statutory benefit ceilings failed to keep pace with rapidly rising wages. Large proportions of claimants were compensated at a flat amount, the ceiling, which replaced less than half their prior weekly wage. In the 1960s, and more so in the 1970s, states acted more frequently and effectively, not only to prevent further erosion of their ceilings but also to make up

---

19. SUB plans became well established in such industries as auto, rubber, and steel manufacturing, which were especially significant in states bordering the Great Lakes.

for ground lost earlier. The flexible maximum, which automatically adjusts the benefit ceiling for average wage level changes, eventually caught on in many states to help overcome the erosion problem. Benefit formulas used to calculate the weekly amounts payable below the ceiling had moved toward simplification in the program's early years (see chapter 7) and consequently away from close adherence to the original concept of replacing at least half the claimant's recent full-time weekly wage, admittedly difficult to administer in practice. Some states had oversimplified by adopting an annual wage formula that produced weekly amounts far removed from the original weekly wage replacement idea. After World War II, the trend shifted toward formulas designed to better approximate that concept. A number of state benefit provisions have taken account of the claimant's dependents, but this approach never became very widespread. By the 1980s, financial strains and fund insolvency led some states to trim back or partially reverse the weekly benefit improvements they had made over previous years.

Weekly Benefit Amount (WBA) Formulas

Relating the benefit to the claimant's base-period high-quarter wages has continued to be the method most widely used for setting the individual's WBA below the maximum. Its popularity diminished somewhat after the 1940s, particularly among the large states, as some turned to the more direct measure of the average weekly wage over the claimant's actual weeks of employment. After peaking at eleven states in 1980, the number using the average weekly wage formula fell off to six as of 1990, although the large states that had been using it tended to hold to this approach. The annual wage formula, more commonly used prior to 1948, has continued to decline to a small group of states (table 10.5).

First used in the State of Washington in 1977, a variation of the high-quarter wage formula developed to significant proportions during the 1980s. By 1990, about one-fourth of the states had adopted it. Table 10.5 lists this variation separately under the heading "multiquarter wages." Most states using this formula total the wages earned by the claimant in the two highest quarters of the base period and calculate the weekly benefit amount as a fraction of that total. For example, 1/52

Table 10.5 Distribution of States by Weekly Benefit Amount Formulas 1948, 1971, 1990

Type of formula (base period earnings measure and percent or fraction applied)[a]	Number of states					
	1948		1971		1990	
Total - all states (10 largest states)[b]	51	(10)	52	(10)	53	(10)
Average weekly wage[c]	2	(1)	10	(6)	6	(5)
50%	0	(0)	6	(3)	4[f]	(3)
55-66-2/3%	0	(0)	2	(1)	2	(2)[g]
Weighted[d]	2	(1)	2	(2)	0	(0)
High-quarter wages	41	(9)	37	(4)	28	(3)
1/26-1/25	15	(3)	25	(1)	15	(1)
1/24-1/20	17	(4)	5	(0)	7	(0)
Weighted[d]	9	(2)	7	(3)	6	(2)
Multiquarter wages[e]					14	(2)
1/52-1/50 (1/26-1/25)					9[h]	(2)[h]
1/48-1/44 (1/24-1/22)					4	(0)
Weighted[d]					1	(0)
Annual wages	8	(0)	5	(0)	5	(0)
1.00%-1.25%	0	(0)	1	(0)	2	(0)
Weighted[d]	8	(0)	4	(0)	3	(0)

SOURCES: *Comparison of State Unemployment Laws*: for 1948, the October 1948 edition issued by the Federal Security Agency, p. 44; for 1971, the edition reflecting revisions issued August 31, 1971, by the USDOL, Manpower Administration, pp. BT-7 and BT-8; for 1990, the edition reflecting revisions issued January 7, 1990, by the USDOL, Employment and Training Administration, pp. 3-35 to 3-38, table 304 .

a. Excludes allowances for dependents.

b. See table 10.1 for ten largest states in these years.

c. No state applied percentages between 50 and 55 percent in these years.

d. Percentages or fractions applied vary inversely with level of wages.

e. Not applicable in 1948 or 1971; based on wages in two highest quarters, except North Dakota which also added half the wages earned in third highest quarter; fractions shown in parentheses are equivalents of high-quarter wage formula fractions.

f. Includes Montana at 49 percent of claimant's average weekly wage.

g. Includes Michigan at 70 percent of claimant's average weekly after-tax wage.

h. Includes Illinois at 49 percent of 1/26 of total wages in two highest quarters of claimant's base period; and Massachusetts at 1/52 of wages in two highest quarters for claimants with average weekly wages in excess of $66 but 1/26 of high quarter for such claimants with earnings in only two quarters, while for those with lower average weekly wage, 1/21-1/26 of high-quarter earnings.

of the high two-quarter wage total would correspond with (or be considered equivalent to) 1/26 of a single high quarter.[20] The multiquarter wage formula does not always yield the same WBA as that produced by the single high-quarter formula using the equivalent fraction. Wages earned in the two highest quarters of the base period are in many cases likely to be unevenly divided between them. One quarter may reflect a pay raise, overtime pay, or a bonus payment not affecting earnings in the other quarter; the latter, on the other hand, may reflect less than full-time employment for part of the quarter. A WBA based on two quarters of sufficiently unequal wage totals will be less than one based on the total in the single highest quarter, using an equivalent fraction. It can be argued that a shift to a multiquarter wage formula helps to compensate for any overstatement of normal full-time weekly wage caused by including overtime or bonus pay in the single high quarter; but it can also understate it by averaging down the effect of a pay raise that began after the second high quarter or by including weeks of partial or nonemployment in the second quarter. In any case, the effect of multiquarter in place of a single high-quarter wage formula is to lower the calculated WBA for some, perhaps many claimants. The shift also reduces total benefit outlays, a major objective of state legislation in the 1980s.

While a benefit equal to half the weekly wage was broadly regarded as the norm, the majority of the states in 1948 and 1971, excluding the annual-wage-formula states, had WBA formulas designed to replace at least a little better than half the claimant's lost weekly wage (or more than 1/26 of high-quarter wages), and as much as 60 percent or more in a few cases. These include states with weighted formulas that paid better than half the weekly wage to claimants at relatively low wage levels. The number of states with such replacement rates declined over time. Before the 1980s, only one or two states restricted the rate of

---

20. A state may instead apply a single high-quarter fraction to the quarterly average of the two high quarters, or derive an average wage from total earnings over the 26 weeks of the two high quarters and apply a percentage to the result, presuming equivalence to using an average weekly wage formula.

wage-loss replacement to slightly less than half at WBA levels below the benefit ceiling; in 1990, four states did so.[21]

One notable innovation took place in Michigan in 1980 when that state adopted for its average weekly wage formula an after-tax wage basis for calculating the WBA. Federal, state, and local income taxes, based on exemptions claimed, and the applicable federal Social Security contribution were subtracted from the gross weekly wages reported for the claimant. The state changed its benefit-wage fraction from 60 percent on the gross wage basis to 70 percent on the after-tax wage basis. The widespread use of privately bargained supplemental unemployment benefit plans in Michigan, based on after-tax wages, was a major factor in encouraging this approach.[22]

Dependents' Allowances

In 1990, about a fourth (fourteen) of the states (including five of the ten largest) paid higher weekly benefits to claimants with dependents, an increase from ten states in 1971 and five in 1948.[23] All counted as dependents minor children, usually under age 18, and most also included a claimant's dependent nonworking spouse. Half the states added a specified amount per dependent to the basic WBA up to a limited number of dependents, or up to a proportion of the basic weekly benefit, or some other limit. In several states, the amount added varied with both the level of wages earned and number of dependents according to a schedule. In Michigan, the effect of dependents on the weekly benefit operated through the amount of income taxes deducted from gross pay to obtain the after-tax wage, the taxes being determined by

---

21. For example, among states with weighted formulas, the range of fractions applied to high-quarter wages went as low as 1/28 in Ohio in 1948 and 1/27 in California in 1971; in 1990, Montana and Illinois replaced 49 percent of the weekly wage (see footnotes f and h on table 10.5) while the weighted high-quarter formula ranged to as low as 1/33 in California and as low as 1/32 of a quarterly average in Tennessee's multiquarter formula.

22. Two other unique early provisions are worthy of mention, though they no longer apply. One was used by Utah in the 1940s to adjust the WBA by changes in the cost-of-living index published by the U.S. Bureau of Labor Statistics; the provision was dropped at the start of the 1950s. The other was adopted by Colorado in 1951 to increase a claimant's WBA by 25 percent if the claimant had earned over $1000 in the state in each of the prior five years and had drawn no benefits during that time; the provision was no longer in effect in 1963.

23. Eight of the fourteen states in 1990 were concentrated along the Northeastern seaboard and five in the North Central region; only Alaska stood apart among the fourteen.

the number of dependents claimed. In 1990, all but four of the states allowing for dependents provided higher benefit ceilings for claimants with dependents; in Maryland, Michigan, New Jersey, and the District of Columbia, the ceiling was the same for all claimants with or without dependents. In four other states (Illinois, Indiana, Iowa, and Ohio), benefits higher than the basic maximum WBA were payable only to claimants with dependents if the claimants also had earnings higher than the minimum level required for the basic ceiling.

Maximum WBA

Weekly benefit ceilings limit the extent to which the wage replacement rates intended by the WBA formulas can apply. As wage levels rise over time, proportionately more claimants qualify for the maximum weekly amount unless the latter also rises.

Wage levels have increased persistently over the life of the program, and quite substantially in some periods. The following figures trace the trend in the U.S. average weekly covered wage (*Unemployment Insurance Financial Data 1938-1982*) since 1940 in five-year intervals. Inflation accounts for much of the large increases that have occurred.

Year	Average weekly covered wage	Percent rise over prior 5 years
1940	$27.02	--
1945	45.11	67.0
1950	60.31	33.7
1955	78.12	29.5
1960	93.30	19.4
1965	109.99	17.9
1970	141.09	28.3
1975	190.28	34.9
1980	276.84	45.5
1985	365.38	32.0
1990	446.68	22.3

Before 1949, every state set its benefit ceiling by statute at a fixed dollar level. Few departed from this approach during the next decade.

Most states altered their ceilings infrequently and by small amounts. As a result, given the steady and rapid rise in wages during the 1940s and early 1950s, most benefit ceilings declined steeply in relation to state average wage levels. In 1941, the maximum WBA was $20 or less in all states but it was at least half the state average weekly wage in all but eight states.[24] By 1948, benefit ceilings were below $25 in forty-two states and less than half the average wage in all but four states (table 10.6). Weekly benefit amounts claimants received increasingly clustered at the ceilings. For example, 60 percent of all claimants who qualified for benefits throughout the country in 1952 were assigned the maximum. For many states, the proportion was well above this level; in effect they were close to being flat-rate benefit programs (USDOL, Bureau of Employment Security 1958, tables B-2 and B-5).

Further serious erosion of benefit ceilings had largely ended by the mid-1950s and a few signs of improvement slowly emerged. More states raised their maximums more often and by somewhat larger amounts than before. The major development was the gradual spread of the "flexible maximum" provision which sets the ceiling at a specified percentage of the state average weekly wage. The ceiling's dollar amount is adjusted periodically, usually once a year, to maintain the percentage relationship and without any further legislative action. Kansas pioneered the idea in 1949 when it pegged its maximum at 50 percent of its average weekly wage.[25] The approach took hold very slowly at first but grew increasingly popular in the 1960s and 1970s. By 1971, half the states (but only two of the ten largest) had adopted the provision. Almost all of them specified that the maximum be maintained at 50 percent or more of the average wage. A trend developed, especially during the 1970s, to set the percentage level higher. By the end of the 1970s, thirty-six states were automatically adjusting their benefit ceilings to keep pace with average wage increases and twelve of them maintained a 65 percent level or better. The flexible maximum

---

24. Based on data for 1941 in *Unemployment Insurance Financial Data, 1938-1982* and *Comparison of State Unemployment Insurance Laws as of December 31, 1941*, Federal Security Agency, December 1941, p. 86.

25. Soon after, however, Kansas limited the adjustment so that the ceiling did not exceed a specified dollar amount, which was reached by 1951. Utah was next to adopt the flexible maximum, in 1955.

Table 10.6   Distributions of States by Maximum Weekly Benefit Amount (WBA) and Maximum as Percent of State Average Weekly Wage (AWW)—All States and Flexible Maximum States, 1948, 1971, 1990

Maximum WBA and maximum as percent of state AWW	1948[d] All states	1971 All states	1971 Flexible states[d]	1990 All states	1990 Flexible states[d]
Total - all states, flexible maximum states (10 largest states)[a]	51[e] (10)	52[e] (10)	26 (2)	53 (10)	36 (6)
Maximum WBA[b]					
Less than $50	51 (10)	7 (3)	0 (0)	- -	- -
$50-$99	- -	45 (7)	26 (2)	1 (0)	0 (0)
$100-$149	- -	- -	- -	4 (0)	2 (0)
$150-$199	- -	- -	- -	23 (3)	14 (2)
$200-$249	- -	- -	- -	16 (4)	11 (1)
$250 and over	- -	- -	- -	9[e] (3)	9[e] (3)
Percent of state AWW[c]					
Less than 35.0%	12 (4)	6 (4)	0 (0)	2 (0)	0 (0)
35.0%-44.9%	27 (5)	10 (3)	0 (0)	11 (3)	2 (2)[g]
45.0%-49.9%	8 (1)	10 (1)	2 (0)	7 (1)	3[h] (0)
50.0%-54.9%	4 (0)	14 (2)	14 (2)	9 (2)	7 (0)
55.0%-64.9%	- -	10 (0)	8[f] (0)	16 (2)	16 (2)
65.0 and over	- -	2 (0)	2 (0)	8 (2)	8 (2)

SOURCES: *Comparison of State Unemployment Insurance Laws*: for 1948, the October 1948 edition issued by the Federal Security Agency, p. 44; for 1971, the edition reflecting revisions issued august 31, 1971, by the USDOL, Manpower Administration, pp. BT-7 through BT-9; for 1990, the edition reflecting revisions issued January 7, 1990, by the USDOL, Employment and Training Administration, pp. 3-35 to 3-40, tables 304 and 305; for average weekly covered wage data, *Unemployment Insurance Financial Data, 1938-1982,* and annual supplements.

a. See table 10.1 for ten largest states in these years.

b. Does not reflect higher maximum WBA for claimants with dependents; maximum WBA for 1948 as of October, for 1971 as of August, and for 1990 as of January.

c. States distributed by percentages specified in flexible maximum provisions, if any, except as noted; other states by percentages based on state AWW for 1948, 1971, and 1989 for the three years presented.

d. States with flexible maximum provisions requiring annual or semiannual adjustment of maximum WBA to maintain specified percentage relationship to state AWW (see footnote f for Ohio and Vermont); no flexible maximum provisions in 1948.

e. No state more than $26 in 1948, less than $40 in 1971, or more than $293 in 1990.

f. Includes Vermont which in 1971 specified a flexible maximum at 50 percent of AWW plus $9 yielding 57.5 percent of 1971 AWW.

g. Includes Illinois with flexible maximum provision specifying 49 percent of AWW but 1990 ceiling frozen to wage level set by statute so that the ceiling equaled 43.2 percent of 1989 AWW; and Ohio with no percentage specified but applying annual percentage change in AWW to adjust maximum which in 1990 equaled 43.6 percent of its 1989 AWW.

h. Includes Louisiana and South Dakota with flexible maximum provisions in 1990 specifying 66-2/3 and 62 percent, respectively, of AWW but with ceilings frozen indefinitely at earlier dollar levels which were 47.0 and 48.1 percent, respectively, of their 1989 AWWs; and Vermont with flexible provisions which called for applying annual percentage change in the average wage to adjust the ceiling (adjustment suspended at times) so that in 1990 it equaled 48.2 percent of its 1989 AWW.

approach had indeed caught on. Federal pressures, including the threat of minimum benefit standards, helped to motivate the states to raise their ceilings to reasonable levels and maintain them there. Even the majority of the largest states joined the parade.

Further progress, however, stalled in the 1980s in the face of financial difficulties. To restrain benefit outlays, several states suspended the operation of their flexible maximum provisions, freezing their ceilings at existing levels for a year or more, or indefinitely. A few reduced somewhat the percentage to be maintained, and one state abandoned the approach altogether. In 1990, the number of states with flexible provisions stood at thirty-six, the same as a decade earlier; four of the ten largest states continued to stand apart from this approach.[26] It should be noted that eleven of the fourteen states that in 1990 paid higher WBAs to claimants with dependents also provided for flexible maximums.[27]

Minimum WBA

Statutory minimum weekly amounts also failed to keep pace with the rise in wages in the program's earlier years. Paid to relatively small numbers of claimants, very few of whom are likely to be regular full-time workers, minimum WBAs have drawn scant legislative attention. Because of their limited impact, minimum benefit provisions tended to be ignored for long periods. In 1948, the states paid weekly minimums ranging from $3 to $10 with thirty-one states no higher than $6. As wage levels rose sharply over the ensuing years, benefit floors lagged, as did ceilings. Minimum state qualifying requirements also eroded to the extent they were based on minimum base-period earnings, especially in states that applied a test of such earnings as a multiple of the weekly benefit amount. In 1971, eighteen states still paid minimum

---

26. Included among the four largest states were California, Florida, and New York, as well as Texas which applied a provision to increase the benefit ceiling by $7 each year if the average weekly wage of production workers in manufacturing in the state exceeded the 1976 average by $10 or more.

27. Of the three nonflexible states, Alaska and Indiana had basic benefit ceilings in 1990 that were, respectively, under 35 percent and under 25 percent of their 1989 average weekly wage levels, the only states so low; with maximum dependents allowed and enough added wages in Indiana, the weekly benefit amount payable could go as high as 48 percent of the average wage in Alaska and 40 percent in Indiana.

weekly amounts of from $3 to $10; a dozen states paid as high as $20 to $25. While the flexible maximum provision was becoming widespread, a similar provision to adjust the minimum had emerged in only three states by 1971. These states set their minimum WBAs at from 10 percent to 15 percent of the average weekly wage, although two of the states accomplished this result indirectly by setting the minimum as a percentage of the flexible maximum amount. Flexible minimum provisions applied in only eight states in 1990, all falling between 10 percent and 15 percent of the average weekly wage. The majority of states had benefit floors of from $30 to $59; a few still paid minimums of $10 or less. Among the ten largest states, minimums ranged from $10 to $59, and none was flexible. In general, benefit floors appeared to have improved somewhat in relation to benefit ceilings and average wage levels.

Benefits for Partial Unemployment

All states provide for the payment of a partial weekly benefit to encourage unemployed workers to take some part-time work until they can regain regular employment. The conditions and benefit computation rules that apply, however, frequently have operated to restrict or block the incentive to take such work. Partial benefit provisions generally concern two key elements: the definition of partial unemployment that can be compensated and the manner of offsetting part-time earnings against the WBA. By and large, because these elements have been so limiting, claimants who earn in a week part-time wages equal to their full WBAs, or perhaps slightly more, have not been eligible for any benefits. Claimants with part-time earnings below those levels usually have received little advantage for their efforts since all but a small portion of the earnings is offset against the full WBA to determine the partial benefit amount payable.

Many of the states have tried to improve the incentives inherent in their partial benefit provisions over the years by allowing some benefit when earnings were over the level of the full weekly benefit, and by disregarding a larger portion of earnings when offsetting them against the WBA. In 1990, about half the states (four of the ten largest) paid a partial benefit to claimants who earned more than the WBA, compared with only one-fourth in 1948. In the earlier year, few states disregarded more than a small dollar amount of earnings ($3 or less) when offsetting part-time earnings against the WBA. By 1990, fewer than a third of the states disregarded a flat dollar amount, most of them $15 or less. About half the states ignored earnings up to a specified proportion of the WBA ranging from 20 to 60 percent. Others disregarded a specified proportion of the earnings themselves. By and large, however, the provisions of most states accommodated the claimant's retention of only minor amounts of part-time earnings while drawing a partial benefit.

Short-time Compensation

A later development that appeared first in California in 1978 was a provision for short-time or worksharing compensation. This approach covers an arrangement, agreed to by the employer and employees and approved by the state agency, whereby the usual full-time work schedule for the week is reduced for all workers in the operation in order to avoid total layoffs of some of them. The reduction amounts to a loss of a uniform number of days or hours of work a week for all workers covered by the agreement. The usual partial benefit provisions would not cover the situation. Short-time compensation, instead, provides that a proportion of the WBA be paid to match the proportion of the regular workweek lost because of the reduction. For example, a 25 percent reduction of the normally scheduled weekly hours would produce a partial WBA equal to 25 percent of the WBA otherwise payable for a full week of unemployment. The work reduction is expected to be temporary, bridging a period of slack business workload or budget shortfall. The number of weeks of short-time compensation allowed in a year is limited. The usual availability-for-work and job-search requirements are not applied but the worker must return to full-time work when the employer schedules it. Special financing provisions may also apply.

As of 1990, short-time compensation provisions existed in fourteen states, including four of the ten largest. Federal legislation adopted in 1982 called for the U.S. Department of Labor to assist states in developing such provisions and to evaluate the experience (see chapter 9).

Waiting Period

Most states do not compensate the first week of insured unemployment in a benefit year. Until the 1980s, the trend had been toward reduction or elimination of the waiting period. In 1948, eight states still had a two-week wait, and one state had none at all; the rest required one waiting week. In 1971, no state required more than a one-week wait before paying benefits and six states had no waiting period;[28] in six other states the waiting week became payable retroactively if the claimant received benefits or was unemployed for a specified period ranging from three to twelve successive weeks.

The trend toward elimination or retroactive payment of the waiting week continued during the 1970s. It peaked in 1980 when twelve states had no waiting period and nine states paid it retroactively; six of these twenty-one states were among the ten largest. Resistance to the trend grew in many states as they encountered financial problems. The relative cost of eliminating the waiting week was not insignificant. In 1980, Congress amended the federal-state extended benefits program to preclude federal sharing of the cost of the first week of extended benefits in a state that did not apply a waiting week for regular benefits, including states that paid it retroactively. During the 1980s, the trend toward waiting week elimination stopped and retroactive payment provisions were repealed in some states. As of 1990, only four states still paid the waiting week retroactively, while twelve states imposed no waiting week at the outset. These states included three of the ten largest.

Duration of Benefits

States continued to liberalize their regular benefit duration provisions throughout the 1950s and 1960s. These efforts focused on increasing the maximum number of weeks of benefits allowed, eventu-

---

28. The waiting period for partial benefits, usually the same as for full weekly benefits, was a week longer in a few states; in 1971, Alabama imposed a one-week wait for partial benefits but none for total unemployment.

ally reaching at least twenty-six weeks in a benefit year nearly everywhere. Variable duration formulas, used by most states to determine the number of weeks payable to individual claimants up to the maximum allowed, have varied widely, and they have tended to be relatively restrictive. As the maximum duration limit was rising, fewer states provided uniform duration, which allows the same maximum number of weeks to all eligible claimants. The major problem that emerged after most states had moved up to a ceiling of 26 weeks for regular benefits was the inadequacy of this much protection during recession periods when much longer term unemployment became so widespread and slow to subside. The solution adopted was to extend benefit duration during such times. This step was taken by some states and promoted elsewhere by the federal government as a temporary measure during the 1958 recession. Temporary extension was then federally mandated for all states during the 1961 recession. Extending benefit duration during high unemployment periods became a permanent federal-state program in 1970. Financial strains led some states to cut back somewhat on their regular duration provisions in the 1980s, as with other benefit and eligibility provisions.

Regular Duration

By the early 1960s, the maximum number of weeks payable had risen to virtually a standard level of twenty-six weeks; some states moved even beyond that level. On the other hand, fewer states applied a uniform duration provision. Table 10.7 shows the progress in statutory maximum duration and the fall off in uniform duration from 1948 to 1971. As of 1990, only Illinois and New York among the ten largest states provided uniform duration, along with seven other states. In Puerto Rico alone was the regular duration ceiling under twenty-six weeks.[29] During the 1980s, the number of states with maximum regular duration limits in excess of twenty-six weeks declined to two, at least partly the consequence of financial strains in state reserve funds. As many as ten states paid more than twenty-six weeks of regular ben-

---

29. In 1992, Puerto Rico increased the number of weeks allowed under its uniform duration provision from twenty to twenty-six weeks.

Table 10.7   Distribution of States by Maximum Regular Uniform and Variable Duration Provisions—1948, 1971, 1990

Type of provision and maximum number of weeks payable	Number of states					
	1948		1971		1990	
Total - all states (10 largest)[a]	51	(10)	52	(10)	53	(10)
Uniform duration total	15	(1)	8	(1)	9	(2)
Less than 20 weeks	6	(0)	0	(0)	0	(0)
20-25 weeks	8	(0)	1[b]	(0)	1[b]	(0)
26 weeks	1	(1)	7	(1)	8	(2)
Variable duration total	36	(9)	44	(9)	44	(8)
Under 20 weeks	5	(1)	0	(0)	0	(0)
20-25 weeks	25	(5)	0	(0)	0	(0)
26 weeks	6	(3)	35	(7)	42	(8)
27 or more weeks	0	(0)	9[c]	(2)	2[d]	(0)

SOURCES: *Comparison of State Unemployment Insurance Laws*: for 1948, the October 1948 edition issued by the Federal Security Agency, p. 52; for 1971, the edition reflecting revisions issued August 31, 1971, by the USDOL, Manpower Administration , pp. BT-14 and BT-15; for 1990, the edition reflecting revisions issued January 7, 1990, by the USDOL, Employment and Training Administration, pp. 3-45 to 3-48, table 309.

a. See table 10.1 for ten largest states in these years.

b. Puerto Rico at twenty weeks.

c. Range of state maximums from twenty-eight to thirty-six weeks.

d. Massachusetts and Washington at thirty weeks.

efits as late as 1980, including one (Iowa) that paid as many as thirty-nine weeks.[30]

Besides the overall maximum limit on regular duration, the majority of states with variable duration formulas have also limited the total amount of benefits payable to a claimant to a specific fraction of the claimant's base-period earnings—to one-third or less in most of these states. Only a few allowed up to one-half or more of base-period earnings. The total of benefits allowed, so calculated, is divided by the claimant's weekly benefit amount to determine the number of weeks payable, up to the overall maximum. In 1990, twenty-seven of thirty-four states that varied duration on this basis used a fraction of one-third or less of base-period earnings. Five of the eight largest states that varied duration based the number of weeks payable on the claimant's weeks of employment in the base period, such as one week of benefit for each two weeks of work in Florida, and three weeks for four weeks of work in Michigan and New Jersey.[31] The remaining variable duration states provided more than a third of base period earnings or used other types of formulas, most of them designed to limit duration allowed for workers with largely seasonal employment.[32] The minimum number of weeks of benefits payable under variable duration formulas has generally derived from the minimum qualifying requirement. In 1990, minimum potential duration among the variable duration states ranged from six to twenty-four weeks, with the majority in the ten to fifteen weeks range.

The result of this diversity among the states in their regular duration provisions is that claimants around the country with similar base-period employment and earnings experience may qualify for considerably different levels of potential weeks of protection. Moreover, to

---

30. Oklahoma had also specified a thirty-nine-week regular duration limit in the 1960s, but its variable duration formula was so restrictive that relatively few claimants could qualify for it.

31. Included in this group were: Ohio which provided twenty weeks of benefits for twenty weeks of work (its minimum qualifying requirement) plus 1 week for each additional week of work up to the overall duration maximum of twenty-six weeks; and Pennsylvania, which qualified claimants with only sixteen or seventeen weeks of work for up to sixteen weeks of benefits and all those with eighteen or more weeks of work for up to the twenty-six-week limit.

32. For example, of the ten largest states, California allowed total benefits equal to 50 percent of the claimant's base-period earnings up to twenty-six weeks, and North Carolina multiplied the base-period to high-quarter earnings multiple by eight to determine weeks payable, subject to the twenty-six-week maximum.

qualify for twenty-six weeks of regular benefits can require very different base-period experience, depending on the state, ranging from as little as sixteen weeks of work in Pennsylvania or $150 in earnings (thirty times the minimum weekly benefit amount) in Hawaii to as much as fifty-two weeks of employment in Florida.

State Extended Benefits

During the 1958 recession, a number of states adopted temporary extended benefit provisions and operated them independently of the federal Temporary Unemployment Compensation program enacted for that time. In 1959, a half dozen states established permanent provisions to extend benefits during periods of high unemployment, triggered on and off by the level of the state insured unemployment rate. The extension was usually 50 percent of the duration of regular benefits. It was in 1959 also that another group of states chose to raise the maximums of their regular duration provisions above twenty-six weeks. In 1961-62, when the federal Temporary Extended Unemployment Compensation program applied and was financed fully by a temporary addition to the Federal Unemployment Tax, the costs of regular state benefits paid beyond the twenty-sixth week during the period were reimbursed by the federal program.

In mid-1970, shortly before the adoption of the Extended Unemployment Compensation Act which set up the permanent federal-state shared program, a total of ten states had their own extended benefit provisions. Most of these provisions were repealed in subsequent years. As of 1990, only two states (California and Connecticut) remained from that group. During the recession years of the early 1980s, several states adopted temporary extension provisions to pay added weeks of benefits to claimants exhausting their regular benefits when the federal-state program was not triggered on in the state. Alaska and Oregon adopted extended benefit provisions later in the 1980s to assure such benefits to claimants unable to meet the stiffer qualifying requirements added to the federal-state program. Hawaii, Minnesota, and Puerto Rico have provided for extended benefits in special unemployment situations within the state.[33] Developments in the 1970s and 1980s pointed increasingly to a much smaller role for the states in providing benefit protection beyond the twenty-sixth week.

Seasonal Provisions

During the early years of the program, as many as thirty-three states had adopted special provisions to limit the benefit entitlement of workers employed in seasonal activities (Murray 1972, p. 29). The principal motivations for these provisions were (1) the fears that benefits claimed by such workers during their off-season would drain reserve funds and threaten solvency, and (2) the fears of employers of such workers that the heavy costs of off-season benefits would make their tax rates very high due to experience rating (Murray 1972, p. 28). The application of these seasonal provisions, however, generally proved to be difficult and generated various anomalies, inequities, and administrative problems. Over the years, the trend has been toward the abandonment of seasonal provisions. By 1971, only sixteen states had them; in 1990, the number was thirteen, including three of the ten largest states.

Seasonal provisions spell out the basis for special restrictions on a worker's benefit rights. The usual process is to define or designate a specific industry, occupation, operation, or employer as "seasonal." The particular period during which the employment activity regularly recurs each year may be defined for each industry or operation. These definitions and designations are determined administratively, on a case-by-case basis, after investigation or hearings, and sometimes on request. Most states with seasonal provisions do not allow workers

---

33. Hawaii added thirteen weeks when a disaster, as declared by the governor, increased unemployment substantially; Minnesota provided six additional weeks for claimants losing jobs due to a large permanent layoff in a county with an unemployment rate of 10 percent or more; and Puerto Rico allowed up to thirty-two more weeks of added benefits beyond its regular uniform twenty-week duration in specific industries, establishments, or occupations determined to be adversely affected by technological or other structural change.

with seasonal employment, so designated, to draw benefits during the off-season on the basis of that employment or the earnings from it. The designations of seasonal activities do not tend to apply to a broad scope of industries or to large significant industries in a state. Considering the cumbersome and somewhat political nature of the process, limited application is not surprising and helps to account for the lessening appeal of this approach to the problem.

The reasonable alternative to special seasonal provisions is a qualifying requirement that effectively screens out workers with very limited base-period employment concentrated in less than fifteen weeks or so, or in a single calendar quarter, and diligent application of the current availability and work search requirements for continuing eligibility. As noted in chapter 9, however, federal provisions adopted in the 1970s required the states to deny benefits to professional athletes during the off-season of their sport and to school employees between school years or terms unless they had no reasonable assurance of resuming their employment.

State Benefit Financing

The states came out of the first half of the 1940s with more abundant benefit reserves, relative to their total covered payrolls, than they were to have since that time. Their response was to lower payroll tax rates through experience rating, the only means available for the purpose. From 1940 to 1948, the yearly U.S. average of state employer tax rates fell from 2.7 to 1.24 percent of taxable payrolls. After rising for a few years to 1.58 in 1951, it resumed its decline, reaching 1.12 percent by 1954. Throughout this period, despite substantial increases in wage levels, the taxable wage base continued unchanged at $3,000. The taxable proportion of all covered payrolls nationwide fell from over 90 percent in 1940 to less than 70 percent by 1955. As a result, the *effective* average tax rate, measured on the basis of *total* payrolls, declined to about 0.8 percent by the mid-1950s. Table 10.8 summarizes the trends in the national averages for several of these key statistics in five-year intervals from 1940.

Table 10.8 Selected U.S. Unemployment Insurance Financial Trends: Five-Year Intervals, 1940-1990

Year	Average employer tax rates[a] as a percent of		Aggregate of taxable payrolls as percent of total payrolls	Aggregate of year-end reserves as percent of total payrolls
	Total payrolls	Taxable payrolls[b]		
1940	2.50	2.70	92.8	5.60
1945	1.50	1.71	87.9	10.38
1950	1.18	1.50	79.1	6.76
1955	.81	1.18	68.3	5.56
1960	1.15	1.88	61.1	3.29
1965	1.18	2.12	55.8	3.17
1970	.64	1.34	47.7	3.11
1975	.89	1.98	45.2	.53
1980	1.06	2.37	44.7	.64
1985	1.29	3.12	41.1	.68[c]
1990	.73	1.95	37.6	1.88[c]

SOURCES: *Unemployment Insurance Financial Data, 1938-1982* and annual supplements.

a. Tax rates are those imposed by states on subject employers.

b. Based on state taxable wages.

c. Based on reserves net of outstanding debt owed by states to the Federal Unemployment Account (loan fund).

The four recessions that marked the post-World War II period through 1961 altered the financial scene in many states. Diminishing reserve funds encountered heavy demands for benefits in those downturns, accelerating the decline. Increasingly, states began to face problems of potential fund inadequacy and the need for careful financial planning. From a low point of 0.79 in 1954, the U.S. average tax rate climbed, to peak at about 1.4 percent of total payrolls in 1962, a level not seen since the early 1940s, before experience rating had taken full effect. The great majority of states held to the $3,000 tax base so that less than 60 percent of all payrolls was taxed in 1962.

The tax rate trend turned down again through the boom years of the 1960s. The U.S. average fell to 0.64 percent of total payrolls by 1970, its lowest level. Only 45 percent of all payrolls was taxed in 1971, the year before the federal tax base increased to $4,200. The increase raised the taxable proportion to 52 percent in 1972. The aggregate of state reserve funds, which had recovered from under 3 percent of total payrolls in the early 1960s, was falling again in 1970 and 1971. Those reserves were severely battered during the next dozen years and completely wiped out in the majority of states, at least at some time in this period. Aggregate reserves, net of outstanding loans, fell to as low as 0.13 percent of all payrolls at the end of 1976. After some limited recovery in the late 1970s, state funds as a whole were negative by over $2.6 billion by the close of 1982 and by $5.8 billion a year later. Legislating tax reforms became increasingly painful as the states struggled to repay federal loans, rebuild reserve funds, and allocate the burden in an atmosphere charged with taxpayer hostility, strained by competing interest groups, and clouded by economic uncertainty.

Tax rates moved up again after 1975, the national average reaching above 1.4 percent of total payrolls in 1979 before subsiding for a few years. Tax bases finally began to move up in more states, but not enough to raise the U.S. proportion of payrolls taxed to as much as half any time after 1973. That proportion dropped below 45 percent in 1983 and below 40 percent in 1988. Amendments of financing provisions by many states in 1982 and 1983 helped raise average tax rates for a while and by more than the experience rating schedules alone would have raised them. By 1985, however, the national average rate was moving down again, despite generally thin reserve positions. Restrained benefit outlays reflected improved economic conditions, but also tightened eligibility rules and pared benefit amount and duration provisions. The resulting net surplus revenues enabled states to pay off their debts and accumulate some reserves.

The scope of the financial crisis in state reserve funds during the 1970s and 1980s warrants a little closer look. The recessions that plagued much of this period resulted in benefit outlays well in excess of current tax revenues. Benefit reserve funds eventually proved insufficient to cover the difference in most states. Moreover, the permanent federal-state extended benefit program enacted in 1970 came into play in the recession that followed soon after; by 1972, all states were paying extended benefits to exhaustees of regular benefits. Half the cost of the benefits also came out of state reserve funds thereby accelerating their depletion. All but fourteen states ran out of funds at some time, beginning with Connecticut in 1972, requiring them to borrow from the federal loan fund in order to continue paying benefits. Insolvency became widespread as successive recessions allowed little time in between to repay the loans and replenish reserves from surplus tax revenues in nonrecession years.

States varied as to the length of time their funds were insolvent in the 1970s and 1980s. Of the thirty-nine states that borrowed in these years, eight did so for short periods, repaying their loans by the end of the year in which they were drawn. Some state funds were insolvent for only a few years; others were insolvent for as many as ten or more years in this period. At least one state fund was insolvent at the end of each year from 1972 through 1987, with the number rising to twenty by the end of 1977, declining to nine after the next two years, then rising again to twenty-three at the end of 1982 and 1983. The table below gives some indication of the length of time state funds were insolvent during the sixteen-year period beginning with 1972 as measured by their year-end reserve fund positions. It shows a distribution of the states (and of the ten largest states) by the number of years from 1972 to 1987 that their year end reserves, net of outstanding loans were negative, i.e., insolvent.[34]

---

34. Information about state reserve fund loans and insolvency based on *Unemployment Insurance Financial Data, 1938-1982*, and annual supplements.

Number of years insolvent	Number of states	
	All states	Ten largest*
Total	53	10
None	22	2
1-3	8	1
4-6	9	2
7-9	6	1
10-13	8	4

*As of 1971; see table 10.1.

Among the ten largest states, California never borrowed in this period, while Florida did but briefly, repaying the debt before the end of the year the loan was made. New York borrowed in 1977 and 1978 but repaid all its debt by 1979. Massachusetts ended each of four years in the 1970s with insolvent reserve funds, and Texas had five such years in the 1980s; in neither state, however, did the amount by which the year-end reserve was negative ever exceed 1 percent of total covered payrolls. Ohio's fund was insolvent at the end of each of seven years during the 1980s and negative by more than 1 percent of total payrolls in all of them except 1980, more than 3 percent in 1982 and 1983. The remaining four large states had insolvent year-end reserve funds in both decades—Illinois and Pennsylvania for twelve years, Michigan for eleven, and New Jersey for ten years. Connecticut's fund was insolvent the longest—thirteen years, finally paying off its debt in full in 1985. In all of the states noted with ten or more years of insolvency, their year-end reserve funds were often negative by more than 1, 2, or 3 percent of total payrolls. Other states with year-end insolvent funds for seven or more years include Delaware, District of Columbia, Minnesota, Puerto Rico, Rhode Island, Vermont, Virgin Islands, and West Virginia. The fourteen states with seven or more years of negative year-end reserves represent the most serious experience with insolvency. While most states came through the financial crisis with comparatively moderate insolvency, or none at all, the concentration of large states among the worst cases magnified the overall problem.[35]

---

35. For additional discussion and analysis of the debt and insolvency of state funds, see Vroman (1986).

Trends in state benefit financing provisions are reviewed against the national trends in key financing measures shown in table 10.8. Table 10.9 extends the data in table 10.8 by presenting how the states were distributed by several of these measures for selected years in the period. The data show that average tax rates tend to be high in most states, as in 1983, after a recession period when experience rating accounts need to be replenished, while average rates move to lower levels, as in 1990, after a period of business expansion when experience rating accounts have been restored to more substantial positions.

Employer Tax Rates and Experience Rating

By 1948, all states provided for experience rating of employer taxes.[36] The key factor in assigning rates is the way an individual employer's experience with unemployment is measured in comparison with that of other employers, and how that measure is related to tax rates. Another important element is the range over which the rates can vary in a state as defined by the minimum and maximum rates as specified by law. States vary in the extent benefits are or are not charged to individual employers; noncharging rules and the way ineffectively charged benefits are handled, therefore, also determine the nature of a state's experience rating system.[37] A newly developed experience rating index calculated by the U.S. Department of Labor for each of forty-eight states for 1989 shows that from 38 to 91 percent of the benefits paid in these states that year were effectively charged. The range for 1990, also among forty-eight states, was from 48 to 94 percent.[38]

Federal law initially required that individual employers have at least three years of experience before they could be assigned reduced rates. New employers paid the standard rate until they accumulated the

---

36. For a comprehensive treatment of experience rating, see Becker (1972). A few states temporarily repealed or suspended their experience rating provisions in subsequent years because of financial difficulties, but all eventually restored them when their financial status improved or in conjunction with tax reforms. Puerto Rico and the Virgin Islands entered the federal-state system in 1961 and 1978, respectively, without provision for experience rating, but both have since adopted it.

37. Ineffectively charged benefits are those charged to employers that exceed the taxes they pay because they are at the maximum tax rate or because they go out of business leaving benefit liabilities inadequately covered by their remaining reserve balances, if any.

38. USDOL, Employment and Training Administration Unemployment Insurance Program Letter (1991). See also earlier Program Letter (1990) for more explanation of the index.

Table 10.9   Distribution of States by Selected Unemployment Insurance Financing Measures—1948, 1971, 1983, and 1990

Financing measure	1948		1971		1983		1990	
Total - all states (10 largest)[a]	51	(10)	52	(10)	53	(10)	53	(10)
Average employer tax rate as % of total payrolls								
Less than 0.50%	4	(1)	18	(4)	1	(1)	10	(1)
0.50 - 0.99	13	(4)	26	(4)	13	(1)	31	(7)
1.00 - 1.99	34	(5)	8	(2)	35	(8)	10	(2)
2.00 and over	0	(0)	0	(0)	4	(0)	2	(0)
Taxable wages as % of total payrolls								
Under 40.0 %	-	-	4	(3)	7	(4)	25	(8)
40.0 - 49.9	-	-	27	(7)	28	(6)	13	(1)
50.0 - 59.9	-	-	18	(0)	10	(0)	8	(1)
60.0 - 69.9	-	-	3	(0)	7	(0)	6	(0)
70.0 and over	51[b]	(10)	0	(0)	1	(0)	1	(0)
Year-end reserve[c] as % of total payrolls								
Negative	-	-	0	(0)	23	(6)	0	(0)
0 - 0.99%	-	-	2	(0)	16	(1)	5	(1)
1.00 - 1.99	-	-	10	(5)	11	(3)	19	(6)
2.00 - 2.99	-	-	22	(5)	2	(0)	12	(1)
3.00 and over	51[d]	(10)	18	(0)	1	(0)	17	(2)

SOURCES: *Unemployment Insurance Financial Data, 1938-1982* and annual supplements.
a. See table 10.1 for ten largest states in these years (in 1983, the same as in 1971).
b. States ranged from 76.2 to 90.9 percent.
c. Net of any outstanding federal loans.
d. States ranged from 4.46 to 12.65 percent.

required record. The standard rate was usually 2.7 percent, equal to the full federal tax offset, until the latter doubled to 5.4 percent beginning 1985. A 1954 federal amendment allowed states to reduce the period to one year, a matter of importance to the smaller firms brought under coverage as required by a federal amendment also adopted that year. About half of the states quickly took advantage of the relaxed requirement, usually specifying only one year of coverage before the taxes of new or newly covered employers are experience rated. About a third of the states still required three years of experience in 1971, and about the same proportion did so in 1990. The 1970 federal amendments mandated coverage of employers of one or more workers. They also permitted states to assign newly covered employers a reduced rate immediately, though not less than 1 percent, on a "reasonable basis," without regard to individual experience, until they became eligible for experience rating. As of 1990, all but four states applied reduced rates to new employers using various grounds as a "reasonable basis."[39]

Types of Experience Rating Systems

The method used by about 60 percent of the states to account for employer experience is the *reserve-ratio* method. It aggregates an employer's past tax contributions and subtracts the total of past benefits charged to that employer. The remaining balance or reserve is then calculated as a ratio to the employer's annual payroll. A specified schedule arrays possible tax rates in inverse relation to reserve ratios, and the tax rate is assigned from the schedule according to the employer's reserve ratio—the higher the ratio, the lower the tax rate. Rates are assigned each year after employer reserve accounts and payrolls are updated. The reserve-ratio method has always been the most popular approach to experience rating—used by twenty-nine states in 1948, thirty-two states in 1971, and by thirty-three states in 1990 including six of the ten largest.

The *benefit-ratio* method eliminates contributions as a factor in measuring an employer's unemployment experience. It considers only the recent record rather than the total past. Benefits charged to the employer during the last few, typically three, years are calculated as a ratio to the employer's taxable payrolls in those years. That ratio serves

---

39. These included, for example, average industry tax rates and average statewide benefit cost rates over a period of years, with a 1 percent minimum and, in some cases, an upper limit as well.

as the basis for the assigned tax rate either directly or from a rate schedule. The method has gained adherents over time. It was used by only six states in 1948, nine states in 1971, and by fifteen states in 1990, including four of the ten largest.

Two other methods of experience rating were in use in 1990; both have declined in popularity over the years. The benefit-wage ratio method measures an employer's experience in terms of the base-period wages earned from the employer by separated employees who drew benefits. Only three states still held to this approach in 1990, compared to nine in 1948.[40] The other method measures the percentage *payroll decline* from year to year or between calendar quarters as the basis for comparative employer experience and rate variation. Only Alaska used it in 1990; seven states did so in 1948.

A state may basically follow one of these methods but make use of other factors as well. For example, Michigan's tax structure in 1990 experience rated on the basis of the benefit-ratio approach, but also used the employer's reserve to determine another component of the tax.[41] Over time, the tax structures of many states became increasingly complex as one or more elements were added to the basic experience rated component, making an employer's tax rate a composite.

Range of Employer Tax Rates

Every state sets a tax rate ceiling and usually a minimum as well. As noted before, the major impetus for the rapid application of experience rating in the early 1940s was the massive reserve buildup and the resulting demands for reducing tax rates below the standard 2.7 percent level. The emphasis, therefore, began with getting rates down. Table 10.10 indicates state distributions by the lowest and highest tax rates

---

40. In 1990 Illinois was in the process of converting from a benefit-wage to a reserve-ratio formula and is counted here among the reserve-ratio states for 1990.

41. Michigan's tax rate structure included three components: an experience rated component determined by the employer's benefit ratio which covered charged benefit costs; a fund solvency component determined by the employer's reserve related to a uniform state solvency standard which is to help raise the employer's reserve to the required level; and a uniform rate component added for all employers to cover noncharged benefits.

Table 10.10   Distribution of States by Minimum and Maximum Tax Rates—1948, 1971, 1983, 1990

Tax rate class[a]	1948		1971		1983		1990	
Total - all states (10 largest)[b]	51	(10)	51[c]	(10)	50[c]	(10)	52[c]	(10)
Maximum tax rate[d]								
2.70 - 2.99	38	(6)	12	(0)	2	(0)	-	-
3.00 - 3.99	10	(3)	12	(1)	1	(0)	-	-
4.00 - 4.99	3	(1)	24	(7)	17	(4)	-	-
5.00 and over	0	(0)	3	(2)	30	(6)	-	-
For 1990 distribution:								
5.40 - 5.99	-	-	-	-	-	-	17	(3)
6.00 - 6.99	-	-	-	-	-	-	15	(3)
7.00 - 7.99	-	-	-	-	-	-	5	(2)
8.00 and over	-	-	-	-	-	-	15	(2)
Minimum tax rate[e]								
0	11	(2)	16	(5)	11[f]	(2)	17[f]	(4)
0.01 - 0.19	3	(1)	17	(2)	19	(1)	20	(3)
0.20 - 0.49	8	(1)	8	(1)	12	(6)	9	(3)
0.50	17	(4)	4	(1)	3	(0)	2	(0)
0.51 - 0.99	8	(1)	3	(0)	2	(1)	2	(0)
1.00 and over	4	(1)	3	(1)	3	(0)	2	(0)

SOURCES: *Comparison of State Unemployment Insurance Laws:* for 1948, the October 1948 edition issued by the Federal Security Agency, p. 16, table 5; for 1971, the edition reflecting revisions issued August 31, 1971, by the USDOL, Manpower Administration, pp. TT-1 and TT2, table TT-1; for 1983, the edition reflecting revisions issued September 4, 1983, by the USDOL, Manpower Administration, pp. 2-39 to 2-42, table 206); for 1990, the edition reflecting revisions issued January 7, 1990, by the USDOL, Employment and Training Administration, pp. 2-39 to 2-42, table 206.

a. Minimum and maximum rates apply to taxable payrolls; they generally do not reflect special additions or emergency surtaxes.

b. See table 10.1 for the ten largest states in these years (in 1983, same as 1971).

c. Excludes states that did not experience rate: Puerto Rico in 1971, 1983, and 1990; the Virgin Islands and Washington in 1983.

d. Maximum rate under least favorable rate schedule if more than one schedule provided in law.

e. Minimum rate under most favorable rate schedule.

f. Includes Nebraska in 1983, and Nebraska and Utah in 1990—minimum rate not specified in law but set administratively instead.

that could apply as of four selected years.[42] By 1948, only thirteen states had rates ranging above 2.7 percent even under their least favorable schedules. The lowest possible rates assignable that year could be less than 0.5 percent in all but twelve states.

During the two decades after 1948, with diminishing reserve funds and recession experience to guide them, most states recognized the need to extend rates above the 2.7 standard level. The restricted taxable wage bases reduced the proportion of payrolls that could be taxed, adding further impetus to higher rates to assure adequate revenues. By 1971, the rate ceilings of over half the states, including nine of the ten largest, could go as high as 4.0 percent or more under their least favorable schedules. At the same time, states were more concentrated below 0.5 percent for their lowest possible rates, as compared with 1948. With the financial crises of the 1970s and early 1980s, and the continuing erosion of taxable payrolls, states shifted increasingly toward higher tax rates. Under the least favorable schedules provided as of 1983, no less than thirty states, including six of the ten largest, set their maximum rates at 5.0 percent or more, and most of these ceilings ranged from 6.0 to 10.5 percent. Fewer states could assign a zero rate than in 1971 under their most favorable schedules; under their least favorable schedules in 1983, minimum rates were 1.0 percent or more in about half the states.

After 1984, the federal law effectively required that state tax rate ceilings be at least 5.4 percent to assure full employer tax credit of this amount against the increased federal tax. As of 1990, the least favorable schedules of thirty-five states, including seven of the ten largest, provided rate ceilings of 6.0 percent or more, with fifteen states ranging from 8.0 to 10.0 percent. The most favorable minimum rates were under 0.5 percent in all but six states. While the range of tax rates assignable under experience rating formulas had widened greatly over the years, it is important to remember that in 1990, less than half of all payrolls was taxable in thirty-eight states, including nine of the ten largest, thus effectively narrowing the range sharply in terms of the total payrolls of the employers of most workers.

---

42. Most states have two or more rate schedules depending on the level of the state fund—the lower the fund level, the higher or less favorable the schedule. Some states with only one schedule apply an adjustment factor to the rates to reflect the fund level.

Noncharging of Benefits

All but a small number of states that experience rate employer taxes specify one or more conditions under which benefits may be paid that preclude the charging of such benefits, or of the benefit wages involved, to an individual employer, thereby eliminating their influence on the employer's rate. The primary rationale for noncharging is that it is reasonable to consider such benefits not to be the responsibility of the employer; their payment may be seen to satisfy a social objective and therefore should be financed on a pooled basis. As of 1990, all but about a half dozen of the states that experience rated using the reserve, benefit, or benefit-wage ratio method did not charge individual employers for benefits paid to unemployed workers who left their jobs voluntarily or were discharged for misconduct. Benefits may have been paid if the worker left for acceptable good personal cause, or after a limited period of benefit suspension, or after the worker requalified with some subsequent employment and became unemployed again in the same benefit year. Only fifteen states did not charge benefits paid to claimants who had been disqualified for refusing suitable work. The noncharging of benefits paid under these circumstances became more widespread over the years. Noncharging of the state share of federal-state extended benefit costs, originally the practice for most states, became less prevalent; only fifteen states excluded these costs from charging as of 1990.

Maintaining Adequate Reserves

Once the abundant state reserves of the 1940s were down to much lower levels, the problem of assuring adequate revenues and reserve funds drew more attention. By the mid-1950s, a few states were developing benefit financing difficulties in the wake of recession and depressed segments of their economies.[43] As financing concerns grew, so did the complexity of state tax structures. Provisions were added to protect the integrity of the funds and also to preserve experience rating.

Most states specified minimum fund requirements, along with their experience rated tax structures, to be met before any rate reductions

---

43. Alaska and Rhode Island, for example, discontinued experience rating in the early 1950s, and Alaska exhausted its reserves in 1955.

from the standard rate could apply (or to terminate the reductions if the fund fell below the specified level). About two-thirds of the states had such requirements in 1948. Many applied higher or lower rate schedules according to fund level. Measures used to designate the critical fund level included a flat dollar amount, the fund as a percent of total payrolls, and the fund as a multiple of total benefits paid in a period of time. Over the years, the way these measures were specified became more elaborate and sophisticated in attempts to capture the points at which fund solvency was threatened. They were also used to trigger the application of various types of adjustment or "solvency" factors, usually uniform percentage increases in the basic tax rates or, simply, added flat rates. As of 1990, somewhat over half the states had provisions for such solvency surcharges.[44]

By 1990, only sixteen states still specified fund requirements which, if not satisfied, would lead to a suspension of experience rating; none were among the largest states. Most of these states required a fund of at least a specified.percent of payrolls for reduced rates to continue experience rating, or to resume it if suspended. That was also the most used fund-level measure to trigger rate schedule changes or solvency factor applications. State tax provisions had become so varied as to defy virtually any useful grouping by major characteristics. States facing debt repayment were motivated further during the 1980s to alter their provisions in response to federal requirements to qualify for loan repayment deferrals, to avoid loss of federal tax credits for their employers, and to ease the impact of interest charges on loans. These further changes have tended to make state benefit financing more, rather than less, complex.

Taxable Wage Base

States may set their taxable wage bases without regard to the federal base. In effect, however, the federal base acts as a minimum since employers could lose a portion of their credit against the federal tax if their state had a lower base. No state departed from the $3,000 federal tax base, first applied in 1940, until Nevada went to $3,600 in 1954.[45]

---

44. Some states also provided for special surcharges when needed to finance interest on loans.
45. Nevada had continued to tax total wages from the outset, not going to the $3,000 base until 1946.

By 1960, the tax base was $3,600 or $3,800 in five states and $7,200 in Alaska.[46]

During the next decade, more states joined the move to higher bases. By 1971, their number had grown to twenty-three, including half the ten largest states; five states were at $4,200 or more. The federal base increased to $4,200 in 1972, and to $6,000 in 1978, already exceeded in that year in twelve states. In 1983, when the federal base increased to $7,000, half the states were at higher levels, though only three of the ten largest states were among them. By 1990, all but seventeen states had tax bases above the $7,000 level (including seven of the ten largest); the base was $10,000 or more in nineteen states and over $15,000 in six of them. Table 10.9 indicates that despite these increases, in 1990 taxable wages accounted for less than half of all covered wages in thirty-eight states, including nine of the ten largest; they were less than 40 percent in twenty-five states (eight of the ten largest).

As with any other wage-related aspect of unemployment insurance, the fixed-dollar tax base is soon eroded as wage levels rise. The idea of an automatic adjustment for wage change by a flexible tax base was applied first in Hawaii in 1965. Each year, Hawaii adjusted its base to equal 90 percent of the state's average annual wage.[47] North Dakota followed this approach several years later, and gradually others followed over the next ten years. By 1990, a total of eighteen states had flexible tax bases, most applying percentages ranging from 50 to 100 percent directly to average annual wages.[48] Only two of the large states were among this group. The 1990 taxable wage bases of these states ranged from $9,500 in Oklahoma to $21,300 in Alaska. Even among these states only four taxed more than half of their total payrolls in 1990; none of the thirty-five states with a fixed taxable wage base did so.

---

46. Alaska increased its base several times between 1955 and 1960 as part of its effort to restore and maintain solvency.

47. Hawaii raised its flexible adjustment in the 1970s to 100 percent of its average annual wage, which enabled it to tax about 70 percent of all covered payrolls.

48. Two states accomplished the same result indirectly by using the average weekly wage as the basis for the adjustment. For example, New Jersey set its taxable wage base at twenty-eight times the state average weekly wage, equivalent to about 52 percent of the average annual wage.

Reimbursement Financing

Two major classes of employers—nonprofit organizations and state and local government units—may finance their unemployment benefit costs by reimbursing state funds for benefits charged instead of through the regular state experience-rated tax system. Federal amendments adopted in the 1970s which mandated the states to cover these groups also required the provision of reimbursement as a financing option for nonprofit organizations.[49] In general, the employees of nonprofit and government employers tend to experience less unemployment than do employees of private, for-profit employers. Reimbursement thus avoids the potential use of public funds or charitable contributions, in effect, to subsidize some of the noncharged or ineffectively charged benefit costs of private firms, as payment of unemployment insurance taxes would entail. Given the option, most of these employers have chosen reimbursement. In 1990, reimbursing employers accounted for about 18 percent of all employment and payrolls covered by state programs.

Individual reimbursing employers may form a group to pool their risks and share benefit charges. The state will treat the group as a single employer for reimbursement purposes. Nonprofit hospitals, for example, have formed such groups in a number of states. This plan permits the individual employer to take advantage of the probable low risk yet have some protection against the possibility of an unexpected costly situation.

Nonprofit and state and local government employers are exempt from the Federal Unemployment Tax. Since that tax finances the program's administrative costs, these employers in effect are subsidized for their share of those costs by the taxpaying employers. Nor do they contribute toward the cost of the federal share of extended benefits, also financed by the federal tax.

---

49. Federal law may not prescribe how states must finance the benefit costs of their own or local government units; states are free to adopt whatever approach they prefer, and most have chosen reimbursement.

Employee Contributions

Unlike arrangements in other countries, employee contributions have never been an important source of unemployment insurance financing in the United States. By 1947, only two (Alabama and New Jersey) of the nine states that had an employee payroll tax for this purpose during the program's formative years still retained it. Beginning in 1955, Alaska levied an employee tax to help strengthen its financing structure. A similar purpose moved Pennsylvania and West Virginia to adopt an employee tax in the 1980s. Alabama, however, repealed its employee tax during this period, leaving four states using this financing source as of 1990. The tax rates in Alaska, New Jersey, and Pennsylvania applied to the same taxable wages as used for employer taxes. Rates ranged from 0.5 to 1.0 percent in Alaska, and up to 1.125 percent in New Jersey; the rate was 0.1 percent in Pennsylvania. West Virginia taxed the gross wages of employees up to 0.15 percent if projected employer tax revenues fell short of expected benefit outlays for a coming calendar quarter.

Concluding Observations

This review of state unemployment insurance provisions has illuminated a number of significant trends over the approximately four decades following the economy's reconversion after World War II. States gradually expanded their programs' coverage from limited beginnings so that by the late 1970s, nearly all wage and salary employment was protected, though not without the mandate of federal law. From earlier simplified easy-to-apply formulas, qualifying requirements changed to reflect more closely the minimum amount of employment intended to signify labor force attachment even though most states continued to use earnings as an equivalent measure for employment. In later years, the required level of employment, or its earnings equivalent, rose generally toward twenty weeks of base-period work, and beyond twenty weeks in a few states, compared with earlier levels of fifteen weeks or less in most states. The minimum amount of earnings in the requirements also rose substantially, but much of the increase was to compensate for the rise in wage levels.

Eligibility rules and disqualifications imposed generally stiffened over the period, a trend that accelerated in later years. By the mid-1980s, all but a handful of states denied benefits for the duration of the claimant's unemployment if disqualified for voluntary leaving of work or a misconduct discharge, as compared with the earlier predominant practice of a limited period of benefit suspension. Acceptable "good cause" for voluntary leaving became increasingly restricted to work or employer-related reasons; personal reasons for leaving became less likely to prevent disqualification.

Weekly benefit amounts paid by the states deteriorated badly from their original weekly wage-loss replacement rates of half or more because fixed statutory benefit ceilings failed to keep up with rapidly rising wage levels. By the mid-1950s, in most states, the majority of claimants were paid the maximum weekly benefit amount rather than the wage-related benefits the state formulas intended. The proportion of wage loss compensated ranged well below half. Further deterioration ceased as states increased their maximum weekly amounts more often though usually not enough to recover lost ground. States enacted larger increases in the 1970s and, more important, the flexible maximum approach was spreading. These improvements went far toward the goal of compensating the great majority of the insured unemployed for half their lost weekly wages. Some slippage occurred during the 1980s, however. A number of states revised their benefit formulas so that more claimants received a smaller weekly amount than the previous formulas would have paid; even at benefit levels below the ceiling, amounts were reduced to less than half the wage loss for some claimants.

From their original maximum duration levels generally at fifteen weeks of benefits payable, the states gradually raised their duration limits until they were at least twenty-six weeks everywhere (except in Puerto Rico) by the end of the 1960s. A number of states provided more than twenty-six weeks, some on a regular basis at all times and others only during periods of high unemployment. When the federal-state extended benefits program came into play in the 1970s, most of these states dropped back to a regular twenty-six-week limit.

The reserve-ratio system was the most popular approach for experience rating state employer payroll tax rates, and became even more so over time. The benefit-wage ratio method also held its adherents. Other approaches diminished in favor or disappeared. With overabundant reserves after World War II, the states applied experience rating mainly to reduce tax rates to below the 2.7 percent standard rate which became the maximum rate in most states. The taxable wage base remained unchanged at $3000 for many years with few exceptions, despite rising wages. The range of effective tax rates based on total payrolls grew very narrow as a result. Reserves declined sharply when periodic recessions swelled benefit outlays. By the late 1950s, adequate benefit financing was seen by more states as a serious problem area. Rates above the 2.7 percent level became more common and tax bases began moving up in some states. The recessions of the 1970s and early 1980s produced a crisis in state reserve funds with most requiring advances from the federal loan fund to sustain benefit payments. The effects of this experience were multiple and profound. While all state reserve funds regained solvency by the end of the 1980s, few were adequate to withstand the impact of another severe recession.

The concept that the states could serve as experimental laboratories for applying new ideas in unemployment insurance has proven to be a valuable feature of the federal-state system. Several approaches used successfully in one or two states spread widely throughout the country or became the basis for federal legislation. Prominent among these initiatives were the flexible weekly benefit ceiling in Kansas, the triggered extended benefits developed in a few states in the late 1950s, and the indexed or flexible taxable wage base pioneered by Hawaii. Some initiatives did not catch on, such as Utah's short-lived cost-of-living adjustment for weekly benefit amounts, and New York's unique alternative qualifying requirement using a two-year base period. Several program ideas were adopted by a limited group of states but have not become more widespread. Among these are dependents' allowances, uniform duration, and short-time compensation. Others, once in favor, declined in use or significance—for example, special seasonal provisions, the flat annual earnings qualifying requirement, and the annual wage benefit formula. Employee contributions, applied by only three states for about thirty-five years, saw a small revival of interest during the late 1980s.

The largest states showed about the same patterns as the other states with respect to most of the significant provisions. Notable exceptions have been the flexible maximum weekly benefit provision and the flexible taxable wage base. The largest states have been less inclined toward adopting those automatic adjustments; therefore, they have tended to provide lower benefit ceilings, relative to their state average wage levels, and taxed a more limited portion of covered payrolls.

Each state has developed its own unemployment insurance program, subject to some important federal requirements to be sure, but nevertheless able to evolve in particular ways to reflect particular economic needs and political tendencies. No two state laws are exactly alike in all respects and many differ widely from each other. In an economy that operates to a large degree on a broad regional or national basis, some of these differences pose questions of equity for workers in different states. For example, two workers laid off from the same type of jobs, perhaps even by the same employer though in different states, and each with identical wage and employment experience, may qualify for very different benefits and face different job-search and eligibility rules. The remedy of a single uniform system advanced by some interests, such as organized labor, has never gained much political support. Instead, federal requirements have been adopted, from time to time, to prohibit state provisions regarded as extreme or to require provisions in all state laws to assure desired national policy. Efforts to impose uniform federal rules or standards usually meet stiff resistance, and for some issues, such as minimum benefit standards, they have never succeeded. Basically, the protection of state prerogatives in the federal-state system remains strong as of 1990. The most vulnerable area for the states in this regard has been a weak financial situation, a legacy of the 1970s and early 1980s.

The states have taken an active and significant role in shaping the character of the federal-state unemployment insurance system. As a scheme for shared responsibility and powers for applying a complex program affecting millions of workers and their employers nationwide, it has worked reasonably well over the long span of years despite inevitable tensions between the two levels of government and between organized labor and employers. The prevailing urge to preserve the state role has led more often to working out the tensions and resolving the conflicts within the framework of the system. Widespread and heavy state reserve fund indebtedness to the federal loan fund has been the most serious path to federal manipulation or control of state laws and real danger to the existing partnership. While a long recession-free period enabled the states to regain solvency by the close of the 1980s, their status remains precarious without much more adequate buildup of reserves and some overall backup reinsurance or equalization fund to avoid resorting to heavy costly borrowing.

The problem of how and when to compensate the long-term unemployed also remains unsettled and unsettling. Total federal responsibility for benefits beyond those payable under the federal-state extended benefit program seems well established by actions adopted in the recessions of the 1970s and 1980s, though with very different approaches each time. The weakening of the federal-state extensions during the early 1980s makes the long-term benefit question more murky and more urgent in recessions. The result is to stimulate far-reaching proposals that could alter the program in some fundamental respects.

State legislative approaches alone are not enough to deal with some of the broad compelling problems and weaknesses in unemployment insurance in this country. Strictly federal solutions, in turn, may forgo important values and advantages of state involvement. The partnership has worked fairly well for over half a century. To continue striving to keep the partnership viable and active while developing remedies for the system's problems would appear to be the course of wisdom.

Epilogue

The early 1990s began to leave their mark on the unemployment insurance program as this volume neared completion and publication. The major economic development was the ninth recession since World War II. It started in the last half of 1990, ending a span of about eight years since the previous downturn. By comparison with that one and the slump of the mid-1970s, the latest recession has been less severe, at least in terms of unemployment rates experienced. It has, however, been more prolonged. By mid-1992, some weak signs of recovery had appeared, though the outlook remained uncertain. The current and long-term health of the economy, central issues in the 1992 Presidential election campaign, engendered broad concern about the nation's ability to adjust to fundamental change and provide adequate employment for its labor force.

The total unemployment rate, which in 1989 reached a sixteen-year low of 5.2 percent (annual average), rose toward 7.0 percent during 1991 and continued to climb, reaching a peak of 7.8 percent by mid-1992, compared to a peak of 10.7 percent in two months during the 1982 recession. The increase in the insured unemployment rate has been similarly less acute when compared with the prior recession experience. As usual, however, long-term unemployment levels rose sharply. Insured unemployed workers who exhausted their regular state benefits totaled less than two million in 1989. Their numbers increased to more than three million in 1991. During that year, only nine states triggered on to pay benefits under the permanent federal-state extended benefit program in which the benefit costs are shared equally by the federal and state governments. Besides the less elevated insured unemployment rates, the more demanding trigger requirements adopted in the early 1980s also limited use of this program in 1991.

Political pressures began to mount in 1990 to provide an emergency federal program of additional unemployment benefits for regular benefit exhaustees. The administration at first resisted the idea as too costly and not necessary—President Bush rejected two bills passed by Congress for the purpose in 1991.[1] In November of that year, however, the President relented and accepted the Emergency Unemployment Compensation Act of 1991.

This Epilogue briefly summarizes the temporary emergency program of 1991 and a number of other legislative changes of importance for unemployment insurance adopted in the early 1990s.

Emergency Unemployment Compensation

The Emergency Unemployment Compensation (EUC) Act of 1991 (P.L. 102-164, as Amended)

The EUC program went into effect shortly after its November enactment. It was to be a temporary measure, set to terminate June 13, 1992. The Act provided for additional weeks of benefits to insured unemployed workers who had exhausted their regular benefits or whose benefit years had expired after February 1991, provided they were not eligible for benefits in a new benefit year or from any other federal or state program. Claimants eligible for EUC could draw up to thirteen weeks, but in states with unemployment rates high enough to equal or exceed specified levels, the maximum was twenty weeks.[2] An amendment adopted in February 1992 (P.L. 102-244) increased these duration limits by thirteen weeks—to twenty-six weeks, and to thirty-three weeks in high unemployment states. The amendment also extended the program from June 13 through July 4, 1992 but with the duration limits lowered to thirteen and twenty weeks during this brief extension.

Two alternative unemployment rates were designated to determine if the higher EUC maximum duration was payable in a state. One was the state's total unemployment rate: if this rate averaged 9.0 percent or more over a six-month period, the higher duration limit would apply. The alternative was the state's insured unemployment rate (IUR) aver-

---

1. The first bill required the President to declare an emergency for it to go into effect, but he refused to do so; he vetoed the second bill.

2. The Act's original provisions called for three different maximum duration levels of EUC depending on state unemployment rates, but an amendment adopted a few weeks after the program began simplified the structure to the two levels described.

aged over a thirteen-week period, adjusted by adding to the count of the insured unemployed in the calculation the total number of claimants who exhausted regular benefits during the last three calendar months for which data were available. If this adjusted IUR averaged at least 5.0 percent over a thirteen-week period, the higher EUC duration maximum would become applicable.

State eligibility and benefit amount provisions applicable for the federal-state shared extended benefit program applied for EUC. The special, restrictive federal requirements adopted in the early 1980s with respect to shared extended benefits were also applicable for EUC. This meant, for example, that claimants who qualified for regular benefits with less than 20 weeks of base-period employment (or the equivalent in an acceptable earnings test) would not be eligible for EUC. It also meant that EUC claimants were subject to stiffer federal rules with regard to their availability for work, the definition of suitable work, and job-search requirements than was the case under state provisions for regular benefits. Any federal-state shared extended benefits paid to claimants served to reduce their EUC entitlement. The Act, however, gave state governors the option to terminate any extended benefit periods that had triggered on in their states under the extended benefit program while EUC was payable.

Federal funds financed the entire cost of EUC benefits. The state governors, therefore, were motivated to call off extended benefit periods so as to avoid charges against state reserve accounts for the state share of extended benefit costs. The funds to pay for EUC were drawn from the Extended Unemployment Compensation Account in the Unemployment Trust Fund.[3] This account had a total of nearly $7.8 billion on September 30, 1991, shortly before the EUC program began. At the outset, EUC costs were estimated to total about $5 billion.[4] The increase in EUC duration limits adopted in February 1992 was expected to add over $2.5 billion more in EUC costs.

---

3. The Extended Unemployment Compensation Account reserve was accumulated from specified allocations of federal unemployment tax revenues to finance the federal share of extended benefits.

4. Estimates of Extended Unemployment Compensation Account reserve level and EUC outlays from USDOL, Employment and Training Administration (1992).

Extension of EUC Program

As the program was about to expire in early July 1992, enactment of the Unemployment Compensation Amendments of 1992 (P.L. 102-318) extended EUC to March 6, 1993, but with several important changes. The EUC duration limits were set at twenty-six weeks in the high unemployment states, using the same unemployment rate measures as before, and at twenty weeks in the other states.[5] These limits were to be lowered further when the national total unemployment rate averaged 7.0 percent or less for two consecutive months—to fifteen weeks and ten weeks, respectively, for high-unemployment and other states. They would fall to thirteen and seven weeks if this rate dropped below 6.8 percent for two months. EUC benefits paid under the extension provided by this Act also were wholly financed by the federal government, but out of general revenues instead of the Extended Unemployment Compensation Account. Another change specified that claimants eligible for EUC who could qualify for regular benefits in a new benefit year could choose to draw EUC if, for example, the weekly amount was higher. Formerly, they had to draw regular benefits first.

Again, shortly before the program's termination and with the urging of the new Clinton administration, Congress extended EUC for another six months (P.L. 103-6). No other changes were made apart from setting a new expiration date in early October 1993, followed by a phase-out period to end in January 1994.[6]

Other Federal Unemployment Insurance Legislation

Some of the changes described here were provided in the laws enacted for the EUC program.

---

5. . These new limits were made retroactive to June 14, 1992 when the limits had been reduced to twenty and thirteen weeks, respectively.

6. EUC claimants drawing benefits up to the program's expiration in October 1993 (formerly March 1993) and with EUC entitlement remaining could continue to draw their benefits, if still unemployed, during a phase-out period lasting three months ending in January 1994 (formerly June 1993).

Extension of Federal Unemployment Tax Increase

In 1977, the net federal unemployment tax rate was raised temporarily 0.2 percent to help repay the federal costs of extended benefits and emergency supplemental benefits. The Extended Unemployment Compensation Account in the Unemployment Trust Fund had to borrow heavily from the U.S. Treasury to cover these costs in the mid-1970s, never having been able to accumulate surplus reserves for the purpose beforehand. Once the account was free of debt, the temporary tax increase was to terminate. Additional heavy extended benefit outlays in the early 1980s delayed this event. The debt was fully repaid by 1987 and the account began to build a reserve. The federal budget deficit problem was so severe, however, that the prospect of any revenue loss evoked congressional resistance to the termination of the tax increase. The scheduled expiration of the 0.2 percent tax increase, therefore, was postponed for three years—through 1990.

As 1990 neared its close, Congress and the administration were struggling to resolve the federal budget for 1991 with the deficit problem worse than ever. Moreover, a slipping economy and proposals afloat for emergency unemployment benefit extension made a strong case for continuing the tax increase again. It was estimated that the 0.2 percent segment was generating more than $1 billion a year in added Federal Unemployment Tax revenues. Accordingly, a provision in the Omnibus Budget Reconciliation Act of 1990 (P.L. 101-508), adopted November 1990, extended the temporary tax increase through 1995. A year later, the EUC Act of 1991 added yet another year to this extension, continuing the increase through 1996.

Restored Protection for Ex-Servicemembers (UCX)

Unemployed men and women recently separated from the armed forces are entitled to file for UCX benefits in accordance with the regular unemployment insurance provisions of the state in which they file. All UCX benefit costs are financed by federal general revenues. In 1982, this program was cut back by federal changes which preempted regular state provisions with respect to UCX claims in two key areas. One change instituted a noncompensable four-week waiting period— no state required more than a one-week wait. The other limited the maximum duration of UCX benefits allowed an individual to thirteen weeks instead of the usual twenty-six weeks for regular state benefits.

A provision of the Emergency Unemployment Compensation Act of 1991 repealed these two special UCX restrictions of 1982. Thereafter, UCX claimants were again treated the same as regular state claimants with regard to the waiting period and benefit duration. In addition, the same provision of the EUC Act revised a special UCX qualifying requirement applicable to military reservists filing for benefits on the basis of a period of active duty. The requirement had specified a minimum of 180 days of active duty service to qualify for UCX. Many reservists activated for duty during the Persian Gulf conflict in 1990-1991 were deactivated after serving less than six months. The 1991 Act changed the minimum requirement for reservists to ninety days instead.

State Option to Pay Benefits to School Employees

When unemployment insurance coverage was extended to school employees in the 1970s,[7] a distinction was made between professional and nonprofessional employees in regard to potential benefit rights during nonwork periods between school years or terms. The federal law prohibited payment of benefits to professional school employees during such periods if they had a contract or some other reasonable assurance of continued employment when school resumed. The same prohibition did not apply to nonprofessional employees. States had the option to determine whether or not benefits could be paid to these employees in similar circumstances. Some states did allow payment; others did not. In 1983, the federal law was amended, removing the state option and including nonprofessional school employees in the federal prohibition of benefit payment between terms. The EUC Act of 1991 repealed the 1983 amendment thereby restoring the option to the states with respect to nonprofessional employees.

---

7. School employees were covered when employment for nonprofit organizations and state and local government came under coverage, as required by federal law.

New Advisory Council

The EUC Act of 1991 also provided for a new Advisory Council on Unemployment Compensation with members appointed by the President and by the heads of both houses of Congress, an arrangement similar to that used for the National Commission on Unemployment Compensation in 1978. The Council's task is to review, study, and evaluate the federal-state unemployment insurance system and to report its findings, conclusions, and recommendations to the President and Congress. A new Council would be reinstituted every four years. The legislation called for the Council to make its first report by February 1, 1994.

Changes in the Extended Benefit Program

The Unemployment Compensation Amendments of 1992, which extended the EUC program until March 6, 1993, also included a few provisions which bear significantly on the permanent federal-state extended benefit program. The latter program, in effect, was not operative while EUC benefits were payable.

One provision of the 1992 Amendments suspended the more stringent federal rules relating to claimant availability for work, job search, and suitable work as these apply to current eligibility for extended benefits. Also suspended was the federal requirement for a minimum amount of work or earnings in employment following a disqualification in order to become eligible for benefits again. During the period of suspension of the federal requirements, state provisions covering these matters with regard to regular benefits were to apply for extended benefits. The suspension would not begin until after the EUC program's expiration date in March 1993, and it would continue through 1994. The question of what to do about the federal rules after 1994 was assigned to the Advisory Council on Unemployment Compensation.

Another change modified the federal qualifying requirement for extended benefits which specifies a minimum of twenty weeks of base-period employment or the equivalent in base-period earnings of at least one-and-one-half times high-quarter earnings or forty times the weekly benefit amount. The application of the federal requirement depends on which of these three types of qualifying tests the state uses. If a state uses none of them, it must choose one to apply the federal minimum to extended benefit claimants. The change made by the 1992 amendments permits each state to provide, by law, at its option, the use of any one or more of the three acceptable types of requirements to determine whether the extended benefit claimant meets the minimum test. While the change appears to be modest and subtle, it can be important for some claimants.[8]

Yet another amendment offered the states a new extended benefit trigger option. The existing trigger mechanism is based on the state insured unemployment rate (IUR) averaged over a thirteen-week period. (In this calculation, only claims for regular benefits are counted; extended benefit claims or exhaustees are not included.) Under existing provisions, an extended benefit period triggers on in a state when that rate equals 5.0 percent or more and is at least 120 percent of the IUR average for the corresponding thirteen-week periods of the two preceding years. The states also have the option to specify in their laws that the 120 percent requirement is suspended if the thirteen-week IUR averages at least 6.0 percent. The 1992 amendments added another trigger option based on the state's *total* unemployment rate (TUR), seasonally adjusted. If this rate, averaged over three successive months, equals or exceeds 6.5 percent and is at least 110 percent of the corresponding three-month average in either of the two prior years, the state may trigger on an extended benefit period. Moreover, if a state chooses this option and its three-month average TUR rises to 8.0 percent or more and satisfies the 110 percent requirement, the state must pay up to an additional seven weeks of extended benefits, raising the duration limit for such benefits from thirteen to twenty weeks.

Authorizing Short-time Compensation

The Unemployment Compensation Amendments of 1992 also dealt with short-time compensation, or worksharing benefits. Legislation was enacted in 1982 to encourage and assist states to develop and implement provisions which would accommodate worksharing plans agreed to by employers and their employees to avoid layoffs during temporary slack periods (see chapter 9). As of 1992, seventeen states provided for short-time compensation when these plans were in effect.

---

8. Thus, if an extended benefit claimant fails to meet one test, the state may then apply one (or both) of the alternative tests which the claimant might be able to meet.

State laws generally define a week of insured unemployment as one in which the claimant was not employed and had no earnings or had limited part-time work with earnings less than a specified amount, in which case a partial unemployment benefit might be paid. Under short-time compensation, the recipient remains employed though on a reduced work schedule which could amount to as much as 90 percent of the employee's normal workweek. Moreover, short-time compensation recipients are not subject to the usual availability and work search requirements. Strictly speaking, short-time compensation payments out of state unemployment insurance trust funds raise a question of their validity in view of the federal standard tracing back to the original law (Title IX of the 1935 Social Security Act) which prohibits withdrawal of such funds for any purpose other than the compensation of unemployment.

The 1982 legislation authorized the development of short-time compensation as a temporary experimental program, with provision for review and evaluation of the experience, a task accomplished in the mid-1980s. The authority for this program expired in 1985. No further federal legislation on the subject followed until the 1992 amendments. One of these permanently authorized the payment of short-time compensation out of state unemployment insurance trust funds, provided that the relevant state law covered several conditions specified in the federal law. For such compensation to be payable, the state provisions must stipulate that the worksharing plan's reduction in the normal workweeks of employees is in lieu of temporary layoffs, that the reduction must be at least 10 percent of the normal workweek that the amount of short-time compensation paid be an equivalent proportion of the full weekly benefit payable for a week of total unemployment, and that recipients of the compensation not be subject to the availability and work search requirements, though they must be available for employment at their normal work schedule. As an option, states may allow employees, while on reduced workweeks and receiving short-time compensation, to participate in state-approved, employer-sponsored training designed to improve their job skills.

State Programs

While some states altered their unemployment insurance provisions between 1990 and 1992, the overall patterns among them did not change much from those described in chapter 10 as of 1990. Weekly benefit ceilings went up in many states especially where flexible maximum provisions were used, although in some cases the ceilings remained frozen at earlier levels or were restrained from rising as much as the percentage setting specified because trust fund levels were too low. The ten largest states showed no changes from 1990 to 1992 in their formulas to apply qualifying requirements or to determine claimant weekly benefit amounts and the number of weeks of benefits payable. Taxable wage bases remained at $7,000 in fifteen states in 1992, compared with seventeen in 1990; they were $10,000 or more in nineteen states, the same as in 1990. Of the ten largest states, three were at $7,000 and two at $10,000 or more in 1992.

A few of the other states altered their provisions somewhat. No general trends are discernible among these changes. Perhaps the most noteworthy changes came in Puerto Rico, which ended its long-held unique positions in two areas—taxes and duration of benefits. Starting in 1992, Puerto Rico applied experience rating to assign individual employer tax rates. It had been the only jurisdiction in the nation not to have experience rating. The doubling of the full federal tax credit allowed for experience rating, beginning in 1985, meant that all employers in Puerto Rico went from a state tax of 2.7 to 5.4 percent. No employer could pay less without experience rating and qualify for the full tax credit against the federal unemployment tax. Revenues increased well beyond levels needed to assure adequate reserves, even though Puerto Rico has tended to be a high benefit-cost state. (Its taxable wage base was at the minimum $7,000 level.) As did many states in the 1940s, Puerto Rico turned to experience rating as the only way to reduce the inflow of unneeded revenues. The other major change was to increase the uniform duration payable from twenty to twenty-six weeks for regular benefits. In no jurisdiction is the regular duration limit now less than twenty-six weeks.

In 1990, total state benefit outlays from all state reserve funds exceeded total unemployment tax revenues by about $3 billion. With reserves totaling over $38 billion, the interest earned made up the difference. Eleven states, however, saw their reserves decline over the year, several sharply. These included all the New England states, except for Vermont, plus the large states of Florida, Michigan, and New York.[9] The picture worsened substantially in the next two years when total benefits paid exceeded total state tax revenues by about $10 billion in 1991 and $8 billion in 1992. The aggregate of state benefit reserve funds at the end of 1992 was about $26 billion net of $1.3 billion in outstanding loans. About half of this debt was owed by Connecticut and the rest mostly by Massachusetts and Michigan, with less than $20 million by the District of Columbia.

The much milder effects of the recession of the early 1990s on the state programs compared with the heavy impacts of the downturns in the early 1980s and mid-1970s was at least partly due to the virtual replacement of shared extended benefits by the totally federally funded EUC benefits. From its start in November 1991 through December 1992, the EUC program paid out a total of $14.3 billion in benefits. In effect, the complete national pooling of long-term unemployment benefit costs has supplied an element of reinsurance for the state programs, besides helping to sustain millions of jobless workers through prolonged periods of unemployment during the recession and slow, weak recovery.[10]

---

9. The 1990 data are from the annual supplement for 1990 to USDOL *Handbook of Unemployment Insurance Financial Data, 1938-1982*.

10. The data for 1991 and 1992 are from *UI Data Summary*, 4th quarter cy 1991, pp. 9 and 13, and 4th quarter cy 1992, pp. 8, 9, and 13, U.S. Department of Labor, Employment and Training Administration.

References

Altmeyer, Arthur J. 1966. *The Formative Years of Social Security*. Madison: University of Wisconsin Press.

Becker, Joseph M. 1959. *Shared Government in Employment Security*. New York: Columbia University Press.

_____. 1972a. *Experience Rating in Unemployment Insurance: Competitive Socialism*. Baltimore: Johns Hopkins University Press.

_____. 1972b. *Experience Rating in Unemployment Insurance: Virtue or Vice*. Kalamazoo, MI: W. E. Upjohn Institute for Employment Research.

Bendick, Marc, Jr., and Mary Lou Egan. 1987. "Transfer Payment Diversion for Small Business Development," *Industrial and Labor Relations Review* 4 (July), pp. 528-42.

Best, Fred. 1981. *Work Sharing: The Issues, Policy Options and Prospects*. Kalamazoo, MI: W. E. Upjohn Institute for Employment Research.

Beveridge, William H. 1930. *Unemployment; A Problem of Industry*. New York: Longmans, Green, new edition.

_____. 1942. *Social Insurance and Allied Services*. London: His Majesty's Stationary Office.

_____. 1953. *Power and Influence*. London: Hodder and Stoughton.

Birch, David L. 1981. "Who Creates Jobs?" *The Public Interest* 65 (Fall), pp. 3-14.

Blank, Rebecca M., and David E. Card. 1991. "Recent Trends in Insured and Uninsured Unemployment: Is There an Explanation?" *Quarterly Journal of Economics* (November), pp. 1157-89.

Blaustein, Saul J. 1968. *Unemployment Insurance Objectives and Issues: An Agenda for Research and Evaluation*. Kalamazoo, MI: W. E. Upjohn Institute for Employment Research, November.

_____. 1979. "Insured Unemployment Data." In *Data Collection, Processing, and Presentation: National and Local,* Appendix Volume II to Counting the Labor Force. Washington, DC: National Commission on Employment and Unemployment Statistics.

_____. 1981. *Job and Income Security of Unemployed Workers*. Kalamazoo, MI: W. E. Upjohn Institute for Employment Research.

Blaustein, Saul J., and Isabel Craig. 1977. *An International Review of Unemployment Insurance Schemes*. Kalamazoo, MI: W. E. Upjohn Institute for Employment Research.

Booth, Philip. 1961. "Temporary Extended Unemployment Compensation Act of 1961—A Legislative History," *Labor Law Journal* (October), pp. 909-21.

Bureau of Labor Statistics News. 1990. "Work Experience of the Population in 1990." U.S. Department of Labor, USDL 91-447.

Bureau of Labor Statistics News. 1991. "The Employment Situation: March 1991." U.S. Department of Labor, USDL 91-147.

Bureau of Labor Statistics News. 1992. "Work Experience of the Population in 1991." U.S. Department of Labor, USDL 92-644, October 9.

Burgess, Paul L., and Jerry L. Kingston. 1978. *The Adequacy of Unemployment Insurance Benefits: An Analysis of Adjustments Undertaken Through Thirteen and Twenty-five Weeks of Unemployment.* U.S. Department of Labor, Employment and Training Administration, Unemployment Insurance Service.

Burns, Eveline M. 1941. *British Unemployment Program, 1920-1938.* Washington, DC: Social Science Research Council.

Burtless, Gary S. 1983. "Why is Insured Unemployment So Low?" *Brookings Papers on Economic Activity* 1, pp. 225-49.

Burtless, Gary S. and Daniel H. Saks. 1984. *The Decline in Insured Unemployment During the 1980s.* Washington, DC: The Brookings Institution, March.

"Business Cycles and Unemployment." 1923. Report of the President's Committee on Unemployment. New York: McGraw-Hill.

Carroll, Mollie Ray. 1930. *Unemployment Insurance in Germany,* 2nd edition, revised. Washington, DC: The Brookings Institution.

Carlson, Valdemar. 1962. *Economic Security in the United States.* New York: McGraw-Hill.

Cohen, Wilbur J., and James L. Calhoun. 1948. "Social Security Legislation, January-June 1948: History and Background," *Social Security Bulletin* (July).

Committee on Long-Range Work and Relief Policies. 1942. "Security, Work, and Relief Policies." Washington, DC: National Resources Planning Board.

Committee on Unemployment Insurance Objectives. 1969. *Unemployment and Income Security: Goals for the 1970s.* Kalamazoo, MI: W. E. Upjohn Institute for Employment Research, July.

Commons, John R. 1922. "Unemployment Prevention," *American Labor Legislation Review* (March).

_____. 1963. *Myself, the Autobiography of John R. Commons.* Madison: University of Wisconsin Press.

Cooper, Sophia. 1960. "Work Experience of the Population in 1959," *Monthly Labor Review* 83, 12 (December), pp. 1272-83.

Corson, Walter, Joan Grossman, and Walter Nicholson. 1986." An Evaluation of the Federal Supplemental Compensation Program." Unemployment

Insurance Service Occasional Paper 86-3, U.S. Department of Labor, Employment and Training Administration.

Corson, Walter, and Walter Nicholson. 1988. "An Examination of Declining UI Claims During the 1980s," Unemployment Insurance Service Occasional Paper 88-3, U.S. Department of Labor, Employment and Training Administration, September.

Curtin, Richard T., and Michael Pouza. 1980. "Attitudes Towards and Experience with Unemployment Compensation Among American Households," *Unemployment Compensation: Studies and Research*, Vol. 3. Washington, DC: National Commission on Unemployment Compensation, July.

Czarnowski, F. B., ed. 1957. *The Eloquence of Winston Churchill.* New York: New American Library.

Danzau, Arthur T., Ronald L. Oaxaca, and Carol A. Taylor. 1979. "The Impact of Unemployment Insurance Benefits on Local Economies-Tucson." Unemployment Insurance Service, U.S. Department of Labor, Employment and Training Administration.

de Schweinitz, Karl. 1943. *England's Road to Social Security.* Philadelphia: University of Pennsylvania Press.

Douglas, Paul H., and Aaron Director. 1931. *The Problem of Unemployment.* New York: Arno Press, reprinted 1976.

Economic Report of the President. Various years. Washington, DC: U.S. Government Printing Office.

Eliot, Thomas H. 1960. "The Social Security Act—25 Years After," *Atlantic Monthly* (August).

Employment and Earnings (E&E). Various monthly issues. U.S. Department of Labor, Bureau of Labor Statistics.

Entes, Ruth. 1977. "Family Support and Expenditures Survey of Unemployment Insurance Claimants in New York State, September 1972-February 1974." Employment Service, U.S. Department of Labor, Employment and Training Administration.

Ewing, John B. 1933. *Job Insurance.* Norman, OK: University of Oklahoma Press.

Federal Security Agency. 1940. *Comparison of State Unemployment Compensation Laws as of March 1, 1940.* Bureau of Employment Security. Employment Security Memorandum No. 8, Social Security Board.

_____. 1941. *Comparison of State Unemployment Insurance Laws as of December 31, 1941.* Bureau of Employment Security, Social Security Board.

_____. 1947. *Unemployment Insurance Abstract: Program Statistics and Legal Provisions, 1937-1947.* Supplement to *Employment Security Activities,* Vol. 3, No. 11. Social Security Administration, November.

_____. 1948. *Comparison of State Unemployment Insurance Laws.* Bureau of Employment Security, Social Security Administration, October

Folsom, Marion B. 1935. "Testimony to the Committee on Economic Security." Hearings on S. 1130, 74th Congress, 1st Session.

Freedman, Audrey. 1980. "Plant Closed—No Jobs," *Across the Board* (August).

Fullerton, Howard N., Jr. 1991. "Labor Force Projections: The Baby Boom Moves On," *Monthly Labor Review* (November), pp. 31-44.

Gilson, Mary B. 1931. *Unemployment Insurance in Great Britain.* New York: Industrial Relations Counselors.

Haber, William, and Merrill G. Murray. 1966. *Unemployment Insurance in the American Economy.* Homewood, IL: Richard D. Irwin.

Hamermesh, Daniel S. 1977. *Jobless Pay and the Economy.* Baltimore: Johns Hopkins University Press.

Handbook of Labor Statistics (HLS). Various issues. Washington, DC: U.S. Bureau of Labor Statistics.

Heffernan, Joseph L. 1932. "The Hungry City: A Mayor's Experience with Unemployment," *Atlantic Monthly* (May).

Henle, Peter. 1980. "The Federal Budget: Removal of State Unemployment Insurance Trust Funds," *Unemployment Compensation: Studies and Research,* Vol. 3. Washington, DC: National Commission on Unemployment Compensation, July.

Historical Statistics of the United States, Colonial Times to 1970, Bicentennial Edition, Part 1. 1979. Washington, DC: U.S. Department of Commerce, Bureau of the Census.

Hohaus, Reinhard. 1948. "Equity, Adequacy and Related Factors in Old Age Security." In *Readings in Social Security,* William Haber and Wilbur J. Cohen. Englewood Cliffs, NJ: Prentice-Hall.

Hunt, H. Allan, and Timothy Hunt. 1983. *The Human Resource Implications of Robotics.* Kalamazoo, MI: W. E. Upjohn Institute for Employment Research.

Industrial Relations Counselors, Inc. 1934. *An Historical Basis for Unemployment Insurance.* Minneapolis, MN: University of Minnesota Press.

International Labour Office. 1955. *Unemployment Insurance Schemes.* Geneva, Switzerland.

Kerachsky, Stuart, Walter Nicholson, and Alan Hershey. 1986. "An Evaluation of Short-Time Compensation Programs." Unemployment Insurance Service Occasional Paper 86-4, U.S. Department of Labor, Employment and Training Administration.

Kiehl, Constance A. 1932. *Unemployment Insurance in Belgium.* New York: Industrial Relations Counselors.

Lampman, Robert J., ed. 1962. *Social Security Perspectives: Essays by Edwin E. Witte.* Madison: University of Wisconsin Press.

Leigh, Duane E. 1989. *Assisting Displaced Workers: Do the States Have a Better Idea?* Kalamazoo, MI: W. E. Upjohn Institute for Employment Research.

Lescohier, Don D., and Florence Peterson. 1931. *The Alleviation of Unemployment in Wisconsin.* Madison: Industrial Commission of Wisconsin, July.

Lester, Richard A. 1962. *The Economics of Unemployment Compensation.* Princeton, NJ: Princeton University, Industrial Relations Section.

Lubove, Roy, ed. 1966. *Social Welfare in Transition: Selected English Documents, 1834-1909.* Pittsburgh: University of Pittsburgh Press.

Malisoff, Harry. 1961. *The Insurance Character of Unemployment Insurance.* Kalamazoo, MI: W. E. Upjohn Institute for Employment Research.

Manual of State Employment Security Legislation. (See U.S. Department of Labor, Bureau of Employment Security, 1950a.)

Mellor, E. F., and W. Parks, II. 1988. "A Year's Work: Labor Force Activity from a Different Perspective," *Monthly Labor Review* 111, 9 (September), pp. 13-18.

Metropolitan Life Insurance Company. 1935. *Unemployment Insurance, A Summary of Some Existing Governmental and Private Plans.* New York: Metropolitan Life Insurance.

Meyers, Charles A. 1945. "Experience Rating in Unemployment Compensation," *American Economic Review* 35 (June), pp. 337-54.

Monthly Labor Review. 1991. "Current Labor Statistics," July.

_____. 1975. "Current Labor Statistics," September.

Murray, Merrill G. 1966. *Proposed Federal Unemployment Insurance Amendments.* Kalamazoo, MI: W. E. Upjohn Institute for Employment Research, February.

_____. 1967. *Should Pensioners Receive Unemployment Compensation?* Kalamazoo, MI: W. E. Upjohn Institute for Employment Research.

_____. 1972. *The Treatment of Seasonal Unemployment Under Unemployment Insurance.* Kalamazoo, MI: W. E. Upjohn Institute for Employment Research, April.

_____. 1974. *The Duration of Unemployment Insurance Benefits.* Kalamazoo, MI: W. E. Upjohn Institute for Employment Research, January.

Myers, Robert J. 1981. *Social Security,* second edition. Homewood, IL: Richard D. Irwin.

National Commission on Unemployment Compensation, *Unemployment Compensation: Final Report*. 1980. Washington, DC: U.S. Government Printing Office, July.

National Industrial Conference Board, Inc. 1932. *Unemployment Insurance in Germany*. New York: National Industrial Conference Board.

Nelson, Daniel. 1969. *Unemployment Insurance: The American Experience, 1915-1935*. Madison: University of Wisconsin Press.

Norman, Colin. 1981. "The New Industrial Revolution: How Microelectronics May Change the Workplace," *The Futurist* (February), pp. 30-32.

Oaxaca, Ronald L., and Carol A. Taylor. 1986. "Estimating the Impacts of Economic Programs on Urban Areas: The Case of Unemployment Insurance Benefits," *Journal of Urban Economics* 19, pp. 23-46.

Ohio Commission on Unemployment Insurance. 1932. "Report." (Report on questions to consider with respect to the unemployment insurance law suitable to conditions in the State of Ohio.) Columbus, OH.

Railroad Unemployment Compensation Committee. 1984. "Report." (Committee established by section 4 of the Railroad Solvency Act of 1983, P.L. 98-16.) June 21.

Raushenbush, Paul. 1931. "Wisconsin's Unemployment Compensation Act," *American Labor Legislation Review* 22.

Raushenbush, Paul A., and Elizabeth Brandeis Raushenbush. 1979. *Our U.C. Story, 1930-1967*. Madison: Raushenbush & Raushenbush.

"Report of the Royal Commission on the Poor Laws and Relief of Distress." 1909. (Cd 4499).

"Report of the Wisconsin Legislative Interim Committee on Unemployment." 1931. Industrial Commission, State of Wisconsin.

"Report to the President of the Committee on Economic Security." 1935. Washington, DC: U.S. Government printing Office.

Rubin, Murray. 1980. "The Proliferation of Special Employee Protection Programs." In *Unemployment Compensation: Studies and Research*, Vol. 3. Washington, DC: National Commission on Unemployment Compensation, July.

_____. 1983. *Federal-State Relations in Unemployment Insurance: A Balance of Power*. Kalamazoo, MI: W. E. Upjohn Institute for Employment Research.

Rubinow, I. M. 1913. *Social Insurance*. New York: Henry Holt.

"Senate Passes Unemployment Bills." 1930. *American Labor Legislation Review*, 20, 125.

Social Security Board. 1936. "Draft Bills for State Unemployment Compensation of Pooled Funds or Employer Reserve Account Types." Mimeo.

_____. 1937. "A Summary of Foreign Experience with Unemployment Insurance." In *Social Security in America: The Factual Background of the Social Security Act as Summarized from Staff Reports to the Committee on Economic Security*. Social Security Board Publication No. 20.

_____. 1942. "Seventh Annual Report of the Social Security Board."

Spates, T. C., and G. S. Rabinovitch. 1931. *Unemployment Insurance in Switzerland*. New York: Industrial Relations Counselors.

Statistical Abstract of the United States. (See U.S. Department of Commerce.)

Stewart, Bryce M. 1930. *Unemployment Benefits in the United States*. New York: Industrial Relations Counselors.

Topel, Robert H. 1984. "Experience Rating of Unemployment Insurance and the Incidence of Unemployment," *Quarterly Journal of Law and Economics* 27 (April), pp. 61-89.

"Unemployment Compensation in a Free Economy." 1952. National Association of Manufacturers, July.

Unemployment Insurance Financial Data, 1938-1982, and annual supplements. U.S. Department of Labor, Employment and Training Administration, ETA Handbook 394.

U.S. Congress, House of Representatives. 1916. Hearings on H.R. 159, Commission to Study Social Insurance and Unemployment, Committee on Labor, 64th Congress, 1st Session.

_____. House of Representatives. 1934. "Unemployment Insurance." Hearings on H.R. 7659 before Subcommittee of the Committee on Ways and Means, 73rd Congress, 2nd Session.

_____. House of Representatives. 1935. Committee on Ways and Means, "Economic Security Act." Hearings on H.R. 4120, 74th Congress, 1st Session.

_____. House of Representatives. 1946. "Issues in Social Security." Report to the Committee on Ways and Means, 79th Congress, 1st Session.

_____. House of Representatives. 1965. "Unemployment Compensation." Hearings on H.R. 8282, Committee on Ways and Means, 89th Congress, 1st Session.

_____. Senate. 1916. "Final Report." Commission on Industrial Relations. 64th Congress, 1st Session, Document No. 415, Vol. 2.

_____. Senate. 1929. "Causes of Unemployment." Report No. 2072, 70th Congress, 2nd Session, February 25.

_____. Senate. 1932a. "Unemployment Insurance." Report No. 629, 72nd Congress, 1st Session, April 29.

_____. Senate. 1932b. "Unemployment Insurance." Report No. 964, 72nd Congress, 1st Session, June 20.

_____. Senate. 1935. "Economic Security Act," Hearings on S. 1130. Committee on Finance, 74th Congress, 1st Session.

_____. Senate. 1937. "Constitutionality of the Social Security Act: Opinions of the Supreme Court of the United States." Document No. 74, 75th Congress, 1st Session, May 26.

_____. Senate. 1950. "Recommendations for Social Security Legislation, Part IV." Advisory Council on Social Security. Reports to the Committee on Finance, Document No. 208, 80th Congress, 2nd Session.

_____. Senate. 1960. "Report of the Senate Special Committee on Unemployment Problems." Report No. 1206, 86th Congress, 2nd Session.

_____. Senate. 1966. "Unemployment Insurance Amendments of 1966." Hearings on H.R. 15119 before the Committee on Finance, 89th Congress, 2nd Session.

U.S. Department of Commerce, *Statistical Abstract of the United States, 1954,* Washington, DC.

U.S. Department of Health and Human Services, Social Security Administration. 1990. *Social Security Programs Throughout the World, 1989.* (Washington, DC: U.S. Government Printing Office.

U.S. Department of Labor, Bureau of Employment Security. 1947. "Unemployment Insurance Legislative Policy, 1947." Supplement to *Manual of State Employment Security Legislation,* Employment Security Memorandum No. 13 Revised, November.

_____. Bureau of Employment Security. 1950a. *Manual of State Employment Security Legislation.* Revised, September.

_____. Bureau of Employment Security. 1950b. "Unemployment Insurance: Purposes and Principles." October.

_____. Bureau of Employment Security. 1950c. "Unemployment Insurance: Purposes and Principles." December.

_____. Bureau of Employment Security. 1955. "Major Objectives of Federal Policy with Respect to the Federal-State Employment Security Program." General Administration Letter No. 305, April 25.

_____. Bureau of Employment Security. 1958. "Adequacy of Benefits Under Unemployment Insurance." Staff report prepared for the Steering Committee of the Federal Advisory Council, Unemployment Insurance Service. October.

_____.Bureau of Employment Security. 1959. "Summary and Appraisal of the Temporary Unemployment Compensation Program." Staff report prepared for the Federal Advisory Council. Mimeo. October.

_____.Bureau of Employment Security. 1962. "Unemployment Insurance Legislative Policy: Recommendations for State Legislation, 1962." BES No. U-212A, October.

_____. Bureau of Employment Security. 1963. "Family Characteristics of the Long-Term Unemployed." Report on a study of claimants under the Temporary Extended Unemployment Compensation Program of 1961-1962. BES No. U-207-4, January.

_____. Bureau of Labor Statistics. 1931. "Unemployment-Benefit Plans in the United States and Unemployment Insurance in Foreign Countries." Bulletin No. 544.

_____. Bureau of Labor Statistics. 1991. "Employment, Hours, and Earnings, United States, 1909-90," Vol. 1. Bulletin 2370, March.

_____. Employment and Training Administration. 1983a. "UI Outlook: FY 1984 Budget—Midsession Review." Division of Actuarial Services, Unemployment Insurance Service, August 5.

_____. Employment and Training Administration. 1983b. *Comparison of State Unemployment Insurance Laws.* Unemployment Insurance Service, September.

_____. Employment and Training Administration. 1990a. *Comparison of State Unemployment Insurance Laws,* Revision No. 4. Unemployment Insurance Service, January.

_____. Employment and Training Administration. 1990b. Unemployment Insurance Program Letter 33-90, June 14.

_____. Employment and Training Administration. 1991. Unemployment Insurance Program Letter 3-92, October 29.

_____. Employment and Training Administration. 1992. "UI Outlook: President's Budget, Fiscal Year 1993." Division of Actuarial Services, Unemployment Insurance Service, January.

_____. Manpower Administration. 1968. *Historical Statistics of Employment Security Activities, 1938-1966.* January 6.

_____. Manpower Administration. 1971. *Comparison of State Unemployment Insurance Laws,* Revision Series 3, No. 3. Unemployment Insurance Service, August.

_____. Manpower Administration. 1972 and 1973 Revised. *Unemployment Insurance: State Laws and Experience,* Unemployment Insurance Service.

_____. Manpower Administration. 1983. *Comparison of State Unemployment Insurance Laws.* Unemployment Insurance Service, September 4.

Vroman, Wayne. 1986. *The Funding Crisis in Unemployment Insurance.* Kalamazoo, MI: W. E. Upjohn Institute for Employment Research.

Wandner, Stephen A. 1989. Unpublished report prepared for the Organization for Economic Cooperation and Development.

Webb, Sidney and Beatrice Webb. 1929. *English Poor Law History: Part II, The Last Hundred Years.* London: Longmans, Green.

Witte, Edwin E. 1936. "An Historical Account of Unemployment Insurance in the Social Security Act," *Law and Contemporary Problems* 3, 1 (January).

_____. 1945. "Development of Unemployment Compensation," *Yale Law Journal* 55, 1 (December).

_____. 1962. *The Development of the Social Security Act.* Madison: University of Wisconsin Press.

Wolman, Leo. 1931. "Unemployment Insurance for the United States," *American Labor Legislation Review* (March).

Young, Anne McDougall. 1979. "Work Experience of the Population in 1978." Special Labor Force Report 236, U.S. Department of Labor, Bureau of Labor Statistics.

Zarnowitz, Victor. 1992. "Business Cycles: Theory, History, Indicators, and Forecasting," *NBER Studies in Business Cycles*, Vol. 27. Chicago: University of Chicago Press.

Index

Abbott, Grace, 137n7
Ability to work concept, 166, 169, 286, 291
Advisory Council on Unemployment Compensation, 334-35
Advisory councils, state, 274
Agricultural labor, 148, 275-76
Aliens, 243
Altmeyer, Arthur J., 133, 138, 140, 155, 156n3, 175nn24,25
American Association for Labor Legislation (AALL), 112-13, 115-16, 120
American Conference on Social Insurance (1913), 113
Andrews, John, 113-14
Antipoverty program, 215
Appeal mechanism, state level, 274-75
Area Redevelopment Act (1961), 30, 214
Athletes, professional, 22, 243, 288, 309
Automotive Products Trade Act (1965), 214
Availability for work concept, 22, 79, 166, 169, 282, 286-87, 291, 301

Baker v. Carr, 272n4
Beaman, Middleton, 146
Becker, Joseph M., 57, 274n5, 314n36
Belgium, 84
Bendick, Marc, Jr., 256n36
Benefit costs
    employer financing, 322
    financed by general not specific revenues, 77-78
    financing of UCX, 333-34
Benefit-ratio method (of experience rating), 316-17
Benefits
    after exhaustion of regular benefits,

201-2
    during and after World War II period, 177-79, 184
    ceiling on weekly, 75, 291-92, 296-98
    child support deductions from, 253
    to claimant with dependents, 76, 295-96
    denial of, 286, 287
    duration of, 163-65, 184-85, 200, 202, 219, 229, 302-8, 324
    earned right basis for, 45, 66, 78-79
    effect of inflation on weekly, 296
    entitlements under original state and federal laws, 162-65
    ineligibility for, 22, 287-88, 309
    noncharging of, 319
    protection of worker's entitlement, 182, 242-43, 285-86
    restrictive standards for, 77, 243-44
    for seasonal workers, 308-9
    Special Unemployment Assistance (1974), 227-28
    state financing of, 309-21
    state qualifying requirements for, 278-82
    suspension during labor disputes, 288-89
    taxing of, 253
    temporary, 181-82
    waiting period for, 302
    See also Eligibility; Extended benefits; Flexible maximum and minimum (benefit) provisions; Partial benefit provisions; Trade Readjustment Allowances; Trigger mechanisms; Wage formulas; Weekly benefit amount (WBA)

351

Manpower Administration. *See* U. S.
Department of Labor
Manpower Development and Training
Act (1962), 30, 214, 215, 223
Marital obligations provisions, 169, 287
Maritime workers, 162, 182, 185
*Mary Ann Turner v. Department of
Employment Security and Board of
Review of the Industrial Commission
of Utah,* 243n23
Massachusetts, 118
Means test, 78-79
See also Needs test
Mellor, E. F., 13n15
Metropolitan Life Insurance Company,
98, 109, 110, 111
Meyers, Charles A., 57
Minnesota, 115
Miscellaneous Revenue Act (1982), 253
Moley, Raymond, 139
Monthly Labor Review, 14-15t, 23n20,
29n26
Moral hazard
in all insurance, 70
in unemployment insurance, 66
in workmen's compensation, 70
Morgenthau, Henry, Jr., 132
Morris Committee, Great Britain, 91
Murray, Merrill G., 22, 155n2, 156n3,
196n9, 212n30, 237n18, 244n25, 308
Myers, Robert J., 67

Nathan, Robert, 140n12
National Assistance Act (1966), Great
Britain, 94
National Commission on Unemployment
Compensation (1978-80), 48,
238n19, 247, 252
National Conference on Economic
Security (1934), 136
National Economy Act (1931), Great
Britain, 93, 95
National Industrial Conference Board,
96n14

National Insurance Act (1911), Great
Britain, 87-90, 112-14
See also National Economy Act
(1931), Great Britain; National
Insurance Act (1946), Great
Britain; Unemployment Insurance
Act (1924, 1927, 1930), Great
Britain
National Insurance Act (1946), Great
Britain, 94
Needs test
substitution of earned right for, 45
use of, 52, 78-80
See also Means test
Nelson, Daniel, 107n1, 114, 138n8
New Federalism, 224
Nicholson, Walter, 35n30, 240n21, 254
Nixon, Robert, 116
Nixon bill, Wisconsin, 116
Nonprofit organizations
benefit costs financing by, 322
coverage in 1972 legislation, 225-26
exemption from Federal
Unemployment Tax, 322
extension of coverage to wages of,
276
initial exclusion from coverage, 148,
162
Norman, Colin, 31n28

Oaxaca, Ronald l., 60
Ohio Commission on Unemployment
Insurance (Ohio plan), 46, 119, 121,
28
Ohio school, 45-46
Ohl, Henry, Jr., 116
Old-age assistance, 146
Old-age insurance, 146, 149, 173-74
Omnibus Budget Reconciliation Act
(1981), 253, 260, 333

Parks, W., II, 13n15
Partial benefit provisions, 165, 300-301
Part-time employment, 300-301

About the Institute

The W.E. Upjohn Institute for Employment Research is a nonprofit research organization devoted to finding and promoting solutions to employment-related problems at the national, state, and local level. It is an activity of the W.E. Upjohn Unemployment Trustee Corporation, which was established in 1932 to administer a fund set aside by the late Dr. W.E. Upjohn, founder of The Upjohn Company, to seek ways to counteract the loss of employment income during economic downturns.

The Institute is funded largely by income from the W.E. Upjohn Unemployment Trust, supplemented by outside grants, contracts, and sales of publications. Activities of the Institute are comprised of the following elements: (1) a research program conducted by a resident staff of professional social scientists; (2) a competitive grant program, which expands and complements the internal research program by providing financial support to researchers outside the Institute; (3) a publications program, which provides the major vehicle for the dissemination of research by staff and grantees, as well as other selected work in the field; and (4) an Employment Management Services division, which manages most of the publicly funded employment and training programs in the local area.

The broad objectives of the Institute's research, grant, and publication programs are to: (1) promote scholarship and experimentation on issues of public and private employment and unemployment policy; and (2) make knowledge and scholarship relevant and useful to policymakers in their pursuit of solutions to employment and unemployment problems.

Current areas of concentration for these programs include: causes, consequences, and measures to alleviate unemployment; social insurance and income maintenance programs; compensation; workforce quality; work arrangements; family labor issues; labor-management relations; and regional economic development and local labor markets.

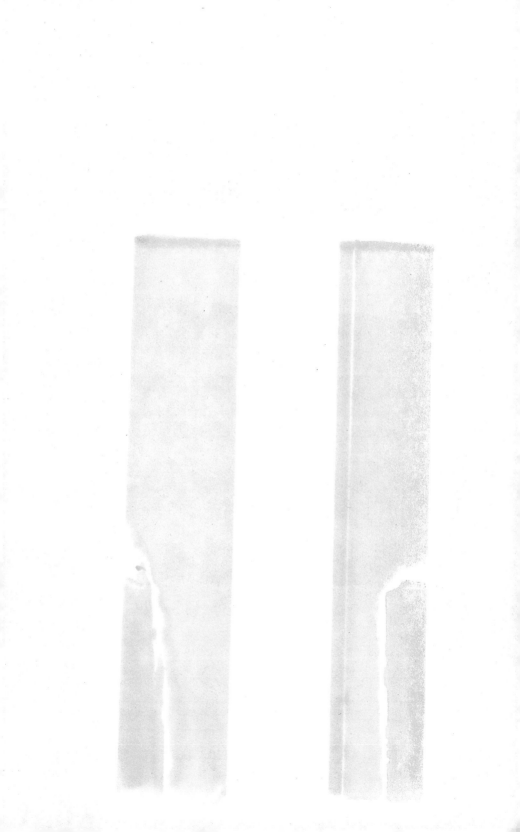

HD 7096 .U5 B5397 1993
Blaustein, Saul J., 1924-
Unemployment insurance in
the United States   76145

VILLA JULIE COLLEGE LIBRARY
STEVENSON, MD 21153

DEMCO